The Giant Book of Poetry

William H. Roetzheim, Editor

Level Four Press, Inc.
San Diego, CA

This book was illustrated by William H. Roetzheim

The author would like to thank Chris McDonald for assistance researching author dates of birth and Marshall Harvey, Will Roetzheim, and Cassandra Rachel Ogle for help with copyediting the manuscript.

Published by Level Four Press, Inc., 13518 Jamul Drive, Jamul, CA91935-1635 USA.
www.Level4Press.com

Library of Congress Cataloging-in-Publication Data
The Giant Book of Poetry
edited by William H. Roetzheim
p. cm.
ISBN 0-9768001-2-8
1. Poetry 2. English poetry. 3. American Poetry. I. Roetzheim, William H.

Library of Congress Control Number:2005903197

This book is printed on acid-neutral archival quality paper.

Dedication

To my wife Marianne—
our relationship is the poetry that matters.

Table of Contents

Notes on the Second Printing

For the second printing of the book, we have reformatted many of the poems to match the format of the original work in terms of line breaks, stanza breaks, indentation, and capitalization. While we don't pretend to perfection, we do believe that the layout of the poems in this printing will be closer to the original intent of the poets represented.

Introduction

This book started out as a flurry of yellow sticky notes. I was new to poetry and as I devoured hundreds of books of poetry over a four year period, I pasted yellow sticky notes on those poems I especially liked, along with jotted notes about my reaction to the poem. Eventually I decided to organize these into a single document to make it easier for me to find a particular poem I was interested in. It was a very small step from that document to this book.

A poetry book is commercially not the most practical book to write, and a broad based anthology such as this one is, perhaps, the least practical of the poetry books. So why do I think there's a place for this book in the market? I see two primary readers for this book. I believe that for a reader relatively new to poetry (as I was a few short years ago), this is a great first book of poetry. It includes a broad cross section of poetry in terms of time written (classic versus modern versus contemporary), poetic form, and author nationality (although there is an emphasis on authors writing in English). In addition, because this book collects together many of the best loved poems of all time I view it as a nice bedside companion for all poetry lovers.

I've included brief notes on many poems in the footnotes on each page. Each footnote includes the form of the poem, defines any unusual words, and where helpful for understanding includes a brief note on interpretation. Poetic meter is covered in an appendix to this book, and the notes on form use terminology from that appendix.

The criteria for being included in this book are three-fold. First, I must have been exposed to the poem somewhere. I'm certainly aware that there are a tremendous number of wonderful poems, and poets, not represented here simply because I have not yet had the pleasure of discovering their work. In those cases, I can only beg forgiveness and hold out the promise of future editions. Second, I must have liked the poem. There were no committees here, just a single editor. This means that the book will be filled with a lot of poems that are the style of poetry that I as a reader enjoy. To the extent that your taste in poetry is like mine, you will agree with my decisions. To the extent that your taste in poetry is unlike mine, you will disagree. Fortunately, my personal taste tends to be relatively broad so you are likely to find a good selection of poetic styles and subjects. Finally, the owner of the rights in the poem must have been willing to grant me the right to reprint the poem.

To better understand what I feel makes a poem good, and thereby to better understand my criteria for inclusion in this book, we need to turn to a document I wrote called "The Level Four Poetry Manifesto".

Level Four Poetry Manifesto

Poetry can be thought of as operating at four levels.

Level One: A poem should communicate clearly to the reader at the denotative level. In other words, with even a casual reading of the poem, a non-sophisticated reader should understand this surface message. The poem should offer something to the reader at level one in payment for their time reading the poem. For example, this might be an interesting story, a memorable image, a surprise ending, or a shared emotion. Multiple readers of the poem should agree on the Level One message of the poem. Level One deals with the concrete. Level One makes the poem successful for the non-skilled reader.

Level Two: A poem should communicate subtly to the reader at the connotative level, creating a desired mood within the reader. This is accomplished through poetic techniques such as word choice with attention to connotative meaning, imagery, and music. Music may include meter, rhyme, consonance, assonance, and attention to the emotional message of various consonants, vowels, and phonemes. Level

Two is focused on the skilled reader of poetry, but adds to the enjoyment for non-skilled readers as well.

Level Three: A poem may offer a separate, "hidden" message to the reader through the use of metaphor or similar techniques. In other words, all or part of the poem may represent something deeper in meaning than the surface description. The Level Three message should be recognizable to the skilled reader, and should be obvious to the non-skilled reader when it is pointed out.

Level Four: The Level Four poetry uses a symbol to offer a separate, "hidden" message to the reader. Metaphors may be symbols, but symbols are not necessarily metaphors. The use of symbols in Level Four poetry has both literal and representative meanings and the representative meaning is flexible with the reader able to fill in the specific meaning that applies most closely to their personal life.

The heart of the Level Four Manifesto is that each level builds on the previous levels, and levels should not be skipped if a poem is to be successful. I say this fully recognizing that some very well known poets have intentionally skipped levels and that many well known poets and poetry journals gravitate toward poetry that skips Level One. For example, Gertrude Stein often skipped Level One and focused on Level Two. Many schools of poetry skipped Levels One and Two and jumped directly to Level Three. However, I would argue that this skipping of levels is exactly why the general readership of poetry shrank during most of the Twentieth Century. New readers of poetry need to begin reading and appreciating a poem at level one, then level two, then level three, and finally fully appreciating it at level four. I believe that all poems that last hundreds of years will operate on Levels One and Two, that most will also operate on Level Three, and that many will operate on Level Four. Similarly, I believe that poets should begin writing at Level One, then add level Two, then Level Three, then Level Four.

Let's look at an example of a successful Level Four poem, Robert Frost's "The Road Not Taken". Here's the poem.

Two roads diverged in a yellow wood,
And sorry I could not travel both
And be one traveler, long I stood
And looked down one as far as I could
To where it bent in the undergrowth;

Then took the other, as just as fair,
And having perhaps the better claim,
Because it was grassy and wanted wear;
Though as for that the passing there
Had worn them really about the same,

And both that morning equally lay
In leaves no step had trodden black.
Oh, I kept the first for another day!
Yet knowing how way leads on to way,
I doubted if I should ever come back.

I shall be telling this with a sigh
Somewhere ages and ages hence:
Two roads diverged in a wood, and I—
I took the one less traveled by,
And that has made all the difference.

On Level One, it's a pleasant story about a walk through the woods. It's an enjoyable poem without delving any deeper into it than this. On Level Two he uses very clear descriptions of the woods and the paths (imagery), meter (iambic tetrameter), and rhyme. On Level Three the path and woods are a metaphor for the narrator's life. Finally, on Level Four the fork in the path is a symbol representing (quoting HowardM2 on the Poetry Free For All Bulletin Board):"a choice between two equally desirable alternatives one of which must be given up in order to have the other". As a symbol, this would obviously apply to many readers and would be personalized to represent individual choices they have had to make during their lives.

Notice that the poem can be appreciated by a reader at any level without any awareness that it is operating at a higher level, but that the more carefully one studies the poem the more meaning is discovered. This is the mark of a successful poem within the Level Four manifesto. All of the poems in this book are successful at levels one and two, most go to level three, and many go to level four.

Meter is an important concept in fully enjoying poetry, whether you are reading it aloud or silently, but fully understanding and appreciating poetic meter can be somewhat intimidating to the new reader. I've included notes on meter in Appendix A for those readers that are ambitious.

Organization of the Poems

The poems are sorted by author date of birth, then alphabetically by author, then alphabetically by poem title. In some cases where poems are related somehow or have a natural order, I've adjusted the order of the poems for a given author. I elected to group them by author date of birth rather than grouping them by subject or author last name for the following reasons:

- It is easier to read a group of poems all written in a single writing style based on the century when written, rather than jumping back and forth between modern English and 16th or 17th century English.

- It is helpful to see the evolution of different schools of poetry over time. Just observing different poetic styles come into and go out of favor over the centuries is insightful.

A Note on Meter

In Appendix A I provide guidance on poetic meter that may be of interest to the advanced reader, however a quick note here is relevant for all readers. For many of the earlier poets writing in English, poetic meter requires that an archaic pronunciation be used for certain words ending in "ed". For example, the work "banished" would be pronounced today in two syllables, or beats—ban-ished, however in old English it would be pronounced in three syllables, or beats—ban-ish-ed. Using the modern pronunciation will throw off the rhythm of these poems. To help the reader, in cases where the "ed" should be unnaturally pronounced as a separate syllable I have spelled it thus: ëd.

A few terms (slightly simplified here) will be especially helpful in reading the footnotes to the poems:

- Iambic: characterized by the pattern da-DUM;

- Dimeter, trimeter, tetrameter, pentameter, hexameter: Having lines with 2, 3, 4, 5, or 6 feet (e.g., iambs) per line;

- Ballad: alternating iambic tetrameter and iambic trimeter lines;

- Blank verse: unrhymed iambic pentameter; and

- Sonnet: Iambic pentameter, 14 lines.

A Request for Understanding and Assistance

Although I've worked hard on this book, it still contains errors. Any work of this size must have errors. I humbly request that you maintain a tolerant attitude toward these errors, and further request that you bring them to my attention so that I can fix them in future printings of the book. I can be reached care of Level Press at 13518 Jamul Drive, Jamul, CA91935, or email at William@Level4Press.com.

I hope that you enjoy reading this book as much as I've enjoyed compiling it!

William H. Roetzheim
Editor

Poems

Unknown (possibly 4,000 BC)

Ishtar[1]
Translated from the Babylonian Cuneiform by Lewis Spence

The unconsecrated foe entered my courts,
Placed his unwashed hands upon me,
And caused me to tremble.
Putting forth his hand
He smote me with fear.

He tore away my robe
And clothed his wife therein;
He stripped off my jewels
And placed them upon his daughter.

Like a quivering dove upon a beam
I sat.
Like a fleeing bird from my cranny
Swiftly I passed

From my temple.
Like a bird
They caused me to fly.

Archilochos (circa 700 BC – 650 BC)

Will, lost in a sea of trouble[2]
translated by Kenneth Rexroth

Will, lost in a sea of trouble,
Rise, save yourself from the whirlpool

---

[1] Form: Free verse
[2] Form: Free verse

Of the enemies of willing.
Courage exposes ambushes.
Steadfastness destroys enemies.
Keep your victories hidden.
Do not sulk over defeat.
Accept good. Bend before evil.
Learn the rhythm which binds all men.

The Bible

Address of Ruth to Naomi[1]

Entreat me not to leave thee,
    Or to return from following after thee:
For whither thou goest, I will go;
    And where thou lodgest, I will lodge.
Thy people shall be my people,
    And thy God my God.
Where thou diest, will I die,
    And there will I be buried.
The Lord do so to me, and more also,
    If ought but death part thee and me.

Mei Sheng (Circe 140 BC)

The Beautiful Toilet[2]
    Translated by Ezra Pound

Blue, blue is the grass about the river
And the willows have overfilled the close garden.
And within, the mistress, in the midmost of her youth,
White, white of face, hesitates, passing the door.
Slender, she puts forth a slender hand;
And she was a courtesan in the old days,
And she has married a sot,
Who now goes drunkenly out
And leaves her too much alone.

---

[1] Form: Free verse
[2] Form: Free verse—Vocabulary: courtesan: Mistress to powerful man; sot: an alcoholic.

Horace (65 BC – 8 BC)

The young bloods come less often now[1]
   Translated from the Latin by James Michie

The young bloods come round less often now,
Pelting your shutters and making a row
And robbing your beauty sleep. Now the door
Clings lovingly close to the jamb—though, before,

It used to move on its hinge pretty fast.
Those were the days—and they're almost past—
When lovers stood out all night long crying,
"Lydia, wake up! Save me! I'm dying!"

Soon your time's coming to be turned down

---

[1] Form: Iambic tetrameter, AABB end rhyme—Vocabulary: Thrace: ancient
region of southeast Balkan Peninsula; raddled: worn out; loins: crotch.

And to feel the scorn of the men about town—
A cheap hag haunting alley places
O moonless nights when the wind from Thrace is

Rising and raging, and so is the fire
In your raddled loins, the brute desire
That drives the mothers of horses mad.
You'll be lonely then and complain how sad

That the gay young boys enjoy the sheen
Of ivy best or the darker green
Of myrtle: dry old leaves they send
As a gift to the east wind, winter's friend.

Norse Myth (circa 50 BC)

from The Longbeards' Saga[1]
Translated by Charles Kingsley

Out of the morning land,
over the snowdrifts,
beautiful Freya came
tripping to Scoring.
White were the moorlands,
and frozen before her;
green were the moorlands,
and blooming behind her.
Out of her gold locks
shaking the spring flowers,
out of her garments
shaking the south wind,
around in the birches
awaking the throstles,
and making chaste housewives all
long for their heroes home.
Loving and love-giving,
came she to Scoring.

---

[1] Form: unrhymed syllabic (count stresses only) dimeter—Vocabulary:
Freya: Female Norse God of love and beauty; Scoring: A place in the
Northland; throstles: A song bird. —Notes: Freya represents the coming of
spring in victory over winter.

Petronius Arbiter (27 AD – 66 AD)

Doing, a filthy pleasure is, and short[1]
Translated from the Latin by Ben Jonson

Doing, a filthy pleasure is, and short;
And done, we straight repent us of the sport:
Let us not rush blindly on unto it,
Like lustful beasts, that only know to do it:
For lust will languish, and that heat decay,
But thus, thus, keeping endless holy-day,
Let us together closely lie, and kiss,
There is no labor, nor no shame in this;
This hath pleased, doth please and long will please; never
Can this decay, but is beginning ever.

Tao Yuan-ming (To-Em-Mei) (365-427)

The Unmoving Cloud[2]
Translated by Ezra Pound

I.
The clouds have gathered, and gathered,
and the rain falls and falls,
the eight ply of the heavens
are all folded into one darkness,
and the wide, flat road stretches out.
I stop in my room toward the East, quiet, quiet,
I pat my new cask of wine.
My friends are estranged, or far distant,
I bow my head and stand still.

II.
Rain, rain, and the clouds have gathered,
the eight ply of the heavens are darkness,
the flat land is turned into river.

---

[1] Form: Iambic pentameter, AABBCC . . . End rhymes—Vocabulary: —
Notes: The virtues of cuddling as opposed to sex.
[2] Form: Free verse—Vocabulary: ply: layers; estranged: on bad terms; —
Notes: Everyone, including even the birds, feels that their sorrow is unique.

"Wine, wine, here is wine!"
I drink by my eastern window.
I think of talking and man,
and no boat, no carriage, approaches.

III.
The trees in my east-looking garden
are bursting out with new twigs,
they try to stir new affection,

and men say the sun and moon keep on moving
because they can't find a soft seat.

IV.
The birds flutter to rest in my tree,
and I think I have heard them saying,
"It is not that there are no other men
But we like this fellow the best,
But however we long to speak
He can not know of our sorrow."

Li Po (701 – 762)

The River-Merchant's Wife: A Letter[1]
Translated from the Chinese by Ezra Pound

While my hair was still cut straight across my forehead
I played at the front gate, pulling flowers.
You came by on bamboo stilts, playing horse,
You walked about my seat, playing with blue plums.
And we went on living in the village of Chokan:
Two small people, without dislike or suspicion.

At fourteen I married My Lord you.
I never laughed, being bashful.
Lowering my head, I looked at the wall.
Called to, a thousand times, I never looked back.

---

[1] Form: Free verse—Vocabulary: —Notes: The wife gave up her dreams to be married, and now her husband is off seeing the world. In her letter she offers to travel a thousand miles to a distant village to meet him, with the subtle message that she still longs to see the world.

At fifteen I stopped scowling,
I desired my dust to be mingled with yours
Forever and forever and forever.
Why should I climb the lookout?

At sixteen you departed,
You went into far Ku-to-en, by the river of swirling eddies,
And you have been gone five months.
The monkeys make sorrowful noise overhead.

You dragged your feet when you went out,
By the gate now, the moss is grown, the different mosses,
Too deep to clear them away!
The leaves fall early this autumn, in wind.
The paired butterflies are already yellow with August
Over the grass in the West garden;
They hurt me. I grow older.
If you are coming down through the narrows of the river
    Kiang,
Please let me know beforehand,
And I will come out to meet you
                    As far as Cho-fu-sa.

Omar Khayam (1044-1123)
    Translated by Edward Fitzgerald

XI[1]

Here with a Loaf of Bread beneath the Bough,
A Flask of Wine, a Book of Verse—and Thou
    Beside me singing in the Wilderness—
And Wilderness is Paradise enow.

---

[1] Form: Iambic pentameter, AAxA end rhymes—Vocabulary: sans: without.

7

XXIII[1]

Ah, make the most of what we yet may spend,
Before we too into the Dust descend;
    Dust into Dust, and under Dust, to lie,
Sans Wine, sans Song, sans Singer, and—sans End!

XXVIII[2]

With them the Seed of Wisdom did I sow,
And with my own hand labor'd it to grow:
    And this was all the Harvest that I reap'd—
"I came like Water, and like Wind I go."

LI[3]

The Moving Finger writes; and, having writ,
Moves on: nor all thy Piety nor Wit
    Shall lure it back to cancel half a Line,
Nor all thy Tears wash out a Word of it.

Moritake (1452 – 1540)

One fallen flower[4]
    Translated from the Japanese by Peter Beilenson

ONE FALLEN FLOWER
    RETURNING TO THE
    BRANCH? . . . OH NO!
A WHITE BUTTERFLY

---

[1] Form: Iambic pentameter, AAxA end rhymes—Notes: "Them" may represent many things. For example, children or people who were given unheeded advice. Alternatively, the narrator may be God and the "them" is really "us".
[2] Form: Iambic pentameter, AAxA end rhymes—Vocabulary: piety: religious devotion—Notes: The moving finger is a central metaphor representing life.
[3] Form: Iambic pentameter, AAxA end rhymes—Vocabulary: bough: branch of tree; enow: enough.
[4] Form: Haiku—Notes: There is a Japanese legend about fallen flowers returning to the tree branch.

Sir Philip Sidney (1554 – 1586)

A Ditty[1]

My true-love hath my heart, and I have his,
By just exchange one for another given:
I hold his dear, and mine he cannot miss,
There never was a better bargain driven:
    My true-love hath my heart, and I have his.

My heart in me keeps him and me in one,
My heart in him his thoughts and senses guides:
He loves my heart, for once it was his own,
I cherish his because in me it bides:
    My true-love hath my heart, and I have his.

Be Your Words Made, Good Sir of Indian Ware[2]

Be your words made, good Sir, of Indian ware,
That you allow me them by so small rate?
Or do you cutted Spartans imitate?
Or do you mean my tender ears to spare
That to my questions you so total are?
When I demand of Phoenix Stella's state,
You say, forsooth, you left her well of late:
O God, think you that satisfies my care?

I would know whether she did sit or walk;
How clothed; how waited on; sighed she or smiled;
Whereof, with whom, how often did she talk;
With what pastime time's journey she beguiled;
If her lips deigned to sweeten my poor name:
Say all; and, all well said, still say the same.

---

[1] Form: Iambic pentameter, ABABA BCBCA end rhymes.
[2] Form: Iambic pentameter, ABBA end rhymes—Vocabulary: Indian Ware: expensive plates; cutted: wounded; Spartans: frugal Greek city state; "so total": giving summary information; Phoenix Stella: narrator's loved one.

Loving in Truth[1]

Loving in truth, and fain in verse my love to show,
That She, dear She, might take some pleasure of my pain;
Pleasure might cause her read,
    reading might make her know,
Knowledge might pity win, and pity grace obtain;
I sought fit words to paint the blackest face of woe,
Studying inventions fine, her wits to entertain;
Oft turning others' leaves, to see if thence would flow
Some fresh and fruitful showers
    upon my sunburned brain.
But words came halting forth, wanting Invention's stay;
Invention, Nature's child, fled step-dame Study's blows;
And others' feet still seemed but strangers in my way.
Thus, great with child to speak, and helpless in my throes,
Biting my truant pen, beating myself for spite.
"Fool," said my Muse to me, "look in thy heart, and write!"

To Sleep[2]

Come, Sleep; O Sleep! the certain knot of peace,
The baiting-place of wit, the balm of woe,
The poor man's wealth, the prisoner's release,
Th' indifferent judge between the high and low;
With shield of proof, shield me from out the prease
Of those fierce darts Despair at me doth throw:
O make in me those civil wars to cease;
I will good tribute pay, if thou do so.

---

[1] Form: Modified sonnet, Iambic hexameter, frequent trochee substitutions at line starts create a driving rhythm, ABAB end rhymes with closing CC couplet—Vocabulary: fain: happily; "turning others' leaves": reading the works of other authors; Invention: imagination; step-dame: stepmother; "great with child": pregnant.

[2] Form: Iambic pentameter, ABAB end rhymes—Vocabulary: baiting-place: applying bait to catch as in fishing; balm: salve; prease: press; garland: wreath of flowers—Notes: The narrator, missing Stella, seeks the escape of sleep, and offers to bribe a personified sleep by trading everything in his bedroom for the alternate world of sleep. He then considers that sleep already has the right to these things, so he sweetens the pot with the promise that after he is asleep then sleep will have the opportunity to see his love, Stella's image.

Take thou of me smooth pillows, sweetest bed,
A chamber deaf to noise and blind to light,
A rosy garland and a weary head:
And if these things, as being thine by right,
Move not thy heavy grace, thou shalt in me,
Livelier than elsewhere, Stella's image see.

Robert Greene (1560 – 1592)

Content[1]

Sweet are the thoughts that savor of content,
   The quiet mind is richer than a crown,
Sweet are the nights in careless slumber spent,
   The poor estate scorns Fortune's angry frown:
Such sweet content, such minds, such sleep, such bliss,
Beggars enjoy, when princes oft do miss.

The homely house that harbors quiet rest,
   The cottage that affords no pride nor care,
The mean that 'grees with country music best,
   The sweet consort of mirth and modest fare,
Obscurëd life sets down a type of bliss:
A mind content both crown and kingdom is.

Michael Drayton (1563-1631)

Love's Farewell[2]

Since there's no help, come let us kiss and part,—
Nay I have done, you get no more of me;
And I am glad, yea, glad with all my heart,
That thus so cleanly I myself can free;
Shake hands for ever, cancel all our vows,

---

[1] Form: Iambic pentameter, ABABCC end rhymes—Vocabulary: savor of: smell of; mean: value; 'grees: agrees.
[2] Form: Sonnet—Vocabulary: jot: smallest bit; decover: revive from death—Notes: He begins by exclaiming that his love for her is dead. He then says that, though it is lying there dead with faith kneeling next to it and innocence closing the dead eyes, even then she could change her mind and bring dead love back to life.

And when we meet at any time again,
Be it not seen in either of our brows
That we one jot of former love retain.
Now at the last gasp of love's latest breath,
When his pulse failing, passion speechless lies,
When faith is kneeling by his bed of death,
And innocence is closing up his eyes,
    —Now if thou would'st when all have given him over,
    From death to life thou might'st him yet decover!

William Shakespeare (1564-1616)

All the World's a Stage[1]

All the world's a stage,
And all the men and women merely players:
They have their exits and their entrances;
And one man in his time plays many parts,
His acts being seven ages. At first the infant,
Mewling and puking in the nurse's arms.
And then the whining school-boy, with his satchel
And shining morning face, creeping like snail
Unwillingly to school. And then the lover,
Sighing like furnace, with a woeful ballad
Made to his mistress' eyebrow. Then a soldier,
Full of strange oaths and bearded like the pard,
Jealous in honor, sudden and quick in quarrel,
Seeking the bubble reputation
Even in the cannon's mouth. And then the justice,
In fair round belly with good capon lined,
With eyes severe and beard of formal cut,
Full of wise saws and modern instances;
And so he plays his part. The sixth age shifts
Into the lean and slippered pantaloon,
With spectacles on nose and pouch on side,
His youthful hose, well saved, a world too wide
For his shrunk shank; and his big manly voice,
Turning again toward childish treble, pipes

---

[1] Form: Unrhymed iambic pentameter (blank verse)—Notes: underlying
message of needing to trust in faith after you have done everything you can
to protect or prepare something (someone) that you love.

12

And whistles in his sound. Last scene of all,
That ends this strange eventful history,
Is second childishness and mere oblivion,
Sans teeth, sans eyes, sans taste, sans everything.

Sonnet XVII[1]

Who will believe my verse in time to come,
If it were filled with your most high deserts?
Though yet, heaven knows, it is but as a tomb
Which hides your life and shows not half your parts.
If I could write the beauty of your eyes,
And in fresh numbers number all your graces,
The age to come would say "this poet lies;
Such heavenly touches ne'er touch'd earthly faces."
So should my papers, yellowed with their age,
Be scorned, like old men of less truth than tongue,
And your true rights be termed a poet's rage
And stretchëd meter of an antique song:
    But were some child of yours alive that time,
    You should live twice—in it, and in my rhyme.

Sonnet XVIII[2]

Shall I compare thee to a summer's day?
Thou art more lovely and more temperate;
Rough winds do shake the darling buds of May,
And summer's lease hath all too short a date:
Sometime too hot the eye of heaven shines,
And often is his gold complexion dimm'd,
And every fair from fair sometime declines,
By chance, or nature's changing course, untrimm'd.
But thy eternal summer shall not fade,
Nor lose possession of that fair thou owest;

---

[1] Form: Sonnet—Vocabulary: deserts: facts deserving reward.

[2] Form: Sonnet—Notes: Here Shakespeare asks if he should compare the object of his love to a summer day, a traditional comparison, and then makes the argument that his love is actually far better than a summer day because a summer day is transient and imperfect as described. He then argues that as long as people are reading this sonnet his love lives through the words in the sonnet, and thereby she achieves permanence far beyond that of a summer day.

Nor shall Death brag thou wanderest in his shade
When in eternal lines to time thou growest.
So long as men can breathe, or eyes can see
So long lives this, and this gives life to thee.

Sonnet XXXII[1]

If Thou survive my well-contented day
When that churl Death my bones with dust shall cover,
And shalt by fortune once more re-survey
These poor rude lines of thy deceasëd lover;
Compare them with the bettering of the time,
And though they be outstripp'd by every pen,
Reserve them for my love, not for their rhyme
Exceeded by the height of happier men.
O then vouchsafe me but this loving thought-
'Had my friend's muse grown with this growing age,
A dearer birth than this his love had brought,
To march in ranks of better equipage:
But since he died, and poets better prove,
Theirs for their style I'll read, his for his love.'

Sonnet LV[2]

Not marble, nor the gilded monuments
Of princes, shall outlive this powerful rhyme;
But you shall shine more bright in these contents
Than unswept stone besmeared with sluttish time.
When wasteful war shall statues overturn,

---

[1] Form: Sonnet—Vocabulary: churl: rude person; bett'ring: best; vouchsafe: grant—Notes: In this sonnet, Shakespeare contemplates the situation where his love outlives him. He considers that as time goes on, poets will write better and better poems until his current attempts are not as good relatively. He then asks his love to consider that if he had continued alive his ability to write verse would have improved as well, and asks that his love look at his sonnet not from the perspective of technical skill with poetry, but because of the deep love that it embodies. He suggests reading the new verse for the technical skills, but his for the emotions.
[2] Form: Sonnet—Vocabulary: broils: heat; enmity: hatred; —Notes: This sonnet shows a hyperbole of confidence, stating that his sonnet will outlast everything physical in proclaiming his love, and that it will not be eclipsed until his love rises up herself at the time of judgment.

And broils root out the work of masonry,
Nor Mars his sword nor war's quick fire shall burn
The living record of your memory.
'Gainst death and all-oblivious enmity
Shall you pace forth; your praise shall still find room
Even in the eyes of all posterity
That wear this world out to the ending doom.
    So, till the judgment that yourself arise,
    You live in this, and dwell in lovers' eyes.

Sonnet CXXX[1]

My mistress' eyes are nothing like the sun;
Coral is far more red, than her lips' red;
If snow be white, why then her breasts are dun;
If hairs be wires, black wires grow on her head.
I have seen roses damasked, red and white,
But no such roses see I in her cheeks;
And in some perfumes is there more delight
Than in the breath that from my mistress reeks.
I love to hear her speak, yet well I know
That music hath a far more pleasing sound;
I grant I never saw a goddess go—
My mistress, when she walks, treads on the ground,
    And yet, by heaven, I think my love as rare,
    As any she belied with false compare.

Sonnet CXXXVIII[2]

When my love swears that she is made of truth,
I do believe her though, I know she lies,
That she might think me some untutored youth,
Unlearnèd in the world's false subtleties.
Thus vainly thinking that she thinks me young,

---

[1] Form: Sonnet—Vocabulary: dun: brownish grey; damasked: used as decoration—Notes: Here Shakespeare makes fun of the various ways poets of the time described their loves through comparisons, concluding that even though his love does not fit the description of women in these other poems, she is actually as beautiful as any of them.
[2] Form: Sonnet—Notes: Although Shakespeare speaks of white lies of love involving his age, his words ring equally true for all of those white lies that we tell loved ones although both of us know they are false.

Although she knows my days are past the best,
Simply I credit her false-speaking tongue;
On both sides thus is simple truth suppressed.
But wherefore says she not she is unjust?
And wherefore say not I that I am old?
O! Love's best habit is in seeming trust,
And age in love, loves not to have years told.
   Therefore I lie with her and she with me,
   And in our faults by lies we flattered be.

Sonnet CXLIII[1]

Lo, as a careful housewife runs to catch
One of her feathered creatures broke away,
Sets down her babe, and makes all swift dispatch
In pursuit of the thing she would have stay;
Whilst her neglected child holds her in chase,
Cries to catch her whose busy care is bent
To follow that which flies before her face,
Not prizing her poor infant's discontent;
So runn'st thou after that which flies from thee,
Whilst I thy babe chase thee afar behind;
But if thou catch thy hope, turn back to me,

---

[1] Form: Sonnet—Vocabulary: feathered creatures: probably a chicken;—
Notes: The poet's love chases after something (another love, her freedom,
her career?) while he waits in the background for her return, wailing like
an infant. Note the pun on Will Shakespeare in the first line of the turn.

16

And play the mother's part, kiss me, be kind;
So will I pray that thou mayst have thy 'Will,'
If thou turn back and my loud crying still.

Sonnet CXLVII[1]

My love is as a fever, longing still,
For that which longer nurseth the disease;
Feeding on that which doth preserve the ill,
The uncertain sickly appetite to please.
My reason, the physician to my love,
Angry that his prescriptions are not kept,
Hath left me, and I desperate now approve
Desire is death, which physic did except.
Past cure I am, now Reason is past care,
And frantic-mad with evermore unrest;
My thoughts and my discourse as madmen's are,
At random from the truth vainly expressed;
For I have sworn thee fair, and thought thee bright,
Who art as black as hell, as dark as night.

Tomorrow, and Tomorrow, and Tomorrow[2]

Tomorrow, and tomorrow, and tomorrow
Creeps in this petty pace from day to day,
To the last syllable of recorded time;
And all our yesterdays have lighted fools
The way to dusty death. Out, out brief candle!
Life's but a walking shadow, a poor player
That struts and frets his hour upon the stage
And then is heard no more: it is a tale
Told by an idiot, full of sound and fury,
Signifying nothing.

---

[1] Form: Sonnet--Vocabulary: longer nurseth: prolongs; physic: medicine--
Notes: His love is the illness. His reason is the physician trying
unsuccessfully to cure him.
[2] Form: Unrhymed iambic pentameter (blank verse).

Thomas Campion (1567 – 1619)

Integer Vitae[1]

The man of life upright,
  Whose guiltless heart is free
From all dishonest deeds,
  Or thought of vanity;

The man whose silent days
  In harmless joys are spent,
Whom hopes cannot delude,
  Nor sorrow discontent;

That man needs neither towers
  Nor armor for defense,
Nor secret vaults to fly
  From thunder's violence:

He only can behold
  With unaffrighted eyes
The horrors of the deep
  And terrors of the skies.

Thus, scorning all the cares
  That fate or fortune brings,
He makes the heaven his book,
  His wisdom heavenly things;

Good thoughts his only friends,
  His wealth a well-spent age,
The earth his sober inn
  And quiet pilgrimage.

---

[1] Form: Iambic trimeter, xAxA end rhymes—Vocabulary: unaffrighted:
unfrightened—Notes: Thomas Campion echoes Robert Greene's feelings
about the happiness of a simple life, but makes his emphasis more the
religious aspects of a simple life unafraid of both worldly things and the
unknown afterlife because of a faith in the afterlife and a view of this life as
simply a pilgrimage.

Sir Henry Wotton (1568 – 1639)

Upon the Death of Sir Albert Morton's Wife[1]

He first deceased; she for a little tried
To live without him, liked it not, and died.

John Donne (1572-1631)

Community[2]

Good we must love, and must hate ill,
For ill is ill, and good good still,
  But there are things indifferent,
Which we may neither hate, nor love,
But one, and then another prove,
  As we shall find our fancy bent.

If then at first wise Nature had
Made women either good or bad,
  Then some we might hate, and some choose,
But since she did them so create,
That we may neither love, nor hate,
  Only this rests, All, all may use

If they were good it would be seen,
Good is as visible as green,
  And to all eyes it self betrays:
If they were bad, they could not last,
Bad doth it self, and others waste,
  So, they deserve nor blame, nor praise.

---

[1] Form: Iambic pentameter, AA end rhyme.
[2] Form: Iambic tetrameter, AABCCB end rhyme—Notes: To get the most
out of this, you need to picture a scene from the early 1600s: A group of
men are in an ale house, sitting around rough hewn wood tables, drinking
by firelight. John stands up, raises his mug, and entertains the group with
this poem to laughs and cheers. He argues that women are not inherently
or consistently either good or bad. He claims that if they were good, then it
would be obvious, while if they were bad then they would naturally die out.
He then makes the leap that women are men's to use as their mood suits
them, and that it is natural to discard them once they are used up.

But they are ours as fruits are ours,
He that but tastes, he that devours,
  And he that leaves all, doth as well:
Changed loves are but changed sorts of meat,
And when he hath the kernel eat,
  Who doth not fling away the shell?

Confined Love[1]

  Some man unworthy to be possessor
Of old or new love, himself being false or weak,
  Thought his pain and shame would be lesser,
If on womankind he might his anger wreak;
      And thence a law did grow,
      One might but one man know;
      But are other creatures so?

  Are sun, moon, or stars by law forbidden
To smile where they list, or lend away their light?
  Are birds divorced or are they chidden
If they leave their mate, or lie abroad a night?
      Beasts do no jointures lose
      Though they new lovers choose;
      But we are made worse than those.

  Who e'er rigged fair ships to lie in harbors,
And not to seek lands, or not to deal with all?
  Or built fair houses, set trees, and arbors,

---

[1] Form: Irregular meter for the first 3 lines of each stanza, ending with 2 lines of iambic trimeter and 1 line of iambic tetrameter starting each with a headless iamb.—Vocabulary: chidden: scolded; jointures: property set aside as inheritance—Notes: Another specialty of John is his poems written to seduce women through logical arguments, although I personally suspect they are either tongue-in-check or written more to the ale house crowds referenced earlier. In this poem, he argues that a weak man created monogamy to deprive women and make himself feel better. John argues that monogamy is not found in nature, that ships are not designed to sit in one harbor but to travel, and good things are meant to be enjoyed by many, not just one.

Only to lock up, or else to let them fall?
     Good is not good, unless
     A thousand it possess,
     But doth waste with greediness.

Death[1]

Death, be not proud, though some have callèd thee
Mighty and dreadful, for thou art not so:
For those whom thou think'st thou dost overthrow
Die not, poor Death; nor yet canst thou kill me.
From Rest and Sleep, which but thy pictures be,
Much pleasure, then from thee much more must flow;
And soonest our best men with thee do go-
Rest of their bones and souls' delivery!
Thou'rt slave to fate, chance, kings, and desperate men,
And dost with poison, war, and sicknesses dwell;
And poppy or charms can make us sleep as well
And better then they stroke. Why swell'st thou then?
     One short sleep past, we wake eternally,
     And Death shall be no more: Death, thou shalt die!

The Computation[2]

For the first twenty years, since yesterday,
     I scarce believed, thou couldst be gone away;
For forty more, I fed on favors past,
     And forty on hopes that thou wouldst they might last;
Tears drowned one hundred, and sighs blew out two;

---

[1] Form: Sonnet with unrhymed Volta.—Vocabulary: poppy: opium—Notes:
Later in his life, John became a priest and presumably gave up
womanizing. His poems transition to spiritual work. In this poem, he
argues that death is not as powerful as many claim. He says that sleep is
a sort of "mini-death" and not so bad. He concludes by saying that
physical death is just a short sleep before eternally awakening, with death
itself the thing that will then die.

[2] Form: Iambic pentameter, AABBCC . . . End rhymes—Notes: A fun way to
describe the seemingless endless hours during absence from his love. The
end is a bit confusing. He says that although time seems to last forever,
she should not think this means he is living a long life. Rather, because he
is dead (in spirit), it is as if he is an immortal ghost. But then, if he is an
immortal ghost, can he die, as he feels like he is dying.

A thousand, I did neither think nor do,
Or not divide, all being one thought of you;
Or in a thousand more, forgot that too.
Yet call not this long life; but think that I
Am, by being dead, immortal; can ghosts die?

The Curse[1]

Whoever guesses, thinks, or dreams, he knows
Who is my mistress, wither by this curse;
     His only, and only his purse
     May some dull whore to love dispose,
And then yield unto all that are his foes;
  May he be scorned by one, whom all else scorn,
  Forswear to others, what to her he hath sworn,
  With fear of missing, shame of getting, torn.

Madness his sorrow, gout his cramp, may he
Make, by but thinking, who hath made him such;
     And may he feel no touch
     Of conscience, but of fame, and be
Anguished, not that 'twas sin, but that 'twas she;
  In early and long scarceness may he rot
  For land which had been his, if he had not
  Himself incestuously an heir begot.

May he dream treason, and believe that he
Meant to perform it, and confesses, and die,
     And no record tell why;
     His sons, which none of his may be,
Inherit nothing but his infamy;
  Or may he so long parasites have fed,
  That he would fain be theirs whom he hath bred,

---

[1] Form: Mostly iambic pentameter, lines 3 and 4 of each stanza are iambic trimeter and iambic tetrameter. ABBAAACCC End rhymes—Vocabulary: dispose: commit; Forswear: renounce; gout: a disease; gamesters: one who plays games; interwish: wish mutually; annexed: added; schedules: appendices—Notes: I think this poem is a wonderful curse John casts on whoever discovers his secret mistress. In the end, he claims that if the victim of his curse is a woman nature has already cursed her more than all the ills of his curse. Again, I'm sure this was very entertaining to his buddies in that ale house.

And at the last be circumcised for bread.

The venom of all step dames, gamesters' gall,
What tyrants and their subjects interwish,
    What plants, mine, beasts, fowl, fish,
    Can contribute, all ill, which all
Prophets or poets spake, and all which shall
    Be annexed in schedules unto this by me,
    Fall on that man; For if it be a she
    Nature beforehand hath out-cursëd me.

William Drummond (1585 – 1649)

Life[1]

This Life, which seems so fair,
Is like a bubble blown up in the air
By sporting children's breath,
Who chase it everywhere
And strive who can most motion it bequeath.
And though it sometimes seem of its own might
Like to an eye of gold to be fix'd there,
And firm to hover in that empty height,
That only is because it is so light.
-But in that pomp it doth not long appear;
For when 'tis most admired, in a thought,
Because it erst was nought, it turns to nought.

Robert Herrick (1591 – 1674)

To the Virgins[2]

Gather ye rosebuds while ye may,
    Old time is still a-flying;
And this same flower that smiles today,
    Tomorrow will be dying.

---

[1] Form: Mostly iambic pentameter, irregular end rhymes—Vocabulary:
bequeath: give; erst: once; nought: nothing.
[2] Form: Ballad, ABAB end rhymes—Vocabulary: coy: flirtatiously shy;
tarry: wait.

The glorious lamp of heaven, the sun,
   The higher he's a-getting,
 The sooner will his race be run,
   And nearer he's to setting.

That age is best which is the first,
   When youth and blood are warmer;
But being spent, the worse, and worst
   Times still succeed the former.

Then be not coy, but use your time,
   And while ye may, go marry;
For having lost but once your prime
   You may for ever tarry.

Upon Julia's Clothes[1]

Whenas in silks my Julia goes,
Then, then, methinks, how sweetly flows
That liquefaction of her clothes.

Next, when I cast mine eyes and see
That brave vibration each way free,
Oh, how that glittering taketh me!

Thomas Carew (1595 – 1639)

Ingrateful Beauty Threatened[2]

Know, Celia, since thou art so proud,
   'Twas I that gave thee thy renown;
Thou had'st in the forgotten crowd
   Of common beauties lived unknown,
Had not my verse exhaled thy name,
And with it imped the wings of Fame.

---

[1] Form: Iambic tetrameter, AAA BBB end rhymes—Vocabulary:
liquefaction: turning to liquid.
[2] Form: Iambic tetrameter, ABABCC end rhymes—Vocabulary: imped:
grafted new feathers onto a falcon to increase speed or repair an injury.

That killing power is none of thine:
    I gave it to thy voice and eyes;
Thy sweets, thy graces, all are mine;
    Thou art my star, shin'st in my skies:
Then dart not from thy borrowed sphere
Lightning on him that fixed thee there.

Tempt me with such affrights no more,
    Lest what I made I uncreate;
Let fools thy mystic forms adore,
    I know thee in thy mortal state:
Wise poets that wrapt Truth in tales,
Knew her themselves through all her veils.

John Milton (1608 – 1674)

On His Blindness[1]

When I consider how my light is spent
   Ere half my days in this dark world and wide,
   And that one talent which is death to hide,
   Lodged with me useless, though my soul more bent
To serve therewith my Maker, and present
   My true account, lest He returning chide,
   'Doth God exact day labor, light denied?'
   I fondly ask. But Patience to prevent
That murmur, soon replies, 'God doth not need
   Either man's work or his own gifts. Who best
   Bear his mild yoke, they serve him best. His state
Is kingly: thousands at his bidding speed,
   And post o'er land and ocean without rest;
   They also serve who only stand and wait.'

Sir John Suckling (1609 – 1642)

Song: Why so pale and wan, fond lover?[2]

Why so pale and wan fond lover?
   Prithee, why so pale?
Will, when looking well can't move her,
   Looking ill prevail?
   Prithee, why so pale?

Why so dull and mute young sinner?

---

[1] Form: Sonnet—Vocabulary: chide: scold mildly—Notes: Milton was
working for many years on his greatest work, "Paradise Lost", a book
length poem written as a tribute to God. While half way done his eyesight
began to fail. Doctors told him to stop working on the book or go blind.
Here he expresses anger at God for putting him in this situation, but then
accepts that his role is to bear whatever God has in store for him.
Ultimately, he did go blind but continued to write using his daughters as
secretaries while he dictated.

[2] Form: Iambic but with many headless iambs at the start of lines, mixture
of tetrameter and trimeter in 4-3-4-3-3 pattern except the last two lines,
which are dimeter for emphasis, ABABB end rhymes—Vocabulary: wan:
depressed; Prithee: expression of polite request.

Prithee, why so mute?
Will, when speaking well can't win her,
    Saying nothing do't?
    Prithee, why so mute?

Quit, quit for shame, this will not move,
    This cannot take her;
If of herself she will not love,
    Nothing can make her;
    The devil take her.

Abraham Cowley (1618 – 1667)

Drinking[1]

The thirsty earth soaks up the rain,
And drinks and gapes for drink again;
The plants suck in the earth, and are
With constant drinking fresh and fair;
The sea itself (which one would think
Should have but little need of drink)
Drinks twice ten thousand rivers up,
So filled that they o'erflow the cup.
The busy Sun (and one would guess
By's drunken fiery face no less)
Drinks up the sea, and when he's done,
The Moon and Stars drink up the Sun:
They drink and dance by their own light,
They drink and revel all the night:
Nothing in Nature's sober found,
But an eternal health goes round.
Fill up the bowl, then, fill it high,
Fill all the glasses there—for why
Should every creature drink but I?
Why, man of morals, tell me why?

---

[1] Form: Iambic tetrameter, AABBCC. . . End rhymes—Vocabulary: By's: by
his.

Richard Lovelace (1618 – 1658)

To Lucasta, On Going to the Wars[1]

Tell me not, Sweet, I am unkind
    That from the nunnery
Of thy chaste breast and quiet mind,
    To war and arms I fly.

True, a new mistress now I chase,
    The first foe in the field;
And with a stronger faith embrace
    A sword, a horse, a shield.

Yet this inconstancy is such
    As you too shall adore;
I could not love thee, Dear, so much,
    Loved I not Honor more.

William Walsh (1663 – 1708)

Love and Jealousy[2]

How much are they deceived who vainly strive,
By jealous fears, to keep our flames alive?
Love's like a torch, which if secured from blasts,
Will faintlier burn; but then it longer lasts.
Exposed to storms of jealousy and doubt,
The blaze grows greater, but 'tis sooner out.

William Congreve (1670 – 1729)

False though she be to me and love[3]

False though she be to me and love,
    I'll ne'er pursue revenge;
For still the charmer I approve
    Though I deplore her change.

---

[1] Form: Ballad.
[2] Form: Iambic pentameter, AABB end rhymes.
[3] Form: Ballad.

In hours of bliss we oft have met:
    They could not always last;
And though the present I regret,
    I'm grateful for the past.

Ryusui (1691 – 1758)

A lost child crying[1]
Translated from the Japanese by Peter Beilenson

A LOST CHILD CRYING
    STUMBLING OVER
    THE DARK FIELDS . . .
CATCHING FIREFLIES

Jokun 助葷 (circa 1700)

Ah! I intended[2]
Translated from the Japanese by Peter Beilenson

AH! I INTENDED
    NEVER NEVER
    TO GROW OLD . . .
LISTEN: NEW YEAR'S BELL!

William Blake (1757 - 1827)

The Garden of Love[3]

I laid me down upon a bank,
Where Love lay sleeping;

---

[1] Form: Haiku.
[2] Form: Haiku.
[3] Form: Iambic, line length varies, irregular end rhymes—Vocabulary: heath: open land with low bushes; chaste: morally pure—Notes: This piece is a clever negative commentary on the Church. The Chapel has suddenly appeared in the garden of love, and the chapel gates are shut and it says "Thou shalt not". In other words, he is excluded and the church lays down laws forbidding things. So he turns to nature (or perhaps, pagan gods), but finds that the priests have destroyed that as well.

I heard among the rushes dank
Weeping, weeping.

Then I went to the heath and the wild,
To the thistles and thorns of the waste;
And they told me how they were beguiled,
Driven out, and compelled to the chaste.

I went to the Garden of Love,
And saw what I never had seen;
A Chapel was built in the midst,
Where I used to play on the green.

And the gates of this Chapel were shut
And "Thou shalt not," writ over the door;
So I turned to the Garden of Love
That so many sweet flowers bore.

And I saw it was filled with graves,
And tombstones where flowers should be;
And priests in black gowns were walking their rounds,
And binding with briars my joys and desires.

The Sick Rose[1]

O Rose, thou art sick!
The Invisible worm,
That flies in the night,
In the howling storm,

Has found out thy bed
Of crimson joy;
And his dark secret love
Does thy life destroy.

---

[1] Form: Roughly equal anapests and iambs, dimeter lines, xAxA end
rhymes—Notes: A classic symbolic metaphor for any evil or ill which
destroys from the inside out.

The Tiger[1]

Tiger, tiger, burning bright,
In the forests of the night,
What immortal hand or eye
Could frame thy fearful symmetry?

In what distant deeps or skies
Burnt the fire of thine eyes?
On what wings dare he aspire?
What the hand dare seize the fire?

And what shoulder and what art
Could twist the sinews of thy heart?
And when thy heart began to beat,
What dread hand and what dread feet?

What the hammer? What the chain?
In what furnace was thy brain?
What the anvil? What dread grasp
Dare its deadly terrors clasp?

When the stars threw down their spears,
And water'd heaven with their tears,
Did He smile His work to see?
Did He who made the lamb make thee?

Tiger, tiger, burning bright
In the forests of the night,
What immortal hand or eye
Dare frame thy fearful symmetry?

To See a World in a Grain of Sand[2]

To see a World in a Grain of Sand

---

[1] Form: Iambic pentameter with lots of headless iambs at the start of lines, AABB end rhymes—Notes: Although not necessarily obvious at first, this is really a religious philosophy piece. Did the same God that made peaceful lambs make the fierce tiger? Broadened, we might ask if the same God that created good is also responsible for creating evil?
[2] Form: Iambic, irregular line length, ABAB end rhymes.

And a Heaven in a Wild Flower,
Hold Infinity in the palm of your hand
And Eternity in an hour.

Robert Burns (1759 1796)

Epitaph for James Smith[1]

Lament him, Mauchline husbands a',
 He aften did assist ye;
For had ye staid hale weeks awa,
 Your wives they ne'er had miss'd ye.

Ye Mauchline bairns, as on ye press
 To school in bands thegither,
O tread ye lightly on his grass—
 Perhaps he was your father!

Epitaph on a Henpecked Squire[2]

As father Adam first was fool'd,
 (A case that's still too common,)
Here lies a man a woman ruled,
 The devil ruled the woman.

Epitaph on William Muir[3]

An honest man here lies at rest
As e'er God with his image blest;
The friend of man, the friend of truth,
The friend of age, and guide of youth:
Few hearts like his, with virtue warmed,
Few heads with knowledge so informed:
If there's another world, he lives in bliss;
If there is none, he made the best of this.

---

[1] Form: Ballad meter (alternating iambic tetrameter and iambic trimeter)—
Vocabulary: Lament: grieve for; Mauchline: village in Scotland; bairns:
children.
[2] Form: Ballad meter, ABAB end rhymes.
[3] Form: Iambic tetrameter, AABBCC. . . End rhymes.

Inconstancy in love[1]

Let not Woman e'er complain
   Of inconstancy in love;
Let not Woman e'er complain
   Fickle Man is apt to rove:
Look abroad thro' Nature's range,
Nature's mighty Law is change,
Ladies, would it not seem strange
   Man should then a monster prove!

Mark the winds, and mark the skies,
   Ocean's ebb, and ocean's flow,
Sun and moon but set to rise,
   Round and round the seasons go.
Why then ask of silly Man
To oppose great Nature's plan?
We'll be constant while we can—
   You can be no more, you know.

To A Louse[2]

ON SEEING ONE ON A LADY'S BONNET AT CHURCH

Ha! Whaur ye gaun, ye crowlin ferlie!
Your impudence protects you sairly;
I canna say but ye strunt rarely,
      Owre gauze and lace;
Tho', faith! I fear ye dine but sparely
      On sic a place.

Ye ugly, creepin, blastit wonner,

---

[1] Form: Iambic tetrameter with lots of headless iambs at the start of lines, ABABCCCB end rhymes.
[2] Form: iambic, 4-4-4-2-4-2 pattern, AAABAB end rhymes—Vocabulary: ferlie: wonder; strunt: swagger; Swith: haste off; haffet: sideburns; sprattle: scramble; bane: poison; grozet: gooseberry; rozet: resin; smeddum: a powder; droddum: the breech; flainen: flannel; aiblins: perhaps; duddie: ragged; wyliecoat: undervest; Lunardi: bonnet; abread: abroad—Notes: Observing a louse crawling around on a fine ladies bonnet, he comments that we would all be more humble if we could only see ourselves as others see us.

33

Detested, shunned by saunt an' sinner,
How daur ye set your fit upon her,
  Sae fine a lady!
Gae somewhere else and seek your dinner,
  On some poor body.

Swith, in some beggar's haffet squattle;
There ye may creep, and sprawl, and sprattle
Wi' ither kindred, jumpin cattle,
  In shoals and nations;
Whare horn or bane ne'er daur unsettle
  Your thick plantations.

Now haud ye there, ye're out o' sight,
Below the fatt'rels, snug an' tight;
Na faith ye yet! Ye'll no be right
  Till ye've got on it,
The vera tapmost, towering height
  O' Miss's bonnet.

My sooth! Right bauld ye set your nose out,

As plump an' grey as onie grozet:
O for some rank, mercurial rozet,
　　　Or fell, red smeddum,
I'd gie ye sic a hearty dose o't,
　　　Wad dress your droddum!

I wad na been surprised to spy
You on an auld wife's flainen toy;
Or aiblins some bit duddie boy,
　　　On's wyliecoat;
But Miss's fine Lunardi!—fie!
　　　How daur ye do't?

O Jenny, dinna toss your head,
An' set your beauties a' abroad!
Ye little ken what cursed speed
　　　The blastie's makin!
Thae winks and finger-ends, I dread,
　　　Are notice takin!

O, wad some Power the giftie gie us
To see oursels as others see us!
It wad frae monie a blunder free us
　　　An' foolish notion:
What airs in dress an' gait wad lea'e us,
　　　And ev'n Devotion!

To A Mountain Daisy[1]

ON TURNING ONE DOWN WITH THE PLOUGH, IN APRIL,
1786

Wee, modest, crimson-tipped flow'r,
Thou's met me in an evil hour;

---

[1] Form: iambic, 4-4-4-2-4-2 pattern, AAABAB end rhymes—Vocabulary:
maun: must; stoure: turmoil (overturned dirt); neebor: neighbor; bonie:
pretty; blithe: carefree; bield: shelter; histie: bare—Notes: The upturned
mountain daisy is observed, and then compared to a woman who is soiled
and lost (loses her virginity), a poet who is ruined (as by the critics), and
ultimately the observation that everyone will die as the daisy before him is
doomed.

For I maun crush amang the stour
               Thy slender stem:
To spare thee now is past my pow'r,
               Thou bonie gem.

Alas! It's no thy neebor sweet,
The bonie lark, companion meet,
Bending thee 'mang the dewy weet,
               Wi' spreckled breast!
When upward-springing, blythe, to greet
               The purpling east.

Cauld blew the bitter-biting north
Upon thy early, humble birth;
Yet cheerfully thou glinted forth
               Amid the storm,
Scarce reared above the parent-earth
               Thy tender form.

The flaunting flow'rs our gardens yield,
High shelt'ring woods and wa's maun shield;
But thou, beneath the random bield
               O' clod or stane,
Adorns the histie stibble-field,
               Unseen, alane.

There, in thy scanty mantle clad,
Thy snawie bosom sun-ward spread,
Thou lifts thy unassuming head
               In humble guise;
But now the share uptears thy bed,
               And low thou lies!

Such is the fate of artless maid,
Sweet flow'ret of the rural shade!
By love's simplicity betrayed,
               And guileless trust,
Till she, like thee, all soiled, is laid
               Low i' the dust.

Such is the fate of simple bard,

On life's rough ocean luckless starred!
Unskillful he to note the card
          Of prudent lore,
Till billows rage, and gales blow hard,
          And whelm him o'er!

Such fate to suffering worth is giv'n,
Who long with wants and woes has striv'n,
By human pride or cunning driv'n
          To mis'ry's brink,
Till wrenched of ev'ry stay but Heav'n,
          He, ruined, sink!

Ev'n thou who mourn'st the Daisy's fate,
That fate is thine—no distant date;
Stern Ruin's ploughshare drives, elate,
          Full on thy bloom,
Till crushed beneath the furrow's weight,
          Shall be thy doom!

William Wordsworth (1770 – 1850)

I Wandered Lonely As A Cloud[1]

I wandered lonely as a Cloud
that floats on high o'er Vales and Hills,
When all at once I saw a crowd,
A host, of golden Daffodils;
Along the Lake, beneath the trees,
Ten thousand dancing in the breeze.

The waves beside them danced, but they
Outdid the sparkling waves in glee:
A Poet could not but be gay
In such a laughing company:
I gazed—and gazed—but little thought
What wealth the show to me had brought:

---

[1] Form: Iambic tetrameter, ABABCC end rhymes—Vocabulary: vales: valley
with a stream; jocund: light hearted.

For oft, when on my couch I lie
In vacant or in pensive mood,
They flash upon that inward eye
Which is the bliss of solitude,
And then my heart with pleasure fills,
And dances with the Daffodils.

Nuns fret not at their convent's narrow room[1]

Nuns fret not at their Convent's narrow room;
And Hermits are contented with their Cells;
And Students with their pensive Citadels;
Maids at the Wheel, the Weaver at his Loom,
Sit blithe and happy; Bees that soar for bloom,
High as the highest Peak of Furness-Fells,
Will murmur by the hour in Foxglove bells:
In truth, the prison, unto which we doom
Ourselves, no prison is: and hence to me,
In sundry moods, 'twas pastime to be bound
Within the Sonnet's scanty plot of ground:
Pleased if some Souls (for such there needs must be)
Who have felt the weight of too much liberty,
Should find brief solace there, as I have found.

The Solitary Reaper[2]

Behold her, single in the field,
Yon solitary Highland Lass!
Reaping and singing by herself;
Stop here, or gently pass!
Alone she cuts and binds the grain,
And sings a melancholy strain;
0 listen! for the vale profound

---

[1] Form: Sonnet—Vocabulary: cells: rooms in a monastery; blithe: carefree; Furness: location in England—Notes: Most poets consider the sonnet the most restrictive of the poetic forms, yet here William writes a sonnet laughing at this attitude, and pointing out other people/things in life that enjoy the metaphorical confinement of a sonnet.

[2] Form: Iambic tetrameter, iambic trimeter for 3rd line in each stanza, ABABCCDD end rhymes—Vocabulary: vale: small valley normally with a stream; chaunt: chant; Hebrides: a group of Islands off the coast of Scotland.

Is overflowing with the sound.

No nightingale did ever chaunt
More welcome notes to weary bands
Of travelers in some shady haunt,
Among Arabian sands:
No sweeter voice was ever heard
In spring-time from the cuckoo-bird,
Breaking the silence of the seas
Among the farthest Hebrides.

Will no one tell me what she sings?
Perhaps the plaintive numbers flow
For old, unhappy, far-off things,
And battles long ago:
Or is it some more humble lay,
Familiar matter of to-day?
Some natural sorrow, loss, or pain,
That has been, and may be again!

Whate'er the theme, the maiden sang
As if her song could have no ending;
I saw her singing at her work,
And o'er the sickle bending;
I listen'd, till I had my fill;
And, as I mounted up the hill,
The music in my heart I bore
Long after it was heard no more.

We are Seven[1]

A simple Child,
That lightly draws its breath,
And feels its life in every limb,
What should it know of death?

I met a little cottage Girl:
She was eight years old she said;

---

[1] Form: Mostly ballad meter—Vocabulary: kerchief: head scarf; porringer: shallow bowl with a handle.

Her hair was thick with many a curl
That clustered round her head.

She had a rustic, woodland air,
And she was wildly clad:
Her eyes were fair, and very fair;
—Her beauty made me glad.

'Sisters and brothers, little Maid,
How many may you be?'
'How many? Seven in all,' she said,
And wondering looked at me.

'And where are they? I pray you tell.'
She answered, 'Seven are we;
And two of us at Conway dwell,
And two are gone to sea.

'Two of us in the church-yard lie,
My sister and my brother;
And, in the church-yard cottage, I
Dwell near them with my mother.'

'You say that two at Conway dwell,
And two are gone to sea,
Yet ye are seven! - I pray you tell,
Sweet Maid, how this may be.'

Then did the little maid reply,
'Seven boys and girls are we;
Two of us in the church-yard lie,
Beneath the church-yard tree.'

'You run above, my little Maid,
Your limbs they are alive;
If two are in the church-yard laid,
Then ye are only five.'

'Their graves are green, they may be seen.'
The little Maid replied,
'Twelve steps or more from my mother's door,

And they are side by side.

'My stockings there I often knit,
My kerchief there I hem;
And there upon the ground I sit,
And sing a song to them.

'And often after sun-set, Sir,
When it is light and fair,
I take my little porringer,
And eat my supper there.

'The first that died was sister Jane;
In bed she moaning lay,
Till God released her of her pain;
And then she went away.

'So in the church-yard she was laid;
And, when the grass was dry,
Together round her grave we played,
My brother John and I.

'And when the ground was white with snow,
And I could run and slide,
My brother John was forced to go,
And he lies by her side.'

'How many are you, then,' said I,
'If they two are in heaven?'
Quick was the little Maid's reply,
'O Master, we are seven.'

'But they are dead; those two are dead!
Their spirits are in heaven!'
'Twas throwing words away; for still
The little Maid would have her will,
And said, 'Nay, we are seven!'

Samuel Taylor Coleridge (1772 – 1834)

The Rime of the Ancient Mariner[1]

PART I

It is an ancient Mariner,
And he stoppeth one of three.
"By thy long beard and glittering eye,
Now wherefore stopp'st thou me?

"The Bridegroom's doors are opened wide,
And I am next of kin;
The guests are met, the feast is set:
May'st hear the merry din."

He holds him with his skinny hand,
"There was a ship,' quoth he.
"Hold off ! Unhand me, grey-beard loon!'
Eftsoons his hand dropt he.

He holds him with his glittering eye—
The Wedding-Guest stood still,
And listens like a three years' child:
The Mariner hath his will.

The Wedding-Guest sat on a stone:
He cannot choose but hear;
And thus spake on that ancient man,
The bright-eyed Mariner.

---

[1] Form: Ballad, xAxA end rhymes—Vocabulary: Eftsoons: soon; kirk: Scottish church; bassoon: wind instrument; minstrelsy: troop of minstrels; ken: recognized; swound: swoon; Albatross: sea bird; vespers: evening prayer time; averred: declared; fathom: six feet; wist: become aware of; water-sprite: nymph that inhabits the water; Gramercy: expression of surprise; Hither: to this place; weal: welfare of the community; gossameres: gauze like fabrics; twain: two; spectre-bark: ghost ship; clomb: climbed; bemocked: mocked; main: ocean; hoary: white with age; wan: pale; sedge: grass-like plant; corses: dead bodies; jargoning: nonsense talking; seraph: type of angel; shrieve: hear confession; trow: think; tod: bushy clump.

"The ship was cheered, the harbor cleared,
Merrily did we drop
Below the kirk, below the hill,
Below the lighthouse top.

"The Sun came up upon the left,
Out of the sea came he!
And he shone bright, and on the right
Went down into the sea.

"Higher and higher every day,
Till over the mast at noon—"
The Wedding-Guest here beat his breast,
For he heard the loud bassoon.

The bride hath paced into the hall,
Red as a rose is she;
Nodding their heads before her goes
The merry minstrelsy.

The Wedding-Guest he beat his breast,
Yet he cannot choose but hear;
And thus spake on that ancient man,
The bright-eyed Mariner.

"And now the Storm-blast came, and he
Was tyrannous and strong:
He struck with his o'ertaking wings,
And chased us south along.

"With sloping masts and dipping prow,
As who pursued with yell and blow
Still treads the shadow of his foe,
And forward bends his head,
The ship drove fast, loud roared the blast,
The southward aye we fled.

"And now there came both mist and snow,
And it grew wondrous cold:
And ice, mast-high, came floating by,
As green as emerald.

"And through the drifts the snowy clifts
Did send a dismal sheen:
Nor shapes of men nor beasts we ken—
The ice was all between.

"The ice was here, the ice was there,
The ice was all around:
It cracked and growled, and roared and howled,
Like noises in a swound!

"At length did cross an Albatross,
Thorough the fog it came;
As if it had been a Christian soul,
We hailed it in God's name.

"It ate the food it ne'er had eat,
And round and round it flew.
The ice did split with a thunder-fit;
The helmsman steered us through!

"And a good south wind sprung up behind;
The Albatross did follow,
And every day, for food or play,
Came to the mariners' hollo!

"In mist or cloud, on mast or shroud,
It perched for vespers nine;
Whiles all the night, through fog-smoke white,
Glimmered the white Moon-shine.'

"God save thee, ancient Mariner!
From the fiends, that plague thee thus!—
Why look'st thou so?"—With my cross-bow
I shot the Albatross.

PART II

The Sun now rose upon the right:
Out of the sea came he,
Still hid in mist, and on the left

Went down into the sea.

And the good south wind still blew behind,
But no sweet bird did follow,
Nor any day for food or play
Came to the mariners' hollo!

And I had done a hellish thing,
And it would work 'em woe:
For all averred, I had killed the bird
That made the breeze to blow.
Ah wretch ! said they, the bird to slay,
That made the breeze to blow!

Nor dim nor red, like God's own head,
The glorious Sun uprist:
Then all averred, I had killed the bird
That brought the fog and mist.
'Twas right, said they, such birds to slay,
That bring the fog and mist.

The fair breeze blew, the white foam flew,
The furrow followed free;
We were the first that ever burst
Into that silent sea.

Down dropt the breeze, the sails dropt down,
'Twas sad as sad could be;
And we did speak only to break
The silence of the sea!

All in a hot and copper sky,
The bloody Sun, at noon,
Right up above the mast did stand,
No bigger than the Moon.

Day after day, day after day,
We stuck, nor breath nor motion;
As idle as a painted ship
Upon a painted ocean.

Water, water, every where,
And all the boards did shrink;
Water, water, every where,
Nor any drop to drink.

The very deep did rot: O Christ!
That ever this should be!
Yea, slimy things did crawl with legs
Upon the slimy sea.

About, about, in reel and rout
The death-fires danced at night;
The water, like a witch's oils,
Burnt green, and blue and white.

And some in dreams assurèd were
Of the Spirit that plagued us so,
Nine fathom deep he had followed us
From the land of mist and snow.

And every tongue, through utter drought.
Was withered at the root;
We could not speak, no more than if
We had been choked with soot.

Ah! well a-day! what evil looks
Had I from old and young!
Instead of the cross, the Albatross
About my neck was hung.

PART III

There passed a weary time. Each throat
Was parched, and glazed each eye.
A weary time! a weary time!
How glazed each weary eye,
When looking westward, I beheld
A something in the sky.

At first it seemed a little speck,
And then it seemed a mist;

It moved and moved, and took at last
A certain shape, I wist.

A speck, a mist, a shape, I wist!
And still it neared and neared:
As if it dodged a water-sprite,
It plunged and tacked and veered.

With throats unslaked, with black lips baked,
We could nor laugh nor wail;
Through utter drought all dumb we stood!
I bit my arm, I sucked the blood,
And cried, A sail! a sail!

With throats unslaked, with black lips baked,
Agape they heard me call:
Gramercy! they for joy did grin,
And all at once their breath drew in,
As they were drinking all.

See! see! (I cried) she tacks no more!
Hither to work us weal;
Without a breeze, without a tide,
She steadies with upright keel!

The western wave was all a-flame.
The day was well nigh done!
Almost upon the western wave
Rested the broad bright Sun;
When that strange shape drove suddenly
Betwixt us and the Sun.

And straight the Sun was flecked with bars,
(Heaven's Mother send us grace!)
As if through a dungeon-grate he peered
With broad and burning face.

Alas! (thought I, and my heart beat loud)
How fast she nears and nears!
Are those her sails that glance in the Sun,
Like restless gossameres?

Are those her ribs through which the Sun
Did peer, as through a grate?
And is that Woman all her crew?
Is that a Death? And are there two?
Is Death that woman's mate?

Her lips were red, her looks were free,
Her locks were yellow as gold:
Her skin was as white as leprosy,
The Night-mare Life-in-Death was she,
Who thicks man's blood with cold.

The naked hulk alongside came,
And the twain were casting dice;
"The game is done! I've won! I've won!"
Quoth she, and whistles thrice.

The Sun's rim dips; the stars rush out:
At one stride comes the dark;
With far-heard whisper, o'er the sea,
Off shot the spectre-bark.

We listened and looked sideways up!
Fear at my heart, as at a cup,

My life-blood seemed to sip!
The stars were dim, and thick the night,

The steerman's face by his lamp gleamed white;
From the sails the dew did drip—
Till clomb above the eastern bar
The horned Moon, with one bright star
Within the nether tip.

One after one, by the star-dogged Moon,
Too quick for groan or sigh,
Each turned his face with a ghastly pang,
And cursed me with his eye.

Four times fifty living men,
(and I heard nor sigh nor groan)
With heavy thump, a lifeless lump,
They dropped down one by one.

The souls did from their bodies fly,—
They fled to bliss or woe!
And every soul, it passed me by,
Like the whizz of my cross-bow!

PART IV

"I fear thee, ancient Mariner!
I fear thy skinny hand!
And thou art long, and lank, and brown,
As is the ribbed sea-sand.

"I fear thee and thy glittering eye,
And thy skinny hand, so brown."—
Fear not, fear not, thou Wedding-Guest!
This body dropt not down.

Alone, alone, all, all alone,
Alone on a wide wide sea!
And never a saint took pity on
My soul in agony.

The many men, so beautiful!
And they all dead did lie:
And a thousand thousand slimy things
Lived on; and so did I.

I looked upon the rotting sea,
And drew my eyes away;
I looked upon the rotting deck,
And there the dead men lay.

I looked to heaven, and tried to pray;
But or ever a prayer had gusht,
A wicked whisper came, and made
My heart as dry as dust.

I closed my lids, and kept them close,
And the balls like pulses beat;
For the sky and the sea, and the sea and the sky
Lay like a load on my weary eye,
And the dead were at my feet.

The cold sweat melted from their limbs,
Nor rot nor reek did they:
The look with which they looked on me
Had never passed away.

An orphan's curse would drag to hell
A spirit from on high;
But oh! more horrible than that
Is the curse in a dead man's eye!
Seven days, seven nights, I saw that curse,
And yet I could not die.

The moving Moon went up the sky,
And no where did abide:
Softly she was going up,
And a star or two beside—

Her beams bemocked the sultry main,
Like April hoar-frost spread;
But where the ship's huge shadow lay,

The charmed water burnt alway
A still and awful red.

Beyond the shadow of the ship,
I watched the water-snakes:
They moved in tracks of shining white,
And when they reared, the elfish light
Fell off in hoary flakes.

Within the shadow of the ship
I watched their rich attire:
Blue, glossy green, and velvet black,
They coiled and swam; and every track
Was a flash of golden fire.

O happy living things! no tongue
Their beauty might declare:
A spring of love gushed from my heart,
And I blessed them unaware:
Sure my kind saint took pity on me,
And I blessed them unaware.

The selfsame moment I could pray;
And from my neck so free
The Albatross fell off, and sank
Like lead into the sea.

PART V

Oh sleep! It is a gentle thing,
Beloved from pole to pole!
To Mary Queen the praise be given!
She sent the gentle sleep from Heaven,
That slid into my soul.

The silly buckets on the deck,
That had so long remained,
I dreamt that they were filled with dew;
And when I awoke, it rained.

My lips were wet, my throat was cold,
My garments all were dank;
Sure I had drunken in my dreams,
And still my body drank.

I moved, and could not feel my limbs:
I was so light—almost
I thought that I had died in sleep,
And was a blessed ghost.

And soon I heard a roaring wind:
It did not come anear;
But with its sound it shook the sails,
That were so thin and sere.

The upper air burst into life!
And a hundred fire-flags sheen,
To and fro they were hurried about!
And to and fro, and in and out,
The wan stars danced between.

And the coming wind did roar more loud,
And the sails did sigh like sedge;
And the rain poured down from one black cloud;
The Moon was at its edge.

The thick black cloud was cleft, and still
The Moon was at its side:
Like waters shot from some high crag,
The lightning fell with never a jag,
A river steep and wide.

The loud wind never reached the ship,
Yet now the ship moved on!
Beneath the lightning and the Moon
The dead men gave a groan.

They groaned, they stirred, they all uprose,
Nor spake, nor moved their eyes;
It had been strange, even in a dream,
To have seen those dead men rise.

The helmsman steered, the ship moved on;
Yet never a breeze up-blew;
The mariners all 'gan work the ropes,
Where they were wont to do;
They raised their limbs like lifeless tools—
We were a ghastly crew.

The body of my brother's son
Stood by me, knee to knee:
The body and I pulled at one rope,
But he said nought to me.

"I fear thee, ancient Mariner!"
Be calm, thou Wedding-Guest!
'Twas not those souls that fled in pain,
Which to their corses came again,
But a troop of spirits blest:

For when it dawned—they dropped their arms,
And clustered round the mast;
Sweet sounds rose slowly through their mouths,
And from their bodies passed.

Around, around, flew each sweet sound,
Then darted to the Sun;
Slowly the sounds came back again,
Now mixed, now one by one.

Sometimes a-dropping from the sky
I heard the sky-lark sing;
Sometimes all little birds that are,
How they seemed to fill the sea and air
With their sweet jargoning!

And now 'twas like all instruments,
Now like a lonely flute;
And now it is an angel's song,
That makes the heavens be mute.

It ceased; yet still the sails made on
A pleasant noise till noon,
A noise like of a hidden brook
In the leafy month of June,
That to the sleeping woods all night
Singeth a quiet tune.

Till noon we quietly sailed on,
Yet never a breeze did breathe:
Slowly and smoothly went the ship,
Moved onward from beneath.

Under the keel nine fathom deep,
From the land of mist and snow,
The spirit slid: and it was he
That made the ship to go.
The sails at noon left off their tune,
And the ship stood still also.

The Sun, right up above the mast,
Had fixed her to the ocean:
But in a minute she 'gan stir,
With a short uneasy motion—
Backwards and forwards half her length
With a short uneasy motion.

Then like a pawing horse let go,
She made a sudden bound:
It flung the blood into my head,
And I fell down in a swound.

How long in that same fit I lay,
I have not to declare;
But ere my living life returned,
I heard and in my soul discerned
Two voices in the air.

"Is it he?" quoth one, "Is this the man?
By him who died on cross,
With his cruel bow he laid full low
The harmless Albatross.

"The spirit who bideth by himself
In the land of mist and snow,
He loved the bird that loved the man
Who shot him with his bow."

The other was a softer voice,
As soft as honey-dew:
Quoth he, "The man hath penance done,
And penance more will do."

PART VI

FIRST VOICE
"But tell me, tell me! Speak again,
Thy soft response renewing—
What makes that ship drive on so fast?
What is the ocean doing?"

SECOND VOICE
"Still as a slave before his lord,
The ocean hath no blast;
His great bright eye most silently
Up to the moon is cast—

"If he may know which way to go;
For she guides him smooth or grim.
See, brother, see! How graciously
She looketh down on him."

FIRST VOICE
"But why drives on that ship so fast,
Without or wave or wind?"

SECOND VOICE

"The air is cut away before,
And closes from behind.

"Fly, brother, fly! More high, more high!
Or we shall be belated:

For slow and slow that ship will go,
When the Mariner's trance is abated."

I woke, and we were sailing on
As in a gentle weather:
'Twas night, calm night, the moon was high,
The dead men stood together.

All stood together on the deck,
For a charnel-dungeon fitter:
All fixed on me their stony eyes,
That in the Moon did glitter.

The pang, the curse, with which they died,
Had never passed away:
I could not draw my eyes from theirs,
Nor turn them up to pray.

And now this spell was snapt: once more
I viewed the ocean green,
And looked far forth, yet little saw
Of what had else been seen—

Like one, that on a lonesome road
Doth walk in fear and dread,
And having once turned round walks on,
And turns no more his head;
Because he knows, a frightful fiend
Doth close behind him tread.

But soon there breathed a wind on me,
Nor sound nor motion made:
Its path was not upon the sea,
In ripple or in shade.

It raised my hair, it fanned my cheek
Like a meadow-gale of spring—
It mingled strangely with my fears,
Yet it felt like a welcoming.

Swiftly, swiftly flew the ship,
Yet she sailed softly too:
Sweetly, sweetly blew the breeze—
On me alone it blew.

Oh! dream of joy! is this indeed
The light-house top I see?
Is this the hill? is this the kirk?
Is this mine own countree?

We drifted o'er the harbor-bar,
And I with sobs did pray—
O let me be awake, my God!
Or let me sleep alway.

The harbor-bay was clear as glass,
So smoothly it was strewn!
And on the bay the moonlight lay,
And the shadow of the Moon.

The rock shone bright, the kirk no less,
That stands above the rock:
The moonlight steeped in silentness
The steady weathercock.

And the bay was white with silent light
Till rising from the same,
Full many shapes, that shadows were,
In crimson colors came.

A little distance from the prow
Those crimson shadows were:
I turned my eyes upon the deck—
Oh, Christ! what saw I there!

Each corse lay flat, lifeless and flat,
And, by the holy rood!
A man all light, a seraph-man,
On every corse there stood.

This seraph-band, each waved his hand:
It was a heavenly sight!
They stood as signals to the land,
Each one a lovely light;

This seraph-band, each waved his hand,
No voice did they impart—
No voice; but oh! the silence sank
Like music on my heart.

But soon I heard the dash of oars,
I heard the Pilot's cheer;
My head was turned perforce away
And I saw a boat appear.

The Pilot and the Pilot's boy,
I heard them coming fast:
Dear Lord in Heaven! it was a joy
The dead men could not blast.

I saw a third—I heard his voice:
It is the Hermit good!
He singeth loud his godly hymns
That he makes in the wood.
He'll shrieve my soul, he'll wash away
The Albatross's blood.

PART VII

This Hermit good lives in that wood
Which slopes down to the sea.
How loudly his sweet voice he rears!
He loves to talk with mariners
That come from a far countree.

He kneels at morn, and noon, and eve—
He hath a cushion plump:
It is the moss that wholly hides
The rotted old oak-stump.

The skiff-boat neared: I heard them talk,
"Why, this is strange, I trow!
Where are those lights so many and fair,
That signal made but now?"

"Strange, by my faith!" the Hermit said—
"and they answered not our cheer!
The planks looked warped! and see those sails,
How thin they are and sere!
I never saw aught like to them,
Unless perchance it were

"Brown skeletons of leaves that lag
My forest-brook along;
When the ivy-tod is heavy with snow,
And the owlet whoops to the wolf below,
That eats the she-wolf's young."

"Dear Lord! it hath a fiendish look—
(the Pilot made reply)
I am a-feared"—"Push on, push on!"
Said the Hermit cheerily.

The boat came closer to the ship,
But I nor spake nor stirred;
The boat came close beneath the ship,
And straight a sound was heard.

Under the water it rumbled on,
Still louder and more dread:
It reached the ship, it split the bay;
The ship went down like lead.

Stunned by that loud and dreadful sound,
Which sky and ocean smote,
Like one that hath been seven days drowned
My body lay afloat;
But swift as dreams, myself I found
Within the Pilot's boat.

Upon the whirl, where sank the ship,
The boat spun round and round;
And all was still, save that the hill
Was telling of the sound.

I moved my lips—the Pilot shrieked
And fell down in a fit;
The holy Hermit raised his eyes,
And prayed where he did sit.

I took the oars: the Pilot's boy,
Who now doth crazy go,
Laughed loud and long, and all the while
His eyes went to and fro.
"Ha! Ha!" quoth he, "full plain I see,
The Devil knows how to row."

And now, all in my own countree,
I stood on the firm land!
The Hermit stepped forth from the boat,
And scarcely he could stand.

"O shrieve me, shrieve me, holy man!"
The Hermit crossed his brow.
"Say quick," quoth he, "I bid thee say—
What manner of man art thou?"

Forthwith this frame of mine was wrenched
With a woeful agony,
Which forced me to begin my tale;
And then it left me free.

Since then, at an uncertain hour,
That agony returns:
And till my ghastly tale is told,
This heart within me burns.

I pass, like night, from land to land;
I have strange power of speech;
That moment that his face I see,
I know the man that must hear me:

To him my tale I teach.

What loud uproar bursts from that door!
The wedding-guests are there:
But in the garden-bower the bride
And bride-maids singing are:
And hark the little vesper bell
Which biddeth me to prayer!

O Wedding-Guest! This soul hath been
Alone on a wide wide sea:
So lonely 'twas, that God himself
Scarce seemed there to be.

O sweeter than the marriage-feast,
'Tis sweeter far to me,
To walk together to the kirk
With a goodly company!—

To walk together to the kirk,
And all together pray,
While each to his great Father bends,
Old men, and babes, and loving friends
And youths and maidens gay!

Farewell, farewell! but this I tell
To thee, thou Wedding-Guest!
He prayeth well, who loveth well
Both man and bird and beast.

He prayeth best, who loveth best
All things both great and small;
For the dear God who loveth us,
He made and loveth all.

The Mariner, whose eye is bright,
Whose beard with age is hoar,
Is gone: and now the Wedding-Guest
Turned from the bridegroom's door.

He went like one that hath been stunned,
And is of sense forlorn:
A sadder and a wiser man,
He rose the morrow morn.

Robert Southey (1774 – 1843)

After Blenheim[1]

It was a summer evening,
    Old Kaspar's work was done,
And he before his cottage door
    Was sitting in the sun;
And by him sported on the green
His little grandchild Wilhelmine.

She saw her brother Peterkin
    Roll something large and round
Which he beside the rivulet
    In playing there had found;
He came to ask what he had found
That was so large and smooth and round.

Old Kaspar took it from the boy,
    Who stood expectant by;
And then the old man shook his head,
    And with a natural sigh,
"'Tis some poor fellow's skull," said he,
"Who fell in the great victory."

"I find them in the garden,
    For there's many here about;
And often, when I go to plough,
    The ploughshare turns them out;
For many thousand men," said he,
"Were slain in that great victory."

---

[1] Form: iambic, 4-3-4-3-4-4- pattern, xAxABB end rhymes—Vocabulary:
Blenheim: site of battle in 1704 as part of War of Spanish Succession;
childing: pregnant; —Notes: Some wars seem pointless at the time, some
seem pointless only in hindsight, but an argument can be made that from
a long enough historic perspective all wars are pointless.

"Now tell us what 'twas all about,"
    Young Peterkin he cries;
And little Wilhelmine looks up
    With wonder-waiting eyes;
"Now tell us all about the war,
And what they fought each other for."

"It was the English," Kaspar cried,
    "Who put the French to rout;
But what they fought each other for
    I could not well make out.
But everybody said," quoth he,
"That 'twas a famous victory.

"My father lived at Blenheim then,
    Yon little stream hard by;
They burnt his dwelling to the ground,
    And he was forced to fly:
So with his wife and child he fled,
Nor had he where to rest his head.

"With fire and sword the country round
    Was wasted far and wide,
And many a childing mother then
    And newborn baby died;
But things like that, you know, must be
At every famous victory.

"They say it was a shocking sight
    After the field was won;
For many thousand bodies here
    Lay rotting in the sun;
But things like that, you know, must be
After a famous victory.

"Great praise the Duke of Marlbro' won,
　　And our good Prince Eugene."
"Why, 'twas a very wicked thing!"
　　Said little Wilhelmine.
"Nay...nay... My little girl," quoth he,
"It was a famous victory.

"And everybody praised the Duke
　　Who this great fight did win."
"But what good came of it at last?"
　　Quoth little Peterkin.
"Why that I cannot tell," said he,
"But 'twas a famous victory."

The Scholar[1]

My days among the Dead are past;
Around me I behold,
Where'er these casual eyes are cast,
The mighty minds of old:
My never-failing friends are they,
With whom I converse day by day.

With them I take delight in weal
And seek relief in woe;

---

[1] Form: Iambic, 4-3-4-3-4-4 pattern; ABABCC end rhymes—Vocabulary:
weal: well being; —Notes: The narrator seeks companionship in books, and
hopes that his writing will grant him some measure of immortal life, as the
authors around him have achieved some degree of immortality.

And while I understand and feel
How much to them I owe,
My cheeks have often been bedewed
With tears of thoughtful gratitude.

My thoughts are with the Dead; with them
I live in long-past years,
Their virtues love, their faults condemn,
Partake their hopes and fears,
And from their lessons seek and find
Instruction with an humble mind.

My hopes are with the Dead; anon
My place with them will be,
And I with them shall travel on
Through all Futurity;
Yet leaving here a name, I trust,
That will not perish in the dust.

Walter Savage Landor (1775 – 1864)

On His Seventy-Fifth Birthday[1]

I strove with none; for none was worth my strife;
Nature I loved, and next to Nature, Art;
I warmed both hands before the fire of life;
It sinks, and I am ready to depart.

Well I Remember[2]

Well I remember how you smiled
    To see me write your name upon
The soft sea-sand . . . "*O! What a child!*
    You think you're writing upon stone!"

I have since written what no tide
    Shall ever wash away, what men
Unborn shall read o'er ocean wide

---

[1] Form: Iambic pentameter, ABAB end rhymes.
[2] Form: Iambic tetrameter, ABAB end rhymes—Notes: Another example in
the "eternal life through poetry" theme.

And find Ianthe's name again.

Thomas Moore (1779 – 1852)

An Argument[1]

I've oft been told by learned friars,
    That wishing and the crime are one,
And Heaven punishes desires
    As much as if the deed were done.

If wishing damns us, you and I
    Are damned to all our heart's content;
Come, then, at least we may enjoy
    Some pleasure for our punishment!

Tis the Last Rose of Summer[2]

'Tis the last rose of Summer,
    Left blooming alone;
All her lovely companions
    Are faded and gone;
No flower of her kindred,
    No rosebud is nigh,
To reflect back her blushes,
    Or give sigh for sigh!

I'll not leave thee, thou lone one,
    To pine on the stem;
Since the lovely are sleeping,
    Go, sleep thou with them.
Thus kindly I scatter
    Thy leaves o'er the bed
Where thy mates of the garden
    Lie scentless and dead.

---

[1] Form: Iambic tetrameter, ABAB end rhymes.
[2] Form: Anapestic dimeter, xAxAxBxB end rhymes—Notes: The last, lonely rose in a flowerbed is compared to the narrator, who is similarly at the end of his life with all of his companions dead and gone.

So soon may I follow,
    When friendships decay,
And from Love's shining circle
    The gems drop away!
When true hearts lie withered,
    And fond ones are flown,
Oh! Who would inhabit
    This bleak world alone?

George Gordon, Lord Byron (1788 – 1824)

She Walks in Beauty[1]

She walks in beauty, like the night
Of cloudless climes and starry skies;
And all that's best of dark and bright
Meet in her aspect and her eyes:
Thus mellowed to that tender light
Which heaven to gaudy day denies.

One shade the more, one ray the less,
Had half impaired the nameless grace
Which waves in every raven tress,
Or softly lightens o'er her face;
Where thoughts serenely sweet express
How pure, how dear their dwelling-place.

And on that cheek, and o'er that brow,
So soft, so calm, yet eloquent,
The smiles that win, the tints that glow,
But tell of days in goodness spent,
A mind at peace with all below,
A heart whose love is innocent!

---

[1] Form: Iambic tetrameter, ABABAB end rhymes—Vocabulary: raven: black and shiny.

So, we'll go no more a-roving[1]

So, we'll go no more a-roving
    So late into the night,
Though the heart still be as loving,
    And the moon still be as bright.

For the sword outwears its sheath,
    And the soul outwears the breast,
And the heart must pause to breathe,
    And love itself have rest.

Though the night was made for loving,
    And the day returns too soon,
Yet we'll go no more a-roving
    By the light of the moon.

Percy Bysshe Shelley (1792 – 1822)

Music[2]

Music, when soft voices die,
Vibrates in the memory;
Odors, when sweet violets sicken,
Live within the sense they quicken.

Rose leaves, when the rose is dead,
Are heaped for the beloved's bed;
And so thy thoughts, when thou art gone,
Love itself shall slumber on.

---

[1] Form: Iambic trimeter, ABAB end rhymes—Notes: In this case, the we is the narrator, now too old to spend the night in amorous adventures.
[2] Form: Iambic tetrameter xxAA end rhymes—Vocabulary: quicken: stimulate.

Mutability[1]

The flower that smiles today
    Tomorrow dies;
All that we wish to stay
    Tempts and then flies.
What is this world's delight?
Lightning that mocks the night,
    Brief even as bright.

Virtue, how frail it is!
    Friendship how rare!
Love, how it sells poor bliss
    For proud despair!
But we, though soon they fall,
Survive their joy, and all
    Which ours we call.

Whilst skies are blue and bright,
    Whilst flowers are gay,
Whilst eyes that change ere night
    Make glad the day;
Whilst yet the calm hours creep,
Dream thou—and from thy sleep
    Then wake to weep.

Ozymandias[2]

---

[1] Form: Iambic, 3-2-3-2-3-3-2 pattern, ABABCCC end rhymes—Notes: Most of this poem has a fairly straight-forward "carpe diem", or "seize the day" theme, beginning with the fleeting nature of nature's delights, then moving to the fleeting nature of human interactions and traits, and entreating the reader to seize the day. The last two lines, however, are a significant shift in tone and deepening of the message. My personal interpretation is that Shelley is telling us to enjoy the beauty that we see around us now, because like a dream, it will suddenly vanish and leave us weeping.

[2] Form: Sonnet—Vocabulary: Ozymandias; Greek translation of Egyptian Ramesses the Great; visage: expression—Notes: The message of the poem involves both the transience of earthly power, and also the fact that what comes closest to giving lasting life is art. The actual inscription on the tomb in Egypt reads: "King of Kings am I, Osymandias. If anyone would know how great I am and where I lie, let him surpass one of my works."

I met a traveler from an antique land
Who said: `Two vast and trunk-less legs of stone
Stand in the desert. Near them, on the sand,
Half sunk, a shattered visage lies, whose frown,
And wrinkled lip, and sneer of cold command,
Tell that its sculptor well those passions read
Which yet survive, stamped on these lifeless things,
The hand that mocked them and the heart that fed.
And on the pedestal these words appear—
"My name is Ozymandias, king of kings:
Look on my works, ye Mighty, and despair!"
Nothing beside remains. Round the decay
Of that colossal wreck, boundless and bare
The lone and level sands stretch far away.'

Song from Charles the First[1]

A widow bird sate mourning for her love
    Upon a wintry bough;
The frozen wind crept on above,
    The freezing stream below.

There was no leaf upon the forest bare,
    No flower upon the ground,
And little motion in the air
    Except the mill-wheel's sound.

---

[1] Form: Ballad—Notes: The poem creates a mood of loneliness and
approaching death, with even the bird left alone with it's companion dead.
The mill wheel both contributes to the mood and may represent the
inexorable march of time.

70

John Clare (1793 – 1864)

Badger[1]

When midnight comes a host of dogs and men
Go out and track the badger to his den,
And put a sack within the hole, and lie
Till the old grunting badger passes by.
He comes an hears—they let the strongest loose.
The old fox hears the noise and drops the goose.
The poacher shoots and hurries from the cry,
And the old hare half wounded buzzes by.
They get a forked stick to bear him down
And clap the dogs and take him to the town,
And bait him all the day with many dogs,
And laugh and shout and fright the scampering hogs.
He runs along and bites at all he meets:
They shout and hollo down the noisy streets.

He turns about to face the loud uproar
And drives the rebels to their very door.
The frequent stone is hurled where'er they go;
When badgers fight, then everyone's a foe.
The dogs are clapped and urged to join the fray'
The badger turns and drives them all away.
Though scarcely half as big, demure and small,
He fights with dogs for hours and beats them all.
The heavy mastiff, savage in the fray,
Lies down and licks his feet and turns away.
The bulldog knows his match and waxes cold,
The badger grins and never leaves his hold.
He drives the crowd and follows at their heels
And bites them through—the drunkard swears and reels

The frighted women take the boys away,
The blackguard laughs and hurries on the fray.
He tries to reach the woods, and awkward race,

---

[1] Form: Iambic pentameter, AABBCC . . . End rhymes—Vocabulary: waxes: grows increasingly; blackguard: scoundrel; cudgels: club—Notes: The poem describes a popular form of entertainment in the middle-ages.

But sticks and cudgels quickly stop the chase.
He turns again and drives the noisy crowd
And beats the many dogs in noises loud.
He drives away and beats them every one,
And then they loose them all and set them on.
He falls as dead and kicked by boys and men,
Then starts and grins and drives the crowd again;
Till kicked and torn and beaten out he lies
And leaves his hold and crackles, groans, and dies.

William Cullen Bryant (1794 – 1878)

A Presentiment[1]

"Oh father, let us hence—for hark,
    A fearful murmur shakes the air;
The clouds are coming swift and dark;—
    What horrid shapes they wear!
A wingëd giant sails the sky;
Oh father, father, let us fly!"

"Hush, child; it is a grateful sound,
    That beating of the summer shower;
Here, where the boughs hang close around,
    We'll pass a pleasant hour,
Till the fresh wind, that brings the rain,
Has swept the broad heaven clear again."

"Nay, father, let us haste—for see,
    That horrid thing with hornëd brow—
His wings o'erhang this very tree,
    He scowls upon us now;
His huge black arm is lifted high;
Oh father, father, let us fly!"

"Hush, child"; but, as the father spoke,
    Downward the livid firebolt came,
Close to his ear the thunder broke,

---

[1] Form: Mostly iambic tetrameter, ABABCC end rhymes—Vocabulary:
boughs: tree limbs.

And, blasted by the flame,
The child lay dead; while dark and still
Swept the grim cloud along the hill.

Mutation[1]

They talk of short-lived pleasure—be it so—
  Pain dies as quickly: stern, hard-featured pain
Expires, and lets her weary prisoner go.
  The fiercest agonies have shortest reign;
  And after dreams of horror, comes again
The welcome morning with its rays of peace.
  Oblivion, softly wiping out the stain,
Makes the strong secret pangs of shame to cease.
Remorse is virtue's root; its fair increase
  Are fruits of innocence and blessedness:
Thus joy, o'erborne and bound, doth still release
  His young limbs from the chains that round him press.
Weep not that the world changes—did it keep
A stable changeless state, 'twere cause indeed to weep.

Thanatopsis[2]

To him who in the love of nature holds
Communion with her visible forms, she speaks
A various language; for his gayer hours
She has a voice of gladness, and a smile
And eloquence of beauty; and she glides
Into his darker musings, with a mild
And healing sympathy that steals away
Their sharpness ere he is aware. When thoughts
Of the last bitter hour come like a blight

---

[1] Form: Sonnet—Notes: similar to the biblical reference to the phrase "This too shall pass", applying to both good things and bad things.
[2] Form: Blank verse (unrhymed iambic pentameter)—Vocabulary: Thanatopsis: a meditation upon death; shroud: burial cloth; pall: coffin; swain: country lad; mold: earth of a grave; patriarchs: Abraham, Isaac, Jacob, or any of Jacob's 12 sons; hoary: grey or white with age; sepulcher: burial vault; vales: valley, typically with a stream—Notes: Considered by many to be the first American poem of significance, this was written when he was 17 years old. His father found the manuscript in a desk and submitted it to the "North American Review" on his son's behalf.

Over thy spirit, and sad images
Of the stern agony, and shroud, and pall,
And breathless darkness, and the narrow house,
Make thee to shudder, and grow sick at heart;—
Go forth, under the open sky, and list
To Nature's teachings, while from all around—
Earth and her waters, and the depths of air—
Comes a still voice. Yet a few days, and thee
The all-beholding sun shall see no more
In all his course; nor yet in the cold ground,
Where thy pale form was laid, with many tears,
Nor in the embrace of ocean, shall exist
Thy image. Earth, that nourished thee, shall claim
Thy growth, to be resolved to earth again,
And, lost each human trace, surrendering up
Thine individual being, shalt thou go
To mix forever with the elements,
To be a brother to the insensible rock
And to the sluggish clod, which the rude swain
Turns with his share, and treads upon. The oak
Shall send his roots abroad, and pierce thy mold.
Yet not to thine eternal resting-place
Shalt thou retire alone, nor couldst thou wish
Couch more magnificent. Thou shalt lie down
With patriarchs of the infant world—with kings,
The powerful of the earth—the wise, the good,
Fair forms, and hoary seers of ages past,
All in one mighty sepulcher. The hills
Rock-ribbed and ancient as the sun,—the vales
Stretching in pensive quietness between;
The venerable woods—rivers that move
In majesty, and the complaining brooks
That make the meadows green; and, poured round all,
Old Ocean's gray and melancholy waste,—
Are but the solemn decorations all
Of the great tomb of man. The golden sun,
The planets, all the infinite host of heaven,
Are shining on the sad abodes of death
Through the still lapse of ages. All that tread
The globe are but a handful to the tribes
That slumber in its bosom.—Take the wings

Of morning, pierce the Barcan wilderness,
Or lose thyself in the continuous woods
Where rolls the Oregon, and hears no sound,
Save his own dashings—yet the dead are there:
And millions in those solitudes, since first
The flight of years began, have laid them down
In their last sleep—the dead reign there alone.
So shalt thou rest—and what if thou withdraw
Unheeded by the living—and no friend
Take note of thy departure? All that breathe
Will share thy destiny. The gay will laugh
When thou art gone, the solemn brood of care
Plod on, and each one as before will chase
His favorite phantom; yet all these shall leave
Their mirth and their employments, and shall come
And make their bed with thee. As the long train
Of ages glides away, the sons of men—
The youth in life's fresh spring, and he who goes
In the full strength of years, matron and maid,
The speechless babe, and the gray-headed man—
Shall one by one be gathered to thy side,
By those, who in their turn, shall follow them.

So live, that when thy summons comes to join
The innumerable caravan, which moves
To that mysterious realm, where each shall take
His chamber in the silent halls of death,
Thou go not, like the quarry-slave at night,
Scourged to his dungeon, but, sustained and soothed
By an unfaltering trust, approach thy grave
Like one who wraps the drapery of his couch
About him, and lies down to pleasant dreams.

The Hurricane[1]

Lord of the winds! I feel thee nigh,
I know thy breath in the burning sky!
And I wait, with a thrill in every vein,

---

[1] Form: Iambic tetrameter, AABBCC. . . End rhymes—Vocabulary: lurid:
pallid in color; covert: shelter.

For the coming of the hurricane!

And lo! On the wing of the heavy gales,
Through the boundless arch of heaven he sails.
Silent and slow, and terribly strong,
The mighty shadow is borne along,
Like the dark eternity to come;
While the world below, dismayed and dumb,
Through the calm of the thick hot atmosphere
Looks up at its gloomy folds with fear.

They darken fast; and the golden blaze
Of the sun is quenched in the lurid haze,
And he sends through the shade a funeral ray—
A glare that is neither night nor day,
A beam that touches, with hues of death,
The cloud above and the earth beneath.
To its covert glides the silent bird,
While the hurricane's distant voice is heard
Uplifted among the mountains round,
And the forests hear and answer the sound.

He is come! He is come! Do ye not behold
His ample robes on the wind unrolled?
Giant of air! We bid thee hail!—
How his gray skirts toss in the whirling gale;
How his huge and writhing arms are bent
To clasp the zone of the firmament,
And fold at length, in their dark embrace,
From mountain to mountain the visible space.

Darker,—still darker! The whirlwinds bear
The dust of the plains to the middle air;
And hark to the crashing, long and loud,
Of the chariot of God in the thunder-cloud!
You may trace its path by the flashes that start
From the rapid wheels where'er they dart,
As the fire-bolts leap to the world below,
And flood the skies with a lurid glow.

What roar is that?—'t is the rain that breaks
In torrents away from the airy lakes,
Heavily poured on the shuddering ground,
And shedding a nameless horror round.
Ah! Well-known woods, and mountains, and skies,
With the very clouds!—ye are lost to my eyes.
I seek ye vainly, and see in your place
The shadowy tempest that sweeps through space,
A whirling ocean that fills the wall
Of the crystal heaven, and buries all.
And I, cut off from the world, remain
Alone with the terrible hurricane.

The Murdered Traveler[1]

When spring, to woods and wastes around,
    Brought bloom and joy again,
The murdered traveler's bones were found,
    Far down a narrow glen.

The fragrant birch, above him, hung
    Her tassels in the sky;
And many a vernal blossom sprung,
    And nodded careless by.

The red-bird warbled, as he wrought
    His hanging nest o'erhead,
And fearless, near the fatal spot,
    Her young the partridge led.

But there was weeping far away,
    And gentle eyes, for him,
With watching many an anxious day,
    Were sorrowful and dim.

They little knew, who loved him so,
    The fearful death he met,

---

[1] Form: Ballad—Vocabulary: vernal: spring; wrought: built; bier: coffin and stand.

77

When shouting o'er the desert snow,
   Unarmed, and hard beset;—

Nor how, when round the frosty pole
   The northern dawn was red,
The mountain wolf and wild-cat stole
   To banquet on the dead;

Nor how, when strangers found his bones,
   They dressed the hasty bier,
And marked his grave with nameless stones,
   Unmoistened by a tear.

But long they looked, and feared, and wept,
   Within his distant home;
And dreamed, and started as they slept,
   For joy that he was come.

So long they looked—but never spied
   His welcome step again,
Nor knew the fearful death he died
   Far down that narrow glen.

The Poet[1]

Thou, who wouldst wear the name
   Of poet mid thy brethren of mankind,
And clothe in words of flame
   Thoughts that shall live within the general mind!
Deem not the framing of a deathless lay
The pastime of a drowsy summer day.

But gather all thy powers,
   And wreak them on the verse that thou dost weave,
And in thy lonely hours,
   At silent morning or at wakeful eve,
While the warm current tingles through thy veins
Set forth the burning words in fluent strains.

---

[1] Form: Iambic, 3-5-3-5-5-5 pattern, ABABCC end rhymes—Vocabulary:
lay: ballad; languid: lacking energy; limn: describe.

78

No smooth array of phrase
  Artfully sought and ordered though it be,
Which the cold rhymer lays
  Upon his page with languid industry
Can wake the listless pulse to livelier speed,
Or fill with sudden tears the eyes that read.

The secret wouldst thou know
  To touch the heart or fire the blood at will?
Let thine own eyes o'erflow;
  Let thy lips quiver with the passionate thrill;
Seize the great thought, ere yet its power be past,
And bind, in words, the fleet emotion fast.

Then, should thy verse appear
  Halting and harsh, and all unaptly wrought,
Touch the crude line with fear,
  Save in the moment of impassioned thought;
Then summon back the original glow and mend
The strain with rapture that with fire was penned.

Yet let no empty gust
  Of passion find an utterance in thy lay,
A blast that whirls the dust
  Along the howling street and dies away;
But feelings of calm power and mighty sweep,
Like currents journeying through the windless deep.

Seek'st thou, in living lays,
  To limn the beauty of the earth and sky?
Before thine inner gaze
  Let all that beauty in clear vision lie,
Look on it with exceeding love, and write
The words inspired by wonder and delight.

Of tempest wouldst thou sing,
  Or tell of battles—make thyself a part
Of the great tumult; cling
  To the tossed wreck with terror in thy heart;
Scale, with the assault host, the rampart's height

And strike and struggle in the thickest fight.

So shalt thou frame a lay
    That haply may endure from age to age,
And they who read shall say;
    "what witchery hangs upon this poet's page!
What art is this the written spells to find
That sway from mood to mood the willing mind!"

The Strange Lady[1]

The summer morn is bright and fresh, the birds are darting
    by,
As if they loved to breast the breeze that sweeps the cool
    clear sky;
Young Albert, in the forest's edge, has heard a rustling sound
An arrow slightly strikes his hand and falls upon the ground.

A dark-haired woman from the wood comes suddenly in
    sight;
Her merry eye is full and black, her cheek is brown and
    bright;
Her gown is of the mid-sea blue, her belt with beads is
    strung,
And yet she speaks in gentle tones, and in the English
    tongue.

"It was an idle bolt I sent, against the villain crow;
Fair sir, I fear it harmed thy hand; beshrew my erring bow!"
"Ah! Would that bolt had not been spent, then, lady, might I
    wear
A lasting token on my hand of one so passing fair!"

"Thou art a flatterer like the rest, but wouldst thou take with
    me
A day of hunting in the wilds, beneath the greenwood tree,
I know where most the pheasants feed, and where the red-
    deer herd,

---

[1] Form: Ballad—Vocabulary: breast: rise over; beshrew: curse; meet: fitting;
boughs: tree limbs; hopples: piles of stone; cornels: type of tree; wist:
knew.

And thou shouldst chase the nobler game, and I bring down
    the bird."

Now Albert in her quiver lays the arrow in its place,
And wonders as he gazes on the beauty of her face:
`Those hunting-grounds are far away, and, lady, 'twere not
    meet
That night, amid the wilderness, should overtake thy feet."

"Heed not the night, a summer lodge amid the wild is mine,
'Tis shadowed by the tulip-tree, 'tis mantled by the vine;
The wild plum sheds its yellow fruit from fragrant thickets
    nigh,
And flowery prairies from the door stretch till they meet the
    sky.
"There in the boughs that hide the roof the mock-bird sits
    and sings,
And there the hang-bird's brood within its little hammock
    swings;
A pebbly brook, where rustling winds among the hopples
    sweep,
Shall lull thee till the morning sun looks in upon thy sleep."

Away, into the forest depths by pleasant paths they go,
He with his rifle on his arm, the lady with her bow,
Where cornels arch their cool dark boughs o'er beds of
    wintergreen,
And never at his father's door again was Albert seen.

That night upon the woods came down a furious hurricane,
With howl of winds and roar of streams and beating of the
    rain;
The mighty thunder broke and drowned the noises in its
    crash;
The old trees seemed to fight like fiends beneath the
    lightning-flash.

Next day, within a mossy glen, mid moldering trunks were
    found
The fragments of a human form, upon the bloody ground;
White bones from which the flesh was torn, and locks of
    glossy hair;
They laid them in the place of graves, yet wist not whose they
    were.

And whether famished evening wolves had mangled Albert so,
Or that strange dame so gay and fair were some mysterious
    foe,
Or whether to that forest lodge, beyond the mountains blue,
He went to dwell with her, the friends who mourned him
    never knew.

To a Waterfowl[1]

    Whither, 'midst falling dew,
While glow the heavens with the last steps of day,
Far, through their rosy depths, dost thou pursue
    Thy solitary way?

    Vainly the fowler's eye
Might mark thy distant flight to do thee wrong,
As, darkly painted on the crimson sky,
    Thy figure floats along.

    Seek'st thou the plashy brink
Of weedy lake, or marge of river wide,

---

[1] Form: Iambic, 3-5-5-3 pattern, ABAB end rhymes—Vocabulary: Whither:
where are you going; fowler: hunter of birds; plashy: watery; marge: edge;
billows: waves; illimitable: limitless—Notes: If God is able to guide a
migrating goose, then he will also guide the narrator through his life.

Or where the rocking billows rise and sink
    On the chafed ocean side?

There is a Power whose care
Teaches thy way along that pathless coast,—
The desert and illimitable air,—
    Lone wandering, but not lost.

All day thy wings have fann'd
At that far height, the cold thin atmosphere:
Yet stoop not, weary, to the welcome land,
    Though the dark night is near.

And soon that toil shall end,
Soon shalt thou find a summer home, and rest,
And scream among thy fellows; reed shall bend
    Soon o'er thy sheltered nest.

Thou'rt gone, the abyss of heaven
Hath swallowed up thy form; yet, on my heart
Deeply hath sunk the lesson thou hast given,
    And shall not soon depart.

He, who, from zone to zone,
Guides through the boundless sky thy certain flight,
In the long way that I must tread alone,
    Will lead my steps aright.

John Keats (1795 – 1821)

Isabella[1]

I.

Fair Isabel, poor simple Isabel!
   Lorenzo, a young palmer in Love's eye!
They could not in the self-same mansion dwell
   Without some stir of heart, some malady;
They could not sit at meals but feel how well
   It soothed each to be the other by;
They could not, sure, beneath the same roof sleep
But to each other dream, and nightly weep.

II.

---

[1] Form: Iambic pentameter, ABABABCC end rhymes—Vocabulary: palmer:
pilgrim who carries a palm branch from the holy land; malady: illness; rill:
small brook; broidery: needlework; vespers: evening prayers; boon: favor;
shrive: confess; clime: climate; erewhile: heretofore; zephyr: gentle breeze;
ditty: short song; honeyed dart: cupid's arrow; bower: shaded recess;
Theseus: king of Athens who slew the Minotaur; Dido: queen and founder
of Carthage, who rescued Aeneas, then killed herself when Aeneas
abandoned her; almsmen: one dependent on alms for support; swelt: faint
from heat; Ceylon: Sri Lanka; racks: torture implement; lazar: leper;
panniered: saddlebags or wicker baskets like saddlebags; ducats: coins;
ledger-men: accountants; covetous: desirous; Boccaccio: Italian poet (1351
- 1353), wrote the Decameron; gittern: Middle-Ages guitar; blithe: carefree;
balustrade: railing; Bestride: straddle; Apennine: mountain chain in Italy;
eglantine: wild, pink rose; matin: morning; fain: gladly; Arno: river near
Florence, flowing from the Apennines; bream: freshwater fish; freshets:
sudden overflows from the stream; wan: pale; 'scape: escape; roundelay:
poem or song with recurring theme; Hinnom's vale: valley between Mount
Zion and the Hill of Evil Counsel. Idolatrous Jews burned their children
alive as sacrifices to Moloch and Baal, and since that time the valley has
been used to dump waste and a fire has been constantly burning, and has
come to symbolize corruption and evil; lute: ancient stringed instrument;
lorn: forlorn; loamed: covered with dirt; miry: muddy; Languor: exhaustion;
palsied: trembling; Druid: ancient Celtic priest; sepulchral: near tombs;
woof: the crosswise threads in a fabric, perpendicular to the warp; avarice:
insatiable greed; heather: evergreen shrub; knelling: ring slowly; Seraph: a
type of angel; spangly: sparkly; hie: hasten; Champaign: plain; betide:
befall; mould: soil; hoar: white with age; travail: strenuous work; plaining:
poetic complaint; Lethean: from the river of forgetfulness (Greek);
Melpomene: the muse of tragedy; Baalites: worshiper of Baal; pelf:
dishonestly acquired wealth; shrift: confession; guerdon: reward; burthen:
burden.

With every morn their love grew tenderer,
   With every eve deeper and tenderer still;
He might not in house, field, or garden stir,
   But her full shape would all his seeing fill;
And his continual voice was pleasanter
   To her, than noise of trees or hidden rill;
Her lute-string gave an echo of his name,
She spoilt her half-done broidery with the same.

III.
He knew whose gentle hand was at the latch
   Before the door had given her to his eyes;
And from her chamber-window he would catch
   Her beauty farther than the falcon spies;
And constant as her vespers would he watch,
   Because her face was turned to the same skies;
And with sick longing all the night outwear,
To hear her morning-step upon the stair.

IV.
A whole long month of May in this sad plight
   Made their cheeks paler by the break of June:
"Tomorrow will I bow to my delight,
   Tomorrow will I ask my lady's boon."—
"O may I never see another night,
   Lorenzo, if thy lips breathe not love's tune."—
So spake they to their pillows; but, alas,
Honeyless days and days did he let pass;

V.
Until sweet Isabella's untouched cheek
   Fell sick within the rose's just domain,
Fell thin as a young mother's, who doth seek
   By every lull to cool her infant's pain:
"How ill she is," said he, "I may not speak,
   And yet I will, and tell my love all plain:
If looks speak love-laws, I will drink her tears,
And at the least 'twill startle off her cares."

VI.
So said he one fair morning, and all day
   His heart beat awfully against his side;
And to his heart he inwardly did pray
   For power to speak; but still the ruddy tide
Stifled his voice, and pulsed resolve away—
   Fevered his high conceit of such a bride,
Yet brought him to the meekness of a child:
Alas! When passion is both meek and wild!

VII.
So once more he had waked and anguishëd
   A dreary night of love and misery,
If Isabel's quick eye had not been wed
   To every symbol on his forehead high;
She saw it waxing very pale and dead,
   And straight all flushed; so, lispëd tenderly,
"Lorenzo!"—here she ceased her timid quest,
But in her tone and look he read the rest.

VIII.
"O Isabella, I can half perceive
   That I may speak my grief into thine ear;
If thou didst ever anything believe,
   Believe how I love thee, believe how near
My soul is to its doom: I would not grieve
   Thy hand by unwelcome pressing, would not fear
Thine eyes by gazing; but I cannot live
Another night, and not my passion shrive."

IX.
"Love! Thou art leading me from wintry cold,
   Lady! Thou leadest me to summer clime,
And I must taste the blossoms that unfold
   In its ripe warmth this gracious morning time."
So said, his erewhile timid lips grew bold,
   And poised with hers in dewy rhyme:
Great bliss was with them, and great happiness
Grew, like a lusty flower in June's caress.

X.
Parting they seemed to tread upon the air,
    Twin roses by the zephyr blown apart
Only to meet again more close, and share
    The inward fragrance of each other's heart.
She, to her chamber gone, a ditty fair
    Sang, of delicious love and honeyed dart;
He with light steps went up a western hill,
And bade the sun farewell, and joyed his fill.

XI.
All close they met again, before the dusk
    Had taken from the stars its pleasant veil,
All close they met, all eves, before the dusk
    Had taken from the stars its pleasant veil,
Close in a bower of hyacinth and musk,
    Unknown of any, free from whispering tale.
Ah! Better had it been for ever so,
Than idle ears should pleasure in their woe.

XII.
Were they unhappy then?—It cannot be—
    Too many tears for lovers have been shed,
Too many sighs give we to them in fee,
    Too much of pity after they are dead,
Too many doleful stories do we see,
    Whose matter in bright gold were best be read;
Except in such a page where Theseus' spouse
Over the pathless waves towards him bows.

XIII.
But, for the general award of love,
    The little sweet doth kill much bitterness;
Though Dido silent is in under-grove,
    And Isabella's was a great distress,
Though young Lorenzo in warm Indian clove
    Was not embalmed, this truth is not the less—
Even bees, the little almsmen of spring-bowers,
Know there is richest juice in poison-flowers.

XIV.

With her two brothers this fair lady dwelt,
    Enrichëd from ancestral merchandize,
And for them many a weary hand did swelt
    In torchëd mines and noisy factories,
And many once proud-quivered loins did melt
    In blood from stinging whip;—with hollow eyes
Many all day in dazzling river stood,
To take the rich-ored driftings of the flood.

XV.

For them the Ceylon diver held his breath,
    And went all naked to the hungry shark;
For them his ears gushed blood; for them in death
    The seal on the cold ice with piteous bark
Lay full of darts; for them alone did seethe
    A thousand men in troubles wide and dark:
Half-ignorant, they turned an easy wheel,
That set sharp racks at work, to pinch and peel.

XVI.

Why were they proud? Because their marble founts
    Gushed with more pride than do a wretch's tears?—
Why were they proud? Because fair orange-mounts
    Were of more soft ascent than lazar stairs?—
Why were they proud? Because red-lined accounts
    Were richer than the songs of Grecian years?—
Why were they proud? Again we ask aloud,
Why in the name of Glory were they proud?

XVII.

Yet were these Florentines as self-retired
    In hungry pride and gainful cowardice,
As two close Hebrews in that land inspired,
    Paled in and vineyarded from beggar-spies;
The hawks of ship-mast forests—the untired
    And panniered mules for ducats and old lies—
Quick cat's-paws on the generous stray-away,—
Great wits in Spanish, Tuscan, and Malay.

XVIII.

How was it these same ledger-men could spy
    Fair Isabella in her downy nest?
How could they find out in Lorenzo's eye
    A straying from his toil? Hot Egypt's pest
Into their vision covetous and sly!
    How could these money-bags see east and west?—
Yet so they did—and every dealer fair
Must see behind, as doth the hunted hare.

XIX.

O eloquent and famed Boccaccio!
    Of thee we now should ask forgiving boon,
And of thy spicy myrtles as they blow,
    And of thy roses amorous of the moon,
And of thy lilies, that do paler grow
    Now they can no more hear thy gittern's tune,
For venturing syllables that ill beseem
The quiet glooms of such a piteous theme.

XX.

Grant thou a pardon here, and then the tale
    Shall move on soberly, as it is meet;
There is no other crime, no mad assail
    To make old prose in modern rhyme more sweet:
But it is done—succeed the verse or fail—
    To honor thee, and thy gone spirit greet;
To stead thee as a verse in English tongue,
An echo of thee in the north-wind sung.

XXI.

These brethren having found by many signs
    What love Lorenzo for their sister had,
And how she loved him too, each unconfines
    His bitter thoughts to other, well nigh mad
That he, the servant of their trade designs,
    Should in their sister's love be blithe and glad,
When 'twas their plan to coax her by degrees
To some high noble and his olive-trees.

XXII.
And many a jealous conference had they,
    And many times they bit their lips alone,
Before they fixed upon a surest way
    To make the youngster for his crime atone;
And at the last, these men of cruel clay
    Cut Mercy with a sharp knife to the bone;
For they resolvèd in some forest dim
To kill Lorenzo, and there bury him.

XXIII.
So on a pleasant morning, as he leant
    Into the sun-rise, o'er the balustrade
Of the garden-terrace, towards him they bent
    Their footing through the dews; and to him said,
"You seem there in the quiet of content,
    Lorenzo, and we are most loath to invade
Calm speculation; but if you are wise,
Bestride your steed while cold is in the skies.

XXIV.
To-day we purpose, aye, this hour we mount
    To spur three leagues towards the Apennine;
Come down, we pray thee, ere the hot sun count
    His dewy rosary on the eglantine."
Lorenzo, courteously as he was wont,
    Bowed a fair greeting to these serpents' whine;
And went in haste, to get in readiness,
With belt, and spur, and bracing huntsman's dress.

XXV.
And as he to the court-yard passed along,
    Each third step did he pause, and listened oft
If he could hear his lady's matin-song,
    Or the light whisper of her footstep soft;
And as he thus over his passion hung,
    He heard a laugh full musical aloft;
When, looking up, he saw her features bright
Smile through an in-door lattice, all delight.

XXVI.
"Love, Isabel!" Said he, "I was in pain
   Lest I should miss to bid thee a good morrow:
Ah! What if I should lose thee, when so fain
   I am to stifle all the heavy sorrow
Of a poor three hours' absence? But we'll gain
   Out of the amorous dark what day doth borrow.
Good bye! I'll soon be back."—"Good bye!" Said she:—
And as he went she chanted merrily.

XXVII.
So the two brothers and their murdered man
   Rode past fair Florence, to where Arno's stream
Gurgles through straitened banks, and still doth fan
   Itself with dancing bulrush, and the bream
Keeps head against the freshets. Sick and wan
   The brothers' faces in the ford did seem,
Lorenzo's flush with love.—They passed the water
Into a forest quiet for the slaughter.

XXVIII.
There was Lorenzo slain and buried in,
   There in that forest did his great love cease;
Ah! When a soul doth thus its freedom win,
   It aches in loneliness—is ill at peace
As the break-covert blood-hounds of such sin:
   They dipped their swords in the water, and did tease
Their horses homeward, with convulsèd spur,
Each richer by his being a murderer.

XXIX.
They told their sister how, with sudden speed,
   Lorenzo had ta'en ship for foreign lands,
Because of some great urgency and need
   In their affairs, requiring trusty hands.
Poor Girl! Put on thy stifling widow's weed,
   And 'scape at once from Hope's accursèd bands;
To-day thou wilt not see him, nor to-morrow,
And the next day will be a day of sorrow.

XXX.
She weeps alone for pleasures not to be;
   Sorely she wept until the night came on,
And then, instead of love, O misery!
   She brooded o'er the luxury alone:
His image in the dusk she seemed to see,
   And to the silence made a gentle moan,
Spreading her perfect arms upon the air,
And on her couch low murmuring "Where? O where?"

XXXI.
But Selfishness, Love's cousin, held not long
   Its fiery vigil in her single breast;
She fretted for the golden hour, and hung
   Upon the time with feverish unrest—
Not long—for soon into her heart a throng
   Of higher occupants, a richer zest,
Came tragic; passion not to be subdued,
And sorrow for her love in travels rude.

XXXII.
In the mid days of autumn, on their eves
   The breath of Winter comes from far away,
And the sick west continually bereaves
   Of some gold tinge, and plays a roundelay
Of death among the bushes and the leaves,
   To make all bare before he dares to stray
From his north cavern. So sweet Isabel
By gradual decay from beauty fell,

XXXIII.
Because Lorenzo came not. Oftentimes
   She asked her brothers, with an eye all pale,
Striving to be itself, what dungeon climes
   Could keep him off so long? They spake a tale
Time after time, to quiet her. Their crimes
   Came on them, like a smoke from Hinnom's vale;
And every night in dreams they groaned aloud,
To see their sister in her snowy shroud.

XXXIV.
And she had died in drowsy ignorance,
　　But for a thing more deadly dark than all;
It came like a fierce potion, drunk by chance,
　　Which saves a sick man from the feathered pall
For some few gasping moments; like a lance,
　　Waking an Indian from his cloudy hall
With cruel pierce, and bringing him again
Sense of the gnawing fire at heart and brain.

XXXV.
It was a vision.—In the drowsy gloom,
　　The dull of midnight, at her couch's foot
Lorenzo stood, and wept: the forest tomb
　　Had marred his glossy hair which once could shoot
Luster into the sun, and put cold doom
　　Upon his lips, and taken the soft lute
From his lorn voice, and past his loamèd ears
Had made a miry channel for his tears.

XXXVI.
Strange sound it was, when the pale shadow spake;
　　For there was striving, in its piteous tongue,
To speak as when on earth it was awake,
　　And Isabella on its music hung:
Languor there was in it, and tremulous shake,
　　As in a palsied Druid's harp unstrung;
And through it moaned a ghostly under-song,
Like hoarse night-gusts sepulchral briars among.

XXXVII.
Its eyes, though wild, were still all dewy bright
　　With love, and kept all phantom fear aloof
From the poor girl by magic of their light,
　　The while it did unthread the horrid woof
Of the late darkened time,—the murderous spite
　　Of pride and avarice,—the dark pine roof
In the forest,—and the sodden turfèd dell,
Where, without any word, from stabs he fell.

XXXVIII.
Saying moreover, "Isabel, my sweet!
    Red whortle-berries droop above my head,
And a large flint-stone weighs upon my feet;
    Around me beeches and high chestnuts shed
Their leaves and prickly nuts; a sheep-fold bleat
    Comes from beyond the river to my bed:
Go, shed one tear upon my heather-bloom,
And it shall comfort me within the tomb."

XXXIX.
"I am a shadow now, alas! Alas!
    Upon the skirts of human-nature dwelling
Alone: I chant alone the holy mass,
    While little sounds of life are round me knelling,
And glossy bees at noon do field ward pass,
    And many a chapel bell the hour is telling,
Paining me through: those sounds grow strange to me,
And thou art distant in Humanity."

XL.
"I know what was, I feel full well what is,
    And I should rage, if spirits could go mad;
Though I forget the taste of earthly bliss,
    That paleness warms my grave, as though I had
A Seraph chosen from the bright abyss
    To be my spouse: thy paleness makes me glad;
Thy beauty grows upon me, and I feel
A greater love through all my essence steal."

XLI.
The Spirit mourned "Adieu!"—dissolved and left
    The atom darkness in a slow turmoil;
As when of healthful midnight sleep bereft,
    Thinking on rugged hours and fruitless toil,
We put our eyes into a pillowy cleft,
    And see the spangly gloom froth up and boil:
It made sad Isabella's eyelids ache,
And in the dawn she started up awake;

94

XLII.
"Ha! Ha!" Said she, "I knew not this hard life,
    I thought the worst was simple misery;
I thought some Fate with pleasure or with strife
    Portioned us—happy days, or else to die;
But there is crime—a brother's bloody knife!
    Sweet Spirit, thou hast schooled my infancy:
I'll visit thee for this, and kiss thine eyes,
And greet thee morn and even in the skies."

XLIII.
When the full morning came, she had devised
    How she might secret to the forest hie;
How she might find the clay, so dearly prized,
    And sing to it one latest lullaby;
How her short absence might be unsurmised,
    While she the inmost of the dream would try.
Resolved, she took with her an agëd nurse,
And went into that dismal forest-hearse.

XLIV.
See, as they creep along the river side,
    How she doth whisper to that aged Dame,
And, after looking round the champaign wide,
    Shows her a knife.—"What feverous hectic flame
Burns in thee, child?—What good can thee betide,
    That thou should'st smile again?"—The evening came,
And they had found Lorenzo's earthy bed;
The flint was there, the berries at his head.

XLV.
Who hath not loitered in a green church-yard,
    And let his spirit, like a demon-mole,
Work through the clayey soil and gravel hard,
    To see skull, coffined bones, and funeral stole;
Pitying each form that hungry Death hath marred
    And filling it once more with human soul?
Ah! This is holiday to what was felt
When Isabella by Lorenzo knelt.

XLVI.
She gazed into the fresh-thrown mould, as though
    One glance did fully all its secrets tell;
Clearly she saw, as other eyes would know
    Pale limbs at bottom of a crystal well;
Upon the murderous spot she seemed to grow,
    Like to a native lily of the dell:
Then with her knife, all sudden, she began
To dig more fervently than misers can.

XLVII.
Soon she turned up a soiled glove, whereon
    Her silk had played in purple fantasies,
She kissed it with a lip more chill than stone,
    And put it in her bosom, where it dries
And freezes utterly unto the bone
    Those dainties made to still an infant's cries:
Then 'gan she work again; nor stayed her care,
But to throw back at times her veiling hair.

XLVIII.
That old nurse stood beside her wondering,
    Until her heart felt pity to the core
At sight of such a dismal laboring,
    And so she kneeled, with her locks all hoar,
And put her lean hands to the horrid thing:
    Three hours they labored at this travail sore;
At last they felt the kernel of the grave,
And Isabella did not stamp and rave.

XLIX.
Ah! Wherefore all this wormy circumstance?
    Why linger at the yawning tomb so long?
O for the gentleness of old Romance,
    The simple plaining of a minstrel's song!
Fair reader, at the old tale take a glance,
    For here, in truth, it doth not well belong
To speak:—O turn thee to the very tale,
And taste the music of that vision pale.

L.
With duller steel than the Persean sword
　　They cut away no formless monster's head,
But one, whose gentleness did well accord
　　With death, as life. The ancient harps have said,
Love never dies, but lives, immortal Lord:
　　If Love impersonate was ever dead,
Pale Isabella kissed it, and low moaned.
'Twas love; cold,—dead indeed, but not dethroned.

LI.
In anxious secrecy they took it home,
　　And then the prize was all for Isabel:
She calmed its wild hair with a golden comb,
　　And all around each eye's sepulchral cell
Pointed each fringed lash; the smearèd loam
　　With tears, as chilly as a dripping well,
She drenched away:—and still she combed, and kept
Sighing all day—and still she kissed, and wept.

LII.
Then in a silken scarf,—sweet with the dews
　　Of precious flowers plucked in Araby,
And divine liquids come with odorous ooze
　　Through the cold serpent-pipe refreshfully,—
She wrapped it up; and for its tomb did choose
　　A garden-pot, wherein she laid it by,
And covered it with mould, and o'er it set
Sweet Basil, which her tears kept ever wet.

LIII.
And she forgot the stars, the moon, and sun,
　　And she forgot the blue above the trees,
And she forgot the dells where waters run,
　　And she forgot the chilly autumn breeze;
She had no knowledge when the day was done,
　　And the new morn she saw not: but in peace
Hung over her sweet Basil evermore,
And moistened it with tears unto the core.

LIV.
And so she ever fed it with thin tears,
 Whence thick, and green, and beautiful it grew,
So that it smelt more balmy than its peers
 Of Basil-tufts in Florence; for it drew
Nurture besides, and life, from human fears,
 From the fast mouldering head there shut from view:
So that the jewel, safely casketed,
Came forth, and in perfumed leafits spread.

LV.
O Melancholy, linger here awhile!
 O Music, Music, breathe despondingly!
O Echo, Echo, from some somber isle,
 Unknown, Lethean, sigh to us—O sigh!
Spirits in grief, lift up your heads, and smile;
 Lift up your heads, sweet Spirits, heavily,
And make a pale light in your cypress glooms,
Tinting with silver wan your marble tombs.

LVI.
Moan hither, all ye syllables of woe,
 From the deep throat of sad Melpomene!
Through bronzëd lyre in tragic order go,
 And touch the strings into a mystery;
Sound mournfully upon the winds and low;
 For simple Isabel is soon to be
Among the dead: She withers, like a palm
Cut by an Indian for its juicy balm.

LVII.
O leave the palm to wither by itself;
 Let not quick Winter chill its dying hour!—
It may not be—those Baalites of pelf,
 Her brethren, noted the continual shower
From her dead eyes; and many a curious elf,
 Among her kindred, wondered that such dower
Of youth and beauty should be thrown aside
By one marked out to be a Noble's bride.

LVIII.
And, furthermore, her brethren wondered much
    Why she sat drooping by the Basil green,
And why it flourished, as by magic touch;
    Greatly they wondered what the thing might mean:
They could not surely give belief, that such
    A very nothing would have power to wean
Her from her own fair youth, and pleasures gay,
And even remembrance of her love's delay.

LIX.
Therefore they watched a time when they might sift
    This hidden whim; and long they watched in vain;
For seldom did she go to chapel-shrift,
    And seldom felt she any hunger-pain;
And when she left, she hurried back, as swift
    As bird on wing to breast its eggs again;
And, patient as a hen-bird, sat her there
Beside her Basil, weeping through her hair.

LX.
Yet they contrived to steal the Basil-pot,
    And to examine it in secret place;
The thing was vile with green and livid spot,
    And yet they knew it was Lorenzo's face:
The guerdon of their murder they had got,
    And so left Florence in a moment's space,
Never to turn again.—Away they went,
With blood upon their heads, to banishment.

LXI.
O Melancholy, turn thine eyes away!
    O Music, Music, breathe despondingly!
O Echo, Echo, on some other day,
    From isles Lethean, sigh to us—O sigh!
Spirits of grief, sing not your "Well-a-way!"
    For Isabel, sweet Isabel, will die;
Will die a death too lone and incomplete,
Now they have ta'en away her Basil sweet.

LXII.
Piteous she looked on dead and senseless things,
    Asking for her lost Basil amorously;
And with melodious chuckle in the strings
    Of her lorn voice, she oftentimes would cry
After the Pilgrim in his wanderings,
    To ask him where her Basil was; and why
'Twas hid from her: "For cruel 'tis," said she,
"to steal my Basil-pot away from me."

LXIII.
And so she pined, and so she died forlorn,
    Imploring for her Basil to the last.
No heart was there in Florence but did mourn
    In pity of her love, so overcast.
And a sad ditty of this story born
    From mouth to mouth through all the country passed:
Still is the burthen sung—"O cruelty,
To steal my Basil-pot away from me!"

La Belle Dame Sans Merci[1]

Ah, what can ail thee, wretched wight,
    Alone and palely loitering;
The sedge is wither'd from the lake,
    And no birds sing.

Ah, what can ail thee, wretched wight,
    So haggard and so woe-begone?
The squirrel's granary is full,
    And the harvest's done.

I see a lily on thy brow,
    With anguish moist and fever dew;

---

[1] Form: Iambic tetrameter, irregular line length for last line in each stanza, xAxA end rhymes—Vocabulary: wight: living being; sedge: grasslike plant; meads: meadows; grot: grotto; thrall: servitude; gloam: twilight; sojourn: reside temporarily —Notes: He has experienced the beauty of the mysterious woman, but now she is gone and he is doomed to suffer perpetual misery searching for her rather than appreciating the beauty in the rest of the world.

100

And on thy cheek a fading rose
    Fast withereth too.

I met a lady in the meads
    Full beautiful, a fairy's child;
Her hair was long, her foot was light,
    And her eyes were wild.

I set her on my pacing steed,
    And nothing else saw all day long;
For sideways would she lean, and sing
    A fairy's song.

I made a garland for her head,
    And bracelets too, and fragrant zone;
She look'd at me as she did love,
    And made sweet moan.

She found me roots of relish sweet,
    And honey wild, and manna dew;
And sure in language strange she said,
    "I love thee true."

She took me to her elfin grot,
    And there she gaz'd and sighed deep,
And there I shut her wild sad eyes—
    So kiss'd to sleep.

And there we slumber'd on the moss,
    And there I dream'd, ah woe betide,
The latest dream I ever dream'd
    On the cold hill side.

I saw pale kings, and princes too,
    Pale warriors, death-pale were they all;
Who cry'd—"La belle Dame sans merci
    Hath thee in thrall!"

I saw their starv'd lips in the gloam
    With horrid warning gapèd wide,

And I awoke, and found me here
   On the cold hill side.

And this is why I sojourn here
   Alone and palely loitering,
Though the sedge is wither'd from the lake,
   And no birds sing.

O Blush Not So[1]

I.
O blush not so! O blush not so!
   Or I shall think you knowing;
And if you smile the blushing while,
   Then maidenheads are going.

II.
There's a blush for want, and a blush for shan't,
   And a blush for having done it;
There's a blush for thought, and a blush for nought,
   And a blush for just begun it.

III.
O sigh not so! O sigh not so!
   For it sounds of Eve's sweet pippin;
By these loosened lips you have tasted the pips
   And fought in an amorous nipping.

IV.
Will you play once more at nice-cut-core,
   For it only will last our youth out,
And we have the prime of the kissing time,
   We have not one sweet tooth out.

V.
There's a sigh for aye, and a sigh for nay,
   And a sigh for "I can't bear it!"

---

[1] Form: Ballad—Vocabulary: maidenhead: virginity; nought: nothing;
pippin: a type of apple; pips: seeds; nipping: biting or pinching.

O what can be done, shall we stay or run?
   O cut the sweet apple and share it!

Ode on a Grecian Urn[1]

I.
Thou still unravished bride of quietness,
   Thou foster child of silence and slow time,
Sylvan historian, who canst thus express
   A flowery tale more sweetly than our rhyme:
What leaf-fringed legend haunts about thy shape
   Of deities or mortals, or of both,
      In Tempe or the dales of Arcady?
   What men or gods are these? What maidens loath?
What mad pursuit? What struggle to escape?
   What pipes and timbrels? What wild ecstasy?

II.
Heard melodies are sweet, but those unheard
   Are sweeter; therefore, ye soft pipes, play on;
Not to the sensual ear, but, more endeared,
   Pipe to the spirit ditties of no tone.
Fair youth, beneath the trees, thou canst not leave
   Thy song, nor ever can those trees be bare;
      Bold Lover, never, never canst thou kiss,
Though winning near the goal—-yet, do not grieve;
      She cannot fade, though thou hast not thy bliss
   For ever wilt thou love, and she be fair!

III.
Ah, happy, happy boughs! That cannot shed
   Your leaves, nor ever bid the Spring adieu;
And, happy melodist, unwearied,

---

1 Form: Iambic pentameter, irregular but frequent end rhymes—
Vocabulary: Sylvan: woodland; deities: Gods; Tempe: a valley in Greece
near Mt. Olympus; dales: valleys; Arcady: a region of ancient Greece;
timbrels: ancient instrument similar to a tambourine; ditties: simple songs;
boughs: tree limb; cloyed: sick of; lowing: mooing; citadel: stronghold;
pious: reverent; brede: ornamental braiding; trodden: stepped on; Pastoral:
rural scene—Notes: A careful descriptions of the scenes from an ancient
urn, where he is congratulating the figures on being frozen through
eternity and describing the benefits of this frozen state.

For ever piping songs forever new;
More happy love! More happy, happy love!
   For ever warm and still to be enjoyed,
      For ever panting, and forever young;
All breathing human passion far above,
   That leaves a heart high-sorrowful and cloyed,
      A burning forehead, and a parching tongue.

IV.
Who are these coming to the sacrifice?
   To what green altar, O mysterious priest,
Lead'st thou that heifer lowing at the skies,
   And all her silken flanks with garlands dressed?
What little town by river or sea shore,
   Or mountain-built with peaceful citadel,
      Is emptied of this folk, this pious morn?
And, little town, thy streets for evermore
   Will silent be; and not a soul to tell
      Why thou art desolate, can e'er return.

V.
O Attic shape! Fair attitude! With brede
   Of marble men and maidens overwrought,
With forest branches and the trodden weed;
   Thou, silent form, dost tease us out of thought
As doth eternity. Cold Pastoral!
   When old age shall this generation waste,
      Thou shalt remain, in midst of other woe

Than ours, a friend to man, to whom thou say'st,
"Beauty is truth, truth beauty"—that is all
    Ye know on earth, and all ye need to know.

This living hand, now warm and capable[1]

This living hand, now warm and capable
Of earnest grasping, would, if it were cold
And in the icy silence of the tomb,
So haunt thy days and chill thy dreaming nights
That thou wouldst wish thine own heart dry of blood
So in my veins red life might stream again,
And thou be conscience-calmed—see here it is—
I hold it towards you.

Thomas Hood (1799 – 1845)

The Poet's Fate[2]

What is a modern Poet's fate?
To write his thoughts upon a slate;
The Critic spits on what is done,
Gives it a wipe—and all is gone.

---

[1] Form: Iambic pentameter, unrhymed.— Notes: Notice that the last line is incomplete, left hanging much like the poem is left hanging. The hand held toward the reader is embodied in the poem itself.
[2] Form: Iambic tetrameter, AABB end rhymes.

Ralph Waldo Emerson (1803 – 1882)

Days[1]

Daughters of Time, the hypocritic Days,
Muffled and dumb like barefoot dervishes,
And marching single in an endless file,
Bring diadems and faggots in their hands.
To each they offer gifts after his will,
Bread, kingdoms, stars, and sky that holds them all.
I, in my pleachëd garden, watched the pomp,
Forgot my morning wishes, hastily
Took a few herbs and apples, and the Day
Turned and departed silent. I, too late,
Under her solemn fillet saw the scorn.

Hamatreya[2]

Bulkeley, hunt, willard, hosmer, meriam, flint,
Possessed the land which rendered to their toil
Hay, corn, roots, hemp, flax, apples, wool and wood.
Each of these landlords walked amidst his farm,
Saying, "'tis mine, my children's and my name's.
How sweet the west wind sounds in my own trees!
How graceful climb those shadows on my hill!
I fancy these pure waters and the flags
Know me, as does my dog: we sympathize;
And, i affirm, my actions smack of the soil.'

Where are these men? Asleep beneath their grounds:
And strangers, fond as they, their furrows plough.
Earth laughs in flowers, to see her boastful boys
Earth-proud, proud of the earth which is not theirs;

---

[1] Form: Blank verse—Vocabulary: dervishes: Muslim monk; diadems: crowns; faggots: bundle of sticks; pleachëd: shaded by interwoven branches or vines; fillet: narrow strip of color on the heraldry of the chief— Notes: Day is personified as a line of daughters of time, each offering us gifts. The narrator realizes too late that he has wasted the gifts offered to him that day.
[2] Form: Iambic pentameter with some variations; earth song is irregular meter—Vocabulary: sitfast: stationary; mould: dust; heritors: inheritor; avarice: immoderate desire for things.

Who steer the plough, but cannot steer their feet
Clear of the grave.
They added ridge to valley, brook to pond,
And sighed for all that bounded their domain;
'This suits me for a pasture; that's my park;
We must have clay, lime, gravel, granite-ledge,
And misty lowland, where to go for peat.
The land is well,—lies fairly to the south.
'Tis good, when you have crossed the sea and back,
To find the sitfast acres where you left them.'
Ah! The hot owner sees not death, who adds
Him to his land, a lump of mould the more.
Hear what the earth says:—

> *Earth-song*
>
> 'Mine and yours;
> Mine, not yours,
> Earth endures;
> Stars abide—
> Shine down in the old sea;
> Old are the shores;
> But where are old men?
> I who have seen much,
> Such have I never seen.
>
> 'The lawyer's deed
> Ran sure,
> In tail,
> To them, and to their heirs
> Who shall succeed,
> Without fail,
> Forevermore.
>
> 'Here is the land,
> Shaggy with wood,
> With its old valley,
> Mound and flood.
> But the heritors?—
> Fled like the flood's foam.
> The lawyer, and the laws,

107

And the kingdom,
Clean swept herefrom.

'They called me theirs,
Who so controlled me;
Yet every one
Wished to stay, and is gone,
How am i theirs,
If they cannot hold me,
But I hold them?'

When I heard the earth-song,
I was no longer brave;
My avarice cooled
Like lust in the chill of the grave.

The Rhodora[1]

*On being asked, Whence is the
flower?*

In May, when sea-winds pierced our solitudes,
I found the fresh Rhodora in the woods,
Spreading its leafless blooms in a damp nook,
To please the desert and the sluggish brook.
The purple petals, fallen in the pool,
Made the black water with their beauty gay;
Here might the red-bird come his plumes to cool,
And court the flower that cheapens his array.
Rhodora! If the sages ask thee why
This charm is wasted on the earth and sky,
Tell them, dear, that if eyes were made for seeing,
Then Beauty is its own excuse for being:
Why thou wert there, O rival of the rose!
I never thought to ask, I never knew:

---

[1] Form: Iambic pentameter, AABBCDCD end rhymes—Vocabulary:
Rhodora: plant with rose-purple flowers; wert: were.—Notes: This poem
notes that a higher entity is responsible for both the big things and the
little things, and that beauty exists with or without observations of the
beauty by people.

But, in my simple ignorance, suppose
The self-same Power that brought me there brought you.

The Snow-Storm[1]

Announced by all the trumpets of the sky,
Arrives the snow, and, driving o'er the fields,
Seems nowhere to alight: the whitëd air
Hides hill and woods, the river, and the heaven,
And veils the farmhouse at the garden's end.
The sled and traveler stopped, the courier's feet
Delayed, all friends shut out, the housemates sit
Around the radiant fireplace, enclosed
In a tumultuous privacy of storm.

Come see the north wind's masonry.
Out of an unseen quarry evermore
Furnished with tile, the fierce artificer
Curves his white bastions with projected roof
Round every windward stake, or tree, or door.
Speeding, the myriad-handed, his wild work
So fanciful, so savage, naught cares he
For number or proportion. Mockingly,
On coop or kennel he hangs Parian wreaths;
A swan-like form invests the hidden thorn;
Fills up the farmer's lane from wall to wall,
Maugre the farmer's sighs; and at the gate
A tapering turret overtops the work.
And when his hours are numbered, and the world
Is all his own, retiring, as he were not,
Leaves, when the sun appears, astonished Art
To mimic in slow structures, stone by stone,
Built in an age, the mad wind's night-work,
The frolic architecture of the snow.

---

[1] Form: Blank verse (unrhymed iambic pentameter)—Vocabulary: Delated:
carried; artificer: craftsman; bastions: projecting parts of a fortress;
naught: nothing; coop: cage for poultry or small animals; Parian: fine white
marble or porcelain; Maugre: notwithstanding.

Elizabeth Barrett Browning (1806 – 1861)

Sonnets from the Portuguese – I[1]

I thought once how Theocritus had sung
Of the sweet years, the dear and wished for years,
Who each one in a gracious hand appears
To bear a gift for mortals, old or young:
And, as I mused it in his antique tongue,
I saw, in gradual vision through my tears,
The sweet, sad years, the melancholy years,
Those of my own life, who by turns had flung
A shadow across me. Straightway I was 'ware,
So weeping, how a mystic Shape did move
Behind me, and drew me backward by the hair;
And a voice said in mastery, while I strove,
"Guess now who holds thee ?" - "Death," I said.
        But, there,
The silver answer rang,—"Not Death, but Love."

Sonnets from the Portuguese – XIV[2]

If thou must love me, let it be for nought
Except for love's sake only. Do not say
"I love her for her smile—her look—her way
Of speaking gently,—for a trick of thought
That falls in well with mine, and certes brought
A sense of pleasant ease on such a day"—
For these things in themselves, Beloved, may
Be changed, or change for thee,—and love, so wrought,
May be unwrought so. Neither love me for
Thine own dear pity's wiping my cheeks dry,—
A creature might forget to weep, who bore
Thy comfort long, and lose thy love thereby!
But love me for love's sake, that evermore
Thou mayst love on, through love's eternity.

---

[1] Form: Sonnet—Vocabulary: Theocritus: Greek poet.
[2] Form: Sonnet—Vocabulary: certes: certainly.

Sonnets from the Portuguese – XX[1]

Belovëd, my Belovëd, when I think
That thou wast in the world a year ago,
What time I sat alone here in the snow
And saw no footprint, heard the silence sink
No moment at thy voice, but, link by link,
Went counting all my chains as if that so
They never could fall off at any blow
Struck by thy possible hand,—why, thus I drink
Of life's great cup of wonder! Wonderful,
Never to feel thee thrill the day or night
With personal act or speech,—nor ever cull
Some prescience of thee with the blossoms white
Thou sawest growing! Atheists are as dull,
Who cannot guess God's presence out of sight.

Sonnets from the Portuguese – XLIII[2]

How do I love thee? Let me count the ways.
I love thee to the depth and breadth and height
My soul can reach, when feeling out of sight
For the ends of Being and ideal Grace.
I love thee to the level of everyday's
Most quiet need, by sun and candle-light.
I love thee freely, as men strive for Right;
I love thee purely, as they turn from Praise.
I love thee with the passion put to use
In my old griefs, and with my childhood's faith.
I love thee with a love I seemed to lose
With my lost saints,—I love thee with the breath,
Smiles, tears, of all my life!—and, if God choose,
I shall but love thee better after death.

---

[1] Form: Sonnet—Vocabulary: cull: pick out; prescience: premonition—
Notes: A brilliant Volta, changing and deepening the direction of the piece.
We start with the wonderful, romantic message of the depressed person
later realizing that throughout this dark time their true love was in the
world waiting to be discovered. The message is then broadened with a
parallel to atheists not realizing that God is present in the world waiting for
them to discover him.
[2] Form: Sonnet.

Henry Wadsworth Longfellow (1807 – 1882)

A Nameless Grave[1]

"A soldier of the Union mustered out,"
    Is the inscription on an unknown grave
    At Newport News, beside the salt-sea wave,
    Nameless and dateless; sentinel or scout
Shot down in skirmish, or disastrous rout
    Of battle, when the loud artillery drave
    Its iron wedges through the ranks of brave
    And doomed battalions, storming the redoubt.
Thou unknown hero sleeping by the sea
    In thy forgotten grave! With secret shame
    I feel my pulses beat, my forehead burn,
When I remember thou hast given for me
    All that thou hadst, thy life, thy very name,
    And I can give thee nothing in return.

Jugurtha[2]

How cold are thy baths, Apollo!
    Cried the African monarch, the splendid,
As down to his death in the hollow
    Dark dungeons of Rome he descended,
    Uncrowned, unthroned, unattended;
How cold are thy baths, Apollo!

How cold are thy baths, Apollo!
    Cried the Poet, unknown, unbefriended,
As the vision, that lured him to follow,
    With the mist and the darkness blended,
    And the dream of his life was ended;
How cold are thy baths, Apollo!

---

[1] Form: Sonnet.
[2] Form: Anapestic trimeter, ABABBA end rhymes—Vocabulary: Jugurtha: Berber King of Numidia, 156-104 BC—Notes: Jugurtha was held in the Rome in the prison Tullianum, also called the Mamertine Prison. It was originally created as a cistern for a spring located in the prison, and used to prepare and wash dead bodies prior to its conversion to use as a prison.

Killed at the Ford[1]

He is dead, the beautiful youth,
The heart of honor, the tongue of truth,
He, the life and light of us all,
Whose voice was blithe as a bugle-call,
Whom all eyes followed with one consent,
The cheer of whose laugh, and whose pleasant word,
Hushed all murmurs of discontent.

Only last night, as we rode along,
Down in the dark of the mountain gap,
To visit the picket-guard at the ford,
Little dreaming of any mishap,
He was humming the words of some old song:
"Two red roses he had on his cap
And another he bore at the point of his sword."

Sudden and swift a whistling ball
Came out of a wood, and the voice was still;
Something I heard in the darkness fall,
And for a moment my blood grew chill;
I spake in a whisper, as he who speaks
In a room where some one is lying dead;
But he made no answer to what I said.

We lifted him up to his saddle again,
And through the mire and the mist and the rain
Carried him back to the silent camp,
And laid him as if asleep on his bed;
And I saw by the light of the surgeon's lamp
Two white roses upon his cheeks,
And one, just over his heart, blood red!

And I saw in a vision how far and fleet
That fatal bullet went speeding forth,
Till it reached a town in the distant North,
Till it reached a house in a sunny street,

---

[1] Form: Iambic tetrameter, irregular but frequent end rhymes—Vocabulary:
blithe: carefree.

Till it reached a heart that ceased to beat
Without a murmur, without a cry;
And a bell was tolled in that far-off town,
For one who had passed from cross to crown,
And the neighbors wondered that she should die.

King Witlaf's Drinking-Horn[1]

Witlaf, a king of the Saxons,
    Ere yet his last he breathed,
To the merry monks of Croyland
    His drinking-horn bequeathed,—

That, whenever they sat at their revels,
    And drank from the golden bowl,
They might remember the donor,
    And breathe a prayer for his soul.

So sat they once at Christmas,
    And bade the goblet pass;
In their beards the red wine glistened
    Like dew-drops in the grass.

They drank to the soul of Witlaf,
    They drank to Christ the Lord,
And to each of the Twelve Apostles,
    Who had preached his holy word.

They drank to the Saints and Martyrs
    Of the dismal days of yore,
And as soon as the horn was empty
    They remembered one Saint more.

And the reader droned from the pulpit
    Like the murmur of many bees,
The legend of good Saint Guthlac,
    And Saint Basil's homilies;

---

[1] Form: Iambic trimeter, xAxA end rhymes—Vocabulary: Croyland: abbey
in Lincolnshire, England; Saint Guthlac: lived in Croyland circa 700 AD;
Saint Basil: lived 329 AD - 379 AD; Bartholomaeus: Monk from Touraine,
France (1478-1535); Guthlac and Bartholomaeus: names of the two bells.

Till the great bells of the convent,
    From their prison in the tower,
Guthlac and Bartholomaeus,
    Proclaimed the midnight hour.

And the Yule-log cracked in the chimney,
    And the Abbot bowed his head,
And the flamelets flapped and flickered,
    But the Abbot was stark and dead.

Yet still in his pallid fingers
    He clutched the golden bowl,
In which, like a pearl dissolving,
    Had sunk and dissolved his soul.

But not for this their revels
    The jovial monks forbore,
For they cried, "Fill high the goblet!
    We must drink to one Saint more!"

Nature[1]

As a fond mother, when the day is o'er,
Leads by the hand her little child to bed,
Half willing, half reluctant to be led,
And leave his broken playthings on the floor,
Still gazing at them through the open door,
Nor wholly reassured and comforted
By promises of others in their stead,
Which, though more splendid, may not please him more;
So Nature deals with us, and takes away
Our playthings one by one, and by the hand
Leads us to rest so gently, that we go
Scarce knowing if we wish to go or stay,
Being too full of sleep to understand
How far the unknown transcends the what we know.

---

[1] Form: Sonnet—Notes: A sonnet helping us to see how we are all children before the unknowns of life and death. Nature takes things away from us as we get older, but promises new and better things for us.

The Beleaguered City[1]

I have read, in some old, marvelous tale,
    Some legend strange and vague,
That a midnight host of specters pale
    Beleaguered the walls of Prague.

Beside the Moldau's rushing stream,
    With the wan moon overhead,
There stood as in an awful dream,
    The army of the dead.

White as a sea-fog, landward bound,
    The spectral camp was seen,
And, with a sorrowful, deep sound,
    The river flowed between.

No other voice nor sound was there,
    Nor drum, nor sentry's pace;
The mist-like banners clasped the air,
    As clouds with clouds embrace.

But when the old cathedral bell
    Proclaimed the morning prayer,
The white pavilions rose and fell
    On the alarmëd air.

Down the broad valley fast and far
    The troubled army fled;
Up rose the glorious morning star,
    The ghastly host was dead.

I have read, in the marvelous heart of man,
    That strange and mystic scroll,

---

[1] Form: Ballad, ABAB end rhymes—Vocabulary: Beleaguered: besieged; specters: ghosts; Prague: capital of what is now the Czech Republic; Moldau: Currently called the Vltava river; wan: pale; vale: valley—Notes: The story of ghosts being disbursed by church bells is then expanded to the idea that people are haunted by their own "ghosts" in life and that religion can dispel those ghosts as well.

That an army of phantoms vast and wan
　　Beleaguer the human soul.

Encamped beside Life's rushing stream,
　　In Fancy's misty light,
Gigantic shapes and shadows gleam,
　　Portentous through the night.

Upon its midnight battle-ground
　　The spectral camp is seen,
And, with sorrowful, deep sound
　　Flows the River of Life between.

No other voice nor sound is there,
　　In the army of the grave;
No other challenge breaks the air,
　　But the rushing of Life's wave.

And when the solemn and deep church-bell
　　Entreats the soul to pray,
The midnight phantoms feel the spell,
　　The shadows sweep away.

Down the broad Vale of Tears afar,
　　The spectral camp is fled;
Faith shineth as a morning star,
　　Our ghastly fears are dead.

The Fire of Drift-Wood[1]

We sat within the farm-house old,
　　Whose windows, looking o'er the bay,
Gave to the sea-breeze, damp and cold,
　　An easy entrance, night and day.

Not far away we saw the port,—
　　The strange, old-fashioned, silent town,—
The lighthouse—the dismantled fort,—
　　The wooden houses, quaint and brown.

---

[1] Form: Iambic tetrameter, ABAB end rhymes.

117

We sat and talked until the night,
    Descending, filled the little room;
Our faces faded from the sight,—
    Our voices only broke the gloom.

We spake of many a vanished scene,
    Of what we once had thought and said,
Of what had been, and might have been,
    And who was changed, and who was dead;

And all that fills the hearts of friends,
    When first they feel, with secret pain,
Their lives thenceforth have separate ends,
    And never can be one again;

The first slight swerving of the heart,
    That words are powerless to express,
And leave it still unsaid in part,
    Or say it in too great excess.

The very tones in which we spake
    Had something strange, I could but mark;
The leaves of memory seemed to make
    A mournful rustling in the dark.

Oft died the words upon our lips,
    As suddenly, from out the fire
Built of the wreck of stranded ships,
    The flames would leap and then expire.

And, as their splendor flashed and failed,
    We thought of wrecks upon the main,—
Of ships dismasted, that were hailed
    And sent no answer back again.

The windows, rattling in their frames,—
    The ocean, roaring up the beach,—
The gusty blast—the bickering flames,—
    All mingled vaguely in our speech;

Until they made themselves a part
Of fancies floating through the brain,—
The long-lost ventures of the heart,
That send no answers back again.

0 flames that glowed! 0 hearts that yearned!
They were indeed too much akin,—
The drift-wood fire without that burned,
The thoughts that burned and glowed within.

The Landlord's Tale[1]

Listen, my children, and you shall hear
Of the midnight ride of Paul Revere,
On the eighteenth of April, in Seventy-five;
Hardly a man is now alive
Who remembers that famous day and year.

He said to his friend, "If the British march
By land or sea from the town to-night,
Hang a lantern aloft in the belfry arch
Of the North Church tower as a signal light,—
One, if by land, and two, if by sea;
And I on the opposite shore will be,
Ready to ride and spread the alarm
Through every Middlesex village and farm
For the country folk to be up and to arm,"

Then he said, "Good night!" and with muffled oar
Silently rowed to the Charlestown shore,
Just as the moon rose over the bay,
Where swinging wide at her moorings lay
The Somerset, British man-of-war;
A phantom ship, with each mast and spar
Across the moon like a prison bar,
And a huge black hulk, that was magnified
By its own reflection in the tide.

---

[1] Form: Iambic tetrameter, irregular but frequent end rhymes.

Meanwhile, his friend, through alley and street,
Wanders and watches with eager ears,
Till in the silence around him he hears
The muster of men at the barrack door,
The sound of arms, and the tramp of feet,
And the measured tread of the grenadiers,
Marching down to their boats on the shore.

Then he climbed the tower of the Old North Church,
By the wooden stairs, with stealthy tread,
To the belfry-chamber overhead,
And startled the pigeons from their perch
On the somber rafters, that round him made
Masses and moving shapes of shade,—
By the trembling ladder, steep and tall
To the highest window in the wall,
Where he paused to listen and look down
A moment on the roofs of the town,
And the moonlight flowing over all.

Beneath, in the churchyard, lay the dead,
In their night-encampment on the hill,
Wrapped in silence so deep and still
That he could hear, like a sentinel's tread,
The watchful night-wind, as it went
Creeping along from tent to tent
And seeming to whisper, "All is well!"
A moment only he feels the spell
Of the place and the hour, and the secret dread
Of the lonely belfry and the dead;
For suddenly all his thoughts are bent
On a shadowy something far away,
Where the river widens to meet the bay,—
A line of black that bends and floats
On the rising tide, like a bridge of boats.

Meanwhile, impatient to mount and ride,
Booted and spurred, with a heavy stride
On the opposite shore walked Paul Revere.
Now he patted his horse's side,
Now gazed at the landscape far and near,

Then, impetuous, stamped the earth,
And turned and tightened his saddle-girth;
But mostly he watched with eager search
The belfry-tower of the Old North Church,
As it rose above the graves on the hill,
Lonely and spectral and somber and still.
And lo! As he looks, on the belfry's height
A glimmer, and then a gleam of light!
He springs to the saddle, the bridle he turns,
But lingers and gazes, till full on his sight
A second lamp in the belfry burns!

A hurry of hoofs in a village street,
A shape in the moonlight, a bulk in the dark,
And beneath, from the pebbles, in passing, a spark
Struck out by a steed flying fearless and fleet:
That was all! And yet, through the gloom and the light,
The fate of a nation was riding that night;
And the spark struck out by that steed, in his flight,
Kindled the land into flame with its heat.
He has left the village and mounted the steep,
And beneath him, tranquil and broad and deep,
Is the Mystic, meeting the ocean tides;
And under the alders, that skirt its edge,
Now soft on the sand, now loud on the ledge,
Is heard the tramp of his steed as he rides.

It was twelve by the village clock
When he crossed the bridge into Medford town.
He heard the crowing of the cock,
And the barking of the farmer's dog,

And felt the damp of the river fog,
That rises after the sun goes down.

It was one by the village clock,
When he galloped into Lexington.
He saw the gilded weathercock
Swim in the moonlight as he passed,
And the meeting-house windows, blank and bare,
Gaze at him with a spectral glare,
As if they already stood aghast
At the bloody work they would look upon.

It was two by the village clock,
When he came to the bridge in Concord town.
He heard the bleating of the flock,
And the twitter of birds among the trees,
And felt the breath of the morning breeze
Blowing over the meadows brown.
And one was safe and asleep in his bed
Who at the bridge would be first to fall,
Who that day would be lying dead,
Pierced by a British musket-ball.

You know the rest. In the books you have read,
How the British Regulars fired and fled,—
How the farmers gave them ball for ball,
From behind each fence and farm-yard wall,
Chasing the red-coats down the lane,
Then crossing the fields to emerge again
Under the trees at the turn of the road,
And only pausing to fire and load.

So through the night rode Paul Revere;
And so through the night went his cry of alarm
To every Middlesex village and farm,—
A cry of defiance and not of fear,
A voice in the darkness, a knock at the door,
And a word that shall echo forevermore!
For, borne on the night-wind of the Past,
Through all our history, to the last,
In the hour of darkness and peril and need,

The people will waken and listen to hear
The hurrying hoof-beats of that steed,
And the midnight message of Paul Revere.

The Phantom Ship[1]

In mather's magnalia christi,
    Of the old colonial time,
May be found in prose the legend
    That is here set down in rhyme.

A ship sailed from new haven,
    And the keen and frosty airs,
That filled her sails in parting
    Were heavy with good men's prayers.

"O lord! If it be thy pleasure"—
    Thus prayed the old divine—
"To bury our friends in the ocean,
    Take them, for they are thine!"

But master lamberton muttered,
    And under his breath said he,
"This ship is so crank and walty
    I fear our grave she will be!"

And the ships that came from england
    When the winter months were gone,
Brought no tidings of this vessel!
    Nor of master lamberton.

This put the people to praying
    That the lord would let them hear
What in his greater wisdom
    He had done to friends so dear.

---

[1] Form: Iambic tetrameter, xAxA end rhymes—Vocabulary: Mather: Cotton Mather (1663-1728); Magnalia Christi: the book "Magnalia Christi Americana"; crank: unstable; walty: liable to roll over; mould: the earth of a grave.

And at last our prayers were answered:
    It was in the month of june
An hour before sunset
    Of a windy afternoon.

When, steadily steering landward,
    A ship was seen below,
And they knew it was lamberton, master,
    Who sailed so long ago.

On she came with a cloud of canvas,
    Right against the wind that blew,
Until the eye could distinguish
    The faces of the crew.

Then fell her straining topmasts,
    Hanging tangled in the shrouds,
And her sails were loosened and lifted,
    And blown away like clouds.

And the masts, with all their rigging,
    Fell slowly, one by one,
And the hulk dilated and vanished,
    As a sea-mist in the sun!

And the people who saw thus marvel
    Each said unto his friend,
That this was the mould of their vessel,
    And thus her tragic end.

And the pastor of the village
    Gave thanks to god in prayer,
That, to quiet their troubled spirits,
    He had sent this ship of air.

The Potter's Wheel[1]

Turn, turn, my wheel! Turn round and round
Without a pause, without a sound:
   So spins the flying world away!
This clay, well mixed with marl and sand,
Follows the motion of my hand;
Far some must follow, and some command,
   Though all are made of clay!

Turn, turn, my wheel! All things must change
To something new, to something strange;
   Nothing that is can pause or stay;
The moon will wax, the moon will wane,
The mist and cloud will turn to rain,
The rain to mist and cloud again,
   Tomorrow be to-day.

Turn, turn, my wheel! All life is brief;
What now is bud wilt soon be leaf,
   What now is leaf will soon decay;
The wind blows east, the wind blows west;
The blue eggs in the robin's nest
Will soon have wings and beak and breast,
   And flutter and fly away.

---

[1] Form: Iambic tetrameter except last line of each stanza iambic trimeter, AABCCCB end rhymes—Vocabulary: marl: mixture of clay and limestone; wax: increase in size; wane; decrease in size; Coptic: afro-Asian (especially Egyptian); potsherds: fragments of broken pottery—Notes: Note the circle between the pots (metaphor for people, or perhaps even societies) making a full circle from clay to pot to fragments of pots and back to clay to begin again.

Turn, turn, my wheel! This earthen jar
A touch can make, a touch can mar;
   And shall it to the Potter say,
What makest thou? Thou hast no hand?
As men who think to understand
A world by their Creator planned,
   Who wiser is than they.

Turn, turn, my wheel! 'T is nature's plan
The child should grow into the man,
   The man grow wrinkled, old, and gray;
In youth the heart exults and sings,
The pulses leap, the feet have wings;
In age the cricket chirps, and brings
   The harvest home of day.

Turn, turn, my wheel! The human race,
Of every tongue, of every place,
   Caucasian, Coptic, or Malay,
All that inhabit this great earth,
Whatever be their rank or worth,
Are kindred and allied by birth,
   And made of the same clay.

Turn, turn, my wheel! What is begun
At daybreak must at dark be done,
    To-morrow will be another day;
To-morrow the hot furnace flame
Will search the heart and try the frame,
And stamp with honor or with shame
    These vessels made of clay.

Stop, stop, my wheel! Too soon, too soon
The noon will be the afternoon,
    Too soon to-day be yesterday;
Behind us in our path we cast
The broken potsherds of the past,
And all are ground to dust at last,
    And trodden into clay!

The Rainy Day[1]

The day is cold, and dark, and dreary;
It rains, and the wind is never weary;
The vine still clings to the mouldering wall,
But at every gust the dead leaves fall,
    And the day is dark and dreary.

My life is cold, and dark, and dreary;
It rains, and the wind is never weary;
My thoughts still cling to the mouldering Past,
But the hopes of youth fall thick in the blast,
    And the days are dark and dreary.

Be still, sad heart! and cease repining;
Behind the clouds is the sun still shining;
Thy fate is the common fate of all,
Into each life some rain must fall,
    Some days must be dark and dreary.

---

[1] Form: Iambic tetrameter, AABBC end rhymes—Vocabulary: mouldering: crumbling; blast: gusts of wind in this case; repining: being discontented.

The Three Silences of Molinos[1]

To John Greenleaf Whittier

Three Silences there are: the first of speech,
    The second of desire, the third of thought;
    This is the lore a Spanish monk, distraught
    With dreams and visions, was the first to teach.
These Silences, commingling each with each,
    Made up the perfect Silence that he sought
    And prayed for, and wherein at times he caught
    Mysterious sounds from realms beyond our reach.
O thou, whose daily life anticipates
    The life to come, and in whose thought and word
    The spiritual world preponderates.
Hermit of Amesbury! Thou too hast heard
    Voices and melodies from beyond the gates,
    And speakest only when thy soul is stirred!

Travels by the Fireside[2]

The ceaseless rain is falling fast,
    And yonder gilded vane,
Immovable for three days past,
    Points to the misty main,

It drives me in upon myself
    And to the fireside gleams,
To pleasant books that crowd my shelf,
    And still more pleasant dreams,

I read whatever bards have sung
    Of lands beyond the sea,
And the bright days when I was young
    Come thronging back to me.

---

[1] Form: Sonnet—Vocabulary: Molinos: Miguel de Molinos (1640 - 1696);commingling: blending; Amesbury: town in Massachusetts—Notes: The concepts here are very zen-like.
[2] Form: Ballad—Vocabulary: gilded: covered with gold foil; climes: climates.

In fancy I can hear again
   The Alpine torrent's roar,
The mule-bells on the hills of Spain,
   The sea at Elsinore.

I see the convent's gleaming wall
   Rise from its groves of pine,
And towers of old cathedrals tall,
   And castles by the Rhine.

I journey on by park and spire,
   Beneath centennial trees,
Through fields with poppies all on fire,
   And gleams of distant seas.

I fear no more the dust and heat,
   No more I feel fatigue,
While journeying with another's feet
   O'er many a lengthening league.

Let others traverse sea and land,
   And toil through various climes,
I turn the world round with my hand
   Reading these poets' rhymes.

From them I learn whatever lies
   Beneath each changing zone,
And see, when looking with their eyes,
   Better than with mine own.

Twilight[1]

The twilight is sad and cloudy,
   The wind blows wild and free,
And like the wings of sea-birds
   Flash the white caps of the sea.

But in the fisherman's cottage
   There shines a ruddier light,

---

[1] Form: Iambic trimeter, xAxA end rhymes.

And a little face at the window
　　Peers out into the night.

Close, close it is pressed to the window,
　　As if those childish eyes
Were looking into the darkness,
　　To see some form arise.

And a woman's waving shadow
　　Is passing to and fro,
Now rising to the ceiling,
　　Now bowing and bending low.

What tale do the roaring ocean,
　　And the night-wind, bleak and wild,
As they beat at the crazy casement,
　　Tell to that little child?

And why do the roaring ocean,
　　And the night-wind, wild and bleak,
As they beat at the heart of the mother,
　　Drive the color from her cheek?

John Greenleaf Whittier (1807 – 1892)

Autumn Thoughts[1]

Gone hath the Spring, with all its flowers,
　　And gone the Summer's pomp and show,
And Autumn, in his leafless bowers,
　　Is waiting for the Winter's snow.

I said to Earth, so cold and gray,
　　"An emblem of myself thou art."
"Not so," the Earth did seem to say,
　　"For Spring shall warm my frozen heart.

---

[1] Form: Iambic tetrameter, ABAB end rhymes—Vocabulary: bowers:
shaded recess—Notes: The narrator compares his hold age with the winter
of the forest, but nature replies that, unlike him, she will renew in the
spring.

I soothe my wintry sleep with dreams
    Of warmer sun and softer rain,
And wait to hear the sound of streams
    And songs of merry birds again."

"But thou, from whom the Spring hath gone,
    For whom the flowers no longer blow,
Who standest blighted and forlorn,
    Like Autumn waiting for the snow;"

"no hope is thine of sunnier hours,
    Thy Winter shall no more depart;
No Spring revive thy wasted flowers,
    Nor Summer warm thy frozen heart."

By their Works[1]

Call him not heretic whose works attest
His faith in goodness by no creed confessed.
Whatever in love's name is truly done
To free the bound and lift the fallen one
Is done to Christ. Whoso in deed and word
Is not against Him labors for our Lord.
When He, who, sad and weary, longing sore
For love's sweet service, sought the sisters' door,
One saw the heavenly, one the human guest,
But who shall say which loved the Master best?

Forgiveness[2]

My heart was heavy, for its trust had been
    Abused, its kindness answered with foul wrong;
So, turning gloomily from my fellow-men,
    One summer Sabbath day I strolled among
The green mounds of the village burial-place;

---

[1] Form: Iambic pentameter, AABB end rhymes—Vocabulary: creed: formal statement of religious belief—Notes: This poem refers to a biblical story in which Jesus visits two sisters (Mary and Martha). One sees only his human form and spends her efforts being a host to his earthly needs. One sees in him God and, ignoring his earthly needs, listens to his teachings.
[2] Form: Sonnet—Vocabulary: meekened: made meek.

Where, pondering how all human love and hate
　　Find one sad level; and how, soon or late,
Wronged and wrongdoer, each with meekened face,
　　And cold hands folded over a still heart,
Pass the green threshold of our common grave,
　　Whither all footsteps tend, whence none depart,
Awed for myself, and pitying my race,
Our common sorrow, like a mighty wave,
Swept all my pride away, and trembling I forgave!

Trust[1]

The same old baffling questions! O my friend,
I cannot answer them. In vain I send
My soul into the dark, where never burn
　　The lamps of science, nor the natural light
Of Reason's sun and stars! I cannot learn
Their great and solemn meanings, nor discern
The awful secrets of the eyes which turn
　　Evermore on us through the day and night
　　With silent challenge and a dumb demand,
Proffering the riddles of the dread unknown,
Like the calm Sphinxes, with their eyes of stone,
　　Questioning the centuries from their veils of sand!
I have no answer for myself or thee,
Save that I learned beside my mother's knee;
"All is of God that is, and is to be;
　　And God is good." Let this suffice us still,
　　Resting in childlike trust upon His will
Who moves to His great ends unthwarted by the ill.

---

[1] Form: Iambic pentameter, irregular but frequent end rhymes—
Vocabulary: unthwarted: unstopped—Notes: He cannot answer his own or
other's questions about what lies beyond the grave, other than to rely on
faith he learned as a child from his mother.

Oliver Wendell Holmes (1809 – 1894)

Sun and Shadow[1]

As I look from the isle, o'er its billows of green,
To the billows of foam-crested blue,
Yon bark, that afar in the distance is seen,
Half dreaming, my eyes will pursue:
Now dark in the shadow, she scatters the spray
As the chaff in the stroke of the flail;
Now white as the sea-gull, she flies on her way,
The sun gleaming bright on her sail.

Yet her pilot is thinking of dangers to shun,—
Of breakers that whiten and roar;
How little he cares, if in shadow or sun
They see him who gaze from the shore!
He looks to the beacon that looms from the reef,
To the rock that is under his lee,
As he drifts on the blast, like a wind-wafted leaf,
O'er the gulfs of the desolate sea.

Thus drifting afar to the dim-vaulted caves
Where life and its ventures are laid,
The dreamers who gaze while we battle the waves
May see us in sunshine or shade;
Yet true to our course, though the shadows grow dark,
We'll trim our broad sail as before,

---

[1] Form: Anapestic, alternating tetrameter and trimeter, ABAB end rhymes—Vocabulary: billows: waves; bark: sailing ship; chaff: stems after seeds are removed; flail: manual threshing device—Notes: This poem looks at perspectives. From the perspective of the shore the boat moves between sun and shadow, while from the perspective of the boat's pilot the boat moves between beacons (buoys) to avoid shoals and other sources of danger. Similarly, the narrator moves between goals which are internal, and the others looking from shore do not understand these goals and measure progress by different criteria. For example, the narrator's goals may be related to writing poetry while the people on shore are critics. Another example would be the narrator's goals being happiness in life while the people on shore are relatives measuring success by financial criteria.

And stand by the rudder that governs the bark,
Nor ask how we look from the shore!

Edgar Allan Poe (1809 – 1849)

Annabel Lee[1]

It was many and many a year ago,
   In a kingdom by the sea,
That a maiden there lived whom you may know
   By the name of Annabel Lee;
And this maiden she lived with no other thought
   Than to love and be loved by me.

I was a child and she was a child,
   In this kingdom by the sea:
But we loved with a love that was more than love—
   I and my Annabel Lee;
With a love that the winged seraphs of heaven
   Coveted her and me.

And this was the reason that, long ago,
   In this kingdom by the sea,
A wind blew out of a cloud, chilling
   My beautiful Annabel Lee;
So that her highborn kinsman came
   And bore her away from me,
To shut her up in a sepulcher
   In this kingdom by the sea.

The angels, not half so happy in heaven,
   Went envying her and me—
Yes!—that was the reason (as all men know,
   In this kingdom by the sea)
That the wind came out of the cloud by night,
   Chilling and killing my Annabel Lee.

---

[1] Form: Anapestic lines 7 feet long (split here to 4-3), AAA end rhymes—
Vocabulary: seraphs: type of angel; dissever: separate—Notes: The
narrator's childhood sweetheart died (probably of a fever), and the narrator
continues to mourn next to her tomb by the sea.

But our love it was stronger by far than the love
    Of those who were older than we—
    Of many far wiser than we—
And neither the angels in heaven above,
    Nor the demons down under the sea,
Can ever dissever my soul from the soul
    Of the beautiful Annabel Lee:

For the moon never beams, without bringing me dreams
    Of the beautiful Annabel Lee;
And the stars never rise, but I feel the bright eyes
    Of the beautiful Annabel Lee;
And so, all the night-tide, I lie down by the side
Of my darling—my darling—my life and my bride,
    In her sepulcher there by the sea,
    In her tomb by the side of the sea.

For Annie[1]

Thank Heaven! The crisis—
    The danger is past,
And the lingering illness
    Is over at last—
And the fever called "Living"
    Is conquered at last.

Sadly, I know
    I am shorn of my strength,
And no muscle I move
    As I lie at full length—
But no matter!—I feel
    I am better at length.

And I rest so composedly,
    Now, in my bed,
That any beholder
    Might fancy me dead—

---

[1] Form: Anapestic dimeter xAxAxA end rhymes where the last two rhyming words are the same word.—Vocabulary: naphthalene: flammable product of coal tar—Notes: In this poem the narrator is dead, yet still thinks of his last moments with his love, Annie.

Might start at beholding me,
   Thinking me dead.

The moaning and groaning,
   The sighing and sobbing,
Are quieted now,
   With that horrible throbbing
At heart:—ah, that horrible,
   Horrible throbbing!

The sickness—the nausea—
   The pitiless pain—
Have ceased, with the fever
   That maddened my brain—
With the fever called "Living"
   That burned in my brain.

And oh! Of all tortures
   That torture the worst
Has abated—the terrible
   Torture of thirst
For the naphthalene river
   Of Passion accurst:—
I have drank of a water
   That quenches all thirst:—

Of a water that flows,
   With a lullaby sound,
From a spring but a very few
   Feet under ground—
From a cavern not very far
   Down under ground.

And ah! Let it never
   Be foolishly said
That my room it is gloomy
   And narrow my bed;
For man never slept
   In a different bed—
And, to sleep, you must slumber
   In just such a bed.

My tantalized spirit
   Here blandly reposes,
Forgetting, or never
   Regretting its roses—
Its old agitations
   Of myrtles and roses:

For now, while so quietly
   Lying, it fancies
A holier odor
   About it, of pansies—
A rosemary odor,
   Commingled with pansies—
With rue and the beautiful
   Puritan pansies.

And so it lies happily,
   Bathing in many
A dream of the truth
   And the beauty of Annie—
Drowned in a bath
   Of the tresses of Annie.

She tenderly kissed me,
   She fondly caressed,
And then I fell gently
   To sleep on her breast—
Deeply to sleep
   From the heaven of her breast.

When the light was extinguished,
   She covered me warm,
And she prayed to the angels
   To keep me from harm—
To the queen of the angels
   To shield me from harm.

And I lie so composedly,
   Now in my bed,
(Knowing her love)

That you fancy me dead—
And I rest so contentedly,
   Now in my bed,
(With her love at my breast)
   That you fancy me dead—
That you shudder to look at me,
   Thinking me dead:—

But my heart it is brighter
   Than all of the many
Stars in the sky,
   For it sparkles with Annie—
It glows with the light
   Of the love of my Annie—
With the thought of the light
   Of the eyes of my Annie.

The Raven[1]

Once upon a midnight dreary, while I pondered, weak and
     weary,
Over many a quaint and curious volume of forgotten lore—
While I nodded, nearly napping, suddenly there came a
     tapping,
As of some one gently rapping, rapping at my chamber door.
"'Tis some visitor," I muttered, "tapping at my chamber
     door—
   Only this and nothing more."

Ah, distinctly I remember it was in the bleak December,

---

[1] Form: Trochaic octameter, or as formatted here, trochaic tetrameter,
AAxBCCCBxBB—Vocabulary: surcease: stop; obeisance: gesture of
deference; mien: bearing or manner; Pallas: Greek goddess of wisdom and
useful arts, guardian of Athens; shorn: clipped; craven: cowardly;
Plutonian: related to the god Pluto, god of Hades; dirges: funeral lament;
censer: container burning incense for religious festivals; Respite: short
interval of relief; nepenthe: drug to reduce grief (Odyssey); quaff: drink;
balm in Gilead: healing sap from shrub grown only in Palestine; Aidenn:
heaven—Notes: The narrator, in his depression, is creating his own form of
hell. He realizes early on that the bird only says one word, and then begins
to pose questions where that one word will contribute to his haunting
depression.

And each separate dying ember wrought its ghost upon the
 floor.
Eagerly I wished the morrow;—vainly I had sought to borrow
From my books surcease of sorrow—sorrow for the lost
 Lenore—
For the rare and radiant maiden whom the angels name
 Lenore—
 Nameless *here* for evermore.

And the silken sad uncertain rustling of each purple curtain
Thrilled me—filled me with fantastic terrors never felt before;
So that now, to still the beating of my heart, I stood repeating
"Tis some visitor entreating entrance at my chamber door—
Some late visitor entreating entrance at my chamber door;
 This it is and nothing more."

Presently my soul grew stronger; hesitating then no longer,
"Sir," said I, "or Madam, truly your forgiveness I implore;
But the fact is I was napping, and so gently you came
 rapping,
And so faintly you came tapping, tapping at my chamber
 door,
That I scarce was sure I heard you"—here I opened wide the
 door;——
 Darkness there and nothing more.

Deep into that darkness peering, long I stood there
 wondering, fearing,
Doubting, dreaming dreams no mortals ever dared to dream
 before;
But the silence was unbroken, and the stillness gave no
 token,
And the only word there spoken was the whispered word,
 "Lenore!"
This I whispered, and an echo murmured back the word,
 "Lenore!"—
 Merely this, and nothing more.

Back into the chamber turning, all my soul within me
 burning,
Soon I heard again a tapping somewhat louder than before.

139

"Surely," said I, "surely that is something at my window
      lattice;
Let me see, then, what thereat is, and this mystery explore—
Let my heart be still a moment and this mystery explore;—
   "Tis the wind and nothing more!"

Open here I flung the shutter, when, with many a flirt and
      flutter,
In there stepped a stately Raven of the saintly days of yore;
Not the least obeisance made he; not an instant stopped or
      stayed he;
But, with mien of lord or lady, perched above my chamber
      door—
Perched upon a bust of Pallas just above my chamber door—
   Perched, and sat, and nothing more.

Then this ebony bird beguiling my sad fancy into smiling,
By the grave and stern decorum of the countenance it wore,
"Though thy crest be shorn and shaven, thou," I said, "art
      sure no craven,
Ghastly grim and ancient raven wandering from the Nightly
      shore—
Tell me what thy lordly name is on the Night's Plutonian
      shore!"
   Quoth the Raven "Nevermore."

Much I marveled this ungainly fowl to hear discourse so
      plainly,
Though its answer little meaning—little relevancy bore;
For we cannot help agreeing that no living human being
Ever yet was blessed with seeing bird above his chamber
      door—
Bird or beast upon the sculptured bust above his chamber
      door,
   With such name as "Nevermore."

But the Raven, sitting lonely on the placid bust, spoke only
That one word, as if his soul in that one word he did outpour.
Nothing farther then he uttered—not a feather then he
      fluttered—

Till I scarcely more than muttered"Other friends have flown
    before—
On the morrow *he* will leave me, as my hopes have flown
    before."
    Then the bird said "Nevermore."

Startled at the stillness broken by reply so aptly spoken,
"Doubtless," said I, "what it utters is its only stock and store
Caught from some unhappy master whom unmerciful
    Disaster
Followed fast and followed faster till his songs one burden
    bore—
Till the dirges of his Hope that melancholy burden bore
    Of "Never—nevermore."

But the raven still beguiling all my sad soul into smiling,
Straight I wheeled a cushioned seat in front of bird, and bust
    and door;
Then, upon the velvet sinking, I betook myself to linking
Fancy unto fancy, thinking what this ominous bird of yore—
What this grim, ungainly, ghastly, gaunt and ominous bird of
    yore
    Meant in croaking "Nevermore."

This I sat engaged in guessing, but no syllable expressing
To the fowl whose fiery eyes now burned into my bosom's
    core;
This and more I sat divining, with my head at ease reclining
On the cushion's velvet lining that the lamplight gloated o'er,
But whose velvet violet lining with the lamplight gloating o'er,
    She shall press, ah, nevermore!

Then, me thought, the air grew denser, perfumed from an
    unseen censer
Swung by Angels whose faint foot-falls tinkled on the tufted
    floor.
"Wretch," I cried, "thy God hath lent thee—by these angels he
    hath sent thee
Respite—respite and nepenthe from thy memories of Lenore;
Quaff, oh quaff this kind nepenthe and forget this lost
    Lenore!"

Quoth the Raven, "Nevermore."

"Prophet!" said I, "thing of evil!—prophet still, if bird or
     devil!—
Whether Tempter sent, or whether tempest tossed thee here
     ashore,
Desolate yet all undaunted, on this desert land enchanted—
On this home by Horror haunted—tell me truly, I implore—
Is there—*is* there balm in Gilead?—tell me—tell me, I
     implore!"
    Quoth the Raven, "Nevermore."

"Prophet!" said I, "thing of evil—prophet still, if bird or devil!
By that Heaven that bends above us—by that God we both
     adore—
Tell this soul with sorrow laden if, within the distant Aidenn,
It shall clasp a sainted maiden whom the angels name
     Lenore—
Clasp a rare and radiant maiden whom the angels name
     Lenore."
    Quoth the Raven, "Nevermore."

"Be that word our sign of parting, bird or fiend!" I shrieked,
     upstarting—
"Get thee back into the tempest and the Night's Plutonian
     shore!
Leave no black plume as a token of that lie thy soul hath
     spoken!
Leave my loneliness unbroken!—quit the bust above my door!
Take thy beak from out my heart, and take thy form from off
     my door!"
    Quoth the Raven, "Nevermore."

And the Raven, never flitting, still is sitting, still is sitting
On the pallid bust of Pallas just above my chamber door;
And his eyes have all the seeming of a demon's that is
     dreaming,
And the lamp-light o'er him streaming throws his shadow on
     the floor;

And my soul from out that shadow that lies floating on the
    floor
  Shall be lifted—nevermore!

Alfred, Lord Tennyson (1809 – 1892)

Come Not, When I am Dead[1]

Come not, when I am dead,
    To drop thy foolish tears upon my grave,
To trample round my fallen head,
    And vex the unhappy dust thou wouldst not save.
There let the wind sweep and the plover cry;
    But thou, go by.

Child, if it were thine error or thy crime
    I care no longer, being all unblest:
Wed whom thou wilt, but I am sick of Time,
    And I desire to rest.
Pass on, weak heart, and leave me where I lie:
    Go by, go by.

Home They Brought Her Warrior Dead[2]

Home they brought her warrior dead:
    She nor swooned, nor uttered cry:
All her maidens, watching, said,
    'She must weep or she will die.'

Then they praised him, soft and low,
    Called him worthy to be loved,
Truest friend and noblest foe;
    Yet she neither spoke nor moved.

Stole a maiden from her place,
    Lightly to the warrior stepped,

---

[1] Form: Iambic pentameter with some lines using other lengths for
emphasis and rhythm, ABABCC end rhymes—Vocabulary: vex: annoy;
plover: large, wading bird.
[2] Form: Iambic tetrameter, ABAB end rhymes.

Took the face-cloth from the face;
　　Yet she neither moved nor wept.

Rose a nurse of ninety years,
　　Set his child upon her knee—
Like summer tempest came her tears—
　　'Sweet my child, I live for thee.'

The Charge of the Light Brigade[1]

Half a league, half a league,
Half a league onward,
All in the valley of Death
　　Rode the six hundred.
'Forward, the Light Brigade!
Charge for the guns!' he said:
Into the valley of Death
　　Rode the six hundred.

'Forward, the Light Brigade!'
Was there a man dismayed?
Not tho' the soldier knew
　　Some one had blunderëd:
Theirs not to make reply,
Theirs not to reason why,
Theirs but to do and die:
Into the valley of Death
　　Rode the six hundred.

Cannon to right of them,
Cannon to left of them,
Cannon in front of them
　　Volleyed and thundered;
Stormed at with shot and shell,
Boldly they rode and well,
Into the jaws of Death,
Into the mouth of Hell
　　Rode the six hundred.

---

[1] Form: Iambic trimeter but with a large number of lines starting with a trochee or headless iamb, mostly AAxxBB end rhymes—Notes: This poem describes an actual charge during the Crimean war in 1854.

Flashed all their sabers bare,
Flashed as they turned in air
Sabring the gunners there,
Charging an army, while
    All the world wondered:
Plunged in the battery-smoke
Right thro' the line they broke;
Cossack and Russian
Reeled from the sabre-stroke
    Shattered and sundered.
Then they rode back, but not
    Not the six hundred.

Cannon to right of them,
Cannon to left of them,
Cannon behind them
    Volleyed and thundered;
Stormed at with shot and shell,
While horse and hero fell,
They that had fought so well
Came thro' the jaws of Death,
Back from the mouth of Hell,
All that was left of them,
    Left of six hundred.

When can their glory fade?
O the wild charge they made!

All the world wondered.
Honor the charge they made!
Honor the Light Brigade,
    Noble six hundred!

Vivien's Song[1]

"In Love, if Love be Love, if Love be ours,
Faith and unfaith can ne'er be equal powers:
Unfaith in aught is want of faith in all.

"It is the little rift within the lute,
That by and by will make the music mute,
And ever widening slowly silence all.

"The little rift within the lover's lute,
Or little pitted speck in garnered fruit,
That rotting inward slowly molders all.

"It is not worth the keeping: let it go;
But shall it? Answer, darling, answer, no.
And trust me not at all or all in all."

Robert Browning (1812 – 1889)

A Toccata of Galuppi's[2]

Oh Galuppi Baldassare, this is very sad to find!
I can hardly misconceive you; it would prove me deaf and
    blind;

---

[1] Form: Iambic pentameter, AAB CCB DDB end rhymes where B is a
repeated word—Vocabulary: aught: anything; rift: narrow opening or tear;
lute: stringed instrument; garnered: gathered; molders: crumbles to dust.
[2] Form: Iambic tetrameter, xAxAxA end rhymes—Vocabulary: Toccata:
freestyle virtuoso for keyboard instrument; Galuppi Baldassare: Venetian
composer; misconceive: misunderstand; Saint Mark: cathedral in Venice
holding the bones of St. Mark; Doges: chief magistrate of Venice; Shylock's
bridge: famous pedestrian bridge over the main canal in Venice; clavichord:
similar to a piano; lesser thirds, sixths diminished, suspensions, solutions,
sevenths, dominants: musical terms referring to chords and chord
progressions.

But although I take your meaning, 'tis with such a heavy
    mind!

Here you come with your old music, and here's all the good it
    brings.
What, they lived once thus at Venice where the merchants
    were the kings,
Where Saint Mark's is, where the Doges used to wed the sea
    with rings?

Ay, because the sea's the street there; and 'tis arched by
    . . . what you call
. . . Shylock's bridge with houses on it, where they kept the
    carnival:
I was never out of England—it's as if I saw it all.

Did young people take their pleasure when the sea was warm
    in May?
Balls and masks begun at midnight, burning ever to mid-day,
When they made up fresh adventures for the morrow, do you
    say?

Was a lady such a lady, cheeks so round and lips so red,—
On her neck the small face buoyant, like a bell-flower on its
    bed,
O'er the breast's superb abundance where a man might base
    his head?

Well, and it was graceful of them—they'd break talk off and
    afford
—She, to bite her mask's black velvet—he, to finger on his
    sword,
While you sat and played Toccatas, stately at the clavichord?

What? Those lesser thirds so plaintive, sixths diminished,
    sigh on sigh,
Told them something? Those suspensions, those solutions—
    "Must we die?"
Those commiserating sevenths—"Life might last! we can but
    try!"

147

"Were you happy?" —"Yes." —"And are you still as happy?" —
  "Yes. And you?"
—"Then, more kisses!" —"Did *I* stop them, when a million
  seemed so few?"
Hark, the dominant's persistence till it must be answered to!

So, an octave struck the answer. Oh, they praised you, I dare
  say!
"Brave Galuppi! that was music! Good alike at grave and gay!
"I can always leave off talking when I hear a master play!"

Then they left you for their pleasure: till in due time, one by
  one,
Some with lives that came to nothing, some with deeds as
  well undone,
Death stepped tacitly and took them where they never see the
  sun.

But when I sit down to reason, think to take my stand nor
  swerve,
While I triumph o'er a secret wrung from nature's close
  reserve,
In you come with your cold music till I creep thro' every
  nerve.

Yes, you, like a ghostly cricket, creaking where a house was
  burned:
"Dust and ashes, dead and done with, Venice spent what
  Venice earned.
The soul, doubtless, is immortal—where a soul can be
  discerned."

"Yours for instance: you know physics, something of geology,
Mathematics are your pastime; souls shall rise in their
  degree;   `
Butterflies may dread extinction, —you'll not die, it cannot
  be!"

As for Venice and her people, merely born to bloom and drop,
Here on earth they bore their fruitage, mirth and folly were
  the crop:

What of soul was left, I wonder, when the kissing had to
    stop?

"Dust and ashes!" So you creak it, and I want the heart to
    scold.
Dear dead women, with such hair, too—what's become of all
    the gold
Used to hang and brush their bosoms? I feel chilly and grown
    old.

Meeting at Night[1]

The grey sea and the long black land;
And the yellow half-moon large and low;
And the startled little waves that leap
In fiery ringlets from their sleep,
As I gain the cove with pushing prow,
And quench its speed i' the slushy sand.

Then a mile of warm sea-scented beach;
Three fields to cross till a farm appears;
A tap at the pane, the quick sharp scratch
And blue spurt of a lighted match,
And a voice less loud, thro' its joys and fears,
Than the two hearts beating each to each!

My Last Duchess[2]

That's my last duchess painted on the wall,
Looking as if she were alive. I call

---

[1] Form: Iambic tetrameter, ABCCBA end rhymes.
[2] Form: Iambic pentameter, AABBCC . . . End rhymes—Vocabulary: Fra
Pandolf: fictitious painter; officious: interfering; forsooth: in truth;
munificence: generosity; Claus of Innsbruck: fictitious sculptor—Notes: the
Duke had his wife killed because she took pleasures in simple things and
treated all people with equal kindness, which meant that her attitude
toward him and his gifts was not special and unique so he was insulted.
Even worse, he killed her without ever telling her what was bothering him
because the act of telling her would be stooping, something he refuses to
do. He's now impressing the emissary negotiating terms for his next wife,
both showing off his possessions and also making clear his expectations
for his new wife's attitude.

That piece a wonder, now; Fra Pandolf's hands
Worked busily a day, and there she stands.
Will't please you sit and look at her? I said
"Fra Pandolf" by design, for never read
Strangers like you that pictured countenance,
That depth and passion of its earnest glance,
But to myself they turned (since none puts by
The curtain drawn for you, but I)
And seemed as they would ask me, if they durst,
How such a glance came there; so not the first
Are you to turn and ask thus. Sir, 't was not
Her husband's presence only, called that spot
Of joy into the Duchess' cheek: perhaps
Fra Pandolf chanced to say "Her mantle laps
Over my lady's wrist too much" or "Paint
Must never hope to reproduce the faint
Half-flush that dies along her throat:" such stuff
Was courtesy, she thought, and cause enough
For calling up that spot of joy. She had
A heart—how shall I say? —too soon made glad,
Too easily impressed: she liked whate'er
She looked on, and her looks went everywhere.
Sir, 't was all one! My favor at her breast,
The dropping of the daylight in the West,
The bough of cherries some officious fool
Broke in the orchard for her, the white mule
She rode with round the terrace—all and each
Would draw from her alike the approving speech,
Or blush, at least. She thanked men—good! But thanked
Somehow—I know not how—as if she ranked
My gift of a nine-hundred-years-old name
With anybody's gift. Who'd stoop to blame
This sort of trifling? Even had you skill
In speech— (which I have not) —to make your will
Quite clear to such a one, and say, "Just this
Or that in you disgusts me; here you miss
Or there exceed the mark"—and if she let
Herself be lessoned so, nor plainly set
Her wits to yours, forsooth, and made excuse
—e'en then would be some stooping; and I choose
Never to stoop. Oh sir, she smiled, no doubt,

150

Whene'er I passed her; but who passed without
Much the same smile? This grew; I gave commands;
Then all smiles stopped together. There she stands
As if alive. Will 't please you rise? We'll meet
The company below, then. I repeat,
The Count your master's known munificence
Is ample warrant that no just pretence
Of mine for dowry will be disallowed;
Though his fair daughter's self, as I avowed
At starting is my object. Nay, we'll go
Together down, sir. Notice Neptune, though,
Taming a sea-horse, thought a rarity,
Which Claus of Innsbruck cast in bronze for me.

Never the Time and the Place[1]

Never the time and the place
   And the loved one all together!
This path—how soft to pace!
   This May—what magic weather!
Where is the loved one's face?
In a dream that loved one's face meets mine,
   But the house is narrow, the place is bleak
Where, outside, rain and wind combine
   With a furtive ear, if I strive to speak,
   With a hostile eye at my flushing cheek,
With a malice that marks each word, each sign!

---

[1] Form: Iambic trimeter, irregular but frequent end rhymes—Notes: The story of a man who's loved one (wife?) has died (the narrow house) and he is now being moved inexorably toward his own death in the near future so that he can be near her in the ground.

O enemy sly and serpentine,
   Uncoil thee from the waking man!
      Do I hold the Past
      Thus firm and fast
Yet doubt if the Future hold I can?
This path so soft to pace shall lead
Thro' the magic of May to herself indeed!
Or narrow if needs the house must be,
Outside are the storms and strangers: we—
Oh, close, safe, warm, sleep I and she, I and she.

Porphyria's Lover[1]

The rain set early in tonight,
   The sullen wind was soon awake,
It tore the elm-tops down for spite,
   And did its worst to vex the lake:
I listened with heart fit to break.
When glided in Porphyria; straight
   She shut the cold out and the storm,
And kneeled and made the cheerless grate
   Blaze up, and all the cottage warm;
Which done, she rose, and from her form
Withdrew the dripping cloak and shawl,
   And laid her soiled gloves by, untied
Her hat and let the damp hair fall,
   And, last, she sat down by my side
And called me. When no voice replied,
She put my arm about her waist,
   And made her smooth white shoulder bare,
And all her yellow hair displaced,
   And, stooping, made my cheek lie there,
And spread, o'er all, her yellow hair,

---

[1] Form: Iambic tetrameter, ABABB end rhymes—Vocabulary: dissever: sever; oped: opened; tress: Long lock of hair—Notes: Like reading a Dean Koontz novel, we enter the mind of a madman. Here, the main character has a moment of wonderful, illicit and forbidden love with Porphyria. Porphyria is upper class, and has too much pride to have a true relationship with the narrator—but she gives in to passion occasionally and visits in the evening. To attempt to capture and retain that moment, he kills her and uses her corpse as a prop in his fantasy of a long term relationship.

Murmuring how she loved me—she
    Too weak, for all her heart's endeavor,
To set its struggling passion free
    From pride, and vainer ties dissever,
And give herself to me forever.
But passion sometimes would prevail,
    Nor could tonight's gay feast restrain
A sudden thought of one so pale
    For love of her, and all in vain:
So, she was come through wind and rain.
Be sure I looked up at her eyes
    Happy and proud; at last I knew
Porphyria worshiped me: surprise
    Made my heart swell, and still it grew
While I debated what to do.
That moment she was mine, mine, fair,
    Perfectly pure and good: I found
A thing to do, and all her hair
    In one long yellow string I wound
Three times her little throat around,
And strangled her. No pain felt she;
    I am quite sure she felt no pain.
As a shut bud that holds a bee,
    I warily oped her lids: again
Laughed the blue eyes without a stain.
And I untightened next the tress
    About her neck; her cheek once more
Blushed bright beneath my burning kiss:
    I propped her head up as before,
Only, this time my shoulder bore
Her head, which droops upon it still:
    The smiling rosy little head,
So glad it has its utmost will,
    That all it scorned at once is fled,
And I, its love, am gained instead!
Porphyria's love: she guessed not how
    Her darling one wish would be heard.
And thus we sit together now,
    And all night long we have not stirred,
And yet God has not said a word!

The Confessional[1]

It is a lie—their Priests, their Pope,
Their Saints, their...all their fear or hope
Are lies, and lies—there! Through my door
And ceiling, there! And walls and floor.
There, lies, they lie—shall still be hurled
Till spite of them I reach the world!

You think priests just and holy men!
Before they put me in this den
I was a human creature too,
With flesh and blood like one of you,
A girl that laughed in beauty's pride
Like lilies in your world outside.

I had a lover, shame avaunt!
This poor wrenched body, grim and gaunt,
Was kissed all over till it burned,
By lips the truest love e'er turned
His heart's own tint: one night they kissed
My soul out in a burning mist

So, next day when the accustomed train
Of things grew round my sense again,
"That is a sin" I said: and slow
With downcast eyes to church I go,
And pass to the confession-chair,
And tell the old mild father there.

But when I falter Beltran's name,
"Ha?" Quoth the father; "much I blame
The sin; yet whereof idly grieve?
Despair not, strenuously retrieve!
Nay, I will turn this love of thine

---

[1] Form: Iambic tetrameter, AABBCC. . . End rhymes—Vocabulary: avaunt: away; scourge: whip—Notes: The priest betrays the confidence of confession to capture, convict, and hang heretics, including the boyfriend of the woman who initially confessed to him. She writes this from prison, where she is presumably held to prevent her telling the world what has happened.

154

To lawful love, almost divine;

For he is young, and led astray,
This Beltran, and he schemes, men say,
To change the laws of church and state;
So, thine shall be an angel's fate
Who, ere the thunder breaks, should roll
Its cloud away and save his soul."

"For, when he lies upon thy breast,
Thou mayst demand and be possessed
Of all his plans, and next day steal
To me, and all those plans reveal,
That I and every priest, to purge
His soul may fast and use the scourge."

That father's beard was long and white,
With love and truth his brow seemed bright;
I went back; all on fire with joy,
And, that same evening, bade the boy
Tell me, as lovers should, heart-free,
Something to prove his love of me.

He told me what he would not tell
For hope of heaven or fear of hell;
And I lay listening in such pride!
And, soon as he had left my side,
Tripped to the church by morning-light
To save his soul in his despite.

I told the father all his schemes
Who were his comrades, what their dreams;
"And now make haste," I said, "to pray
The one spot from his soul away;
To-night he comes, but not the same
Will look." At night he never came.

Nor next night; on the after-morn,
I went forth with a strength new-born.
The church was empty; something drew
My steps into the street; I knew

It led me to the market-place;
Where, lo, on high, the fathers face!

That horrible back scaffold dressed,
That stapled block...God sink the rest!
That head strapped back, that blinding vest,
Those knotted hands and naked breast,
Till near one busy hangman pressed,
And, on the neck these arms caressed...

No part in aught they hope or fear!
No heaven with them, no hell! – and here,
No earth, not so much space as pens
My body in their worst of dens
But shall bear God and man my cry,
Lies—lies, again—and still, they lie!

The Pied Piper of Hamelin[1]

A Child's Story

I.
   Hamelin Town's in Brunswick,
By famous Hanover city;
   The river Weser, deep and wide,
   Washes its wall on the southern side;

---

[1] Form: Iambic tetrameter, irregular but frequent end rhymes—
Vocabulary: Brunswick: region in north central Germany; Corporation: The
financial administration of the city; ditty: simple song; sprats: small fish;
noddy: fool; ermine: weasel; Rouse: arise; guilder: unit of currency; kith
and kin: kindred more or less remote; newt: salamander; viper: type of
poisonous snake; vesture: clothing; old-fangled: gaudy in an old fashion;
Tartary: region of eastern Europe and northern Asia; Cham: a Tartar or
Mogul Kahn; Nizam: ruler of Hyderabad, India; tripe: lining of stomach
used as food; psaltery: an ancient stringed instrument; drysaltery:
preserved foods; nuncheon: light snack; puncheon: large cask (about 100
gallons); Claret, Moselle, Vin-de-Grave, Hock: types of wine; butt: a large
cask holding about 126 gallons; Rhenish: a sweet Rhine wine; poke: sack;
Bagdat: Baghdad; pottage: thick soup or stew; Caliph: leader of Arabic
region; bate: reduce; stiver: a coin worth 1/20 of a guilder; ribald: vulgar,
lewdly funny person; vesture: clothing; piebald: patches of bright colors;
fallow: resting; burgher: citizen of a city; pate: head; tabor: small drum to
accompany a pipe; hostelry: inn; trepanned: trapped.

A pleasanter spot you never spied;
But, when begins my ditty,
   Almost five hundred years ago,
   To see the townsfolk suffer so
      From vermin, was a pity.

II.

   Rats!
They fought the dogs, and killed the cats,
   And bit the babies in the cradles,
And ate the cheeses out of the vats,
   And licked the soup from the cook's own ladles,
Split open the kegs of salted sprats,
Made nests inside men's Sunday hats,
And even spoiled the women's chats,
   By drowning their speaking
   With shrieking and squeaking
In fifty different sharps and flats.

III.

At last the people in a body
   To the Town Hall came flocking:
"Tis clear," cried they, "our Mayor's a noddy;
   And as for our Corporation—shocking
To think we buy gowns lined with ermine
For dolts that can't or won't determine
What's best to rid us of our vermin!
You hope, because you're old and obese,
To find in the furry civic robe ease?
Rouse up, Sirs! Give your brains a racking
To find the remedy we're lacking,
Or, sure as fate, we'll send you packing!"
At this the Mayor and Corporation
Quaked with a mighty consternation.

IV.

An hour they sate in council,
   At length the Mayor broke silence:
"For a guilder I'd my ermine gown sell;
   I wish I were a mile hence!
It's easy to bid one rack one's brain—

I'm sure my poor head aches again
I've scratched it so, and all in vain.
Oh for a trap, a trap, a trap!"
Just as he said this, what should hap
At the chamber door but a gentle tap?
"Bless us," cried the Mayor, "what's that?"
(With the Corporation as he sat,
Looking little though wondrous fat;
Nor brighter was his eye, nor moister
Than a too-long-opened oyster,
Save when at noon his paunch grew mutinous
For a plate of turtle green and glutinous)
"Only a scraping of shoes on the mat?
Anything like the sound of a rat
Makes my heart go pit-a-pat!"

V.
"Come in!" —the Mayor cried, looking bigger:
And in did come the strangest figure!
His queer long coat from heel to head
Was half of yellow and half of red;
And he himself was tall and thin,
With sharp blue eyes, each like a pin,
And light loose hair, yet swarthy skin,
No tuft on cheek nor beard on chin,
But lips where smiles went out and in—
There was no guessing his kith and kin!
And nobody could enough admire
The tall man and his quaint attire:
Quoth one: "It's as my great-grandsire,
Starting up at the Trump of Doom's tone,
Had walked this way from his painted tombstone!"

VI.
He advanced to the council-table:
And, "Please your honors," said he, "I'm able,
By means of a secret charm, to draw
All creatures living beneath the sun,
That creep or swim or fly or run,
After me so as you never saw!
And I chiefly use my charm

158

On creatures that do people harm,
The mole and toad and newt and viper;
And people call me the Pied Piper."
(And here they noticed round his neck
A scarf of red and yellow stripe,
To match with his coat of the selfsame cheque;
And at the scarf's end hung a pipe;
And his fingers, they noticed, were ever straying
As if impatient to be playing
Upon this pipe, as low it dangled
Over his vesture so old-fangled.)
"Yet," said he, "poor piper as I am,
In Tartary I freed the Cham,
Last June, from his huge swarms of gnats;
I eased in Asia the Nizam
Of a monstrous brood of vampire-bats;
And, as for what your brain bewilders,
If I can rid your town of rats
Will you give me a thousand guilders?"
"One? Fifty thousand!" —was the exclamation
Of the astonished Mayor and Corporation.

VII.
Into the street the Piper stepped,
    Smiling first a little smile,
As if he knew what magic slept
    In his quiet pipe the while;
Then, like a musical adept,
To blow the pipe his lips he wrinkled,
And green and blue his sharp eyes twinkled
Like a candle flame where salt is sprinkled;
And ere three shrill notes the pipe uttered,
You heard as if an army muttered;
And the muttering grew to a grumbling;
And the grumbling grew to a mighty rumbling;
And out of the houses the rats came tumbling.
Great rats, small rats, lean rats, brawny rats,
Brown rats, black rats, grey rats, tawny rats,
Grave old plodders, gay young friskers,
    Fathers, mothers, uncles, cousins,
Cocking tails and pricking whiskers,

Families by tens and dozens,
Brothers, sisters, husbands, wives—
Followed the Piper for their lives.
From street to street he piped advancing,
And step for step they followed dancing,
Until they came to the river Weser,
Wherein all plunged and perished!
—Save one who, stout a Julius Caesar,
Swam across and lived to carry
(As he, the manuscript he cherished)
To Rat-land home his commentary:
Which was, "At the first shrill notes of the pipe
I heard a sound as of scraping tripe,
And putting apples, wondrous ripe,
Into a cider-press's gripe:
And a moving away of pickle-tub-boards,
And a leaving ajar of conserve-cupboards,
And a drawing the corks of train-oil-flasks,
And a breaking the hoops of butter-casks;
And it seemed as if a voice
(Sweeter far than by harp or by psaltery
Is breathed) called out `Oh, rats, rejoice!
The world is grown to one vast drysaltery!
So munch on, crunch on, take your nuncheon,
Breakfast, supper, dinner, luncheon!'
And just as a bulky sugar-puncheon,
All ready staved, like a great sun shone
Glorious scarce and inch before me,
Just as me thought it said `Come, bore me!'
—Found the Weser rolling o'er me."

VIII.
You should have heard the Hamelin people
Ringing the bells till they rocked the steeple.
"Go," cried the Mayor, "and get long poles!
Poke out the nests and block up the holes!
Consult with carpenters and builders,
And leave in our town not even a trace
Of the rats!" —when suddenly, up the face
Of the Piper perked in the market-place,
With a, "First, if you please, my thousand guilders!"

160

IX.
A thousand guilders! The Mayor looked blue;
So did the Corporation too.
For council dinners made rare havoc
With Claret, Moselle, Vin-de-Grave, Hock;
And half the money would replenish
Their cellar's biggest butt with Rhenish.
To pay this sum to a wandering fellow
With a gypsy coat of red and yellow!
"Beside," quoth the Mayor with a knowing wink,
"Our business was done at the river's brink;
We saw with our eyes the vermin sink,
And what's dead can't come to life, I think.
So, friend, we're not the folks to shrink
From the duty of giving you something for drink,
And a matter of money to put in your poke;
But, as for the guilders, what we spoke
Of them, as you very well know, was in joke.
Beside, our losses have made us thrifty.
A thousand guilders! Come, take fifty!"

X.
The Piper's face fell, and he cried
"No trifling! I can't wait, beside!
I've promised to visit by dinner-time
Bagdat, and accept the prime
Of the Head Cook's pottage, all he's rich in,
For having left, in the Caliph's kitchen,
Of a nest of scorpions no survivor—
With him I proved no bargain-driver,
With you, don't think i'll bate a stiver!
And folks who put me in a passion
May find me pipe to another fashion."

XI.
"How?" cried the Mayor, "d'ye think i'll brook
Being worse treated than a Cook?
Insulted by a lazy ribald
With idle pipe and vesture piebald?
You threaten us, fellow? Do your worst,

161

Blow your pipe there till you burst!"

XII.
Once more he stepped into the street;
   And to his lips again
Laid his long pipe of smooth straight cane;
   And ere he blew three notes (such sweet
Soft notes as yet musician's cunning
   Never gave the enraptured air)
There was a rustling, that seemed like a bustling
Of merry crowds justling at pitching and hustling,
Small feet were pattering, wooden shoes clattering,
Little hands clapping and little tongues chattering,
And, like fowls in a farmyard when barley is scattering,
Out came the children running.
All the little boys and girls,
With rosy cheeks and flaxen curls,
And sparkling eyes and teeth like pearls,
Tripping and skipping, ran merrily after
The wonderful music with shouting and laughter.

XIII.
The Mayor was dumb, and the Council stood
As if they were changed into blocks of wood,

Unable to move a step, or cry
To the children merrily skipping by
—Could only follow with the eye
That joyous crowd at the Piper's back.
But how the Mayor was on the rack,
And the wretched Council's bosoms beat,
As the Piper turned from the High Street
To where the Weser rolled its waters
Right in the way of their sons and daughters!
However he turned from South to West,
And to Koppelberg Hill his steps addressed,
And after him the children pressed;
Great was the joy in every breast.
"He never can cross that mighty top!
He's forced to let the piping drop,
And we shall see our children stop!"
When, lo, as they reached the mountain's side,
A wondrous portal opened wide,
As if a cavern was suddenly hollowed;
And the Piper advanced and the children followed,
And when all were in to the very last,
The door in the mountain-side shut fast.
Did I say, all? No! One was lame,
And could not dance the whole of the way;
And in after years, if you would blame
His sadness, he was used to say,—
"It's dull in our town since my playmates left!
I can't forget that I'm bereft
Of all the pleasant sights they see,
Which the Piper also promised me:
For he led us, he said, to a joyous land,
Joining the town and just at hand,
Where waters gushed and fruit-trees grew,
And flowers put forth a fairer hue,
And everything was strange and new;
The sparrows were brighter than peacocks here,
And their dogs outran our fallow deer,
And honey-bees had lost their stings,
And horses were born with eagles' wings:
And just as I became assured
My lame foot would be speedily cured,

The music stopped and I stood still,
And found myself outside the hill,
Left alone against my will,
To go now limping as before,
And never hear of that country more!"

XIV.
Alas, alas for Hamelin!
    There came into many a burgher's pate
    A text which says, that Heaven's Gate
    Opes to the Rich at as easy rate
As the needle's eye takes a camel in!
The Mayor sent East, West, North, and South,
To offer the Piper, by word of mouth,
    Wherever it was men's lot to find him,
Silver and gold to his heart's content,
If he'd only return the way he went,
    And bring the children behind him.
But when they saw 'twas a lost endeavor,
And Piper and dancers were gone for ever,
They made a decree that lawyers never
    Should think their records dated duly
If, after the day of the month and year,
These words did not as well appear,
"And so long after what happened here
    On the Twenty-second of July,
Thirteen hundred and seventy-six":
And the better in memory to fix
The place of the children's last retreat,
They called it, the Pied Piper's Street—
Where any one playing on pipe or tabor
Was sure for the future to lose his labor.
Nor suffered they hostelry or tavern
    To shock with mirth a street so solemn;
But opposite the place of the cavern
    They wrote the story on a column,
And on the great Church-Window painted
The same, to make the world acquainted
How their children were stolen away;
And there it stands to this very day.
And I must not omit to say

That in Transylvania there's a tribe
Of alien people that ascribe
The outlandish ways and dress
On which their neighbors lay such stress,
To their fathers and mothers having risen
Out of some subterraneous prison
Into which they were trepanned
Long time ago in a mighty band
Out of Hamelin town in Brunswick land,
But how or why, they don't understand.

XV.
So, Willy, let you and me be wipers
Of scores out with all men—especially pipers!
And, whether they pipe us free, from rats or from mice,
If we've promised them aught, let us keep our promise.

Edward Lear (1812 – 1888)

The Owl and the Pussy-Cat[1]

I
The Owl and the Pussy-cat went to sea
   In a beautiful pea-green boat,
They took some honey, and plenty of money,
   Wrapped up in a five-pound note.
The Owl looked up to the stars above,
   And sang to a small guitar
'O lovely Pussy! O Pussy, my love,
   What a beautiful Pussy you are,
      You are,
      You are!
   What a beautiful Pussy you are!

---

[1] Form: Ballad—Vocabulary: five pound: British pounds sterling; mince: finely chopped food; quince: a fruit; runcible: made up word, although since used by others as a kind of fork with three broad prongs or tines, one having a sharp edge, curved like a spoon, used with pickles, etc.

II

Pussy said to the Owl, 'You elegant fowl!
    How charmingly sweet you sing!
O let us be married! too long have we tarried;
    But what shall we do for a ring?'
They sailed away, for a year and a day,
    To the land where the Bong-tree grows
And there in the wood a Piggy-wig stood
    With a ring at the end of his nose,
            His nose,
            His nose,
    With a ring at the end of his nose.

III

'Dear Pig, are you willing to sell for one shilling
    Your ring?' Said the Piggy, 'I will.'
So they took it away, and were married next day
    By the Turkey who lives on the hill.
They dined on mince, and slices of quince,
    Which they ate with a runcible spoon;
And hand in hand, on the edge of the sand,
    They danced by the light of the moon,
            The moon,
            The moon,
    They danced by the light of the moon.

Emily Bronte (1818 – 1848)

I am the Only Being Whose Doom[1]

I am the only being whose doom
No tongue would ask no eye would mourn
I never caused a thought of gloom
A smile of joy since I was born

---

[1] Form: Iambic tetrameter, ABAB end rhymes—Vocabulary: natal: birth;
drear: dreary—Notes: The narrator looks down on those around her, and
withdraws into her own world as a recluse. Now, no longer youthful or
attractive, she realizes too late that the corruption in the world she was
hiding from is equally present in her own mind.

In secret pleasure—secret tears
This changeful life has slipped away
As friendless after eighteen years
As lone as on my natal day

There have been times I cannot hide
There have been times when this was drear
When my sad soul forgot its pride
And longed for one to love me here

But those were in the early glow
Of feelings since subdued by care
And they have died so long ago
I hardly now believe they were

First melted off the hope of youth
Then Fancy's rainbow fast withdrew
And then experience told me truth
In mortal bosoms never grew

'Twas grief enough to think mankind
All hollow servile insincere
But worse to trust to my own mind
And find the same corruption there

Charles Kingsley (1819 – 1875)

Young and Old[1]

When all the world is young, lad,
    And all the trees are green;
And every goose a swan, lad,
    And every lass a queen;
Then hey for boot and horse, lad,
    And round the world away;
Young blood must have its course, lad,
    And every dog his day.

---

[1] Form: Ballad—Vocabulary: "hey for boot and horse": Hello to traveling by
foot and horse.

When all the world is old, lad,
    And all the trees are brown;
And all the sport is stale, lad,
    And all the wheels run down;
Creep home, and take your place there,
    The spent and maimed among:
God grant you find one face there,
    You loved when all was young.

Walt Whitman (1819 – 1892)

Darest Thou Now O Soul[1]

Darest thou now O soul,
Walk out with me toward the unknown region,
Where neither ground is for the feet nor any path to follow?

No map there, nor guide,
Nor voice sounding, nor touch of human hand,
Nor face with blooming flesh, nor lips, nor eyes, are in that
    land.

I know it not O soul,
Nor dost thou, all is a blank before us,
All waits undreamed of in that region, that inaccessible land.

Till when the ties loosen,
All but the ties eternal, Time and Space,
Nor darkness, gravitation, sense, nor any bounds bounding
    us.

Then we burst forth, we float,
In Time and Space O soul, prepared for them,
Equal, equipped at last, (O joy! O fruit of all!) Them to fulfill O
    soul.

---

[1] Form: Free verse—Notes: The poem deals with death and the subsequent liberation of the soul.

I Saw in Louisiana a Live-Oak Growing[1]

I saw in Louisiana a live-oak growing,
All alone stood it and the moss hung down from the
    branches,
Without any companion it grew there uttering joyous leaves
    of dark green,
And its look, rude, unbending, lusty, made me think of
    myself,
But I wondered how it could utter joyous leaves standing
    alone there without its friend near, for I knew I could not,
And I broke off a twig with a certain number of leaves upon
    it, and twined around it a little moss,
And brought it away,
And I have placed it in sight in my room,
It is not needed to remind me as of my own dear friends,
(For I believe lately I think of little else than of them,)
Yet it remains to me a curious token, it makes me think of
    manly love;
For all that, and though the live-oak glistens there in
    Louisiana solitary in a wide flat space,
Uttering joyous leaves all its life without a friend or lover
    near,
I know very well I could not.

---

[1] Form: Free verse—Vocabulary: moss: Spanish moss.

My Legacy[1]

The business man the acquirer vast,
After assiduous years surveying results, preparing for
  departure,
Devises houses and lands to his children, bequeaths stocks,
  goods, funds for a school or hospital,
Leaves money to certain companions to buy tokens,
souvenirs of gems and gold.

But I, my life surveying, closing,
With nothing to show to devise from its idle years,
Nor houses nor lands, nor tokens of gems or gold for my
  friends,
Yet certain remembrances of the war for you, and after you,
And little souvenirs of camps and soldiers, with my love,
I bind together and bequeath in this bundle of songs.

O Captain! My Captain[2]

O Captain! my Captain! our fearful trip is done,
The ship has weathered every rack, the prize we sought is
      won,
The port is near, the bells I hear, the people all exulting,
While follow eyes the steady keel, the vessel grim and daring;
        But O heart! heart! heart!
          O the bleeding drops of red,
            Where on the deck my Captain lies,
              Fallen cold and dead.

O Captain! my Captain! rise up and hear the bells;
Rise up—for you the flag is flung—for you the bugle trills,
For you bouquets and ribboned wreaths—for you the shores
  a-crowding,

---

[1] Form: Free verse.
[2] Form: Mostly ballad meter with substitutions for emphasis, unrhymed—
Vocabulary: trills: fluttering sound—Notes: Originally written about Lincoln
after he was assassinated. The ship refers to the Union after the civil war
(the ship of state). However, the metaphor works for any situation where
the leader is successful but does not live to see their success.

For you they call, the swaying mass, their eager faces
    turning;
        Here Captain! dear father!
           This arm beneath your head!
              It is some dream that on the deck,
                You've fallen cold and dead.

My Captain does not answer, his lips are pale and still,
My father does not feel my arm, he has no pulse nor will,
The ship is anchored safe and sound, its voyage closed and
    done,
From fearful trip the victor ship comes in with object won;
        Exult O shores, and ring O bells!
          But I with mournful tread,
             Walk the deck my Captain lies,
              Fallen cold and dead.

Song of Prudence[1]

Manhattan's streets I sauntered pondering,
On Time, Space, Reality—on such as these, and abreast with
    them Prudence.

The last explanation always remains to be made about
    prudence,
Little and large alike drop quietly aside from the prudence
    that suits immortality.

The soul is of itself,
All verges to it, all has reference to what ensues,
All that a person does, says, thinks, is of consequence,
Not a move can a man or woman make, that affects him or
    her in a day, month, any part of the direct lifetime, or the
    hour of death,
But the same affects him or her onward afterward through
    the indirect lifetime.

The indirect is just as much as the direct,

---

[1] Form: Free verse—Vocabulary: onanist: masturbator; peculation:
embezzlement; literat: literati.

The spirit receives from the body just as much as it gives to
the body, if not more.

Not one word or deed, not venereal sore, discoloration,
privacy of the onanist,
Putridity of gluttons or rum-drinkers, peculation, cunning,
betrayal, murder, seduction, prostitution,
But has results beyond death as really as before death.

Charity and personal force are the only investments worth
any thing.

No specification is necessary, all that a male or female does,
That is vigorous, benevolent, clean, is so much profit to him
or her,
In the unshakable order of the universe and through the
whole scope of it forever.

Who has been wise receives interest,
Savage, felon, President, judge, farmer, sailor, mechanic,
literat, young, old, it is the same,
The interest will come round—all will come round.

Singly, wholly, to affect now, affected their time, will forever
affect, all of the past and all of the present and all of the
future,
All the brave actions of war and peace,
All help given to relatives, strangers, the poor, old,
sorrowful,young children, widows, the sick, and to
shunned persons,
All self-denial that stood steady and aloof on wrecks, and saw
others fill the seats of the boats,
All offering of substance or life for the good old cause, or for a
friend's sake, or opinion's sake,
All pains of enthusiasts scoffed at by their neighbors,
All the limitless sweet love and precious suffering of mothers,
All honest men baffled in strifes recorded or unrecorded,
All the grandeur and good of ancient nations whose
fragments we inherit,
All the good of the dozens of ancient nations unknown to us
by name, date, location,

All that was ever manfully begun, whether it succeeded or no,
All suggestions of the divine mind of man or the divinity of
    his mouth, or the shaping of his great hands,
All that is well thought or said this day on any part of the
    globe, or on any of the wandering stars, or on any of the
    fix'd stars, by those there as we are here,
All that is henceforth to be thought or done by you whoever
    you are, or by any one,
These inure, have inured, shall inure, to the identities from
    which they sprang, or shall spring.

Did you guess any thing lived only its moment?
The world does not so exist, no parts palpable or impalpable
    so exist,
No consummation exists without being from some long
    previous consummation, and that from some other,
Without the farthest conceivable one coming a bit nearer the
    beginning than any.

Whatever satisfies souls is true;
Prudence entirely satisfies the craving and glut of souls,
Itself only finally satisfies the soul,
The soul has that measureless pride which revolts from every
    lesson but its own.

Now I breathe the word of the prudence that walks abreast
    with time, space, reality,
That answers the pride which refuses every lesson but its
    own.

What is prudence is indivisible,
Declines to separate one part of life from every part,
Divides not the righteous from the unrighteous or the living
    from the dead,
Matches every thought or act by its correlative,
Knows no possible forgiveness or deputed atonement,
Knows that the young man who composedly periled his life
    and lost it has done exceedingly well for himself without
    doubt,

That he who never periled his life, but retains it to old age in
    riches and ease, has probably achieved nothing for himself
    worth mentioning,
Knows that only that person has really learned who has
    learned to prefer results,
Who favors body and soul the same,
Who perceives the indirect assuredly following the direct,
Who in his spirit in any emergency whatever neither hurries
    nor avoids death.

This Compost[1]

1

Something startles me where I thought I was safest,
I withdraw from the still woods I loved,
I will not go now on the pastures to walk,
I will not strip the clothes from my body to meet my lover the
    sea,
I will not touch my flesh to the earth as to other flesh to
    renew me.

O how can it be that the ground itself does not sicken?
How can you be alive you growths of spring?
How can you furnish health you blood of herbs, roots,
    orchards, grain?
Are they not continually putting distempered corpses within
    you?
Is not every continent worked over and over with sour dead?

Where have you disposed of their carcasses?
Those drunkards and gluttons of so many generations?
Where have you drawn off all the foul liquid and meat?
I do not see any of it upon you today, or perhaps I am
    deceived,
I will run a furrow with my plough, I will press my spade
    through the sod and turn it up underneath,
I am sure I shall expose some of the foul meat.

---

[1] Form: Free verse—Vocabulary: distempered: an animal disease; mould:
earth of a grave; visage: face.

174

2

Behold this compost! Behold it well!
Perhaps every mite has once formed part of a sick person—
    yet behold!
The grass of spring covers the prairies,
The bean bursts noiselessly through the mould in the
garden,
The delicate spear of the onion pierces upward,
The apple-buds cluster together on the apple-branches,
The resurrection of the wheat appears with pale visage out of
    its graves,
The tinge awakes over the willow-tree and the mulberry-tree,
The he-birds carol mornings and evenings while the she-
birds   sit on their nests,
The young of poultry break through the hatched eggs,
The new-born of animals appear, the calf is dropt from the
    cow, the colt from the mare,
Out of its little hill faithfully rise the potato's dark green
    leaves,
Out of its hill rises the yellow maize-stalk, the lilacs bloom in
    the dooryards,
The summer growth is innocent and disdainful above all
    those strata of sour dead.

What chemistry!
That the winds are really not infectious,
That this is no cheat, this transparent green-wash of the sea
    Which is so amorous after me,
That it is safe to allow it to lick my naked body all over
    With its tongues,
That it will not endanger me with the fevers that have
    deposited themselves in it,
That all is clean forever and forever,
That the cool drink from the well tastes so good,
That blackberries are so flavorous and juicy,
That the fruits of the apple-orchard and the orange-orchard,
That melons, grapes, peaches, plums, will none of them
    poison me,
That when I recline on the grass I do not catch any disease,

Though probably every spear of grass rises out of what was
    once catching disease.

Now I am terrified at the Earth, it is that calm and patient,
It grows such sweet things out of such corruptions,
It turns harmless and stainless on its axis, with such endless
    successions of diseased corpses,
It distills such exquisite winds out of such infused fetor,
It renews with such unwitting looks its prodigal, annual,
    sumptuous crops,
It gives such divine materials to men, and accepts such
    leavings from them at last.

When I heard the Learn'd Astronomer[1]

When I heard the learn'd astronomer;
When the proofs, the figures, were ranged in columns before
    me;
When I was shown the charts and the diagrams, to add,
    divide, and measure them;
When I, sitting, heard the astronomer, where he lectured with
    much applause in the lecture-room,
How soon, unaccountable, I became tired and sick;
Till rising and gliding out, I wandered off by myself,
In the mystical moist night-air, and from time to time,
Looked up in perfect silence at the stars.

Charles Baudelaire (1821 – 1867)

A Carrion[2]
Translated by Sir John Squire

Rememberest thou, my sweet, that summer's day,
How in the sun outspread

---

[1] Form: Free verse.
[2] Form: Alternating iambic pentameter and iambic tetrameter, ABAB end
rhymes—Vocabulary: Carrion: dead, decaying flesh; procreative: generated;
winnowing: separate grain from chaff; moldering: crumbling to dust—
Notes: Charles is commenting on the fact that his lovely companion's flesh
will one day be as rotted as the carcass they saw along the path.

At a path's bend a filthy carcass lay
Upon a pebbly bed?

Like a lewd woman, with its legs in air,
Burned, oozed the poisonous mass;
Its gaping belly, calm and debonair,
Was full of noisome gas.

And steadily upon this rottenness,
As though to cook it brown
And render Nature hundredfold excess,
The sun shone down.

The blue sky thought the carrion marvelous,
A flower most fair to see;
And as we gazed it almost poisoned us—
It stank so horribly.

The flies buzzed on this putrid belly, whence
Black hosts of maggots came,
Which streamed in thick and shining rivers thence
Along that ragged frame.

Pulsating like a wave, spurting about
Bright jets, it seemed to live;
As though it were by some vague wind blown out,
Some breath procreative.

And all this life was strangely musical
Like wind or bubbling spring,
Or corn which moves with rhythmic rise and fall
In time of winnowing.

The lines became indefinite and faint
As a thin dream that dies,
A half-forgotten scene the hand can paint
Only from memories . . .

Behind the rocks there lurked a hungry hound
With melancholy eye,
Longing to nose the morsel he had found

And gnaw it greedily.

Yet thou shalt be as vile a carrion
As this infection dire,
O bright star of my eyes, my nature's sun,
My angel, my desire!

Yea, such, O queen of the graces, shalt thou be
After the last soft breath,
Beneath the grass and the lush greenery
A-moldering in death!

When they sweet flesh the worms devour with kisses,
Tell them, O beauty mine,
Of rotting loves I keep the bodily blisses
And essence all-divine!

from Fuses I – on Art[1]
Translated from the French by Norman Cameron

At a theater or ball, each person is being pleasured by
everybody else.
What is art? Prostitution.
The pleasure of being in a crowd is a mysterious
expression of delight in the multiplication of number.
Number is *all,* and in all, number is within the individual.
Intoxication is a number.

from Fuses I – on Love[2]
Translated from the French by Norman Cameron

Love may arise from a generous sentiment—namely, the
liking for prostitution; but it soon becomes corrupted by the
liking for ownership.
Love seeks to escape from itself, to mingle itself with its
victim, as a victor nation with the vanquished—and yet at the
same time to retain the privileges of a conqueror.

---

[1] Form: Free verse.
[2] Form: Free verse.

The sensual pleasures of a man who keeps a mistress have in them something both of the angel and of the proprietor. Charity and ferocity.

from Fuses I – on God[1]
Translated from the French by Norman Cameron

Even if God did not exist, religion would still be holy and
   divine,
   God is the only being who, in order to rule, does not need
      even to exist.
Creations of the mind are more alive than matter.

Heautontimoroumenos[2]
Translated by Lewis Piaget Shanks

I'll strike thee without enmity
Nor wrath,—like butchers at the block!

---

[1] Form: Free verse.
[2] Form: Iambic tetrameter, ABBA end rhymes—Vocabulary:
Heautontimoroumenos: Latin—the self tormentor—Notes: Charles died of
complications from syphilis. Perhaps the reference to poison blood is
related to this.

As Moses smote the living rock,
—Till from thine eyelids' agony

The springs of suffering shall flow
To slake the desert of my thirst;
And on that flood, my lust accurst
With Hope to fill its sails, shall go

As on the waves, a pitching barge,
And in my bosom quickening,
Thy sobs and tears I love shall ring
Loud as a drum that beats a charge!

For am I not a clashing note
In God's eternal symphony,
Thanks to this vulture, Irony,
Whose talons rend my heart and throat?

She's in my voice, the screaming elf!
My poisoned blood came all from her!
I am the mirror sinister
Wherein the vixen sees herself!

I am the wound and I the knife!
I am the blow I give, and feel!
I am the broken limbs, the wheel,
The hangman and the strangled life!

I am my heart's own vampire, for
I walk alone, condemned, forlorn,
By laughter everlasting torn,
Yet doomed to smile, —ah, nevermore!

Metamorphoses of the Vampire[1]
Translated by George Dillon

Meanwhile from her red mouth the woman, in husky tones,
Twisting her body like a serpent upon hot stones

---

[1] Form: Iambic hexameter, AABBCC. . . End rhymes—Vocabulary: tresses:
long locks of hair; wan: unnaturally pale.

And straining her white breasts from their imprisonment,
Let fall these words, as potent as a heavy scent:
"My lips are moist and yielding, and I know the way
To keep the antique demon of remorse at bay.
All sorrows die upon my bosom. I can make
Old men laugh happily as children for my sake.
For him who sees me naked in my tresses, I
Replace the sun, the moon, and all the stars of the sky!
Believe me, learnëd sir, I am so deeply skilled
That when I wind a lover in my soft arms, and yield
My breasts like two ripe fruits for his devouring—both
Shy and voluptuous, insatiable and loath—
Upon this bed that groans and sighs luxuriously
Even the impotent angels would be damned for me!"

When she had drained me of my very marrow, and cold
And weak, I turned to give her one more kiss—behold,
There at my side was nothing but a hideous
Putrescent thing, all faceless and exuding pus.
I closed my eyes and mercifully swooned till day:
And when I looked at morning for that beast of prey
Who seemed to have replenished her arteries from my own,
The wan, disjointed fragments of a skeleton
Wagged up and   down in a lewd posture where she had
lain,
Rattling with each convulsion like a weathervane
Or an old sign that creaks upon its bracket, right
Mournfully in the wind upon a winter's night.

Spleen[1]
Translated by Lewis Piaget Shanks

November, angry at the capital,
Whelms in a death-chill from her gloomy urn
The pallid dead beneath the graveyard wall,
The death-doomed who in dripping houses yearn.

---

[1] Form: Iambic pentameter, ABAB end rhymes—Vocabulary: grimalkin: an old and female cat; dropsical: suffering from edema (swelling); sinistrously: sinisterly.

Grimalkin prowls, a gaunt and scurvy ghoul,
Seeking a softer spot for her sojourn;
Under the eaves an ancient poet's soul
Shivers and flees and wails at each return.

The grieving church-bell and the sputtering log
Repeat the rusty clock's harsh epilogue;
While in a pack of cards, scent-filled and vile,

Grim relic of a spinster dropsical,
The knave of hearts and queen of spades recall
Their loves, defunct, and sinistrously smile.

The Flask[1]
   Translated by James Huneker

There are some powerful odors that can pass
Out of the stoppered flagon; even glass
To them is porous. Oft when some old box
Brought from the East is opened and the locks
And hinges creak and cry; or in a press
In some deserted house, where the sharp stress
Of odors old and dusty fills the brain;
An ancient flask is brought to light again,
And forth the ghosts of long-dead odors creep.
There, softly trembling in the shadows, sleep
A thousand thoughts, funereal chrysalides,
Phantoms of old the folding darkness hides,
Who make faint flutterings as their wings unfold,
Rose-washed and azure-tinted, shot with gold.

---

[1] Form: Iambic pentameter, AABBCC . . . End rhymes—Vocabulary:
chrysalides: protected as in a cocoon; languor: listlessness; Lazarus: man
raised from the dead by Jesus; shroud: burial cloth; virulence: extremely
infectious, poisonous, or malignant.

A memory that brings languor flutters here:
The fainting eyelids droop, and giddy Fear
Thrusts with both hands the soul towards the pit
Where, like a Lazarus from his winding-sheet,
Arises from the gulf of sleep a ghost
Of an old passion, long since loved and lost.
So I, when vanished from man's memory
Deep in some dark and somber chest I lie,
An empty flagon they have cast aside,
Broken and soiled, the dust upon my pride,
Will be your shroud, beloved pestilence!
The witness of your might and virulence,
Sweet poison mixed by angels; bitter cup
Of life and death my heart has drunken up!

The Ghostly Visitant[1]
Translated by Sir John Squire

Like the mild-eyed angels sweet

---

[1] Form: Iambic tetrameter, AABB end rhymes—Notes: A nice ghost story,
but also a metaphor for many problem relationships.

I will come to thy retreat,
Stealing in without a sound
When the shades of night close round.

I will give thee manifold
Kisses soft and moony-cold,
Gliding, sliding o'er thee like
A serpent crawling round a dike.

When the livid morn creeps on
You will wake and find me gone
Till the evening come again.

As by tenderness and truth
Others rule thy life and youth,
I by terror choose to reign.

The Murderer's Wine[1]
Translated by Sir John Squire

My wife is dead and I am free,
Now I may drink to my content;
When I came back without a cent
Her piteous outcries tortured me.

Now I am happy as a king,
The air is pure, the sky is clear;
Just such a summer as that year,
When first I went a-sweethearting.

A horrible thirst is tearing me,
To quench it I should have to swill
Just as much cool wine as would fill
Her tomb—that's no small quantity.

I threw her down and then began
To pile upon her where she fell

---

[1] Form: Iambic tetrameter, ABAB end rhymes—Vocabulary: sodden:
soaked; shroud: burial cloth; cur: mongrel dog; dray: cart; incontinent:
uncontrolled.

All the great stones around the well—
I shall forget it if I can.

By all the soft vows of our prime,
By those eternal oaths we swore,
And that our love might be once more
As 'twas in our old passionate time,

I begged her in a lonely spot
To come and meet me at nightfall;
She came, mad creature—we are all
More or less crazy, are we not?

She was quite pretty still, my wife,
Though she was very tired, and I,
I loved her too much, that is why
I said to her, 'Come, quit this life.'

No one can grasp my thoughts aright;
Did any of these sodden swine
Ever conceive a shroud of wine
On his most strangely morbid night?

Dull and insensible above
Iron machines, that stupid crew,
Summer or winter, never knew
The agonies of real love.

So now I am without a care!
Dead-drunk this evening I shall be,
Then fearlessly, remorselessly
Shall lie out in the open air

And sleep there like a homeless cur;
Some cart may rumble with a load
Of stones or mud along the road
And crush my head—I shall not stir.

Some heavy dray incontinent
May come and cut me clean in two;

I laugh at thought o't as I do
At Devil, God, and Sacrament.

The Pit[1]
Translated by Wilfrid Thorley

Great Pascal had his pit always in sight.
All is abysmal—deed, desire, or dream
Or speech! Full often over me doth scream
The wind of Fear and blows my hair upright.
By the lone strand, thro' silence, depth and height,
And shoreless space that doth with terrors teem . . .
On my black nights God's finger like a beam
Traces his swarming torments infinite.

Sleep is a monstrous hole that I do dread,
Full of vague horror, leading none knows where;
All windows open on infinity,
So that my dizzy spirit in despair
Longs for the torpor of the unfeeling dead.
Ah! from Time's menace never to win free!

The Vampire[2]
Translated by George Dillon

Thou who abruptly as a knife
Didst come into my heart; thou who,
A demon horde into my life,
Didst enter, wildly dancing, through

The doorways of my sense unlatched
To make my spirit thy domain—

---

[1] Form: Sonnet—Vocabulary: Pascal: French mathematician, philosopher
and inventor; abysmal: unfathomable; torpor: lethargy—Notes: Strong
imagery time centered around two perspectives of an abyss (Pascal's pit
versus sleep, described as a "monstrous hole). Note the use of "abysmal"
to contribute to the sense of the poem. The narrator longs for death as the
only possible escape.
[2] Form: Iambic tetrameter, ABAB end rhymes—Vocabulary: phial: vial—
Notes: We've all at least witnessed a love that was self-destructive, in which
the victim could not escape. In this case, even if the victim tried to escape
by killing his "love" his subsequent kisses would revive her.

Harlot to whom I am attached
As convicts to the ball and chain,

As gamblers to the wheel's bright spell,
As drunkards to their raging thirst,
As corpses to their worms—accurst
Be thou! Oh, be thou damned to hell!

I have entreated the swift sword
To strike, that I at once be freed;
The poisoned phial I have implored
To plot with me a ruthless deed.

Alas! the phial and the blade
Do cry aloud and laugh at me:
"Thou art not worthy of our aid;
Thou art not worthy to be free.

"Though one of us should be the tool
To save thee from thy wretched fate,
Thy kisses would resuscitate
The body of thy vampire, fool!"

Coventry Patmore (1823 – 1896)

The Toys[1]

My little Son, who look'd from thoughtful eyes
And moved and spoke in quiet grown-up wise,
Having my law the seventh time disobey'd,
I struck him, and dismiss'd
With hard words and unkiss'd,
—his Mother, who was patient, being dead.
Then, fearing lest his grief should hinder sleep,
I visited his bed,
But found him slumbering deep,

---

[1] Form: Iambic, irregular line lengths, irregular end rhymes—Vocabulary:
counters: tokens; bluebells: type of flower; —Notes: The child clinging to
worthless toys but obtaining the father's forgiveness is compared with
adults clinging to worthless worldly goods but assured of forgiveness by
God.

With darken'd eyelids, and their lashes yet
From his late sobbing wet.
And I, with moan,
Kissing away his tears, left others of my own;
For, on a table drawn beside his head,
He had put, within his reach,
A box of counters and a red-vein'd stone,
A piece of glass abraded by the beach,
And six or seven shells,
A bottle with bluebells,
And two French copper coins, ranged there with careful art,
To comfort his sad heart.
So when that night I pray'd
To God, I wept, and said:
"Ah, when at last we lie with trancëd breath,
And Thou rememberest of what toys
We made our joys,
How weakly understood
Thy great commanded good,
Then, fatherly not less
Than I whom Thou hast molded from the clay,
Thou'lt leave Thy wrath, and say,
'I will be sorry for their childishness.'"

Richard Henry Stoddard (1805 – 1923)

The Jar[1]

Day and night my thoughts incline
To the blandishments of wine:
Jars were made to drain, I think,
Wine, I know, was made to drink.

When I die, (the day be far!)
Should the potters make a jar
Out of this poor clay of mine,
Let the jar be filled with wine!

---

[1] Form: Iambic tetrameter, AABB end rhymes—Vocabulary:
blandishments: flattery.

Emily Dickinson (1830 – 1886)

A deed knocks first at thought[1]

A deed knocks first at thought,
And then it knocks at will.
That is the manufacturing spot,
And will at home and well.

It then goes out an act,
Or is entombed so still
That only to the ear of God
Its doom is audible.

A narrow fellow in the grass[2]

A narrow fellow in the grass
Occasionally rides;
You may have met him,—did you not,
His notice sudden is.

The grass divides as with a comb,
A spotted shaft is seen;
And then it closes at your feet
And opens further on.

He likes a boggy acre,
A floor too cool for corn.
Yet when a child, and barefoot,
I more than once, at morn,

Have passed, I thought, a whip-lash
Unbraiding in the sun,—
When, stooping to secure it,
It wrinkled, and was gone.

---

[1] Form: Iambic trimeter with tetrameter for line 3 of each stanza. xAxA
slant rhyme—Notes: A deed starts as an idea, where it is manufactured
and refined. It is then either acted on, or not, and if not only God knows
that it ever existed.
[2] Form: Mostly iambic trimeter with a few lines of iambic tetrameter,
irregular slant end rhymes—Notes: Observations about snakes.

Several of nature's people
I know, and they know me;
I feel for them a transport
Of cordiality;

But never met this fellow,
Attended or alone,
Without a tighter breathing,
And zero at the bone.

A word is dead[1]

A word is dead
    When it is said,
Some say.
    I say it just
Begins to live
    That day.

After great pain a formal feeling comes[2]

After great pain, a formal feeling comes—
The Nerves sit ceremonious, like Tombs—
The stiff Heart questions was it He, that bore,
And Yesterday, or Centuries before?

The Feet, mechanical, go round—
Of Ground, or Air, or Ought—
A Wooden way
Regardless grown,
A Quartz contentment, like a stone—

This is the Hour of Lead—
Remembered, if outlived,
As Freezing persons, recollect the Snow—

---

[1] Form: Iambic, 2-2-1 pattern xxA xxA end rhyme pattern.
[2] Form: Free verse with irregular slant rhyme—Notes: A description of grief
with the perceived slowing of time and movement, and then the
comparison of the stages of grief with stages of freezing to death.

First—Chill—then Stupor—then
The letting go—

Apparently with no surprise[1]

Apparently with no surprise
To any happy Flower
The Frost beheads it at its play—
In accidental power—
The blonde Assassin passes on—
The Sun proceeds unmoved
To measure off another Day
For an Approving God.

Because I could not stop for death[2]

Because I could not stop for Death—
He kindly stopped for me—
The Carriage held but just Ourselves—
And Immortality.

We slowly drove—He knew no haste
And I had put away
My labor and my leisure too,
For His Civility—

We passed the School, where Children played
Their lessons scarcely done
We passed the Fields of Gazing Grain—
We passed the Setting Sun—

---

[1] Form: Ballad meter —Vocabulary: —Notes: The death of innocent things (flowers) through natural occurrences (frost). The last line may be read literally as God endorsing the natural death, or ironically as questioning God's awareness and involvement in this death.

[2] Form: Ballad meter—Vocabulary: Gossamer: soft gauzy fabric; Tippet: covering for the shoulders; Tulle: fine net of silk—Notes: The narrator is busy throughout life, so death stops for her and carries her to her final resting place in the cemetery. In route they metaphorically pass a lifetime (childhood, grain as middle-age, and setting-sun as death). Now, the narrator lives in a tomb through the centuries.

We paused before a House that seemed
A Swelling of the Ground—
The Roof was scarcely visible—
The Cornice—but a mound—

Since then—'tis Centuries—but each
Feels shorter than the Day
I first surmised the Horses' Heads
Were toward Eternity—

Hope is the thing with feathers[1]

"Hope" is the thing with feathers—
That perches in the soul—
And sings the tune without the words—
And never stops—at all—

And sweetest—in the Gale—is heard—
And sore must be the storm—
That could abash the little Bird
That kept so many warm—

I've heard it in the chillest land—
And on the strangest Sea—
Yet, never, in Extremity,
It asked a crumb—of Me.

---

[1] Form: Mostly ballad meter.

I felt a funeral in my brain[1]

I felt a Funeral, in my Brain,
   And Mourners to and fro
Kept treading—treading—till it seemed
   That Sense was breaking through—

And when they all were seated,
   A Service, like a Drum—
Kept beating—beating—till I thought
   My Mind was going numb—

And then I heard them lift a Box
   And creak across my Soul
With those same Boots of Lead, again,
   Then Space—began to toll,

As all the Heavens were a Bell,
   And Being, but an Ear,
And I, and Silence, some strange Race
   Wrecked, solitary, here—

I had been hungry all the years[2]

I had been hungry, all the Years—
My Noon had Come—to dine—
I trembling drew the Table near—
And touched the Curious Wine—

'Twas this on Tables I had seen—
When turning, hungry, Home
I looked in Windows, for the Wealth
I could not hope—for Mine—

---

[1] Form: Mostly ballad meter—Notes: The narrator dies, and in spite of logic (reason) finds herself falling to an afterlife. Notice how it ends with suspense, as if the narrator is telling us about the experience but a line is crossed beyond which she is unable to communicate back to the world of the living.

[2] Form: Ballad meter—Notes: This may be interpreted as the discovery of religion, not just in nature but in a more formal church setting.

I did not know the ample Bread—
'Twas so unlike the Crumb
The Birds and I, had often shared
In Nature's—Dining Room—

The Plenty hurt me—'twas so new—
Myself felt ill—and odd—
As Berry—of a Mountain Bush—
Transplanted—to a Road—

Nor was I hungry—so I found
That Hunger—was a way
Of Persons outside Windows—
The Entering—takes away—

I heard a fly buzz when I died[1]

I heard a Fly buzz—when I died—
   The Stillness in the Room
Was like the Stillness in the Air—
   Between the Heaves of Storm—

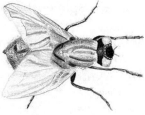

The Eyes around—had wrung them dry—
   And Breaths were gathering firm
For that last Onset—when the King
   Be witnessed—in the Room—

I willed my Keepsakes—Signed away
   What portions of me be
Assignable—and then it was
   There interposed a Fly—

With Blue—uncertain stumbling Buzz—
   Between the light—and me—
And then the Windows failed—and then
   I could not see to see—

---

[1] Form: Ballad—Notes: The narrator is dying the perfect death. Her loved ones are around her, she bequeaths her most precious objects to people, and then . . . everything is ruined as a fly intrudes and becomes the last thing she is aware of before dying.

I like to see it lap the miles[1]

I like to see it lap the miles,
And lick the valleys up,
And stop to feed itself at tanks;
And then, prodigious, step

Around a pile of mountains,
And, supercilious, peer
In shanties by the sides of roads;
And then a quarry pare

To fit its sides, and crawl between,
Complaining all the while
In horrid, hooting stanza;
Then chase itself down hill

And neigh like Boanerges;
Then, punctual as a star,
Stop—docile and omnipotent—
At its own stable door.

---

[1] Form: Mostly iambic trimeter but with some tetrameter lines in ballad
form.—Vocabulary: supercilious: haughty disdain; shanties: shacks; pare:
shave down; Boanerges: a loud orator; —Notes: This poem is an image rich
description of a steam locomotive.

I taste a liquor never brewed[1]

I taste a liquor never brewed—
From Tankards scooped in Pearl—
Not all the Vats upon the Rhine
Yield such an Alcohol!

Inebriate of Air—am I—
And Debauchee of Dew—
Reeling—thro endless summer days—
From inns of Molten Blue—

When "Landlords" turn the drunken Bee
Out of the Foxglove's door—
When Butterflies—renounce their "drams"—
I shall but drink the more!

Till Seraphs swing their snowy Hats—
And Saints—to windows run—
To see the little Tippler
Leaning against the—Sun—

I'm nobody! Who are you?[2]

I'm Nobody! Who are you?
Are you—Nobody—too?
Then there's a pair of us?–Don't tell!
They'd banish us—you know!

How dreary—to be—Somebody!
How public—like a Frog—
To tell your name—the livelong day—
To an admiring Bog!

---

[1] Form: Ballad—Vocabulary: Rhine: area of Germany known for wine;
Inebriate: intoxicated; Debauchee: morally unrestrained person; drams: a
small amount as of alcohol; Seraphs: type of angel.
[2] Form: Free verse—Vocabulary: Bog: wetland area.

I've Known a Heaven, Like a Tent[1]

I've known a Heaven like a tent
To wrap its shining yards,
Pluck up its stakes and disappear
Without the sound of boards
Or rip of nail, or carpenter,
But just the miles of stare
That signalize a show's retreat
In North America.
No trace, no figment of the thing
That dazzled yesterday,
No ring, no marvel;
Men and feats
Dissolved as utterly
As birds' far navigation
Discloses just a hue;
A plash of oars—a gaiety,
Then swallowed up to view.

My life closed twice before its close[2]

My life closed twice before its close—
    It yet remains to see
If Immortality unveil
    A third event to me,

So huge, so hopeless to conceive
    As these that twice befell.
Parting is all we know of heaven,
    And all we need of hell.

---

[1] Form: Iambic, varying line lengths—Notes: The transient nature of the beauty of a sky (perhaps with clouds) is compared to the transient nature of a traveling circus.
[2] Form: Ballad—Notes: Seeing someone die and leave us is the closest we get to seeing heaven (i.e., they have just left for heaven), but also the closest we get to understanding hell.

The Last Night[1]

The last night that she lived,
It was a common night,
Except the dying; this to us
Made nature different.

We noticed smallest things,—
Things overlooked before,
By this great light upon our minds
Italicized, as 't were.

That others could exist
While she must finish quite,
A jealousy for her arose
So nearly infinite.

We waited while she passed;
It was a narrow time,
Too jostled were our souls to speak,
At length the notice came.

She mentioned, and forgot;
Then lightly as a reed
Bent to the water, shivered scarce,
Consented, and was dead.

And we, we placed the hair,
And drew the head erect;
And then an awful leisure was,
Our faith to regulate.

---

[1] Form: Iambic, 3-3-4-3 pattern—Notes: The narrator's life was occupied
with the care of the invalid (mother?), and after her death the grief and void
created a sense of time going by slowly and painfully.

The Props Assist the House[1]

The Props assist the House
Until the House is built
And then the Props withdraw
And adequate, erect,
The House support itself
And cease to recollect
The Auger and the Carpenter—
Just such a retrospect
Hath the perfected Life—
A past of Plank and Nail
And slowness—then the Scaffolds drop
Affirming it a Soul.

The way I read a letter's this[2]

The Way I read a Letter's—this—
'Tis first—I lock the Door—
And push it with my fingers—next—
For transport it be sure—

And then I go the furthest off
To counteract a knock—
Then draw my little Letter forth
And slowly pick the lock—

---

[1] Form: Mostly iambic trimeter with a few lines of iambic tetrameter—
Vocabulary: Auger: hand tool for boring holes—Notes: A metaphor for any
situation of development with support until the support is no longer
needed. This could be read as a religious awakening by Emily.
[2] Form: Ballad.

Then—glancing narrow, at the Wall—
And narrow at the floor
For firm Conviction of a Mouse
Not exorcised before—

Peruse how infinite I am
To no one that You—know—
And sigh for lack of Heaven—but not
The Heaven God bestow—

There came a wind like a bugle[1]

There came a Wind like a Bugle—
It quivered through the Grass
And a Green Chill upon the Heat
So ominous did pass
We barred the Windows and the Doors
As from an Emerald Ghost—
The Doom's electric Moccasin
That very instant passed—
On a strange Mob of panting Trees
And Fences fled away
And Rivers where the Houses ran
Those looked that lived—that Day—
The Bell within the steeple wild
The flying tidings told—
How much can come
And much can go,
And yet abide the World!

There's a certain slant of light[2]

There's a certain Slant of light,
Winter Afternoons—

---

[1] Form: Irregular meter, but iambic trimeter dominates—Notes: A
description of a violent storm, but concluding that the world goes on.
Doom's electric moccasin is lightning. Fences are blown (flee) before the
wind. Houses are washed down rivers.
[2] Form: Irregular meter, mostly iambic trimeter and tetrameter—
Vocabulary: Heft: weight.

That oppresses, like the Heft
Of Cathedral Tunes—

Heavenly Hurt, it gives us—
We can find no scar,
But internal difference,
Where the Meanings, are—

None may teach it—Anything—
'Tis the Seal Despair—
An imperial affliction
Sent us of the air—

When it comes, the Landscape listens—
Shadows—hold their breath—
When it goes, 'tis like the Distance
On the look of Death—

To make a prairie it takes a clover[1]

To make a prairie it takes a clover and one bee,
One clover, and a bee,—
And revery.
The revery alone will do,
If bees are few.

We Grow Accustomed to the Dark[2]

We grow accustomed to the Dark—
When light is put away—
As when the Neighbor holds the Lamp
To witness her Goodbye—

A Moment—We uncertain step
For newness of the night—
Then—fit our Vision to the Dark—
And meet the Road—erect—

---

[1] Form: Iambic, irregular line lengths—Vocabulary: revery: light headed dreaming.
[2] Form: Iambic, irregular line lengths—Notes: This poem describes the process of dealing with grief and loss.

And so of larger—Darkness—
Those Evenings of the Brain—
When not a Moon disclose a sign—
Or Star—come out—within—

The Bravest—grope a little—
And sometimes hit a Tree
Directly in the Forehead—
But as they learn to see—

Either the Darkness alters—
Or something in the sight
Adjusts itself to Midnight—
And Life steps almost straight.

Wild nights! Wild nights![1]

Wild nights—wild nights!
Were i with thee
Wild nights should be
Our luxury!

Futile—the winds—
To a heart in port—
Done with the compass—
Done with the chart!

Rowing in eden—
Ah, the sea!
Might i but moor—
Tonight in thee!

---

[1] Form: Dimeter, roughly equal number of trochees and iambs.

Christina Georgina Rossetti (1830 – 1894)

Goblin Market[1]

Morning and evening
Maids heard the goblins cry:
"Come buy our orchard fruits,
Come buy, come buy:
Apples and quinces,
Lemons and oranges,
Plump unpecked cherries—
Melons and raspberries,
Bloom-down-cheeked peaches,
Swart-headed mulberries,
Wild free-born cranberries,
Crab-apples, dewberries,
Pine-apples, blackberries,
Apricots, strawberries—
All ripe together
In summer weather—
Morns that pass by,
Fair eves that fly;
Come buy, come buy;
Our grapes fresh from the vine,
Pomegranates full and fine,

---

[1] Form: Iambic, irregular line lengths, irregular but frequent end rhymes—
Vocabulary: bullaces: type of plum; greengages: variety of plum; Damsons:
type of plum; bilberries: blueberry; barberries: berry from an ornamental
shrub; Citrons: lemon-like fruit; wombat: similar to a small bear; beck:
small brook; whisk: sweeping; purloin: steal; cloy: be too filling, rich, or
sweet; stone: hard covering containing the seed; upbraidings:
rapprochements; bowers: shady recess; Pellucid: translucent; mead:
meadow; succous: fluid excreted by living tissue; balked: thwarted; waxed:
increased in size; drouth: drought; cankerous: ulcerous; rime: thin coating
of ice; heath: uncultivated open land; furze: evergreen shrub with fragrant
yellow flowers; gobbling: eating greedily; Demure: modest; Ratel: similar to
a badger; Panniers: saddle-bags; pates: tops of their heads; obstreperously:
aggressively; hoary: white or grey with age; scudded: ran before a gale with
no sail; copse: thicket of small trees; dingle: small wooded valley; gibe: jeer;
wormwood: a bitter plant; flagging: weakening—Notes: The primary lesson
is siblings supporting each other. The poem also includes a warning
against the temptations of evil, and could be read in a modern context as a
metaphorical anti-drug message. Some have found hints at lesbian ideas
in the poem.

Dates and sharp bullaces,
Rare pears and greengages,
Damsons and bilberries,
Taste them and try:
Currants and gooseberries,
Bright-fire-like barberries,
Figs to fill your mouth,
Citrons from the South,
Sweet to tongue and sound to eye,
Come buy, come buy."

Evening by evening
Among the brookside rushes,
Laura bowed her head to hear,
Lizzie veiled her blushes:
Crouching close together
In the cooling weather,
With clasping arms and cautioning lips,
With tingling cheeks and finger-tips.
"Lie close," Laura said,
Pricking up her golden head:
We must not look at goblin men,
We must not buy their fruits:
Who knows upon what soil they fed
Their hungry thirsty roots?"
"Come buy," call the goblins
Hobbling down the glen.
"O! Cried Lizzie, Laura, Laura,
You should not peep at goblin men."
Lizzie covered up her eyes
Covered close lest they should look;
Laura reared her glossy head,
And whispered like the restless brook:
"Look, Lizzie, look, Lizzie,
Down the glen tramp little men.
One hauls a basket,
One bears a plate,
One lugs a golden dish
Of many pounds' weight.
How fair the vine must grow
Whose grapes are so luscious;

How warm the wind must blow
Through those fruit bushes."
"No," said Lizzie, "no, no, no;
Their offers should not charm us,
Their evil gifts would harm us."
She thrust a dimpled finger
In each ear, shut eyes and ran:
Curious Laura chose to linger
Wondering at each merchant man.
One had a cat's face,
One whisked a tail,
One tramped at a rat's pace,
One crawled like a snail,
One like a wombat prowled obtuse and furry,
One like a rattle tumbled hurry-scurry.
Lizzie heard a voice like voice of doves
Cooing all together:
They sounded kind and full of loves
In the pleasant weather.

Laura stretched her gleaming neck
Like a rush-imbedded swan,
Like a lily from the beck,
Like a moonlit poplar branch,
Like a vessel at the launch
When its last restraint is gone.

Backwards up the mossy glen
Turned and trooped the goblin men,
With their shrill repeated cry,
"Come buy, come buy."
When they reached where Laura was
They stood stock still upon the moss,
Leering at each other,
Brother with queer brother;
Signaling each other,
Brother with sly brother.
One set his basket down,
One reared his plate;
One began to weave a crown
Of tendrils, leaves, and rough nuts brown

205

(Men sell not such in any town);
One heaved the golden weight
Of dish and fruit to offer her:
"Come buy, come buy," was still their cry.
Laura stared but did not stir,
Longed but had no money:
The whisk-tailed merchant bade her taste
In tones as smooth as honey,
The cat-faced purr'd,
The rat-paced spoke a word
Of welcome, and the snail-paced even was heard;
One parrot-voiced and jolly
Cried "Pretty Goblin" still for "Pretty Polly";
One whistled like a bird.

But sweet-tooth Laura spoke in haste:
"Good folk, I have no coin;
To take were to purloin:
I have no copper in my purse,
I have no silver either,
And all my gold is on the furze
That shakes in windy weather
Above the rusty heather."
"You have much gold upon your head,"
They answered altogether:
"Buy from us with a golden curl."
She clipped a precious golden lock,
She dropped a tear more rare than pearl,
Then sucked their fruit globes fair or red:
Sweeter than honey from the rock,
Stronger than man-rejoicing wine,
Clearer than water flowed that juice;
She never tasted such before,
How should it cloy with length of use?
She sucked and sucked and sucked the more
Fruits which that unknown orchard bore,
She sucked until her lips were sore;
Then flung the emptied rinds away,
But gathered up one kernel stone,
And knew not was it night or day
As she turned home alone.

Lizzie met her at the gate
Full of wise upbraidings:
"Dear, you should not stay so late,
Twilight is not good for maidens;
Should not loiter in the glen
In the haunts of goblin men.
Do you not remember Jeanie,
How she met them in the moonlight,
Took their gifts both choice and many,
Ate their fruits and wore their flowers
Plucked from bowers
Where summer ripens at all hours?
But ever in the moonlight
She pined and pined away;
Sought them by night and day,
Found them no more, but dwindled and grew gray;
Then fell with the first snow,
While to this day no grass will grow
Where she lies low:
I planted daisies there a year ago
That never blow.
You should not loiter so."
"Nay hush," said Laura.
"Nay hush, my sister:
I ate and ate my fill,
Yet my mouth waters still;
To-morrow night I will
Buy more," and kissed her.
"Have done with sorrow;
I'll bring you plums to-morrow
Fresh on their mother twigs,
Cherries worth getting;
You cannot think what figs
My teeth have met in,
What melons, icy-cold
Piled on a dish of gold
Too huge for me to hold,
What peaches with a velvet nap,
Pellucid grapes without one seed:
Odorous indeed must be the mead

Whereon they grow, and pure the wave they drink,
With lilies at the brink,
And sugar-sweet their sap."

Golden head by golden head,
Like two pigeons in one nest
Folded in each other's wings,
They lay down, in their curtained bed:
Like two blossoms on one stem,
Like two flakes of new-fallen snow,
Like two wands of ivory
Tipped with gold for awful kings.
Moon and stars beamed in at them,
Wind sang to them lullaby,
Lumbering owls forbore to fly,
Not a bat flapped to and fro
Round their rest:
Cheek to cheek and breast to breast
Locked together in one nest.

Early in the morning
When the first cock crowed his warning,
Neat like bees, as sweet and busy,
Laura rose with Lizzie:
Fetched in honey, milked the cows,
Aired and set to rights the house,
Kneaded cakes of whitest wheat,
Cakes for dainty mouths to eat,
Next churned butter, whipped up cream,
Fed their poultry, sat and sewed;
Talked as modest maidens should
Lizzie with an open heart,
Laura in an absent dream,
One content, one sick in part;
One warbling for the mere bright day's delight,
One longing for the night.

At length slow evening came—
They went with pitchers to the reedy brook;
Lizzie most placid in her look,
Laura most like a leaping flame.

They drew the gurgling water from its deep
Lizzie plucked purple and rich golden flags,
Then turning homeward said: "The sunset flushes
Those furthest loftiest crags;
Come, Laura, not another maiden lags,
No willful squirrel wags,
The beasts and birds are fast asleep."
But Laura loitered still among the rushes
And said the bank was steep.

And said the hour was early still,
The dew not fallen, the wind not chill:
Listening ever, but not catching
The customary cry,
"Come buy, come buy,"
With its iterated jingle
Of sugar-baited words:
Not for all her watching
Once discerning even one goblin
Racing, whisking, tumbling, hobbling;
Let alone the herds
That used to tramp along the glen,
In groups or single,
Of brisk fruit-merchant men.

Till Lizzie urged, "O Laura, come,
I hear the fruit-call, but I dare not look:
You should not loiter longer at this brook:
Come with me home.
The stars rise, the moon bends her arc,
Each glow-worm winks her spark,
Let us get home before the night grows dark;
For clouds may gather even
Though this is summer weather,
Put out the lights and drench us through;
Then if we lost our way what should we do?"

Laura turned cold as stone
To find her sister heard that cry alone,
That goblin cry,
"Come buy our fruits, come buy."

209

Must she then buy no more such dainty fruit?
Must she no more such succous pasture find,
Gone deaf and blind?
Her tree of life drooped from the root:
She said not one word in her heart's sore ache;
But peering thro' the dimness, naught discerning,
Trudged home, her pitcher dripping all the way;
So crept to bed, and lay
Silent 'til Lizzie slept;
Then sat up in a passionate yearning,
And gnashed her teeth for balked desire, and wept
As if her heart would break.

    Day after day, night after night,
Laura kept watch in vain,
In sullen silence of exceeding pain.
She never caught again the goblin cry:
"Come buy, come buy,"
She never spied the goblin men
Hawking their fruits along the glen:
But when the noon waxed bright
Her hair grew thin and gray;
She dwindled, as the fair full moon doth turn
To swift decay, and burn
Her fire away.

    One day remembering her kernel-stone
She set it by a wall that faced the south;
Dewed it with tears, hoped for a root,
Watched for a waxing shoot,
But there came none;
It never saw the sun,
It never felt the trickling moisture run:
While with sunk eyes and faded mouth
She dreamed of melons, as a traveler sees
False waves in desert drouth
With shade of leaf-crowned trees,
And burns the thirstier in the sandful breeze.

    She no more swept the house,
Tended the fowls or cows,

Fetched honey, kneaded cakes of wheat,
Brought water from the brook:
But sat down listless in the chimney-nook
And would not eat.

    Tender Lizzie could not bear
To watch her sister's cankerous care,
Yet not to share.
She night and morning
Caught the goblins' cry:
"Come buy our orchard fruits,
Come buy, come buy."
Beside the brook, along the glen
She heard the tramp of goblin men,
The voice and stir
Poor Laura could not hear;
Longed to buy fruit to comfort her,
But feared to pay too dear,
She thought of Jeanie in her grave,
Who should have been a bride;
But who for joys brides hope to have
Fell sick and died
In her gay prime,
In earliest winter-time,
With the first glazing rime,
With the first snow-fall of crisp winter-time.

    Till Laura, dwindling,
Seemed knocking at Death's door:
Then Lizzie weighed no more
Better and worse,
But put a silver penny in her purse,
Kissed Laura, crossed the heath with clumps of furze
At twilight, halted by the brook,
And for the first time in her life
Began to listen and look.

    Laughed every goblin
When they spied her peeping:
Came towards her hobbling,
Flying, running, leaping,

Puffing and blowing,
Chuckling, clapping, crowing,
Clucking and gobbling,
Mopping and mowing,
Full of airs and graces,
Pulling wry faces,
Demure grimaces,
Cat-like and rat-like,
Ratel and wombat-like,
Snail-paced in a hurry,
Parrot-voiced and whistler,
Helter-skelter, hurry-skurry,
Chattering like magpies,
Fluttering like pigeons,
Gliding like fishes,—
Hugged her and kissed her;
Squeezed and caressed her;
Stretched up their dishes,
Panniers and plates:
"Look at our apples
Russet and dun,
Bob at our cherries
Bite at our peaches,
Citrons and dates,
Grapes for the asking,
Pears red with basking
Out in the sun,
Plums on their twigs;
Pluck them and suck them,
Pomegranates, figs."

"Good folk," said Lizzie,
Mindful of Jeanie,
"Give me much and many";—
Held out her apron,
Tossed them her penny.
"Nay, take a seat with us,
Honor and eat with us,"
They answered grinning;
"Our feast is but beginning.
Night yet is early,

Warm and dew-pearly,
Wakeful and starry:
Such fruits as these
No man can carry;
Half their bloom would fly,
Half their dew would dry,
Half their flavor would pass by.
Sit down and feast with us,
Be welcome guest with us,
Cheer you and rest with us."
"Thank you," said Lizzie; "but one waits
At home alone for me:
So, without further parleying,
If you will not sell me any
Of your fruits though much and many,
Give me back my silver penny
I tossed you for a fee."
They began to scratch their pates,
No longer wagging, purring,
But visibly demurring,
Grunting and snarling.
One called her proud,
Cross-grained, uncivil;
Their tones waxed loud,
Their looks were evil.
Lashing their tails
They trod and hustled her,
Elbowed and jostled her,
Clawed with their nails,
Barking, mewing, hissing, mocking,
Tore her gown and soiled her stocking,
Twitched her hair out by the roots,
Stamped upon her tender feet,
Held her hands and squeezed their fruits
Against her mouth to make her eat.

White and golden Lizzie stood,
Like a lily in a flood,
Like a rock of blue-veined stone
Lashed by tides obstreperously,—
Like a beacon left alone
In a hoary roaring sea,
Sending up a golden fire,—
Like a fruit-crowned orange-tree
White with blossoms honey-sweet
Sore beset by wasp and bee,—
Like a royal virgin town
Topped with gilded dome and spire
Close beleaguered by a fleet
Mad to tug her standard down.

One may lead a horse to water,
Twenty cannot make him drink.
Though the goblins cuffed and caught her,
Coaxed and fought her,
Bullied and besought her,
Scratched her, pinched her black as ink,
Kicked and knocked her,
Mauled and mocked her,
Lizzie uttered not a word;
Would not open lip from lip
Lest they should cram a mouthful in;

But laughed in heart to feel the drip
Of juice that syruped all her face,
And lodged in dimples of her chin,
And streaked her neck which quaked like curd.
At last the evil people,
Worn out by her resistance,
Flung back her penny, kicked their fruit
Along whichever road they took,
Not leaving root or stone or shoot.
Some writhed into the ground,
Some dived into the brook
With ring and ripple.
Some scudded on the gale without a sound,
Some vanished in the distance.

In a smart, ache, tingle,
Lizzie went her way;
Knew not was it night or day;
Sprang up the bank, tore through the furze,
Threaded copse and dingle,
And heard her penny jingle
Bouncing in her purse,—
Its bounce was music to her ear.
She ran and ran
As if she feared some goblin man
Dogged her with gibe or curse
Or something worse:
But not one goblin scurried after,
Nor was she pricked by fear;
The kind heart made her windy-paced
That urged her home quite out of breath with haste
And inward laughter.

She cried "Laura," up the garden,
"Did you miss me ?
Come and kiss me.
Never mind my bruises,
Hug me, kiss me, suck my juices
Squeezed from goblin fruits for you,
Goblin pulp and goblin dew.
Eat me, drink me, love me;

215

Laura, make much of me:
For your sake I have braved the glen
And had to do with goblin merchant men."

    Laura started from her chair,
Flung her arms up in the air,
Clutched her hair:
"Lizzie, Lizzie, have you tasted
For my sake the fruit forbidden?
Must your light like mine be hidden,
Your young life like mine be wasted,
Undone in mine undoing,
And ruined in my ruin;
Thirsty, cankered, goblin-ridden?"
She clung about her sister,
Kissed and kissed and kissed her:
Tears once again
Refreshed her shrunken eyes,
Dropping like rain
After long sultry drouth;
Shaking with aguish fear, and pain,
She kissed and kissed her with a hungry mouth.

    Her lips began to scorch,
That juice was wormwood to her tongue,
She loathed the feast:
Writhing as one possessed she leaped and sung,
Rent all her robe, and wrung
Her hands in lamentable haste,
And beat her breast.
Her locks streamed like the torch
Borne by a racer at full speed,
Or like the mane of horses in their flight,
Or like an eagle when she stems the light
Straight toward the sun,
Or like a caged thing freed,
Or like a flying flag when armies run.

    Swift fire spread through her veins, knocked at her heart,
Met the fire smoldering there
And overbore its lesser flame,

She gorged on bitterness without a name:
Ah! Fool, to choose such part
Of soul-consuming care!
Sense failed in the mortal strife:
Like the watch-tower of a town
Which an earthquake shatters down,
Like a lightning-stricken mast,
Like a wind-uprooted tree
Spun about,
Like a foam-topped water-spout
Cast down headlong in the sea,
She fell at last;
Pleasure past and anguish past,
Is it death or is it life ?

    Life out of death.
That night long Lizzie watched by her,
Counted her pulse's flagging stir,
Felt for her breath,
Held water to her lips, and cooled her face
With tears and fanning leaves:
But when the first birds chirped about their eaves,
And early reapers plodded to the place
Of golden sheaves,
And dew-wet grass
Bowed in the morning winds so brisk to pass,
And new buds with new day
Opened of cup-like lilies on the stream,
Laura awoke as from a dream,
Laughed in the innocent old way,
Hugged Lizzie but not twice or thrice;
Her gleaming locks showed not one thread of gray,
Her breath was sweet as May,
And light danced in her eyes.

    Days, weeks, months, years
Afterwards, when both were wives
With children of their own;
Their mother-hearts beset with fears,
Their lives bound up in tender lives;
Laura would call the little ones

217

And tell them of her early prime,
Those pleasant days long gone
Of not-returning time:
Would talk about the haunted glen,
The wicked, quaint fruit-merchant men,
Their fruits like honey to the throat,
But poison in the blood;
(Men sell not such in any town;)
Would tell them how her sister stood
In deadly peril to do her good,
And win the fiery antidote:
Then joining hands to little hands
Would bid them cling together,
"For there is no friend like a sister,
In calm or stormy weather,
To cheer one on the tedious way,
To fetch one if one goes astray,
To lift one if one totters down,
To strengthen whilst one stands."

Remember[1]

Remember me when I am gone away,
    Gone far away into the silent land;
    When you can no more hold me by the hand,
Nor I half turn to go, yet turning stay.
Remember me when no more day by day
    You tell me of our future that you planned:
    Only remember me; you understand
It will be late to counsel then or pray.
Yet if you should forget me for a while
    And afterwards remember, do not grieve:
    For if the darkness and corruption leave
    A vestige of the thoughts that once I had,
Better by far you should forget and smile
Than that you should remember and be sad.

---

[1] Form: Sonnet—Vocabulary: vestige: evidence.

Song[1]

When I am dead, my dearest,
   Sing no sad songs for me;
Plant thou no roses at my head,
   Nor shady cypress tree:
Be the green grass above me
   With showers and dewdrops wet;
And if thou wilt, remember,
   And if thou wilt, forget.

I shall not see the shadows,
   I shall not feel the rain;
I shall not hear the nightingale
   Sing on, as if in pain;
And dreaming through the twilight
   That doth not rise nor set,
Haply I may remember,
   And haply may forget.

The First Day[2]

I wish I could remember the first day,
First hour, first moments of your meeting me;
If bright or dim the season, it might be.
Summer or Winter for aught I can say.
So unrecorded did it slip away.
So blind was I to see and to foresee,
So dull to mark the budding of my tree,
That would not blossom for many a May.
If only I could recollect it! Such
A day of days! I let it come and go
As traceless as a thaw of bygone snow.
It seemed to mean so little, meant so much!
If only now I could recall that touch,
First touch of hand in hand!—Did one but know!

---

[1] Form: Iambic trimeter except the 3rd line of each stanza, which is tetrameter, xAxA end rhymes.
[2] Form: Mostly iambic pentameter, ABBA end rhymes.

Lewis Carroll (1832 – 1898)

The Walrus and the Carpenter[1]

The sun was shining on the sea,
 Shining with all his might:
He did his very best to make
 The billows smooth and bright—
And this was odd, because it was
 The middle of the night.

The moon was shining sulkily,
 Because she thought the sun
Had got no business to be there
 After the day was done—
"It's very rude of him," she said,
 "To come and spoil the fun!"

The sea was wet as wet could be,
 The sands were dry as dry.
You could not see a cloud, because
 No cloud was in the sky:
No birds were flying overhead—
 There were no birds to fly.

The Walrus and the Carpenter
 Were walking close at hand;
They wept like anything to see
 Such quantities of sand:
"If this were only cleared away,"
 They said, "it would be grand!"

"If seven maids with seven mops
 Swept it for half a year,
Do you suppose," the Walrus said,
 "That they could get it clear?"
"I doubt it," said the Carpenter,
 And shed a bitter tear.

---

[1] Form: Ballad—Vocabulary: billows: waves; briny: salty; sealing-wax: wax
used to seal letters.

"O Oysters, come and walk with us!"
    The Walrus did beseech.
"A pleasant walk, a pleasant talk,
    Along the briny beach:
We cannot do with more than four,
    To give a hand to each."

The eldest Oyster looked at him,
    But never a word he said:
The eldest Oyster winked his eye,
    And shook his heavy head—
Meaning to say he did not choose
    To leave the oyster-bed.

But four young Oysters hurried up,
    All eager for the treat:
Their coats were brushed, their faces washed,
    Their shoes were clean and neat—
And this was odd, because, you know,
    They hadn't any feet.

Four other Oysters followed them,
    And yet another four;
And thick and fast they came at last,
    And more, and more, and more—
All hopping through the frothy waves,
    And scrambling to the shore.

The Walrus and the Carpenter
    Walked on a mile or so,
And then they rested on a rock
    Conveniently low:
And all the little Oysters stood
    And waited in a row.

"The time has come," the Walrus said,
    "To talk of many things:
Of shoes—and ships—and sealing-wax—
    Of cabbages—and kings—

And why the sea is boiling hot—
    And whether pigs have wings."

"But wait a bit," the Oysters cried,
    "Before we have our chat;
For some of us are out of breath,
    And all of us are fat!"
"No hurry!" said the Carpenter.
    They thanked him much for that.

"A loaf of bread," the Walrus said,
    "Is what we chiefly need:
Pepper and vinegar besides
    Are very good indeed—
Now if you're ready, Oysters dear,
    We can begin to feed."

"But not on us!" the Oysters cried,
    Turning a little blue.
"After such kindness, that would be
    A dismal thing to do!"
"The night is fine," the Walrus said.
    "Do you admire the view?

"It was so kind of you to come!
    And you are very nice!"
The Carpenter said nothing but
    "Cut us another slice:
I wish you were not quite so deaf—
    I've had to ask you twice!"

"It seems a shame," the Walrus said,
    "To play them such a trick,
After we've brought them out so far,
    And made them trot so quick!"
The Carpenter said nothing but
    "The butter's spread too thick!"

"I weep for you," the Walrus said:
    "I deeply sympathize."
With sobs and tears he sorted out

Those of the largest size,
Holding his pocket-handkerchief
Before his streaming eyes.

"O Oysters," said the Carpenter,
"You've had a pleasant run!
Shall we be trotting home again?'
But answer came there none—
And this was scarcely odd, because
They'd eaten every one.

Thomas Hardy (1840 – 1928)

Channel firing[1]

That night your great guns, unawares,
Shook all our coffins as we lay,
And broke the chancel window-squares,
We thought it was the Judgement-day

And sat upright. While drearisome
Arose the howl of wakened hounds:
The mouse let fall the altar-crumb,
The worm drew back into the mounds,

The glebe cow drooled. Till God cried, "No;
It's gunnery practice out at sea
Just as before you went below;
The world is as it used to be:

"All nations striving strong to make
Red war yet redder. Mad as hatters
They do no more for Christés sake
Than you who are helpless in such matters.

"That this is not the judgment-hour
For some of them's a blessed thing,

---

[1] Form: Iambic tetrameter, ABAB end rhymes—Vocabulary: chancel: area around alter of a church; glebe: plot of land by parish for use by the priest; —Notes: The dead buried in a churchyard cemetery are awakened by gunnery practice in preparation for war.

223

For if it were they'd have to scour
Hell's floor for so much threatening. . . .

"Ha, ha. It will be warmer when
I blow the trumpet (if indeed
I ever do; for you are men,
And rest eternal sorely need)."

So down we lay again. "I wonder,
Will the world ever saner be,"
Said one, "than when He sent us under
In our indifferent century!"

And many a skeleton shook his head.
"Instead of preaching forty year,"
My neighbor Parson Thirdly said,
"I wish I had stuck to pipes and beer."

Again the guns disturbed the hour,
Roaring their readiness to avenge,
As far inland as Stourton Tower,
And Camelot, and starlit Stonehenge.

I look into my glass[1]

I look into my glass,
And view my wasting skin,
And say, "Would God it came to pass
My heart had shrunk as thin!"

For then, I, undistrest
By hearts grown cold to me,
Could lonely wait my endless rest
With equanimity.

But Time, to make me grieve,
Part steals, lets part abide;

---

[1] Form: Iambic, 3-3-4-3 pattern, ABAB end rhymes—Vocabulary:
equanimity: calmness—Notes: His body is old, but his heart still longs for
romance.

And shakes this fragile frame at eve
With throbbings of noontide.

The oxen[1]

Christmas Eve, and twelve of the clock.
   'Now they are all on their knees,'
An elder said as we sat in a flock
   By the embers in hearthside ease.

We pictured the meek mild creatures where
   They dwelt in their strawy pen,
Nor did it occur to one of us there
   To doubt they were kneeling then.

So fair a fancy few would weave
   In these years! Yet, I feel,
If someone said on Christmas Eve,
   'Come; see the oxen kneel,

'In the lonely barton by yonder coomb
   Our childhood used to know,'
I should go with him in the gloom,
   Hoping it might be so.

The Ruined Maid[2]

"O'Melia, my dear, this does everything crown!
Who could have supposed I should meet you in Town?
And whence such fair garments, such prosperi-ty?"
"O didn't you know I'd been ruined?" said she.

---

[1] Form: Ballad—Vocabulary: coomb: Hollow in a hillside—Notes: This poem refers to a legend that at midnight on each Christmas Eve oxen kneel in honor of Christ. Notice that if given the chance to observe this, the author would go while hoping that it would be true, implying that he no longer really believes the story. The poem is really about not just questioning faith, but longing for the innocent acceptance of faith.

[2] Form: Anapestic tetrameter, AABB end rhymes—Vocabulary: spudding: digging with a spade; docks: wild greens used in salads; barton: a region in England; hag: an old woman; sock: exclaim; megrims: depression.

— "You left us in tatters, without shoes or socks,
Tired of digging potatoes, and spudding up docks;
And now you've gay bracelets and bright feathers three!"
"Yes: that's how we dress when we're ruined," said she.

— "At home in the barton you said 'thee' and 'thou,'
And 'thik oon,' and 'theäs oon,'' and 't'other'; but now
Your talking quite fits 'ee for high compa-ny!"—
"Some polish is gained with one's ruin," said she.

— "Your hands were like paws then, your face blue and bleak
But now I'm bewitched by your delicate cheek,
And your little gloves fit as on any la-dy!"
"We never do work when we're ruined," said she.

— "You used to call home-life a hag-ridden dream,
And you'd sigh, and you'd sock; but at present you seem
To know not of megrims or melancho-ly!"
"True. One's pretty lively when ruined," said she.

— "I wish I had feathers, a fine sweeping gown,
And a delicate face, and could strut about Town!"
"My dear - a raw country girl, such as you be,
Cannot quite expect that. You ain't ruined," said she.

Sidney Lanier (1842 – 1881)

The Revenge of Hamish[1]

It was three slim does and a ten-tined buck in the bracken
    lay;
    And all of a sudden the sinister smell of a man,
    Awaft on a wind-shift, wavered and ran

---

[1] Form: Anapestic, 6-5-4-6 pattern (note that the 6 foot lines in the printed book have margin forced line breaks), ABBA end rhymes.—Vocabulary: tined: pronged; bracken: ferns; hillock: small hill; waxed: increasingly; glen: valley; henchman: loyal follower; burn: stream; nether: lower; bating: stopping; Brake: held back; gluttonous: greedy; kern: lout; crag: rocky part of a cliff; gillie: hunting guide; gibe: mocking remark—Notes: Perhaps a story written as a lesson regarding abuse of slaves or servants.

Down the hill-side and sifted along through the bracken and
    passed that way.

Then Nan got a-tremble at nostril; she was the daintiest doe;
    In the print of her velvet flank on the velvet fern
    She reared, and rounded her ears in turn.
Then the buck leapt up, and his head as a king's to a crown
    did go

Full high in the breeze, and he stood as if Death had the form
    of a deer;
    And the two slim does long lazily stretching arose,
    For their day-dream slowlier came to a close,
Till they woke and were still, breath-bound with waiting and
    wonder and fear.

Then Alan the huntsman sprang over the hillock, the hounds
    shot by,
    The does and the ten-tined buck made a marvelous
    bound,
    The hounds swept after with never a sound,
But Alan loud winded his horn in sign that the quarry was
    nigh.

For at dawn of that day proud Maclean of Lochbuy to the
    hunt had waxed wild,

And he cursed at old Alan till Alan fared off with the
    hounds
For to drive him the deer to the lower glen-grounds:
"I will kill a red deer," quoth Maclean, "in the sight of the wife
    and the child."

So gaily he paced with the wife and the child to his chosen
    stand;
    But he hurried tall Hamish the henchman ahead: "Go
    turn,"—
    Cried Maclean—"if the deer seek to cross to the burn,
Do thou turn them to me: nor fail, lest thy back be red as thy
    hand."

Now hard-fortuned Hamish, half blown of his breath with the
    height of the hill,
    Was white in the face when the ten-tined buck and the
    does
    Drew leaping to burn-ward; huskily rose
His shouts, and his nether lip twitched, and his legs were
    o'er-weak for his will.

So the deer darted lightly by Hamish and bounded away to
    the burn.
    But Maclean never bating his watch tarried waiting below
    Still Hamish hung heavy with fear for to go
All the space of an hour; then he went, and his face was
    greenish and stern,

And his eye sat back in the socket, and shrunken the
    eyeballs shone,
    As withdrawn from a vision of deeds it were shame to see.
    "Now, now, grim henchman, what is't with thee?"
Brake Maclean, and his wrath rose red as a beacon the wind
    hath upblown.

"Three does and a ten-tined buck made out," spoke Hamish,
    full mild,
    "and I ran for to turn, but my breath it was blown, and
    they passed;
    I was weak, for ye called ere I broke me my fast."

Cried Maclean: "Now a ten-tined buck in the sight of the wife
 and the child

I had killed if the gluttonous kern had not wrought me a
 snail's own wrong!"
 Then he sounded, and down came kinsmen and clansmen
  all:
 "Ten blows, for ten tine, on his back let fall,
And reckon no stroke if the blood follow not at the bite of
 thong!"

So Hamish made bare, and took him his strokes; at the last
 he smiled.
 "Now i'll to the burn," quoth Maclean, "for it still may be,
 If a slimmer-paunched henchman will hurry with me,
I shall kill me the ten-tined buck for a gift to the wife and the
 child!"

Then the clansmen departed, by this path and that; and over
 the hill
 Sped Maclean with an outward wrath for an inward
  shame;
 And that place of the lashing full quiet became;
And the wife and the child stood sad; and bloody-backed
 Hamish sat still.

But look! Red Hamish has risen; quick about and about
 turns he.
 "There is none betwixt me and the crag-top!" he screams
  under breath.
 Then, livid as Lazarus lately from death,
He snatches the child from the mother, and clambers the
 crag toward the sea.

Now the mother drops breath; she is dumb, and her heart
 goes dead for a space,
 Till the motherhood, mistress of death, shrieks, shrieks
  through the glen,
 And that place of the lashing is live with men,
And Maclean, and the gillie that told him, dash up in a
 desperate race.

229

Not a breath's time for asking; an eye-glance reveals all the
    tale untold.
    They follow mad Hamish afar up the crag toward the sea,
    And the lady cries: "Clansmen, run for a fee!—
Yon castle and lands to the two first hands that shall hook
    him and hold

Fast Hamish back from the brink!"—and ever she flies up the
    steep,
    And the clansmen pant, and they sweat, and they jostle
    and strain.
    But, mother, 'tis vain; but, father, 'tis vain;
Stern Hamish stands bold on the brink, and dangles the
    child o'er the deep.

Now a faintness falls on the men that run, and they all stand
    still.
    And the wife prays Hamish as if he were God, on her
    knees,
    Crying: "Hamish! O Hamish! But please, but please
For to spare him!" and Hamish still dangles the child, with a
    wavering will.

On a sudden he turns; with a sea-hawk scream, and a gibe,
    and a song,
    Cries: "So; I will spare ye the child if, in sight of ye all,
    Ten blows on Maclean's bare back shall fall,
And ye reckon no stroke if the blood follow not at the bite of
    the thong!"

Then Maclean he set hardly his tooth to his lip that his tooth
    was red,
    Breathed short for a space, said: "Nay, but it never shall
    be!
    Let me hurl off the damnable hound in the sea!"
But the wife: "Can Hamish go fish us the child from the sea,
    if dead?

Say yea!—Let them lash *me*, Hamish?"—"Nay!"—"Husband,
    the lashing will heal;

But, oh, who will heal me the bonny sweet bairn in his
    grave?
Could ye cure me my heart with the death of a knave?
Quick! Love! I will bare thee—so—kneel!" Then Maclean 'gan
    slowly to kneel

With never a word, till presently downward he jerked to the
    earth.
    Then the henchman—he that smote Hamish—would
        tremble and lag;
    "Strike, hard!" quoth Hamish, full stern, from the crag;
Then he struck him, and "One!" sang Hamish, and danced
    with the child in his mirth.

And no man spake beside Hamish; he counted each stroke
    with a song.
    When the last stroke fell, then he moved him a pace down
        the height,
    And he held forth the child in the heartaching sight
Of the mother, and looked all pitiful grave, as repenting a
    wrong.

And there as the motherly arms stretched out with the
    thanksgiving prayer—
    And there as the mother crept up with a fearful swift pace,
    Till her finger nigh felt of the bairnie's face—
In a flash fierce Hamish turned round and lifted the child in
    the air,

And sprang with the child in his arms from the horrible
    height in the sea,
    Shrill screeching, "Revenge!" in the wind-rush;
        And pallid Maclean,
    Age-feeble with anger and impotent pain,
Crawled up on the crag, and lay flat, and locked hold of dead
    roots of a tree—

And gazed hungrily o'er, and the blood from his back drip-
    dripped in the brine,
    And a sea-hawk flung down a skeleton fish as he flew,
    And the mother stared white on the waste of blue,

And the wind drove a cloud to seaward, and the sun began to
    shine.

The Waving of the Corn[1]

Ploughman, whose gnarly hand yet kindly wheeled
Thy plough to ring this solitary tree
    With clover, whose round plat, reserved a-field,
In cool green radius twice my length may be—
    Scanting the corn thy furrows else might yield,
To pleasure August, bees, fair thoughts, and me,
    That here come oft together—daily I,
    Stretched prone in summer's mortal ecstasy,
Do stir with thanks to thee, as stirs this morn
        With waving of the corn.

Unseen, the farmer's boy from round the hill
Whistles a snatch that seeks his soul unsought,
    And fills some time with tune, howbeit shrill;
The cricket tells straight on his simple thought—
    Nay, 'tis the cricket's way of being still;
The peddler bee drones in, and gossips naught;
    Far down the wood, a one-desiring dove
    Times me the beating of the heart of love:
And these be all the sounds that mix, each morn,
        With waving of the corn.

From here to where the louder passions dwell,
Green leagues of hilly separation roll:
    Trade ends where yon far clover ridges swell.
Ye terrible Towns, ne'er claim the trembling soul
    That, craftless all to buy or hoard or sell,
From out your deadly complex quarrel stole
    To company with large amiable trees,
    Suck honey summer with unjealous bees,
And take Time's strokes as softly as this morn
        Takes waving of the corn.

---

[1] Form: Iambic pentameter, ABABABCCDD end rhymes—Vocabulary: plat:
plot of land—Notes: A hidden sanctuary left in the middle of the corn-field,
and perhaps metaphorically, any peaceful island in a sea of trouble.

To Nannette Falk-Auerbach[1]

Oft as I hear thee, wrapt in heavenly art,
  The massive message of Beethoven tell
With thy ten fingers to the people's heart
  As if ten tongues told news of heaven and hell,—
Gazing on thee, I mark that not alone,
  Ah, not alone, thou sittest: there, by thee,
Beethoven's self, dear living lord of tone,
  Doth stand and smile upon thy mastery.
Full fain and fatherly his great eyes glow:
  He says, "From Heaven, my child, I heard thee call
(For, where an artist plays, the sky is low):
  Yea, since my lonesome life did lack love's all,
    In death, God gives me thee: thus, quit of pain,
    Daughter, Nannette! In thee I live again."

Gerard Manley Hopkins (1844 – 1889)

Binsey Poplars[2]

felled 1879

My aspens dear, whose airy cages quelled,
Quelled or quenched in leaves the leaping sun,
All felled, felled, are all felled;
  Of a fresh and following folded rank
        Not spared, not one
        That dandled a sandaled
    Shadow that swam or sank
On meadow and river and wind-wandering weed-winding
  bank.

  O if we but knew what we do
      When we delve or hew—

---

[1] Form: Sonnet—Vocabulary: fain: happily.
[2] Form: Iambic but irregular line lengths.—Vocabulary: Binsey: location in
England; dandled: bounce child on knee; delve: dig; hew: cut with ax; rack:
torture; únselve: remove; especial: special—Notes: The narrator bemoans
the fact that his beloved grove of aspen trees has been chopped down. This
is best appreciated when sung.

Hack and rack the growing green!
 Since country is so tender
To touch, her being só slender,
That, like this sleek and seeing ball
But a prick will make no eye at all,
Where we, even where we mean
  To mend her we end her,
 When we hew or delve:
After-comers cannot guess the beauty been.
 Ten or twelve, only ten or twelve
  Strokes of havoc únselve
   The sweet especial scene,
  Rural scene, a rural scene,
  Sweet especial rural scene.

Carrion Comfort[1]

Not, I'll not, carrion comfort, Despair, not feast on thee;
Not untwist—slack they may be—these last strands of man
In me ór, most weary, cry I *can no more*. I can;
Can something, hope, wish day come, not choose not to be.
But ah, but O thou terrible, why wouldst thou rude on me
Thy wring-world right foot rock? Lay a lion limb against me?
 scan
With darksome devouring eyes my bruisèd bones? And fan,
O in turns of tempest, me heaped there; me frantic to avoid
 thee and flee?
Why? That my chaff might fly; my grain lie, sheer and clear.
Nay in all that toil, that coil, since (seems) I kissed the rod,
Hand rather, my heart lo! Lapped strength, stole joy, would
 laugh, chéer.
Cheer whom though? The hero whose heaven-handling flung
 me, fóot tród
Me? Or me that fought him? O which one? Is it each one?
 that night, that year

---

[1] Form: Iambic but irregular line lengths.—Vocabulary: Carrion: dead, decaying flesh; rude on: disrespect—Notes: This poem was written as Gerald was undergoing an inner conflict between his role as poet and his role as priest. Like all of his work, it is best appreciated when read aloud or sung.

Of now done darkness I wretch lay wrestling with (my God!)
  my God.

Spring and Fall[1]

To a Young Child

Márgarét, are you gríeving
Over Goldengrove unleaving?
Leaves, like the things of man, you
With your fresh thoughts care for, can you?
Áh! Ás the heart grows older
It will come to such sights colder
By & by, nor spare a sigh
Though worlds of wanwood leafmeal lie;
And yet you wíll weep & know why.
Now no matter, child, the name:
Sórrow's spríngs áre the same.
Nor mouth had, no nor mind, expressed
What héart héard of, ghóst guéssed:
It is the blight man was born for,
It is Margaret you mourn for.

The Windhover[2]

To Christ our Lord

I caught this morning morning's minion, kingdom of
  daylight's dauphin, dapple-dawn-drawn Falcon, in his
  riding
  Of the rolling level underneath him steady air, and striding
High there, how he rung upon the rein of a wimpling wing

---

[1] Form: Iambic but irregular line lengths.—Vocabulary: Goldengrove:
fictitious place in England; unleaving: trees losing leaves; wanwood: Decay
of woods; leafmeal: loss of leaves—Notes: Addressed to a child sad over the
loss of leaves on the trees, the narrator says that this is but a small taste
of the loss she will suffer and that her mourning is really for her lost
innocence.

[2] Form: Iambic but irregular line lengths.—Vocabulary: minion: follower or
dependent; dauphin: eldest son of the king; dapple: mottled; wimpling:
rippling; skate: type of ray (as in sting-ray); chevalier: knight; sillion: strip
of cultivated land; gall: friction burn; vermillion: a reddish-orange color.

In his ecstasy! then off, off forth on swing
    As a skate's heel sweeps smooth on a bow-bend: the hurl
    and gliding
    Rebuffed the big wind. My heart in hiding
Stirred for a bird,—the achieve of; the mastery of the thing!

Brute beauty and valor and act, oh, air, pride, plume, here
    Buckle! and the fire that breaks from thee then, a billion
Times told lovelier, more dangerous, O my chevalier!

    No wonder of it: shéer plód makes plough down sillion
Shine, and blue-bleak embers, ah my dear,
    Fall, gall themselves, and gash gold-vermillion.

Edward Rowland Sill (1847 – 1881)

Five Lives[1]

    Five mites of monads dwelt in a round drop
That twinkled on a leaf by a pool in the sun.
To the naked eye they lived invisible;
Specks, for a world of whom the empty shell
Of a mustard-seed had been a hollow sky.

    One was a meditative monad, called a sage;
And, shrinking all his mind within, he thought:
"Tradition, handed down for hours and hours,
Tells that our globe, this quivering crystal world,
Is slowly dying. What if, seconds hence,
When I am very old, yon shimmering dome
Come drawing down and down, till all things end?"
Then with a weazen smirk he proudly felt
No other mote of God had ever gained
Such giant grasp of universal truth.

    One was a transcendental monad; thin
And long and slim in the mind; and thus he mused:
"Oh, vast, unfathomable monad-souls!

---

[1] Form: Blank verse—Vocabulary: mites: very small creatures; monads: single celled microorganism; wizen: dried up; mote: speck; infusoria: group of micro-organisms; Aeonian: relating to an eon.

236

Made in the image"--a hoarse frog croaks from the pool--
"Hark! 'twas some god, voicing his glorious thought
In thunder music! Yea, we hear their voice,
And we may guess their minds from ours, their work.
Some taste they have like ours, some tendency
To wriggle about, and munch a trace of scum."
He floated up on a pin-point bubble of gas
That burst, pricked by the air, and he was gone.

One was a barren-minded monad, called
A positivist; and he knew positively:
"There is no world beyond this certain drop.
Prove me another! Let the dreamers dream
Of their faint dreams, and noises from without,
And higher and lower; life is life enough."
Then swaggering half a hair's breadth, hungrily
He seized upon an atom of bug, and fed.

One was a tattered monad, called a poet;
And with shrill voice ecstatic thus he sang:
"Oh, the little female monad's lips!
Oh, the little female monad's eyes:
Ah, the little, little, female, female monad!"

The last was a strong-minded monadess,
Who dashed amid the infusoria,
Danced high and low, and wildly spun and dove
Till the dizzy others held their breath to see.

But while they led their wondrous little lives
Aeonian moments had gone wheeling by.
The burning drop had shrunk with fearful speed;
A glistening film--'twas gone; the leaf was dry.
The little ghost of an inaudible squeak
Was lost to the frog that goggled from his stone;
Who, at the huge, slow tread of a thoughtful ox
Coming to drink, stirred sideways fatly, plunged,
Launched backward twice, and all the pool was still.

William Ernest Henley (1849 – 1903)

Invictus[1]

Out of the night that covers me,
  Black as the pit from pole to pole,
I thank whatever gods may be
  For my unconquerable soul.

In the fell clutch of circumstance
  I have not winced nor cried aloud.
Under the bludgeonings of chance
  My head is bloody, but unbowed.

Beyond this place of wrath and tears
  Looms but the Horror of the shade,
And yet the menace of the years
  Finds, and shall find, me unafraid.

It matters not how strait the gate,
  How charged with punishments the scroll,
I am the master of my fate:
  I am the captain of my soul.

Eugene Field (1850 – 1895)

Little Boy Blue[2]

The little toy dog is covered with dust,
  But sturdy and stanch he stands;
And the little toy soldier is red with rust,
  And his musket moulds in his hands.
Time was when the little toy dog was new,
  And the soldier was passing fair;
And that was the time when our Little Boy Blue
  Kissed them and put them there.

---

[1] Form: Iambic tetrameter, ABAB end rhymes—Notes: This beautiful piece
was somewhat spoiled for many when it was read by Oklahoma City
Bomber Timothy McVeigh immediately prior to his execution.
[2] Form: Ballad—Vocabulary: trundle-bed: low bed on wheels.

"Now, don't you go till I come," he said,
    "and don't you make any noise!"
So, toddling off to his trundle-bed,
    He dreamt of the pretty toys;
And, as he was dreaming, an angel song
    Awakened our Little Boy Blue—
Oh! The years are many, the years are long,
    But the little toy friends are true!

Ay, faithful to Little Boy Blue they stand,
    Each in the same old place,
Awaiting the touch of a little hand,
    The smile of a little face;
And they wonder, as waiting the long years through
    In the dust of that little chair,
What has become of our Little Boy Blue,
    Since he kissed them and put them there.

Wynken, Blynken, and Nod[1]

Wynken, Blynken, and Nod one night
    Sailed off in a wooden shoe,—
Sailed on a river of crystal light,
    Into a sea of dew.
"Where are you going, and what do you wish?"
    The old moon asked the three.
"We have come to fish for the herring fish
    That live in this beautiful sea;
    Nets of silver and gold have we!"
        Said Wynken,
        Blynken,
        And Nod.

The old moon laughed and sang a song
    As they rocked in the wooden shoe,
And the wind that sped them all night long
    Ruffled the waves of dew.
The little stars were the herring fish
    That lived in the beautiful sea

---

[1] Form: Ballad.

"Now cast your nets wherever you wish
   Never afeard are we";
  So cried the stars to the fisherman three:
     Wynken,
     Blynken,
     And Nod.

All night long their nets they threw
   To the stars in the twinkling foam
Then down from the skies came the wooden shoe,
   Bringing the fishermen home:
'Twas all so pretty a sail it seemed
   As if it could not be,
And some folks thought 'twas a dream they'd dreamed
   Of sailing that beautiful sea
  But I shall name you the fishermen three:
     Wynken,
     Blynken,
     And Nod.

Wynken and Blynken are two little eyes,
   And Nod is a little head,
And the wooden shoe that sailed the skies
   Is a wee one's trundle-bed;
So shut your eyes while mother sings
   Of wonderful sights that be,
And you shall see the beautiful things
   As you rock in the misty sea
  Where the old shoe rocked the fishermen three:
     Wynken,
     Blynken,
     And Nod.

Robert Louis Stevenson (1850 – 1894)

Requiem[1]

Under the wide and starry sky

---

[1] Form: Iambic but with initial trochees lines 1,2,3 and an initial anapest in line 4 of each stanza. Tetrameter lines for 1,2,3 and trimeter for line 4 of each stanza. AAAB CCCB end rhymes.

Dig the grave and let me lie:
Glad did I live and gladly die,
   And I laid me down with a will.

This be the verse you grave for me:
Here he lies where he longed to be;
Home is the sailor, home from sea,
   And the hunter home from the hill.

Ella Wheeler Wilcox (1850 – 1919)

Solitude[1]

Laugh, and the world laughs with you;
   Weep, and you weep alone.
For the sad old earth must borrow it's mirth,
   But has trouble enough of its own.
Sing, and the hills will answer;
   Sigh, it is lost on the air.
The echoes bound to a joyful sound,
   But shrink from voicing care.

Rejoice, and men will seek you;
   Grieve, and they turn and go.
They want full measure of all your pleasure,
   But they do not need your woe.
Be glad, and your friends are many;
   Be sad, and you lose them all.
There are none to decline your nectared wine,
   But alone you must drink life's gall.

Feast, and your halls are crowded;
   Fast, and the world goes by.
Succeed and give, and it helps you live,
   But no man can help you die.
There is room in the halls of pleasure
   For a long and lordly train,
But one by one we must all file on
   Through the narrow aisles of pain.

---

[1] Form: Iambic, 3-3-4-3 pattern, ABAB end rhymes.

A.E. Housman (1859 – 1936)

Loveliest of trees, the cherry now[1]

Loveliest of trees, the cherry now
Is hung with bloom along the bough,
And stands about the woodland ride
Wearing white for Eastertide.

Now, of my threescore years and ten,
Twenty will not come again,
And take from seventy springs a score,
It only leaves me fifty more.

And since to look at things in bloom
Fifty springs are little room,
About the woodlands I will go
To see the cherry hung with snow.

Terence, This is Stupid Stuff[2]

"Terence, this is stupid stuff:
You eat your victuals fast enough;
There can't be much amiss, 'tis clear,
To see the rate you drink your beer.
But oh, good Lord, the verse you make,
It gives a chap the belly-ache.
The cow, the old cow, she is dead;

---

[1] Form: Iambic tetrameter, AABB end rhymes—Vocabulary: bough: branch;
Eastertide: Easter season; threescore: sixty; score: twenty—Notes: The
narrator meditates on how short life is and the need to enjoy beauty for the
moment.

[2] Form: Iambic tetrameter, AABB end rhymes—Vocabulary: victuals: food;
hop-yard: a field where hops (for beer) are grown; Mithridates: an ancient
king of Pontus—Notes: A friend of Terence begins by complaining that the
poems Terence writes are depressing and asks for something more
cheerful. Terence replies that if cheer is what is desired poems are a bad
choice when compared to beer. However, beer creates a false sense of
happiness. He then goes on to say that his poems reflect the sad reality of
life. Finally, he claims that by reading sad poems the reader is inoculated
against sad events in their life, and thus able to better survive them.

It sleeps well, the hornëd head:
We poor lads, 'tis our turn now
To hear such tunes as killed the cow.
Pretty friendship 'tis to rhyme
Your friends to death before their time
Moping melancholy mad:
Come, pipe a tune to dance to, lad."

Why, if 'tis dancing you would be,
There's brisker pipes than poetry.
Say, for what were hop-yards meant,
Or why was Burton built on Trent?
Oh many a peer of England brews
Livelier liquor than the Muse,
And malt does more than Milton can
To justify God's ways to man.
Ale, man, ale's the stuff to drink
For fellows whom it hurts to think:
Look into the pewter pot
To see the world as the world's not.
And faith, 'tis pleasant till 'tis past:
The mischief is that 'twill not last.
Oh I have been to Ludlow fair
And left my necktie God knows where,
And carried half way home, or near,
Pints and quarts of Ludlow beer:
Then the world seemed none so bad,
And I myself a sterling lad;
And down in lovely muck i've lain,
Happy till I woke again.
Then I saw the morning sky:
Heigho, the tale was all a lie;
The world, it was the old world yet,
I was I, my things were wet,
And nothing now remained to do
But begin the game anew.

Therefore, since the world has still
Much good, but much less good than ill,
And while the sun and moon endure
Luck's a chance, but trouble's sure,

I'd face it as a wise man would,
And train for ill and not for good.
'Tis true, the stuff I bring for sale
Is not so brisk a brew as ale:
Out of a stem that scored the hand
I wrung it in a weary land.
But take it: if the snack is sour,
The better for the embittered hour;
It should do good to heart and head
When your soul is in my soul's stead;
And I will friend you, if I may,
In the dark and cloudy day.

There was a king reigned in the East:
There, when kings will sit to feast,
They get their fill before they think
With poisoned meat and poisoned drink.
He gathered all that springs to birth
From the many-venomed earth;
First a little, thence to more,
He sampled all her killing store;
And easy, smiling, seasoned sound,
Sate the king when healths went round.
They put arsenic in his meat
And stared aghast to watch him eat;
They poured strychnine in his cup
And shook to see him drink it up:
They shook, they stared as white's their shirt:
Them it was their poison hurt.
—I tell the tale that I heard told.
Mithridates, he died old.

They say my Verse is Sad: No Wonder[1]

They say my verse is sad: no wonder.
   Its narrow measure spans
Rue for eternity, and sorrow
   Not mine, but man's.

---

[1] Form: Iambic 4-3-4-2 pattern, xAxA end rhymes—Vocabulary: unbegot: not yet in existence.

244

This is for all ill-treated fellows
   Unborn and unbegot,
For them to read when they're in trouble
   And I am not.

To an Athlete Dying Young[1]

The time you won your town the race
We chaired you through the market-place;
Man and boy stood cheering by,
And home we brought you shoulder-high.

To-day, the road all runners come,
Shoulder high—high we bring you home,
And set you at your threshold down,
Townsman of a stiller town.

Smart lad, to slip betimes away
From fields where glory does not stay
And early though the laurel grows
It withers quicker than the rose.

Eyes the shady night has shut
Cannot see the record cut,
And silence sounds no worse than cheers
After earth has stopped the ears:

Now you will not swell the rout
Of lads that wore their honors out,
Runners whom renown outran
And the name died before the man.

So set, before its echoes fade,
The fleet foot on the sill of shade,
And hold to the low lintel up
The still-defended challenge-cup.

---

[1] Form: Iambic tetrameter, AABB end rhymes—Vocabulary: lintel: horizontal beam—Notes: An athlete died shortly after winning the championship for his town. Housman congratulates him on, in effect, quitting while he was ahead.

And round that early-laurelled head
Will flock to gaze the strengthless dead,
And find unwithered on its curls
The garland briefer than a girl's.

James B Naylor (1860 – 1902)

Authorship[1]

"King David and King Solomon
    Led merry, merry lives,
With many, many lady friends
    And many, many wives;
But when old age crept over them,
    With many, many qualms,
King Solomon wrote the Proverbs
    And King David wrote the Psalms."

Charles Perkins Stetson (1860 – 1935)

An Obstacle[2]

I was climbing up a mountain-path
With many things to do,
Important business of my own,
And other people's too,
When I ran against a Prejudice
That quite cut off the view.

My work was such as could not wait,
My path quite clearly showed,
My strength and time were limited,
I carried quite a load;
And there that hulking Prejudice
Sat all across the road.

---

[1] Form: Ballad.
[2] Form: Alternating iambic tetrameter, iambic trimeter, xAxAxA end
rhymes—Vocabulary: Solomon: King Solomon (Bible); obdurate: hardened
in wrongdoing; Bunker Hill: revolutionary war site; incubus: evil spirit.

So I spoke to him politely,
For he was huge and high,
And begged that he would move a bit
And let me travel by.
He smiled, but as for moving!—
He didn't even try.

And then I reasoned quietly
With that colossal mule:
My time was short—no other path—
The mountain winds were cool.
I argued like a Solomon;
He sat there like a fool.

Then I flew into a passion,
I danced and howled and swore.
I pelted and belabored him
Till I was stiff and sore;
He got mad as I did—
But sat there as before.

And then I begged him on my knees;
I might be kneeling still
If so I hoped to move that mass
Of obdurate ill-will—
As well invite the monument
To vacate Bunker Hill!

So I sat before him helpless,
In an ecstasy of woe—
The mountain mists were rising fast,
The sun was sinking slow—
When a sudden inspiration came,
As sudden winds do blow.

I took my hat, I took my stick,
My load I settled fair,
I approached that awful incubus
With an absent minded air—
And I walked directly through him,
As if he wasn't there!

Black Elk (1863 – 1950)

Everything the Power of the World Does is done in a circle[1]
As spoken to John G. Neihardt

Everything the Power of the World does,
is done in a circle. The sky is round,
and I have heard that the earth is round
like a ball, and so are all the stars.
The wind, in its greatest power, whirls.

Birds make their nests in circles;
for theirs is the same religion as ours.

The sun comes forth and goes down again
in a circle. The moon does the same,
and both are round. Even the seasons
form a great circle in their changing,
and always come back to where they were.

The life of a man is a circle from childhood to childhood.
and so it is with everything where power moves.

Rudyard Kipling (1865 – 1930)

If[2]

If you can keep your head when all about you
    Are losing theirs and blaming it on you;
If you can trust yourself when all men doubt you,
    But make allowance for their doubting too;
If you can wait and not be tired by waiting,
    Or, being lied about, don't deal in lies,

---

[1] Form: Free verse—Vocabulary: —Notes: This extract is taken from a book. After looking at the power of circles (in this extract), Black Elk goes on to say that the white men have forced Indians to live in squares (square house, square cars, square offices, and so on).
[2] Form: Iambic pentameter, ABAB end rhymes—Vocabulary: knaves: deceitful people.

Or, being hated, don't give way to hating,
　　And yet don't look too good, nor talk too wise;

If you can dream - and not make dreams your master;
　　If you can think - and not make thoughts your aim;
If you can meet with triumph and disaster
　　And treat those two imposters just the same;
If you can bear to hear the truth you've spoken
　　Twisted by knaves to make a trap for fools,
Or watch the things you gave your life to broken,
　　And stoop and build 'em up with wornout tools;

If you can make one heap of all your winnings
　　And risk it on one turn of pitch-and-toss,
And lose, and start again at your beginnings
　　And never breath a word about your loss;
If you can force your heart and nerve and sinew
　　To serve your turn long after they are gone,
And so hold on when there is nothing in you
　　Except the Will which says to them: "Hold on!";

If you can talk with crowds and keep your virtue,
　　Or walk with kings—nor lose the common touch;
If neither foes nor loving friends can hurt you;
　　If all men count with you, but none too much;
If you can fill the unforgiving minute
　　With sixty seconds' worth of distance run—
Yours is the Earth and everything that's in it,
　　And—which is more—you'll be a Man my son!

The Way Through the Woods[1]

They shut the road through the woods
Seventy years ago.
Weather and rain have undone it again,
And now you would never know
There was once a road through the woods
Before they planted the trees.

---

[1] Form: Ballad—Vocabulary: coppice: grove of small tress; heath:
uncultivated open land; anemones: type of herb; broods: nests.

It is underneath the coppice and heath
And the thin anemones.
Only the keeper sees
That, where the ring-dove broods,
And the badgers roll at ease,
There was once a road through the woods.

Yet if you enter the woods
Of a summer evening late,
When the night-air cools on the trout-ringed pools
Where the otter whistles his mate,
(They fear not men in the woods,
Because they see so few.)
You will hear the beat of a horse's feet,
And the swish of a skirt in the dew,
Steadily cantering through
The misty solitudes,
As though they perfectly knew
The old lost road through the woods...
But there is no road through the woods.

We and They[1]

Father and Mother, and Me,
   Sister and Auntie say
All the people like us are We,
   And every one else is They.
And They live over the sea,
   While We live over the way,
But-would you believe it?—They look upon We
   As only a sort of They!

We eat pork and beef
   With cow-horn-handled knives.
They who gobble Their rice off a leaf,
   Are horrified out of Their lives;
While they who live up a tree,
   And feast on grubs and clay,
(Isn't it scandalous?) look upon We

---

[1] Form: Primarily iambic trimeter, ABAB end rhymes.

As a simply disgusting They!

We shoot birds with a gun.
    They stick lions with spears.
Their full-dress is un-.
    We dress up to Our ears.
They like Their friends for tea.
    We like Our friends to stay;
And, after all that, They look upon We
    As an utterly ignorant They!

We eat kitcheny food.
    We have doors that latch.
They drink milk or blood,
    Under an open thatch.
We have Doctors to fee.
    They have Wizards to pay.
And (impudent heathen!) They look upon We
    As a quite impossible They!

All good people agree,
    And all good people say,
All nice people, like Us, are We
    And every one else is They:
But if you cross over the sea,
    Instead of over the way,
You may end by (think of it!) Looking on We
    As only a sort of They!

William Butler Yeats (1865 – 1939)

A Dream of Death[1]

I dreamed that one had died in a strange place
Near no accustomed hand,
And they had nailed the boards above her face,
The peasants of that land,
Wondering to lay her in that solitude,

---

[1] Form: Modified ballad, iambic pentameter alternating with iambic
trimeter, ABAB end rhymes.

And raised above her mound
A cross they had made out of two bits of wood,
And planted cypress round;
And left her to the indifferent stars above
Until I carved these words:
She was more beautiful than thy first love,
But now lies under boards.

Politics[1]

'In our time the destiny of man presents its meanings in
political terms.' -Thomas Mann

How can I, that girl standing there,
My attention fix
On Roman or on Russian
Or on Spanish politics?
Yet here's a traveled man that knows
What he talks about,
And there's a politician
That has both read and thought,
And maybe what they say is true
Of war and war's alarms,
But O that I were young again
And held her in my arms.

The Ballad of Father Gilligan[2]

The old priest Peter Gilligan
Was weary night and day;
For half his flock were in their beds,
Or under green sods lay.

Once, while he nodded on a chair,
At the moth-hour of eve,
Another poor man sent for him,
And he began to grieve.

---

[1] Form: Free verse.
[2] Form: Ballad—Vocabulary: moth-hour: time when moths begin flying
(twilight); mavrone: Irish expression of shock; fen: marsh.

'I have no rest, nor joy, nor peace,
For people die and die';
And after cried he, 'God forgive!
My body spake, not I!'

He knelt, and leaning on the chair
He prayed and fell asleep;
And the moth-hour went from the fields,
And stars began to peep.

They slowly into millions grew,
And leaves shook in the wind;
And God covered the world with shade,
And whispered to mankind.

Upon the time of sparrow-chirp
When the moths came once more.
The old priest Peter Gilligan
Stood upright on the floor.

'Mavrone, mavrone! The man has died
While I slept on the chair';
He roused his horse out of its sleep,
And rode with little care.

He rode now as he never rode,
By rocky lane and fen;
The sick man's wife opened the door:
'Father! You come again!'

'And is the poor man dead?' he cried.
'He died an hour ago.'
The old priest Peter Gilligan
In grief swayed to and fro.

'When you were gone, he turned and died
As merry as a bird.'
The old priest Peter Gilligan
He knelt him at that word.

'He Who hath made the night of stars
For souls who tire and bleed,
Sent one of His great angels down
To help me in my need.

'He Who is wrapped in purple robes,
With planets in His care,
Had pity on the least of things
Asleep upon a chair.'

The Indian upon God[1]

I passed along the water's edge below the humid trees,
My spirit rocked in evening light, the rushes round my knees,
My spirit rocked in sleep and sighs; and saw the moor-fowl
    pace
All dripping on a grassy slope, and saw them cease to chase
Each other round in circles, and heard the eldest speak:
Who holds the world between His bill and made us strong or
    weak
Is an undying moorfowl, and He lives beyond the sky.
The rains are from His dripping wing, the moonbeams from His
    eye.
I passed a little further on and heard a lotus talk:
Who made the world and ruleth it, He hangeth on a stalk,
For I am in His image made, and all this tinkling tide
Is but a sliding drop of rain between His petals wide.
A little way within the gloom a roebuck raised his eyes
Brimful of starlight, and he said: *The Stamper of the Skies,*
He is a gentle roebuck; for how else, I pray, could He
Conceive a thing so sad and soft, a gentle thing like me?
I passed a little further on and heard a peacock say:
Who made the grass and made the worms and made my
    feathers gay,
He is a monstrous peacock, and He waveth all the night
His languid tail above us, lit with myriad spots of light.

---

[1] Form: Ballad—Vocabulary: moor-fowl: marsh bird; lotus: a water plant; languid: lacking energy.

The Sad Shepherd[1]

There was a man whom Sorrow named his Friend,
And he, of his high comrade Sorrow dreaming,
Went walking with slow steps along the gleaming
And humming Sands, where windy surges wend:
And he called loudly to the stars to bend
From their pale thrones and comfort him, but they
Among themselves laugh on and sing alway:
And then the man whom Sorrow named his friend
Cried out, *Dim sea, hear my most piteous story!*
The sea swept on and cried her old cry still,
Rolling along in dreams from hill to hill.
He fled the persecution of her glory
And, in a far-off, gentle valley stopping,
Cried all his story to the dewdrops glistening.
But naught they heard, for they are always listening,
The dewdrops, for the sound of their own dropping.
And then the man whom Sorrow named his friend
Sought once again the shore, and found a shell,
And thought, *I will my heavy story tell*
Till my own words, re-echoing, shall send
Their sadness through a hollow, pearly heart;
And my own tale again for me shall sing,
And my own whispering words be comforting,
And lo! My ancient burden may depart.
Then he sang softly nigh the pearly rim;
But the sad dweller by the sea-ways lone
Changed all he sang to inarticulate moan
Among her wildering whirls, forgetting him.

---

[1] Form: Iambic pentameter, ABBA end rhymes—Vocabulary: wend: go;
wildering: wildering: bewildering—Notes: The lesson that people are not
interested in hearing your tales of woe is told through a series of
metaphors.

Shiki (Masaoka Tseunenori) (1867 – 1902)

By that fallen house[1]
Translated from the Japanese by Peter Beilenson

BY THAT FALLEN HOUSE
   THE PEAR-TREE STANDS
   FULL-BLOOMING . . .
AN ANCIENT BATTLE-SITE

Edgar Lee Masters (1868 – 1950)

Alexander Throckmorton[2]

In youth my wings were strong and tireless,
But I did not know the mountains.
In age I knew the mountains
But my weary wings could not follow my vision—
Genius is wisdom and youth.

Aner Clute[3]

Over and over they used to ask me,
While buying the wine or the beer,
In Peoria first, and later in Chicago,
Denver, Frisco, New York, wherever I lived,
How I happened to lead the life,
And what was the start of it.
Well, I told them a silk dress,
And a promise of marriage from a rich man—
(It was Lucius Atherton).
But that was not really it at all.
Suppose a boy steals an apple
From the tray at the grocery store,
And they all begin to call him a thief,
The editor, minister, judge, and all the people—
"A thief," "a thief," "a thief," wherever he goes.
And he can't get work, and he can't get bread

---

[1] Form: Haiku.
[2] Form: Free verse.
[3] Form: Free verse.

Without stealing it, why, the boy will steal.
It's the way the people regard the theft of the apple
That makes the boy what he is.

Conrad Siever[1]

Not in that wasted garden
Where bodies are drawn into grass
That feeds no flocks, and into evergreens
That bear no fruit—
There where along the shaded walks
Vain sighs are heard,
And vainer dreams are dreamed
Of close communion with departed souls—
But here under the apple tree
I loved and watched and pruned
With gnarled hands
In the long, long years;
Here under the roots of this northern-spy
To move in the chemic change and circle of life,
Into the soil and into the flesh of the tree,
And into the living epitaphs
Of redder apples!

Fiddler Jones[2]

The earth keeps some vibration going
There in your heart, and that is you.
And if the people find you can fiddle,
Why, fiddle you must, for all your life.
What do you see, a harvest of clover?
Or a meadow to walk through to the river?
The wind's in the corn; you rub your hands
For beeves hereafter ready for market;
Or else you hear the rustle of skirts
Like the girls when dancing at Little Grove.
To Cooney Potter a pillar of dust
Or whirling leaves meant ruinous drouth;

---

[1] Form: Free verse—Vocabulary: chemic: chemical.
[2] Form: Iambic tetrameter—Vocabulary: beeves: steer ready for slaughter; drouth: drought; till: plow.

They looked to me like Red-Head Sammy
Stepping it off, to "Toor-a-Loor."
How could I till my forty acres
Not to speak of getting more,
With a medley of horns, bassoons and piccolos
Stirred in my brain by crows and robins
And the creak of a wind-mill—only these?
And I never started to plow in my life
That some one did not stop in the road
And take me away to a dance or picnic.
I ended up with forty acres;
I ended up with a broken fiddle—
And a broken laugh, and a thousand memories,
And not a single regret.

Silas Dement[1]

It was moon-light, and the earth sparkled
With new-fallen frost.
It was midnight and not a soul abroad.
Out of the chimney of the court-house
A gray-hound of smoke leapt and chased
The northwest wind.
I carried a ladder to the landing of the stairs
And leaned it against the frame of the trap-door
In the ceiling of the portico,
And I crawled under the roof amid the rafters
And flung among the seasoned timbers
A lighted handful of oil-soaked waste.
Then I came down and slunk away.
In a little while the fire-bell rang—
Clang! Clang! Clang!
And the Spoon River ladder company
Came with a dozen buckets and began to pour water
On the glorious bon-fire, growing hotter,
Higher and brighter, till the walls fell in,
And the limestone columns where Lincoln stood

---

[1] Form: Free verse—Vocabulary: portico: Porch with pillars; Joliet: prison
in Joliet Illinois—Notes: Although this is the story of an arson, it's really
the story of the willingness of some to destroy the old for the new, and the
frequency with which the people trying to do this are punished.

Crashed like trees when the woodman fells them...
When I came back from Joliet
There was a new court house with a dome.
For I was punished like all who destroy
The past for the sake of the future.

Tom Beatty[1]

I was a lawyer like Harmon Whitney
Or Kinsey Keene or Garrison Standard,
For I tried the rights of property,
Although by lamp-light, for thirty years,
In that poker room in the opera house.
And I say to you that Life's a gambler
Head and shoulders above us all.
No mayor alive can close the house.
And if you lose, you can squeal as you will;
You'll not get back your money.
He makes the percentage hard to conquer;
He stacks the cards to catch your weakness
And not to meet your strength.
And he gives you seventy years to play:
For if you cannot win in seventy
You cannot win at all.
So, if you lose, get out of the room—
Get out of the room when your time is up.
It's mean to sit and fumble the cards,
And curse your losses, leaden-eyed,
Whining to try and try.

---

[1] Form: Free verse.

Roka (1868 – 1927)

Winter rain deepens[1]
Translated from the Japanese by Peter Beilenson

WINTER RAIN DEEPENS
   LICHENED LETTERS
   ON THE GRAVE . . .
AND MY OLD SADNESS

Edwin Arlington Robinson (1869 – 1935)

Amaryllis[2]

Once, when I wandered in the woods alone,
An old man tottered up to me and said,
"Come, friend, and see the grave that I have made
For Amaryllis." There was in the tone
Of his complaint such quaver and such moan
That I took pity on him and obeyed,
And long stood looking where his hands had laid
An ancient woman, shrunk to skin and bone.

Far out beyond the forest I could hear
The calling of loud progress, and the bold
Incessant scream of commerce ringing clear;
But though the trumpets of the world were glad,
It made me lonely and it made me sad
To think that Amaryllis had grown old.

An Old Story[3]

Strange that I did not know him then.
   That friend of mine!
I did not even show him then
   One friendly sign;

---

[1] Form: Haiku.
[2] Form: Sonnet.
[3] Form: Iambic, 4-2-4-2 pattern, ABAB end rhymes where A is exact word matches.

But cursed him for the ways he had
    To make me see
My envy of the praise he had
    For praising me.

I would have rid the earth of him
    Once, in my pride...
I never knew the worth of him
    Until he died.

Haunted House[1]

Here was a place where none would ever come
For shelter, save as we did from the rain.
We saw no ghost, yet once outside again
Each wondered why the other should be so dumb;
And ruin, and to our vision it was plain
Where thrift, outshivering fear, had let remain
Some chairs that were like skeletons of home.

There were no trackless footsteps on the floor
Above us, and there were no sounds elsewhere.
But there was more than sound; and there was more
Than just an axe that once was in the air
Between us and the chimney, long before
Our time. So townsmen said who found her there.

John Evereldown[2]

"Where are you going to-night, to-night,—
    Where are you going, John Evereldown?
There's never the sign of a star in sight,
    Nor a lamp that's nearer than Tilbury Town.
Why do you stare as a dead man might?
Where are you pointing away from the light?
And where are you going to-night, to-night,—
    Where are you going, John Evereldown?"

---

[1] Form: Iambic pentameter, irregular but frequent end rhymes.
[2] Form: Iambic tetrameter, ABABAAAB end rhymes—Vocabulary: league: 3 miles.

"Right through the forest, where none can see,
    There's where I'm going, to Tilbury Town.
The men are asleep,— or awake, may be,—
    But the women are calling John Evereldown.
Ever and ever they call for me,
And while they call can a man be free?
So right through the forest, where none can see,
    There's where I'm going, to Tilbury Town."

"But why are you going so late, so late,—
    Why are you going, John Evereldown?
Though the road be smooth and the path be straight,
    There are two long leagues to Tilbury Town.
Come in by the fire, old man, and wait!
Why do you chatter out there by the gate?
And why are you going so late, so late,—
    Why are you going, John Evereldown?"

"I follow the women wherever they call,—
    That's why I'm going to Tilbury Town.
God knows if I pray to be done with it all,
    But God is no friend to John Evereldown.
So the clouds may come and the rain may fall,
The shadows may creep and the dead men crawl,—
But I follow the women wherever they call,
    And that's why I'm going to Tilbury Town."

Karma[1]

Christmas was in the air and all was well
With him, but for a few confusing flaws
In divers of God's images. Because
A friend of his would neither buy nor sell,
Was he to answer for the axe that fell?
He pondered; and the reason for it was,
Partly, a slowly freezing Santa Claus
Upon the corner, with his beard and bell.

Acknowledging an improvident surprise,

---

[1] Form: Sonnet—Vocabulary: divers: diverse.

He magnified a fancy that he wished
The friend whom he had wrecked were here again.
Not sure of that, he found a compromise;
And from the fullness of his heart he fished
A dime for Jesus who had died for men.

Mr. Flood's Party[1]

Old Eben Flood, climbing alone one night
Over the hill between the town below
And the forsaken upland hermitage
That held as much as he should ever know
On earth again of home, paused warily.
The road was his with not a native near;
And Eben, having leisure, said aloud,
For no man else in Tilbury Town to hear:

"Well, Mr. Flood, we have the harvest moon
Again, and we may not have many more;
The bird is on the wing, the poet says,
And you and I have said it here before.
Drink to the bird." He raised up to the light
The jug that he had gone so far to fill,
And answered huskily: "Well, Mr. Flood,
Since you propose it, I believe I will."

Alone, as if enduring to the end
A valiant armor of scarred hopes outworn,
He stood there in the middle of the road
Like Roland's ghost winding a silent horn.
Below him, in the town among the trees,
Where friends of other days had honored him,
A phantom salutation of the dead
Rang thinly till old Eben's eyes were dim.

---

[1] Form: Iambic pentameter, xAxAxBxB end rhymes—Vocabulary:
hermitage: monastery; Roland: French hero killed in 778; Convivially:
festive—Notes: Although once popular, Eben has outlived his friends and is
now alone. Eben recognizes in the fragile nature of his jug the fragile
nature of "most things". But Eben goes on, until even the jug itself is
empty.

Then, as a mother lays her sleeping child
Down tenderly, fearing it may awake,
He set the jug down slowly at his feet
With trembling care, knowing that most things break;
And only when assured that on firm earth
It stood, as the uncertain lives of men
Assuredly did not, he paced away,
And with his hand extended paused again:

"Well, Mr. Flood, we have not met like this
In a long time; and many a change has come
To both of us, I fear, since last it was
We had a drop together. Welcome home!"
Convivially returning with himself,
Again he raised the jug up to the light;
And with an acquiescent quaver said:
"Well, Mr. Flood, if you insist, I might.

"Only a very little, Mr. Flood—
For auld lang syne. No more, sir; that will do."
So, for the time, apparently it did,
And Eben evidently thought so too;
For soon amid the silver loneliness
Of night he lifted up his voice and sang,
Secure, with only two moons listening,
Until the whole harmonious landscape rang—

"For auld lang syne." The weary throat gave out,
The last word wavered; and the song being done,
He raised again the jug regretfully
And shook his head, and was again alone.
There was not much that was ahead of him,
And there was nothing in the town below—
Where strangers would have shut the many doors
That many friends had opened long ago.

Reuben Bright[1]

Because he was a butcher and thereby
Did earn an honest living (and did right),
I would not have you think that Reuben Bright
Was any more a brute than you or I;
For when they told him that his wife must die,
He stared at them, and shook with grief and fright,
And cried like a great baby half that night,
And made the women cry to see him cry.

And after she was dead, and he had paid
The singers and the sexton and the rest,
He packed a lot of things that she had made
Most mournfully away in an old chest
Of hers, and put some chopped-up cedar boughs
In with them, and tore down the slaughter-house.

Richard Cory[2]

Whenever Richard Cory went down town,
We people on the pavement looked at him:
He was a gentleman from sole to crown,
Clean favored, and imperially slim.

And he was always quietly arrayed,
And he was always human when he talked;
But still he fluttered pulses when he said,
"Good-morning," and he glittered when he walked.

And he was rich—yes, richer than a king—
And admirably schooled in every grace;
In fine we thought that he was everything

---

[1] Form: Sonnet—Vocabulary: sexton: functionary of a church—Notes:
There is an obvious message about the tender heart beneath the rough
exterior, but notice that when he was happy at home he was able to
slaughter the animals, but he was not able to do so when he did not have a
happy home to return to after work. Perhaps he needed the happiness at
home to overcome the sadness of killing during the day in the
slaughterhouse.
[2] Form: Iambic pentameter, ABAB end rhymes—Vocabulary: sole: bottom
of his foot; crown: top of his head.

To make us wish that we were in his place.

So on we worked, and waited for the light,
And went without the meat, and cursed the bread;
And Richard Cory, one calm summer night,
Went home and put a bullet through his head.

Souvenir[1]

A vanished house that for an hour I knew
By some forgotten chance when I was young
Had once a glimmering window overhung
With honeysuckle wet with evening dew.
Along the path tall dusky dahlias grew,
And shadowy hydrangeas reached and swung
Ferociously; and over me, among
The moths and mysteries, a blurred bat flew.

Somewhere within there were dim presences
Of days that hovered and of years gone by.
I waited, and between their silences
There was an evanescent faded noise;
And though a child, I knew it was the voice
Of one whose occupation was to die.

Supremacy[2]

There is a drear and lonely tract of hell
From all the common gloom removed afar:
A flat, sad land it is, where shadows are,
Whose lorn estate my verse may never tell.
I walked among them and I knew them well:
Men I had slandered on life's little star
For churls and sluggards; and I knew the scar
Upon their brows of woe ineffable.

---

[1] Form: Sonnet—Vocabulary: evanescent: vanishing like vapor.
[2] Form: Sonnet—Vocabulary: drear: dreary; lorn: forlorn; churls: rude
boorish person; sluggard: lazy person; ineffable: indescribable—Notes:
Those he looked down upon in life were exalted over him in heaven.

But as I went majestic on my way,
Into the dark they vanished, one by one,
Till, with a shaft of God's eternal day,
The dream of all my glory was undone,—
And, with a fool's importunate dismay,
I heard the dead men singing in the sun.

The Dead Village[1]

Here there is death. But even here, they say,—
Here where the dull sun shines this afternoon
As desolate as ever the dead moon
Did glimmer on dead Sardis,—men were gay;
And there were little children here to play,
With small soft hands that once did keep in tune
The strings that stretch from heaven, till too soon
The change came, and the music passed away.

Now there is nothing but the ghosts of things,—
No life, no love, no children, and no men;
And over the forgotten place there clings
The strange and unrememberable light
That is in dreams. The music failed, and then
God frowned, and shut the village from His sight.

The Growth of "Lorraine"[2]

I.
While I stood listening, discreetly dumb,
Lorraine was having the last word with me:
"I know," she said, "I know it, but you see
Some creatures are born fortunate, and some
Are born to be found out and overcome—
Born to be slaves, to let the rest go free;
And if I'm one of them (and I must be)
You may as well forget me and go home.

---

[1] Form: Sonnet—Vocabulary: Sardis: Important city in Asia Minor about 600 BC, destroyed by Tamerlane in 1402.
[2] Form: Iambic pentameter, ABBA end rhymes—Vocabulary: Impenitent: without remorse.

"You tell me not to say these things, I know,
But I should never try to be content:
I've gone too far; the life would be too slow.
Some could have done it—some girls have the stuff;
But I can't do it—I don't know enough.
I'm going to the devil." And she went.

II
I did not half believe her when she said
That I should never hear from her again;
Nor when I found a letter from Lorraine,
Was I surprised or grieved at what i read:
"Dear friend, when you find this, I shall be dead.
You are too far away to make me stop.
They say that one drop—think of it, one drop!—
Will be enough; but I'll take five instead.

"You do not frown because I call you friend;
For I would have you glad that I still keep
Your memory, and even at the end—
Impenitent, sick, shattered—cannot curse
The love that flings, for better or for worse,
This worn-out, cast-out flesh of mine to sleep."

The Mill[1]

The miller's wife had waited long,
   The tea was cold, the fire was dead;
And there might yet be nothing wrong
   In how he went and what he said:
"There are no millers any more,"
   Was all that she had heard him say;
And he had lingered at the door
   So long that it seemed yesterday.

Sick with a fear that had no form
   She knew that she was there at last;
And in the mill there was a warm
   And mealy fragrance of the past.
What else there was would only seem
   To say again what he had meant;
And what was hanging from a beam
   Would not have heeded where she went.

And if she thought it followed her,
   She may have reasoned in the dark
That one way of the few there were
   Would hide her and would leave no mark:
Black water, smooth above the weir
   Like starry velvet in the night,
Though ruffled once, would soon appear
   The same as ever to the sight.

[1] Form: Iambic tetrameter, ABAB end rhymes—Vocabulary: weir: a dam to
divert water for the mill—Notes: The end of mills in the town, and the
double suicide of the miller and his wife.

The Pity of the Leaves[1]

Vengeful across the cold November moors,
Loud with ancestral shame there came the bleak
Sad wind that shrieked, and answered with a shriek,
Reverberant through lonely corridors.
The old man heard it; and he heard, perforce,
Words out of lips that were no more to speak—
Words of the past that shook the old man's cheek
Like dead, remembered footsteps on old floors.

And then there were the leaves that plagued him so!
The brown, thin leaves that on the stones outside
Skipped with a freezing whisper. Now and then
They stopped, and stayed there—just to let him know
How dead they were; but if the old man cried,
They fluttered off like withered souls of men.

The Sheaves[2]

Where long the shadows of the wind had rolled,
Green wheat was yielding to the change assigned;
And as by some vast magic undivined
The world was turning slowly into gold.
Like nothing that was ever bought or sold
It waited there, the body and mind;
And with a mighty meaning of a kind
That tells the more the more it is not told.

So in a land where all days are not fair,
Fair days went on till on another day
A thousand golden sheaves were lying there,
Shining and still, but not for long to stay—
As if a thousand girls with golden hair
Might rise from where they slept and go away.

---

[1] Form: Sonnet—Vocabulary: perforce: by necessity—Notes: The man is
haunted by memories of all of those he knows who are dead, with even the
sound of the leaves sounding like those long gone acquaintances.
[2] Form: Sonnet—Vocabulary: sheaves: bundle of stalks from grain.

270

The Tavern[1]

Whenever I go by there nowadays
And look at the rank weeds and the strange grass,
The torn blue curtains and the broken glass,
I seem to be afraid of the old place;
And something stiffens up and down my face,
For all the world as if I saw the ghost
Of old Ham Amory, the murdered host,
With his dead eyes turned on me all aglaze.

The Tavern has a story, but no man
Can tell us what it is. We only know
That once long after midnight, years ago,
A stranger galloped up from Tilbury Town,
Who brushed, and scared, and all but overran
That skirt-crazed reprobate, John Evereldown.

Stephen Crane (1871 – 1900)

In the desert[2]

In the desert
I saw a creature, naked, bestial,
Who, squatting upon the ground,
Held his heart in his hands,
And ate of it.
I said, "Is it good, friend?"
"It is bitter – bitter", he answered;
"But I like it
Because it is bitter,
And because it is my heart."

---

[1] Form: Sonnet—Vocabulary: rank: growing profusely; reprobate:
predestined to damnation.
[2] Form: Free verse.

W.H. Davies (1871 – 1940)

Leisure[1]

What is this life if, full of care,
We have no time to stand and stare?

No time to stand beneath the boughs,
And stare as long as sheep and cows:

No time to see, when woods we pass,
Where squirrels hide their nuts in grass:

No time to see, in broad daylight,
Streams full of stars, like skies at night:

No time to turn at Beauty's glance,
And watch her feet, how they can dance:

No time to wait till her mouth can
Enrich that smile her eyes began?

A poor life this if, full of care,
We have no time to stand and stare.

Robert Frost (1874 – 1963)

"Out, Out—"[2]

The buzz-saw snarled and rattled in the yard
And made dust and dropped stove-length sticks of wood,
Sweet-scented stuff when the breeze drew across it.
And from there those that lifted eyes could count
Five mountain ranges one behind the other
Under the sunset far into Vermont.
And the saw snarled and rattled, snarled and rattled,

---

[1] Form: Iambic tetrameter, AABB end rhymes.
[2] Form: blank verse (unrhymed iambic pentameter)—Notes:
Understatement at the end is used to underscore the horror of the scene.
Compare the reaction of the boy here with the reaction of the construction
worker in Mark Turpin's poem "Poem".

As it ran light, or had to bear a load.
And nothing happened: day was all but done.
Call it a day, I wish they might have said
To please the boy by giving him the half hour
That a boy counts so much when saved from work.
His sister stood beside them in her apron
To tell them 'Supper'. At the word, the saw,
As if to prove saws knew what supper meant,
Leaped out at the boy's hand, or seemed to leap—
He must have given the hand. However it was,
Neither refused the meeting. But the hand!
The boy's first outcry was a rueful laugh.
As he swung toward them holding up the hand
Half in appeal, but half as if to keep
The life from spilling. Then the boy saw all—
Since he was old enough to know, big boy
Doing a man's work, though a child at heart—
He saw all spoiled. 'Don't let him cut my hand off
The doctor, when he comes. Don't let him, sister!'
So. But the hand was gone already.
The doctor put him in the dark of ether.
He lay and puffed his lips out with his breath.
And then—the watcher at his pulse took fright.
No one believed. They listened at his heart.
Little—less—nothing!—and that ended it.
No more to build on there. And they, since they
Were not the one dead, turned to their affairs.

A Brook in the City[1]

The farm house lingers, though averse to square
With the new city street it has to wear
A number in. But what about the brook
That held the house as in an elbow-crook?
I ask as one who knew the brook, its strength
And impulse, having dipped a finger length
And made it leap my knuckle, having tossed
A flower to try its currents where they crossed.

---

[1] Form: Iambic pentameter, AABBCC . . . End rhymes—Vocabulary:
square: conform.

The meadow grass could be cemented down
From growing under pavements of a town;
The apple trees be sent to hearth-stone flame.
Is water wood to serve a brook the same?
How else dispose of an immortal force
No longer needed? Staunch it at its source
With cinder loads dumped down? The brook was thrown
Deep in a sewer dungeon under stone
In fetid darkness still to live and run—
And all for nothing it had ever done
Except forget to go in fear perhaps.
No one would know except for ancient maps
That such a brook ran water. But I wonder
If from its being kept forever under
The thoughts may not have risen that so keep
This new-built city from both work and sleep.

A Dream Pang[1]

I had withdrawn in forest, and my song
Was swallowed up in leaves that blew alway;
And to the forest edge you came one day
(This was my dream) and looked and pondered long,
But did not enter, though the wish was strong:
You shook your pensive head as who should say,
'I dare not—too far in his footsteps stray—
He must seek me would he undo the wrong.

Not far, but near, I stood and saw it all
Behind low boughs the trees let down outside;
And the sweet pang it cost me not to call
And tell you that I saw does still abide.
But 'tis not true that thus I dwelt aloof,
For the wood wakes, and you are here for proof.

---

[1] Form: Sonnet—Notes: The narrator withdraws, metaphorically to a forest, after a fight. His wife is not able to enter after him, and he sees her as if at a distant.

A Fountain, a Bottle, a Donkey's Ears, and Some Books[1]

Old Davis owned a solid mica mountain
In Dalton that would someday make his fortune.
There'd been some Boston people out to see it:
And experts said that deep down in the mountain
The mica sheets were big as plate-glass windows.
He'd like to take me there and show it to me.

"I'll tell you what you show me. You remember
You said you knew the place where once, on Kinsman,
The early Mormons made a settlement
And built a stone baptismal font outdoors—
But Smith, or someone, called them off the mountain
To go West to a worse fight with the desert.
You said you'd seen the stone baptismal font.
Well, take me there."

     "Someday I will."

     "Today."

"Huh, that old bathtub, what is that to see?
Let's talk about it."

     "Let's go see the place."

'To shut you up i'll tell you what i'll do:
I'll find that fountain if it takes all summer,
And both of our united strengths, to do it."

"You've lost it, then?"

     "Not so but I can find it.
No doubt it's grown up some to woods around it.
The mountain may have shifted since I saw it
In eighty-five."

     "As long ago as that?"

---

[1] Form: Blank verse—Vocabulary: mica: a mineral.

"If I remember rightly, it had sprung
A leak and emptied then. And forty years
Can do a good deal to bad masonry.
You won't see any Mormon swimming in it.
But you have said it, and we're off to find it.
Old as I am, I'm going to let myself
Be dragged by you all over everywhere——"
"I thought you were a guide.”

        "I *am* a guide,
And that's why I can't decently refuse you."

We made a day of it out of the world,
Ascending to descend to reascend.
The old man seriously took his bearings,
And spoke his doubts in every open place.

We came out on a look-off where we faced
A cliff, and on the cliff a bottle painted,
Or stained by vegetation from above,
A likeness to surprise the thrilly tourist.

"Well, if I haven't brought you to the fountain,
At least i've brought you to the famous Bottle."

"I won't accept the substitute. It's empty.”

"So's everything."

        "I want my fountain."

"I guess you'd find the fountain just as empty.
And anyway this tells me where I am.”

"Hadn't you long suspected where you were?"

"You mean miles from that Mormon settlement?
Look here, you treat your guide with due respect
If you don't want to spend the night outdoors.
I vow we must be near the place from where

The two converging slides, the avalanches,
On Marshall, look like donkey's ears.
We may as well see that and save the day."

"Don't donkey's ears suggest we shake our own?"

"For God's sake, aren't you fond of viewing nature?
You don't like nature. All you like is books.
What signify a donkey's ears and bottle,
However natural? Give you your books!
Well then, right here is where I show you books.
Come straight down off this mountain just as fast
As we can fall and keep a-bouncing on our feet.
It's hell for knees unless done hell-for-leather."

Be ready, I thought, for almost anything.

We struck a road I didn't recognize,
But welcomed for the chance to lave my shoes
In dust once more. We followed this a mile,
Perhaps, to where it ended at a house
I didn't know was there. It was the kind
To bring me to for broad-board paneling.
I never saw so good a house deserted.

"Excuse me if I ask you in a window
That happens to be broken, Davis said.
"The outside doors as yet have held against us.
I want to introduce you to the people
Who used to live here. They were Robinsons.
You must have heard of Clara Robinson,
The poetess who wrote the book of verses
And had it published. It was all about
The posies on her inner windowsill,
And the birds on her outer windowsill,
And how she tended both, or had them tended:
She never tended anything herself.
She was 'shut in' for life. She lived her whole
Life long in bed, and wrote her things in bed.
I'll show you how she had her sills extended
To entertain the birds and hold the flowers.

Our business first's up attic with her books."

We trod uncomfortably on crunching glass
Through a house stripped of everything
Except, it seemed, the poetess's poems.
Books, I should say!—-if books are what is needed.
A whole edition in a packing case
That, overflowing like a horn of plenty,
Or like the poetess's heart of love,
Had spilled them near the window, toward the light
Where driven rain had wet and swollen them.
Enough to stock a village library—
Unfortunately all of one kind, though.
They had been brought home from some publisher
And taken thus into the family.
Boys and bad hunters had known what to do
With stone and lead to unprotected glass:
Shatter it inward on the unswept floors.
How had the tender verse escaped their outrage?
By being invisible for what it was,
Or else by some remoteness that defied them
To find out what to do to hurt a poem.
Yet oh! The tempting flatness of a book,
To send it sailing out the attic window
Till it caught wind and, opening out its covers,
Tried to improve on sailing like a tile
By flying like a bird (silent in flight,
But all the burden of its body song),
Only to tumble like a stricken bird,
And lie in stones and bushes unretrieved.
Books were not thrown irreverently about.
They simply lay where someone now and then,
Having tried one, had dropped it at his feet
And left it lying where it fell rejected.
Here were all those the poetess's life
Had been too short to sell or give away.

"Take one," Old Davis bade me graciously.

"Why not take two or three?"

"Take all you want.
Good-looking books like that." He picked one fresh
In virgin wrapper from deep in the box,
And stroked it with a horny-handed kindness.
He read in one and I read in another,
Both either looking for or finding something.

The attic wasps went missing by like bullets.

I was soon satisfied for the time being.

All the way home I kept remembering
The small book in my pocket. It was there.
The poetess had sighed, I knew, in heaven
At having eased her heart of one more copy—
Legitimately. My demand upon her,
Though slight, was a demand. She felt the tug.
In time she would be rid of all her books.

A Late Walk[1]

When I go up through the mowing field,
    The headless aftermath,
Smooth-laid like thatch with the heavy dew,
    Half closes the garden path.

And when I come to the garden ground,
    The whir of sober birds
Up from the tangle of withered weeds
    Is sadder than any words

A tree beside the wall stands bare,
    But a leaf that lingered brown,
Disturbed, I doubt not, by my thought,
    Comes softly rattling down.

I end not far from my going forth
    By picking the faded blue

---

[1] Form: Ballad—Notes: This can be read as a metaphorical look at a walk
through the autumn of the narrator's life.

Of the last remaining aster flower
　To carry again to you.

After Apple-Picking[1]

My long two-pointed ladder's sticking through a tree
Toward heaven still,
And there's a barrel that I didn't fill
Beside it, and there may be two or three
Apples I didn't pick upon some bough.
But I am done with apple-picking now.
Essence of winter sleep is on the night,
The scent of apples: I am drowsing off.
I cannot rub the strangeness from my sight
I got from looking through a pane of glass
I skimmed this morning from the drinking trough
And held against the world of hoary grass.
It melted, and I let it fall and break.
But I was well
Upon my way to sleep before it fell,
And I could tell
What form my dreaming was about to take.
Magnified apples appear and disappear,
Stem end and blossom end,
And every fleck of russet showing clear.
My instep arch not only keeps the ache,
It keeps the pressure of a ladder-round.
I feel the ladder sway as the boughs bend.
And I keep hearing from the cellar bin
The rumbling sound
Of load on load of apples coming in.
For I have had too much
Of apple-picking: I am overtired
Of the great harvest I myself desired.
There were ten thousand thousand fruit to touch,
Cherish in hand, lift down, and not let fall.
For all

---

[1] Form: Mostly iambic pentameter; irregular but frequent end rhymes—
Vocabulary: hoary: white (with dew in this case); russet: reddish brown
type of apple; —Notes: The poem may also be read as a metaphorical
description of someone at the end of a long, productive life.

That struck the earth,
No matter if not bruised or spiked with stubble,
Went surely to the cider-apple heap
As of no worth.
One can see what will trouble
This sleep of mine, whatever sleep it is.
Were he not gone,
The woodchuck could say whether it's like his
Long sleep, as I describe its coming on,
Or just some human sleep.

An Old Man's Winter Night[1]

All out of doors looked darkly in at him
Through the thin frost, almost in separate stars,
That gathers on the pane in empty rooms.
What kept his eyes from giving back the gaze
Was the lamp tilted near them in his hand.
What kept him from remembering what it was
That brought him to that creaking room was age.
He stood with barrels round him—at a loss.
And having scared the cellar under him
In clomping there, he scared it once again
In clomping off;—and scared the outer night,
Which has its sounds, familiar, like the roar
Of trees and crack of branches, common things,
But nothing so like beating on a box.
A light he was to no one but himself
Where now he sat, concerned with he knew what,
A quiet light, and then not even that.
He consigned to the moon, such as she was,
So late-arising, to the broken moon
As better than the sun in any case
For such a charge, his snow upon the roof,
His icicles along the wall to keep;
And slept. The log that shifted with a jolt
Once in the stove, disturbed him and he shifted,
And eased his heavy breathing, but still slept.

---

[1] Form: Blank verse (unrhymed iambic pentameter)—Vocabulary: pane: windowpane, but perhaps a double meaning; consigned: entrusted.

One aged man—one man—can't keep a house,
A farm, a countryside, or if he can,
It's thus he does it of a winter night.

Birches[1]

When I see birches bend to left and right
Across the lines of straighter darker trees,
I like to think some boy's been swinging them.
But swinging doesn't bend them down to stay
As ice-storms do. Often you must have seen them
Loaded with ice a sunny winter morning
After a rain. They click upon themselves
As the breeze rises, and turn many-colored
As the stir cracks and crazes their enamel.
Soon the sun's warmth makes them shed crystal shells
Shattering and avalanching on the snow-crust—
Such heaps of broken glass to sweep away
You'd think the inner dome of heaven had fallen.
They are dragged to the withered bracken by the load,
And they seem not to break; though once they are bowed
So low for long, they never right themselves:
You may see their trunks arching in the woods
Years afterwards, trailing their leaves on the ground
Like girls on hands and knees that throw their hair
Before them over their heads to dry in the sun.
But I was going to say when Truth broke in
With all her matter-of-fact about the ice-storm
I should prefer to have some boy bend them
As he went out and in to fetch the cows—
Some boy too far from town to learn baseball,
Whose only play was what he found himself,
Summer or winter, and could play alone.
One by one he subdued his father's trees
By riding them down over and over again
Until he took the stiffness out of them,
And not one but hung limp, not one was left
For him to conquer. He learned all there was
To learn about not launching out too soon

---

[1] Form: Blank verse—Vocabulary: bracken: a weedy fern.

And so not carrying the tree away
Clear to the ground. He always kept his poise
To the top branches, climbing carefully
With the same pains you use to fill a cup
Up to the brim, and even above the brim.
Then he flung outward, feet first, with a swish,
Kicking his way down through the air to the ground.
So was I once myself a swinger of birches.
And so I dream of going back to be.
It's when I'm weary of considerations,
And life is too much like a pathless wood
Where your face burns and tickles with the cobwebs
Broken across it, and one eye is weeping
From a twig's having lashed across it open.
I'd like to get away from earth awhile
And then come back to it and begin over.
May no fate willfully misunderstand me
And half grant what I wish and snatch me away
Not to return. Earth's the right place for love:
I don't know where it's likely to go better.
I'd like to go by climbing a birch tree,
And climb black branches up a snow-white trunk
Toward heaven, till the tree could bear no more,
But dipped its top and set me down again.
That would be good both going and coming back.
One could do worse than be a swinger of birches.

Death of the Hired Man[1]

Mary sat musing on the lamp-flame at the table
Waiting for Warren. When she heard his step,
She ran on tip-toe down the darkened passage
To meet him in the doorway with the news
And put him on his guard. "Silas is back."
She pushed him outward with her through the door
And shut it after her. "Be kind," she said.
She took the market things from Warren's arms
And set them on the porch, then drew him down

---

[1] Form: Mostly unrhymed iambic pentameter—Vocabulary: piqued: a
feeling of wounded pride.

To sit beside her on the wooden steps.

"When was I ever anything but kind to him?
But I'll not have the fellow back," he said.
"I told him so last haying, didn't I?
'If he left then,' I said, 'that ended it.'
What good is he? Who else will harbor him
At his age for the little he can do?
What help he is there's no depending on.
Off he goes always when I need him most.
'He thinks he ought to earn a little pay,
Enough at least to buy tobacco with,
So he won't have to beg and be beholden.'
'All right,' I say, 'I can't afford to pay
Any fixed wages, though I wish I could.'
'Someone else can.' 'Then someone else will have to.'
I shouldn't mind his bettering himself
If that was what it was. You can be certain,
When he begins like that, there's someone at him
Trying to coax him off with pocket-money,—
In haying time, when any help is scarce.
In winter he comes back to us. I'm done."

"Sh! Not so loud: he'll hear you," Mary said.

"I want him to: he'll have to soon or late."

"He's worn out. He's asleep beside the stove.
When I came up from Rowe's I found him here,
Huddled against the barn-door fast asleep,
A miserable sight, and frightening, too—
You needn't smile—I didn't recognize him—
I wasn't looking for him—and he's changed.
Wait till you see."

            "Where did you say he'd been?"

"He didn't say. I dragged him to the house,
And gave him tea and tried to make him smoke.
I tried to make him talk about his travels.
Nothing would do: he just kept nodding off."

"What did he say? Did he say anything?"

"But little."

      "Anything? Mary, confess
He said he'd come to ditch the meadow for me."

"Warren!"

     "But did he? I just want to know."

"Of course he did. What would you have him say?
Surely you wouldn't grudge the poor old man
Some humble way to save his self-respect.
He added, if you really care to know,
He meant to clear the upper pasture, too.
That sounds like something you have heard before?
Warren, I wish you could have heard the way
He jumbled everything. I stopped to look
Two or three times—he made me feel so queer—
To see if he was talking in his sleep.
He ran on Harold Wilson—you remember—
The boy you had in haying four years since.
He's finished school, and teaching in his college.
Silas declares you'll have to get him back.
He says they two will make a team for work:
Between them they will lay this farm as smooth!
The way he mixed that in with other things.
He thinks young Wilson a likely lad, though daft
On education—you know how they fought
All through July under the blazing sun,
Silas up on the cart to build the load,
Harold along beside to pitch it on."

"Yes, I took care to keep well out of earshot."

"Well, those days trouble Silas like a dream.
You wouldn't think they would. How some things linger!
Harold's young college boy's assurance piqued him.
After so many years he still keeps finding

285

Good arguments he sees he might have used.
I sympathize. I know just how it feels
To think of the right thing to say too late.
Harold's associated in his mind with Latin.
He asked me what I thought of Harold's saying
He studied Latin like the violin
Because he liked it—that an argument!
He said he couldn't make the boy believe
He could find water with a hazel prong—
Which showed how much good school had ever done him.
He wanted to go over that. But most of all
He thinks if he could have another chance
To teach him how to build a load of hay——"

"I know, that's Silas' one accomplishment.
He bundles every forkful in its place,
And tags and numbers it for future reference,
So he can find and easily dislodge it
In the unloading. Silas does that well.
He takes it out in bunches like big birds' nests.
You never see him standing on the hay
He's trying to lift, straining to lift himself."

"He thinks if he could teach him that, he'd be
Some good perhaps to someone in the world.
He hates to see a boy the fool of books.
Poor Silas, so concerned for other folk,
And nothing to look backward to with pride,
And nothing to look forward to with hope,
So now and never any different."

Part of a moon was falling down the west,
Dragging the whole sky with it to the hills.
Its light poured softly in her lap. She saw
And spread her apron to it. She put out her hand
Among the harp-like morning-glory strings,
Taut with the dew from garden bed to eaves,
As if she played unheard the tenderness
That wrought on him beside her in the night.
"Warren," she said, "he has come home to die:
You needn't be afraid he'll leave you this time."

"Home," he mocked gently.

        "Yes, what else but home?
It all depends on what you mean by home.
Of course he's nothing to us, any more
Than was the hound that came a stranger to us
Out of the woods, worn out upon the trail."

"Home is the place where, when you have to go there,
They have to take you in."

        "I should have called it
Something you somehow haven't to deserve."

Warren leaned out and took a step or two,
Picked up a little stick, and brought it back
And broke it in his hand and tossed it by.
"Silas has better claim on us you think
Than on his brother? Thirteen little miles
As the road winds would bring him to his door.
Silas has walked that far no doubt to-day.
Why didn't he go there? His brother's rich,
A somebody—director in the bank."

"He never told us that."

        "We know it though."

"I think his brother ought to help, of course.
I'll see to that if there is need. He ought of right
To take him in, and might be willing to—
He may be better than appearances.
But have some pity on Silas. Do you think
If he'd had any pride in claiming kin
Or anything he looked for from his brother,
He'd keep so still about him all this time?"

"I wonder what's between them."

        "I can tell you.

287

Silas is what he is—we wouldn't mind him—
But just the kind that kinsfolk can't abide.
He never did a thing so very bad.
He don't know why he isn't quite as good
As anybody, worthless though he is.
He won't be made ashamed to please his brother."

"*I* can't think Si ever hurt anyone."

"No, but he hurt my heart the way he lay
And rolled his old head on that sharp-edged chair-back.
He wouldn't let me put him on the lounge.
You must go in and see what you can do.
I made the bed up for him there to-night.
You'll be surprised at him—how much he's broken.
His working days are done; I'm sure of it."

"I'd not be in a hurry to say that."

"I haven't been. Go, look, see for yourself.
But, Warren, please remember how it is:
He's come to help you ditch the meadow.
He has a plan. You mustn't laugh at him.
He may not speak of it, and then he may.
I'll sit and see if that small sailing cloud
Will hit or miss the moon."

    It hit the moon.
Then there were three there, making a dim row,
The moon, the little silver cloud, and she.

Warren returned—too soon, it seemed to her,
Slipped to her side, caught up her hand and waited.

"Warren," she questioned.

    "Dead," was all he answered.

Fire and Ice[1]

Some say the world will end in fire;
Some say in ice.
From what I've tasted of desire
I hold with those who favor fire.
But if it had to perish twice,
I think I know enough of hate
To know that for destruction ice
Is also great
And would suffice.

For Once, Then, Something[2]

Others taught me with having knelt at well-curbs
Always wrong to the light, so never seeing
Deeper down in the well than where the water
Gives me back in a shining surface picture
Me myself in the summer heaven godlike
Looking out of a wreath of fern and cloud puffs.
Once, when trying with chin against a well-curb,
I discerned, as I thought, beyond the picture,
Through the picture, a something white, uncertain,
Something more of the depths—and then I lost it.
Water came to rebuke the too clear water.
One drop fell from a fern, and lo, a ripple
Shook whatever it was lay there at bottom,
Blurred it, blotted it out. What was that whiteness?
Truth? A pebble of quartz? For once, then, something.

---

[1] Form: Mostly iambic tetrameter, irregular but frequent end rhymes.
[2] Form: Iambic pentameter but with an unusually large number of trochees.

Good-by and Keep Cold[1]

This saying good-by on the edge of the dark
And the cold to an orchard so young in the bark
Reminds me of all that can happen to harm
An orchard away at the end of the farm
All winter, cut off by a hill from the house.
I don't want it girdled by rabbit and mouse,
I don't want it dreamily nibbled for browse
By deer, and I don't want it budded by grouse.
(If certain it wouldn't be idle to call
I'd summon grouse, rabbit, and deer to the wall
And warn them away with a stick for a gun.)
I don't want it stirred by the heat of the sun.
(We made it secure against being, I hope,
By setting it out on a northerly slope.)
No orchard's the worse for the wintriest storm;
But one thing about it, it mustn't get warm.
'How often already you've had to be told,
Keep cold, young orchard. Good-by and keep cold.
Dread fifty above more than fifty below.'
I have to be gone for a season or so.
My business awhile is with different trees,
Less carefully nurtured, less fruitful than these,
And such as is done to their wood with an ax—
Maples and birches and tamaracks.
I wish I could promise to lie in the night
And think of an orchard's arboreal plight
When slowly (and nobody comes with a light)
Its heart sinks lower under the sod.
But something has to be left to God.

---

[1] Form: Anapestic tetrameter, AABB end rhymes—Vocabulary: girdled:
bark eaten off in a ring; budded: new buds eaten; grouse: chicken-like bird;
tamaracks: short needled tree; arboreal: relating to trees—Notes: There is
an underlying message of needing to trust in faith after you have done
everything you can to protect or prepare something (someone) that you
love.

Home Burial[1]

He saw her from the bottom of the stairs
Before she saw him. She was starting down,
Looking back over her shoulder at some fear.
She took a doubtful step and then undid it
To raise herself and look again. He spoke
Advancing toward her: 'What is it you see
From up there always—for I want to know.'
She turned and sank upon her skirts at that,
And her face changed from terrified to dull.
He said to gain time: 'What is it you see,'
Mounting until she cowered under him.
'I will find out now—you must tell me, dear.'
She, in her place, refused him any help
With the least stiffening of her neck and silence.
She let him look, sure that he wouldn't see,
Blind creature; and awhile he didn't see.
But at last he murmured, 'Oh,' and again, 'Oh.'

'What is it—what?' she said.

        'Just that I see.'

'You don't,' she challenged. 'Tell me what it is.'

'The wonder is I didn't see at once.
I never noticed it from here before.
I must be wonted to it—that's the reason.
The little graveyard where my people are!
So small the window frames the whole of it.
Not so much larger than a bedroom, is it?
There are three stones of slate and one of marble,
Broad-shouldered little slabs there in the sunlight
On the side hill. We haven't to mind those.
But I understand: it is not the stones,
But the child's mound—'

---

[1] Form: Blank verse (unrhymed iambic pentameter)—Vocabulary: wonted: accustomed.

291

'Don't, don't, don't, don't,' she cried.

She withdrew shrinking from beneath his arm
That rested on the banister, and slid downstairs;
And turned on him with such a daunting look,
He said twice over before he knew himself:
'Can't a man speak of his own child he's lost?'

'Not you! Oh, where's my hat? Oh, I don't need it!
I must get out of here. I must get air.
I don't know rightly whether any man can.'

'Amy! Don't go to someone else this time.
Listen to me. I won't come down the stairs.'
He sat and fixed his chin between his fists.
'There's something I should like to ask you, dear.'

'You don't know how to ask it.'

'Help me, then.'

Her fingers moved the latch for all reply.

'My words are nearly always an offense.
I don't know how to speak of anything
So as to please you. But I might be taught
I should suppose. I can't say I see how.
A man must partly give up being a man
With women-folk. We could have some arrangement
By which I'd bind myself to keep hands off
Anything special you're a-mind to name.
Though I don't like such things 'twixt those that love.
Two that don't love can't live together without them.
But two that do can't live together with them.'
She moved the latch a little. 'Don't—don't go.
Don't carry it to someone else this time.
Tell me about it if it's something human.
Let me into your grief. I'm not so much
Unlike other folks as your standing there
Apart would make me out. Give me my chance.
I do think, though, you overdo it a little.

What was it brought you up to think it the thing
To take your mother—loss of a first child
So inconsolably—in the face of love.
You'd think his memory might be satisfied—'

'There you go sneering now!'

      'I'm not, I'm not!
You make me angry. I'll come down to you.
God, what a woman! And it's come to this,
A man can't speak of his own child that's dead.'

'You can't because you don't know how to speak.
If you had any feelings, you that dug
With your own hand—how could you?—his little grave;
I saw you from that very window there,
Making the gravel leap and leap in air,
Leap up, like that, like that, and land so lightly
And roll back down the mound beside the hole.
I thought, Who is that man? I didn't know you.
And I crept down the stairs and up the stairs
To look again, and still your spade kept lifting.
Then you came in. I heard your rumbling voice
Out in the kitchen, and I don't know why,
But I went near to see with my own eyes.
You could sit there with the stains on your shoes
Of the fresh earth from your own baby's grave
And talk about your everyday concerns.
You had stood the spade up against the wall
Outside there in the entry, for I saw it.'

'I shall laugh the worst laugh I ever laughed.
I'm cursed. God, if I don't believe I'm cursed.'

'I can repeat the very words you were saying.
"Three foggy mornings and one rainy day
Will rot the best birch fence a man can build."
Think of it, talk like that at such a time!
What had how long it takes a birch to rot
To do with what was in the darkened parlor.
You *couldn't* care! The nearest friends can go

With anyone to death, comes so far short
They might as well not try to go at all.
No, from the time when one is sick to death,
One is alone, and he dies more alone.
Friends make pretense of following to the grave,
But before one is in it, their minds are turned
And making the best of their way back to life
And living people, and things they understand.
But the world's evil. I won't have grief so
If I can change it. Oh, I won't, I won't!'

'There, you have said it all and you feel better.
You won't go now. You're crying. Close the door.
The heart's gone out of it: why keep it up.
Amy! There's someone coming down the road!'

'*You*—oh, you think the talk is all. I must go—
Somewhere out of this house. How can I make you—'

'If—you—do! 'She was opening the door wider.
'Where do you mean to go? First tell me that.
I'll follow and bring you back by force. I *will!*—'

In a Disused Graveyard[1]

The living come with grassy tread
To read the gravestones on the hill;
The graveyard draws the living still,
But never anymore the dead.

The verses in it say and say:
"The ones who living come today
To read the stones and go away
Tomorrow dead will come to stay."

So sure of death the marbles rhyme,
Yet can't help marking all the time
How no one dead will seem to come.
What is it men are shrinking from?

---

[1] Form: Iambic tetrameter, irregular but frequent end rhymes.

It would be easy to be clever
And tell the stones: Men hate to die
And have stopped dying now forever.
I think they would believe the lie.

Into My Own[1]

One of my wishes is that those dark trees,
So old and firm they scarcely show the breeze,
Were not, as 'twere, the merest mask of gloom,
But stretched away unto the edge of doom.

I should not be withheld but that some day
Into their vastness I should steal away,
Fearless of ever finding open land,
Or highway where the slow wheel pours the sand.

I do not see why I should e'er turn back,
Or those should not set forth upon my track
To overtake me, who should miss me here
And long to know if still I held them dear.

They would not find me changed from him they knew—
Only more sure of all I thought was true.

Mending Wall[2]

Something there is that doesn't love a wall,
That sends the frozen-ground-swell under it,
And spills the upper boulders in the sun;
And makes gaps even two can pass abreast.
The work of hunters is another thing:

---

[1] Form: Sonnet.
[2] Form: blank verse (unrhymed iambic pentameter)—Notes: This poem is complex in subtle ways. First, it's about the annual rite of coming together with a neighbor to mend a stone fence. Then there's the narrator's insistence that the walls between neighbors are, at least in this case, unnecessary and in all cases counter to nature's inclination, with the neighbor insisting that "good fences make good neighbors." But then, in describing the neighbor it's obvious that the narrator has his own mental fences that separate him from his "stone age" neighbor.

I have come after them and made repair
Where they have left not one stone on a stone,
But they would have the rabbit out of hiding,
To please the yelping dogs. The gaps I mean,
No one has seen them made or heard them made,
But at spring mending-time we find them there.
I let my neighbor know beyond the hill;
And on a day we meet to walk the line
And set the wall between us once again.
We keep the wall between us as we go.
To each the boulders that have fallen to each.
And some are loaves and some so nearly balls
We have to use a spell to make them balance:
'Stay where you are until our backs are turned!'
We wear our fingers rough with handling them.
Oh, just another kind of outdoor game,
One on a side. It comes to little more:
There where it is we do not need the wall:
He is all pine and I am apple orchard.
My apple trees will never get across
And eat the cones under his pines, I tell him.
He only says, 'Good fences make good neighbors.'
Spring is the mischief in me, and I wonder
If I could put a notion in his head:
'*Why* do they make good neighbors? Isn't it
Where there are cows? But here there are no cows.
Before I built a wall I'd ask to know
What I was walling in or walling out,
And to whom I was like to give offense.
Something there is that doesn't love a wall,
That wants it down. 'I could say 'Elves' to him,
But it's not elves exactly, and I'd rather
He said it for himself. I see him there
Bringing a stone grasped firmly by the top
In each hand, like an old-stone savage armed.
He moves in darkness as it seems to me,
Not of woods only and the shade of trees.
He will not go behind his father's saying,
And he likes having thought of it so well
He says again, 'Good fences make good neighbors.'

Misgiving[1]

All crying, 'We will go with you, O Wind!'
The foliage follow him, leaf and stem;
But a sleep oppresses them as they go,
And they end by bidding him stay with them.

Since ever they flung abroad in spring
The leaves had promised themselves this flight,
Who now would fain seek sheltering wall,
Or thicket, or hollow place for the night.

And now they answer his summoning blast
With an ever vaguer and vaguer stir,
Or at utmost a little reluctant whirl
That drops them no further than where they were.

I only hope that when I am free
As they are free to go in quest
Of the knowledge beyond the bounds of life
It may not seem better to me to rest.

On a Tree Fallen Across the Road[2]
(To Hear Us Talk)

The tree the tempest with a crash of wood
Throws down in front of us is not to bar
Our passage to our journey's end for good,
But just to ask us who we think we are

Insisting always on our own way so.
She likes to halt us in our runner tracks,
And make us get down in a foot of snow
Debating what to do without an ax.

---

[1] Form: Iambic tetrameter but an unusually large number of anapests, irregular but frequent end rhymes—Vocabulary: fain: rather—Notes: The leaves operate as a metaphor for the human soul. They anticipate release from the tree (earthly life) to explore that which is beyond, but when the time comes they are tired and end up wanting nothing but to rest in a corner.

[2] Form: Sonnet—Notes: The tree represents obstacles, which are then personified.

And yet she knows obstruction is in vain:
We will not be put off the final goal
We have it hidden in us to attain,
Not though we have to seize earth by the pole

And, tired of aimless circling in one place,
Steer straight off after something into space.

Stopping by Woods on a Snowy Evening[1]

Whose woods these are I think I know.
His house is in the village, though;
He will not see me stopping here
To watch his woods fill up with snow.

My little horse must think it queer
To stop without a farmhouse near
Between the woods and frozen lake
The darkest evening of the year.

He gives his harness bells a shake
To ask if there is some mistake.
The only other sound's the sweep
Of easy wind and downy flake.

The woods are lovely, dark and deep,
But I have promises to keep,
And miles to go before I sleep,
And miles to go before I sleep.

Storm Fear[2]

When the wind works against us in the dark,
And pelts with snow
The lowest chamber window on the east,

---

[1] Form: Iambic tetrameter, AABABBxB end rhymes—Notes: The rest of
death is inviting, but the narrator has more to do in life before he is ready
for death.
[2] Form: Mostly iambic pentameter with substitutions and some lines split
across multiple physical lines.—Vocabulary: chamber: bedroom.

And whispers with a sort of stifled bark,
The beast,
'Come out! Come out!'—
It costs no inward struggle not to go,
Ah, no!
I count our strength,
Two and a child,
Those of us not asleep subdued to mark
How the cold creeps as the fire dies at length,—
How drifts are piled,
Dooryard and road ungraded,
Till even the comforting barn grows far away
And my heart owns a doubt
Whether 'tis in us to arise with day
And save ourselves unaided.

The Aim was Song[1]

Before man came to blow it right
    The wind once blew itself untaught,
And did its loudest day and night
    In any rough place where it caught.

Man came to tell it what was wrong:
    It hadn't found the place to blow;
It blew too hard—the aim was song.
    And listen—how it ought to go!

He took a little in his mouth,
    And held it long enough for north
To be converted into south,
    And then by measure blew it forth.

By measure. It was word and note,
    The wind the wind had meant to be—
A little through the lips and throat.
    The aim was song—the wind could see.

---

[1] Form: Iambic tetrameter, ABAB end rhymes—Vocabulary: hie: go quickly;
bluet: flowering plant—Notes: A silent, hidden observer of things both
living and dead, far and near, day and night.

The Need of Being Versed in Country Things[1]

The house had gone to bring again
To the midnight sky a sunset glow.
Now the chimney was all of the house that stood,
Like a pistil after the petals go.

The barn opposed across the way,
That would have joined the house in flame
Had it been the will of the wind, was left
To bear forsaken the place's name.

No more it opened with all one end
For teams that came by the stony road
To drum on the floor with scurrying hoofs
And brush the mow with the summer load.

The birds that came to it through the air
At broken windows flew out and in,
Their murmur more like the sigh we sigh
From too much dwelling on what has been.

Yet for them the lilac renewed its leaf,
And the aged elm, though touched with fire;
And the dry pump flung up an awkward arm;
And the fence post carried a strand of wire.

For them there was really nothing sad.
But though they rejoiced in the nest they kept,
One had to be versed in country things
Not to believe the phoebes wept.

The Onset[1]

---

[1] Form: Iambic tetrameter, but an unusually large number of anapests, xAxAxBxB... end rhymes—Vocabulary: pistil: sex organ of a flower, normally inside the flower; phoebes: flycatcher (type of bird)—Notes: The decaying farm is viewed from three perspectives, the animals (nature) which are now reclaiming the farm; a normal human; and a human who is sufficiently versed in country things to see the decay from the nature perspective.

Always the same, when on a fated night
At last the gathered snow lets down as white
As may be in dark woods, and with a song
It shall not make again all winter long
Of hissing on the yet uncovered ground,
I almost stumble looking up and round,
As one who overtaken by the end
Gives up his errand, and lets death descend
Upon him where he is, with nothing done
To evil, no important triumph won,
More than if life had never been begun.

Yet all the precedent is on my side:
I know that winter death has never tried
The earth but it has failed: the snow may heap
In long storms an undrifted four feet deep
As measured against maple, birch, and oak,
It cannot check the peeper's silver croak;
And I shall see the snow all go down hill
In water of a slender April rill
That flashes tail through last year's withered brake
And dead weeds, like a disappearing snake.
Nothing will be left white but here a birch,
And there a clump of houses with a church.

The Road Not Taken[2]

Two roads diverged in a yellow wood,
And sorry I could not travel both
And be one traveler, long I stood
And looked down one as far as I could
To where it bent in the undergrowth;

Then took the other, as just as fair,

---

[1] Form: Iambic pentameter, AABBCC . . . End rhymes—Vocabulary:
peeper: type of frog; rill: rivulet; brake: area overgrown with dense brush;
—Notes: A poem about that deals metaphorically with death and renewal.
[2] Form: Iambic tetrameter, ABCCA end rhymes—Notes: The road is a
symbol for any decision in life where both options are roughly equally good,
but the selection of one or the other will have a big impact on the future.

And having perhaps the better claim,
Because it was grassy and wanted wear;
Though as for that the passing there
Had worn them really about the same,

And both that morning equally lay
In leaves no step had trodden black.
Oh, I kept the first for another day!
Yet knowing how way leads on to way,
I doubted if I should ever come back.

I shall be telling this with a sigh
Somewhere ages and ages hence:
Two roads diverged in a wood, and I—
I took the one less traveled by,
And that has made all the difference.

The Vantage Point[1]

If tired of trees I seek again mankind,
    Well I know where to hie me—in the dawn,
    To a slope where the cattle keep the lawn.
There amid lolling juniper reclined,
Myself unseen, I see in white defined
    Far off the homes of men, and farther still,
    The graves of men on an opposing hill,
Living or dead, whichever are to mind.

And if by moon I have too much of these,
    I have but to turn on my arm, and lo,
    The sun-burned hillside sets my face aglow,
My breathing shakes the bluet like a breeze,
    I smell the earth, I smell the bruisëd plant,
    I look into the crater of the ant.

The Wood-Pile[2]

Out walking in the frozen swamp one gray day

---

[1] Form: Sonnet.
[2] Form: Blank verse—Vocabulary: Clematis: vining plant.

I paused and said, 'I will turn back from here.
No, I will go on farther—and we shall see'.
The hard snow held me, save where now and then
One foot went through. The view was all in lines
Straight up and down of tall slim trees
Too much alike to mark or name a place by
So as to say for certain I was here
Or somewhere else: I was just far from home.
A small bird flew before me. He was careful
To put a tree between us when he lighted,
And say no word to tell me who he was
Who was so foolish as to think what *he* thought.
He thought that I was after him for a feather—
The white one in his tail; like one who takes
Everything said as personal to himself.
One flight out sideways would have undeceived him.
And then there was a pile of wood for which
I forgot him and let his little fear
Carry him off the way I might have gone,
Without so much as wishing him good-night.
He went behind it to make his last stand.
It was a cord of maple, cut and split
And piled—and measured, four by four by eight.
And not another like it could I see.
No runner tracks in this year's snow looped near it.
And it was older sure than this year's cutting,
Or even last year's or the year's before.
The wood was gray and the bark warping off it
And the pile somewhat sunken. Clematis
Had wound strings round and round it like a bundle.
What held it, though, on one side was a tree
Still growing, and on one a stake and prop,
These latter about to fall. I thought that only
Someone who lived in turning to fresh tasks
Could so forget his handiwork on which
He spent himself the labor of his ax,
And leave it there far from a useful fireplace
To warm the frozen swamp as best it could
With the slow smokeless burning of decay.

Amy Lowell (1874 – 1925)

A Decade[1]

When you came, you were like red wine and honey,
And the taste of you burnt my mouth with its sweetness.
Now you are like morning bread,
Smooth and pleasant.
I hardly taste you at all for I know your savour,
But I am completely nourished.

New Heavens for Old[2]

I am useless.
What I do is nothing,
What I think has no savour.
There is an almanac between the windows:
It is of the year when I was born.

My fellows call to me to join them,
They shout for me,
Passing the house in a great wind of vermilion banners.
They are fresh and fulminant,
They are indecent and strut with the thought of it,
They laugh, and curse, and brawl,
And cheer a holocaust of "Who comes firsts!" at the iron
    fronts of the houses at the two edges of the street.
Young men with naked hearts jeering between iron
    house-fronts,
Young men with naked bodies beneath their clothes
Passionately conscious of them,
Ready to strip off their clothes,
Ready to strip off their customs, their usual routine,
Clamoring for the rawness of life,
In love with appetite,

---

[1] Form: Free verse—Vocabulary: savor: a distinctive taste or smell.
[2] Form: Free verse—Vocabulary: Savor: distinctive quality; vermilion:
orange red color; fulminant: exploding; hemlock: poison—Notes: The
narrator in the winter of her life, slowly, elegantly committing suicide to
move onto the next plane, while outside the youth are so exuberant and
lustful.

304

Proclaiming it as a creed,
Worshipping youth,
Worshipping themselves.
They call for women and the women come,
They bare the whiteness of their lusts to the dead gaze of the
    old house-fronts,
They roar down the street like flame,
They explode upon the dead houses like new, sharp fire.

But I—
I arrange three roses in a Chinese vase:
A pink one,
A red one,
A yellow one.
I fuss over their arrangement.
Then I sit in a South window
And sip pale wine with a touch of hemlock in it,
And think of Winter nights,
And field-mice crossing and re-crossing
The spot which will be my grave.

Patterns[1]

I walk down the garden paths,
And all the daffodils
Are blowing, and the bright blue squills.
I walk down the patterned garden paths
In my stiff, brocaded gown.
With my powdered hair and jewelled fan,
I too am a rare
Pattern. As I wander down
The garden paths,
My dress is richly figured,
And the train
Makes a pink and silver stain
On the gravel, and the thrift
Of the borders.
Just a plate of current fashion,

---

[1] Form: Iambic, irregular line lengths—Vocabulary: squills: type of flower;
brocaded: heavy fabric with raised design; se'nnight: a week ago.

Tripping by in high-heeled, ribboned shoes.
Not a softness anywhere about me,
Only whalebone and brocade.
And I sink on a seat in the shade
Of a lime tree. For my passion
Wars against the stiff brocade.
The daffodils and squills
Flutter in the breeze
As they please.
And I weep;
For the lime tree is in blossom
And one small flower has dropped upon my bosom.
And the plashing of waterdrops
In the marble fountain
Comes down the garden paths.
The dripping never stops.
Underneath my stiffened gown
Is the softness of a woman bathing in a marble basin,
A basin in the midst of hedges grown
So thick, she cannot see her lover hiding,
But she guesses he is near,
And the sliding of the water
Seems the stroking of a dear
Hand upon her.
What is Summer in a fine brocaded gown!
I should like to see it lying in a heap upon the ground.
All the pink and silver crumpled up on the ground.

I would be the pink and silver as I ran along the paths,
And he would stumble after,
Bewildered by my laughter.
I should see the sun flashing from his sword-hilt and the
    buckles on his shoes.
I would choose
To lead him in a maze along the patterned paths,
A bright and laughing maze for my heavy-booted lover.
Till he caught me in the shade,
And the buttons of his waistcoat bruised my body as he
    clasped me,
Aching, melting, unafraid.
With the shadows of the leaves and the sundrops,

And the plopping of the waterdrops,
All about us in the open afternoon—
I am very like to swoon
With the weight of this brocade,
For the sun sifts through the shade.

Underneath the fallen blossom
In my bosom,
Is a letter I have hid.
It was brought to me this morning by a rider from the Duke
"Madam, we regret to inform you that Lord Hartwell
Died in action Thursday se'nnight."
As I read it in the white, morning sunlight,
The letters squirmed like snakes.
"Any answer, Madam," said my footman.
"No," I told him.
"See that the messenger takes some refreshment.
No, no answer."
And I walked into the garden,
Up and down the patterned paths,
In my stiff, correct brocade.
The blue and yellow flowers stood up proudly in the sun,
Each one.
I stood upright too,
Held rigid to the pattern
By the stiffness of my gown.
Up and down I walked,
Up and down.

In a month he would have been my husband.
In a month, here, underneath this lime,
We would have broke the pattern;
He for me, and I for him,
He as Colonel, I as Lady,
On this shady seat.
He had a whim
That sunlight carried blessing.
And I answered, "It shall be as you have said."
Now he is dead.

In Summer and in Winter I shall walk
Up and down
The patterned garden paths
In my stiff, brocaded gown.
The squills and daffodils
Will give place to pillared roses, and to asters, and to snow.
I shall go
Up and down,
In my gown.
Gorgeously arrayed,
Boned and stayed.
And the softness of my body will be guarded from embrace
By each button, hook, and lace.
For the man who should loose me is dead,
Fighting with the Duke in Flanders,
In a pattern called a war.
Christ! What are patterns for?

Robert Service (1874 – 1958)

Just Think![1]

Just think! Some night the stars will gleam
   Upon a cold, grey stone,
And trace a name with silver beam,
   And lo! 'twill be your own.

This night is speeding on to greet
   Your epitaphic rhyme.
Your life is but a little beat
   Within the heart of Time.

A little gain, a little pain,
   A laugh, lest you may moan;
A little blame, a little fame,
   A star-gleam on a stone.

---

[1] Form: Ballad—Vocabulary: epitaphic: inscription on tombstone.

Lost[1]

"Black is the sky, but the land is white--
(O the wind, the snow and the storm!)--
Father, where is our boy to-night?
Pray to God he is safe and warm."

"Mother, mother, why should you fear?
Safe is he, and the Arctic moon
Over his cabin shines so clear--
Rest and sleep, 'twill be morning soon."

"It's getting dark awful sudden. Say, this is mighty queer!
Where in the world have I got to? It's still and black as a
     tomb.
I reckoned the camp was yonder, I figured the trail was here--
Nothing! Just draw and valley packed with quiet and gloom;
Snow that comes down like feathers, thick and gobby and
     gray;
Night that looks spiteful ugly--seems that I've lost my way.
     "The cold's got an edge like a jackknife--it must be forty
     below;
Leastways that's what it seems like--it cuts so fierce to the
bone.
The wind's getting real ferocious; it's heaving and whirling
the snow;
It shrieks with a howl of fury, it dies away to a moan;
Its arms sweep round like a banshee's, swift and icily white,
And buffet and blind and beat me. Lord! it's a hell of a night.

"I'm all tangled up in a blizzard. There's only one thing to do--
Keep on moving and moving; it's death, it's death if I rest.
Oh, God! if I see the morning, if only I struggle through,
I'll say the prayers I've forgotten since I lay on my mother's
     breast.
I seem going round in a circle; maybe the camp is near.
Say! did somebody holler? Was it a light I saw?

---

[1] Form: Ballad—Vocabulary: banshee: female spirit who wails to warn of
impending death; wan: pale; loon: type of bird.

Or was it only a notion? I'll shout, and maybe they'll hear--
No! the wind only drowns me--shout till my throat is raw.

"The boys are all round the camp-fire wondering when I'll be
   back.
They'll soon be starting to seek me; they'll scarcely wait for
   the light.
What will they find, I wonder, when they come to the end of
   my track--
A hand stuck out of a snowdrift, frozen and stiff and white.
That's what they'll strike, I reckon; that's how they'll find
   their pard,
A pie-faced corpse in a snowbank--curse you, don't be a fool!
Play the game to the finish; bet on your very last card;
Nerve yourself for the struggle. Oh, you coward, keep cool!

I'm going to lick this blizzard; I'm going to live the night.
It can't down me with its bluster--I'm not the kind to be beat.
On hands and knees will I buck it; with every breath will I
   fight;
It's life, it's life that I fight for--never it seemed so sweet.
I know that my face is frozen; my hands are numblike and
   dead;
But oh, my feet keep a-moving, heavy and hard and slow;
They're trying to kill me, kill me, the night that's black
   overhead,
The wind that cuts like a razor, the whipcord lash of the
   snow.
Keep a-moving, a-moving; don't, don't stumble, you fool!
Curse this snow that's a-piling a-purpose to block my way.
It's heavy as gold in the rocker, it's white and fleecy as wool;
It's soft as a bed of feathers, it's warm as a stack of hay.
Curse on my feet that slip so, my poor tired, stumbling feet;
I guess they're a job for the surgeon, they feel so queerlike to
   lift--
I'll rest them just for a moment--oh, but to rest is sweet!
The awful wind cannot get me, deep, deep down in the drift."

"Father, a bitter cry I heard,
Out of the night so dark and wild.
Why is my heart so strangely stirred?

310

'Twas like the voice of our erring child."
"Mother, mother, you only heard
A waterfowl in the locked lagoon--
Out of the night a wounded bird--
Rest and sleep, 'twill be morning soon."

Who is it talks of sleeping? I'll swear that somebody shook
Me hard by the arm for a moment, but how on earth could it
    be?
See how my feet are moving--awfully funny they look--
Moving as if they belonged to a someone that wasn't me.
The wind down the night's long alley bowls me down like a
    pin;
I stagger and fall and stagger, crawl arm-deep in the snow.
Beaten back to my corner, how can I hope to win?
And there is the blizzard waiting to give me the knockout
    blow.
Oh, I'm so warm and sleepy! No more hunger and pain.
Just to rest for a moment; was ever rest such a joy?
Ha! what was that? I'll swear it, somebody shook me again;
Somebody seemed to whisper: "Fight to the last, my boy."
Fight! That's right, I must struggle. I know that to rest means
    death;
Death, but then what does death mean? --ease from a world
    of strife.
Life has been none too pleasant; yet with my failing breath
Still and still must I struggle, fight for the gift of life.
* * * * *

Seems that I must be dreaming! Here is the old home trail;
Yonder a light is gleaming; oh, I know it so well!
The air is scented with clover; the cattle wait by the rail;
Father is through with the milking; there goes the supper-
    bell.
* * * * *

Mother, your boy is crying, out in the night and cold;
Let me in and forgive me, I'll never be bad any more:
I'm, oh, so sick and so sorry: please, dear mother, don't
    scold--
It's just your boy, and he wants you. . . ..Mother, open the
    door. . .

311

"Father, father, I saw a face
Pressed just now to the window-pane!
Oh, it gazed for a moment's space,
Wild and wan, and was gone again!"
"Mother, mother, you saw the snow
Drifted down from the maple tree
(Oh, the wind that is sobbing so!
Weary and worn and old are we)--
Only the snow and a wounded loon--
Rest and sleep, 'twill be morning soon."

My Madonna[1]

I haled me a woman from the street,
    Shameless, but, oh, so fair!
I bade her sit in the model's seat
    And I painted her sitting there.

I hid all trace of her heart unclean;
    I painted a babe at her breast;
I painted her as she might have been
    If the Worst had been the Best.

She laughed at my picture and went away.
    Then came, with a knowing nod,
A connoisseur, and I heard him say;
    "'Tis Mary, the Mother of God."

So I painted a halo round her hair,
    And I sold her and took my fee,
And she hangs in the church of Saint Hillaire,
    Where you and all may see.

---

[1] Form: Ballad.

On the Wire[1]

O God, take the sun from the sky!
It's burning me, scorching me up.
God, can't You hear my cry?
Water! A poor, little cup!
It's laughing, the cursed sun!
See how it swells and swells
Fierce as a hundred hells!
God, will it never have done?
It's searing the flesh on my bones;
It's beating with hammers red
My eyeballs into my head;
It's parching my very moans.
See! It's the size of the sky,
And the sky is a torrent of fire,
Foaming on me as I lie
Here on the wire . . . The wire. . . .

Of the thousands that wheeze and hum
Heedlessly over my head,
Why can't a bullet come,
Pierce to my brain instead,
Blacken forever my brain,
Finish forever my pain?
Here in the hellish glare
Why must I suffer so?
Is it God doesn't care?
Is it God doesn't know?
Oh, to be killed outright,
Clean in the clash of the fight!
That is a golden death,
That is a boon; but this . . .
Drawing an anguished breath
Under a hot abyss,
Under a stooping sky
Of seething, sulphurous fire,

---

[1] Form: Anapestic trimeter, rhyming pairs of lines in various
configurations—Vocabulary: Trussed: tied up tightly; wan: unnaturally
pale—Notes: The wounded soldier is trapped under barbed wire between
lines during WWI.

Scorching me up as I lie
Here on the wire . . . The wire. . . .

Hasten, O God, Thy night!
Hide from my eyes the sight
Of the body I stare and see
Shattered so hideously.
I can't believe that it's mine.
My body was white and sweet,
Flawless and fair and fine,
Shapely from head to feet;
Oh no, I can never be
The thing of horror I see
Under the rifle fire,
Trussed on the wire . . . The wire. . . .

Of night and of death I dream;
Night that will bring me peace,
Coolness and starry gleam,
Stillness and death's release:
Ages and ages have passed,—
Lo! It is night at last.
Night! But the guns roar out.
Night! But the hosts attack.
Red and yellow and black
Geysers of doom upspout.
Silver and green and red
Star-shells hover and spread.
Yonder off to the right
Fiercely kindles the fight;
Roaring near and more near,
Thundering now in my ear;
Close to me, close . . . Oh, hark!
Someone moans in the dark.
I hear, but I cannot see,
I hear as the rest retire,
Someone is caught like me,
Caught on the wire . . . The wire. . . .

Again the shuddering dawn,
Weird and wicked and wan;

Again, and i've not yet gone.
The man whom I heard is dead.
Now I can understand:
A bullet hole in his head,
A pistol gripped in his hand.
Well, he knew what to do,—
Yes, and now I know too. . . .

Hark the resentful guns!
Oh, how thankful am I
To think my beloved ones
Will never know how I die!
I've suffered more than my share;
I'm shattered beyond repair;
I've fought like a man the fight,
And now I demand the right
(God! How his fingers cling!)
To do without shame this thing.
Good! There's a bullet still;
Now I'm ready to fire;
Blame me, God, if You will,
Here on the wire . . . The wire. .

The Ballad of Pious Pete[1]

"The North has got him."—Yukonism.

I tried to refine that neighbor of mine, honest to God, I did.
I grieved for his fate, and early and late I watched over him
  like a kid.
I gave him excuse, I bore his abuse in every way that I could;
I swore to prevail; I camped on his trail; I plotted and planned
  for his good.

---

[1] Form: Ballad—Vocabulary: precept: rule of personal conduct; Gehennas:
hell; sirens: beautiful women who sing to lure sailors to their death on
rocks; scrofulous: morally degenerate; dissolute: lacking moral restraint;
galoot: uncouth person; cant: monotonous talk; cadaverous: deathlike;
pinions: wings of a bird; winnowing: separate wheat from chaff;
gallivanting: roaming about searching for pleasure; malamute: sled dog;
iniquitous: wicked; "Fount of the Law": Bible—Notes: They symptoms of
scurvy, a common ailment in the Yukon, are accurately described.

315

By day and by night I strove in men's sight to gather him into
    the fold,
With precept and prayer, with hope and despair, in hunger
    and hardship and cold.
I followed him into Gehennas of sin, I sat where the sirens
    sit;
In the shade of the Pole, for the sake of his soul, I strove with
    the powers of the Pit.
I shadowed him down to the scrofulous town; I dragged him
    from dissolute brawls;
But I killed the galoot when he started to shoot electricity
    into my walls.

God knows what I did he should seek to be rid of one who
    would save him from shame.
God knows what I bore that night when he swore and bade
    me make tracks from his claim.
I started to tell of the horrors of hell, when sudden his eyes lit
    like coals;
And " Chuck it," says he, " don't persecute me with your cant
    and your saving of souls."
I'll swear I was mild as I'd be with a child, but he called me
    the son of a slut;
And, grabbing his gun with a leap and a run, he threatened
    my face with the butt.
So what could I do (I leave it to you)? With curses he harried
    me forth;
Then he was alone, and I was alone, and over us menaced
    the North.

Our cabins were near; I could see, I could hear; but between
    us there rippled the creek;
And all summer through, with a rancor that grew, he would
    pass me and never would speak.
Then a shuddery breath like the coming of Death crept down
    from the peaks far away;
The water was still; the twilight was chill; the sky was a tatter
    of gray.
Swift came the Big Cold, and opal and gold the lights of the
    witches arose;

The frost-tyrant clinched, and the valley was cinched by the
stark and cadaverous snows.
The trees were like lace where the star-beams could chase,
each leaf with a jewel agleam.
The soft white hush lapped the Northland and wrapped us
round in a crystalline dream;
So still I could hear quite loud in my ear the swish of the
pinions of time;
So bright I could see, as plain as could be, the wings of God's
angels ashine.

As I read in the Book I would oftentimes look to that cabin
just over the creek.
Ah me, it was sad and evil and bad, two neighbors who never
would speak!
I knew that full well like the devil in hell he was hatching out,
early and late,
A system to bear through the frost-spangled air the warm,
crimson waves of his hate.
I only could peer and shudder and fear—'twas ever so ghastly
and still;
But I knew over there in his lonely despair he was plotting
me terrible ill.
I knew that he nursed a malice accurst, like the blast of a
winnowing flame;
I pleaded aloud for a shield, for a shroud—oh, God ! then
calamity came.

Mad ! If I'm mad then you too are mad; but it's all in the
point of view.
If you'd looked at them things gallivantin' on wings, all purple
and green and blue;
If you'd noticed them twist, as they mounted and hissed like
scorpions dim in the dark;
If you'd seen them rebound with a horrible sound, and
spitefully spitting a spark;
If you'd watched It with dread, as it hissed by your bed, that
thing with the feelers that crawls—
You'd have settled the brute that attempted to shoot
electricity into your walls.

Oh, some they were blue, and they slithered right through;
    They were silent and squashy and round;
And some they were green; they were wriggly and lean; They
    writhed with so hateful a sound.
My blood seemed to freeze; I fell on my knees; my face was a
    white splash of dread.
Oh, the Green and the Blue, they were gruesome to view;
But the worst of them all were the Red,
They came through the door,
They came through the floor,
They came through the moss-creviced logs.
They were savage and dire;
they were whiskered with fire;
they bickered like malamute dogs.
They ravined in rings like iniquitous things; They gulped
    down the Green and the Blue.
I crinkled with fear whene'er they drew near, and nearer and
    nearer they drew.

And then came the crown of Horror's grim crown, the
    monster so loathsomely red.
Each eye was a pin that shot out and in, as, squid-like, it
    oozed to my bed;
So softly it crept with feelers that swept and quivered like fine
    copper wire;
Its belly was white with a sulphurous light, its jaws were a-
    drooling with fire.
It came and it came; I could breathe of its flame, but never a
    wink could I look.
I thrust in its maw the Fount of the Law; I fended it off with
    the Book.
I was weak—oh, so weak—but I thrilled at its shriek, as
    wildly it fled in the night;
And deathlike I lay till the dawn of the day. (Was ever so
    welcome the light ?)

I loaded my gun at the rise of the sun; to his cabin so softly I
    slunk.
My neighbor was there in the frost-freighted air, all wrapped
    in a robe in his bunk.

It muffled his moans; it outlined his bones, as feebly he
 twisted about;
His gums were so black, and his lips seemed to crack, and
 his teeth all were loosening out.
'Twas a death's head that peered through the tangle of beard;
'Twas a face I will never forget; sunk eyes full of woe, and
They troubled me so with their pleadings and anguish, and
 yet
As I rested my gaze in a misty amaze on the scurvy
 degenerate wreck,
I thought of the Things with the dragon-fly wings, then laid I
 my gun on his neck.
He gave out a cry that was faint as a sigh, like a perishing
 malamute,
And he says unto me, "I'm converted," says he; "for Christ's
 sake, Peter, don't shoot!"

. . .

They're taking me out with an escort about, and under a
 sergeant's care;
I am humbled indeed, for I'm 'cuffed to a Swede that thinks
 he's a millionaire.
But it's all Gospel true what I'm telling to you—up there
 where the Shadow falls—
That I settled Sam Noot when he started to shoot electricity
 into my walls.

The Ballad of the Black Fox Skin[1]

I

There was Claw-fingered Kitty and Windy Ike living the life of
  shame,
When unto them in the Long, Long Night came the man-who-
  had-no-name;
Bearing his prize of a black fox pelt, out of the Wild he came.

His cheeks were blanched as the flume-head foam when the
  brown spring freshets flow;
Deep in their dark, sin-calcined pits were his somber eyes
  aglow;
They knew him far for the fitful man who spat forth blood on
  the snow.

"Did ever you see such a skin?" quoth he; "there's nought in
  the world so fine—
Such fullness of fur as black as the night, such luster, such
  size, such shine;
It's life to a one-lunged man like me; it's London, it's women,
  it's wine.

"The Moose-hides called it the devil-fox, and swore that no
  man could kill;
That he who hunted it, soon or late, must surely suffer some
  ill;
But I laughed at them and their old squaw-tales. Ha! Ha! I'm
  laughing still.

---

[1] Form: Ballad—Vocabulary: flume-head: head of a narrow gorge with a
stream flowing through it; freshets: a sudden overflow from a stream after
a thaw; calcined: heated to the point of decomposition; Moose-hides:
Indian tribe; fleer: smirk or laugh in contempt; ptarmigan: an arctic game
bird (grouse); sacerdotal: priestly; carded: combed out; vastitudes:
immensity; up-shoaled: made shallow; scathless: unharmed; mushed:
drove a dog sled; Fournier and Labelle: Two characters from other Robert
Service ballads; poke of dust: bag of gold dust; wiles: tricks; malamutes:
sled dogs; Dawson: mining town in Alaska; rind: outer layer of ice;
caromed: bounced; dight: dressed; mail: armor; slough: depression filled
with mud; hooch: inferior liquor; sardonic: mocking; twain: two—Notes:
The devil is often portrayed as having hoofed feet.

"For look ye, the skin—it's as smooth as sin, and black as the
    core of the Pit.
By gun or by trap, whatever the hap, I swore I would capture
    it;
By star and by star afield and afar, I hunted and would not
    quit.

"For the devil-fox, it was swift and sly, and it seemed to fleer
    at me;
I would wake in fright by the camp-fire light, hearing its evil
    glee;
Into my dream its eyes would gleam, and its shadow would I
    see.

"It sniffed and ran from the ptarmigan I had poisoned to
    excess;
Unharmed it sped from my wrathful lead ('twas as if I shot by
    guess);
Yet it came by night in the stark moonlight to mock at my
    weariness.

"I tracked it up where the mountains hunch like the
    vertebrae of the world;
I tracked it down to the death-still pits where the avalanche
    is hurled;
From the glooms to the sacerdotal snows, where the carded
    clouds are curled.

"From the vastitudes where the world protrudes through
    clouds like seas up-shoaled,
I held its track till it led me back to the land I had left of old—
The land I had looted many moons. I was weary and sick and
    cold.

"I was sick, soul-sick, of the futile chase, and there and then
    I swore
The foul fiend fox might scathless go, for I would hunt no
    more;
Then I rubbed mine eyes in a vast surprise—it stood by my
    cabin door.

"A rifle raised in the wraith-like gloom, and a vengeful shot
 that sped;
A howl that would thrill a cream-faced corpse—and the
 demon fox lay dead. . . .
Yet there was never a sign of wound, and never a drop he
 bled.

"So that was the end of the great black fox, and here is the
 prize i've won;
And now for a drink to cheer me up—i've mushed since the
 early sun;
We'll drink a toast to the sorry ghost of the fox whose race is
 run."

II

Now Claw-fingered Kitty and Windy Ike, bad as the worst
 were they;
In their road-house down by the river-trail they waited and
 watched for prey;
With wine and song they joyed night long, and they slept like
 swine by day.

For things were done in the Midnight Sun that no tongue will
 ever tell;
And men there be who walk earth-free, but whose names are
 writ in hell—
Are writ in flames with the guilty names of Fournier and
 Labelle.

Put not your trust in a poke of dust would ye sleep the sleep
 of sin;
For there be those who would rob your clothes ere yet the
 dawn comes in;
And a prize likewise in a woman's eyes is a peerless black fox
 skin.

Put your faith in the mountain cat if you lie within his lair;
Trust the fangs of the mother-wolf, and the claws of the lead-
 ripped bear;
But oh, of the wiles and the gold-tooth smiles of a dance-hall
 wench beware!

322

Wherefore it was beyond all laws that lusts of man restrain,
A man drank deep and sank to sleep never to wake again;
And the Yukon swallowed through a hole the cold corpse of
the slain.

III
The black fox skin a shadow cast from the roof nigh to the
floor;
And sleek it seemed and soft it gleamed, and the woman
stroked it o'er;
And the man stood by with a brooding eye, and gnashed his
teeth and swore.

When thieves and thugs fall out and fight there's fell arrears
to pay;
And soon or late sin meets its fate, and so it fell one day
That Claw-fingered Kitty and Windy Ike fanged up like dogs
at bay.

"The skin is mine, all mine," she cried; "I did the deed alone."
"It's share and share with a guilt-yoked pair", he hissed in a
pregnant tone;
And so they snarled like malamutes over a mildewed bone.

And so they fought, by fear untaught, till haply it befell
One dawn of day she slipped away to Dawson town to sell
The fruit of sin, this black fox skin that had made their lives
a hell.

She slipped away as still he lay, she clutched the wondrous
fur;
Her pulses beat, her foot was fleet, her fear was as a spur;
She laughed with glee, she did not see him rise and follow
her.

The bluffs uprear and grimly peer far over Dawson town;
They see its lights a blaze o' nights and harshly they look
down;
They mock the plan and plot of man with grim, ironic frown.

The trail was steep; 'twas at the time when swiftly sinks the
 snow;
All honey-combed, the river ice was rotting down below;
The river chafed beneath its rind with many a mighty throe.

And up the swift and oozy drift a woman climbed in fear,
Clutching to her a black fox fur as if she held it dear;
And hard she pressed it to her breast—then Windy Ike drew
 near.

She made no moan—her heart was stone—she read his
 smiling face,
And like a dream flashed all her life's dark horror and
 disgrace;
A moment only—with a snarl he hurled her into space.

She rolled for nigh an hundred feet; she bounded like a ball;
From crag to crag she caromed down through snow and
 timber fall; . . .
A hole gaped in the river ice; the spray flashed—that was all.

A bird sang for the joy of spring, so piercing sweet and frail;
And blinding bright the land was dight in gay and glittering
 mail;
And with a wondrous black fox skin a man slid down the
 trail.

IV
A wedge-faced man there was who ran along the river bank,
Who stumbled through each drift and slough, and ever
 slipped and sank,
And ever cursed his Maker's name, and ever "hooch" he
 drank.

He traveled like a hunted thing, hard harried, sore distrest;
The old grandmother moon crept out from her cloud-quilted
 nest;
The aged mountains mocked at him in their primeval rest.

Grim shadows diapered the snow; the air was strangely mild;

The valley's girth was dumb with mirth, the laughter of the
   wild;
The still, sardonic laughter of an ogre o'er a child.

The river writhed beneath the ice; it groaned like one in pain,
And yawning chasms opened wide, and closed and yawned
   again;
And sheets of silver heaved on high until they split in twain.

From out the road-house by the trail they saw a man afar
Make for the narrow river-reach where the swift cross-
   currents are;
Where, frail and worn, the ice is torn and the angry waters
   jar.

But they did not see him crash and sink into the icy flow;
They did not see him clinging there, gripped by the undertow,
Clawing with bleeding finger-nails at the jagged ice and snow.

They found a note beside the hole where he had stumbled in:
"here met his fate by evil luck a man who lived in sin,
And to the one who loves me least I leave this black fox skin."

And strange it is; for, though they searched the river all
   around,
No trace or sign of black fox skin was ever after found;
Though one man said he saw the tread of hoofs deep in the
   ground.

The Cremation of Sam McGee[1]

THERE are strange things done in the midnight sun
  By the men who moil for gold;
The Arctic trails have their secret tales
  That would make your blood run cold;
The Northern Lights have seen queer sights,
  But the queerest they ever did see

---

[1] Form: Ballad—Vocabulary: moil: toil; marge: margin; mushing: driving a
dog sled; Dawson trail: hazardous trail from Whitehorse to Dawson City
along the frozen Yukon river; brawn: muscles.

Was that night on the marge of Lake Lebarge
 I cremated Sam McGee.

Now Sam McGee was from Tennessee, where the cotton
  blooms and blows.

Why he left his home in the South to roam 'round the Pole,
  God only knows.
He was always cold, but the land of gold seemed to hold him
  like a spell;
Though he'd often say in his homely way that 'he'd sooner
  live in hell.'

On a Christmas Day we were mushing our way over the
  Dawson trail.
Talk of your cold! through the parka's fold it stabbed like a
  driven nail.
If our eyes we'd close, then the lashes froze till sometimes we
  couldn't see;
It wasn't much fun, but the only one to whimper was Sam
  McGee.

And that very night, as we lay packed tight in our robes
  beneath the snow,
And the dogs were fed, and the stars o'erhead were dancing
  heel and toe,
He turned to me, and 'Cap,' says he, 'I'll cash in this trip, I
  guess;
And if I do, I'm asking that you won't refuse my last request.'

Well, he seemed so low that I couldn't say no; then he says
  with a sort of moan:
'It's the cursed cold, and it's got right hold till I'm chilled
  clean through to the bone.
Yet 'taint being dead–it's my awful dread of the icy grave that
  pains;
So I want you to swear that, foul or fair, you'll cremate my
  last remains.'

A pal's last need is a thing to heed, so I swore I would not
  fail;

And we started on at the streak of dawn; but God! he looked
ghastly pale.
He crouched on the sleigh, and he raved all day of his home
in Tennessee;

And before nightfall a corpse was all that was left of Sam
McGee.

There wasn't a breath in that land of death, and I hurried,
horror-driven,
With a corpse half hid that I couldn't get rid, because of a
promise given;
It was lashed to the sleigh, and it seemed to say: 'You may
tax your brawn and brains,
But you promised true, and it's up to you to cremate those
last remains.'

Now a promise made is a debt unpaid, and the trail has its
own stern code.
In the days to come, though my lips were dumb, in my heart
how I cursed that load.
In the long, long night, by the lone firelight, while the
huskies, round in a ring,
Howled out their woes to the homeless snows–O God! how I
loathed the thing.

And every day that quiet clay seemed to heavy and heavier
grow;
And on I went, though the dogs were spent and the grub was
getting low;
The trail was bad, and I felt half mad, but I swore I would not
give in;
And I'd often sing to the hateful thing, and it hearkened with
a grin.

Till I came to the marge of Lake Lebarge, and a derelict there
lay;
It was jammed in the ice, but I saw in a trice it was called the
'Alice May.'
And I looked at it, and I thought a bit, and I looked at my
frozen chum;

Then 'Here,' said I, with a sudden cry, 'is my cre-ma-tor-
   eum.'

Some planks I tore from the cabin floor, and I lit the boiler
   fire;
Some coal I found that was lying around, and I heaped the
   fuel higher;

The flames just soared, and the furnace roared–such a blaze
   you seldom see;
And I burrowed a hole in the glowing coal, and I stuffed in
   Sam McGee.

Then I made a hike, for I didn't like to hear him sizzle so;
And the heavens scowled, and the huskies howled, and the
   wind began to blow.
It was icy cold, but the hot sweat rolled down my cheeks, and
   I don't know why;
And the greasy smoke in an inky cloak went streaking down
   the sky.

I do not know how long in the snow I wrestled with grisly
   fear;
But the stars came out and they danced about ere again I
   ventured near;
I was sick with dread, but I bravely said: 'I'll just take a peep
   inside.
I guess he's cooked, and it's time I looked;' . . . then the door
   I opened wide.

And there sat Sam, looking cool and calm, in the heart of the
   furnace roar;
And he wore a smile you could see a mile, and he said:
   'Please close that door.
It's fine in here, but I greatly fear you'll let in the cold and
   storm–
Since I left Plumtree, down in Tennessee, it's the first time
   I've been warm.'

There are strange things done in the midnight sun
   By the men who moil for gold;

The Arctic trails have their secret tales
  That would make your blood run cold;
The Northern Lights have seen queer sights,
  But the queerest they ever did see
Was that night on the marge of Lake Lebarge
  I cremated Sam McGee.

The Shooting of Dan McGrew[1]

A bunch of the boys were whooping it up in the Malamute
    saloon;
The kid that handles the music-box was hitting a jag-time
    tune;
Back of the bar, in a solo game, sat Dangerous Dan mcgrew,
And watching his luck was his light-o'-love, the lady that's
    known as Lou.

When out of the night, which was fifty below, and into the din
    and glare,
There stumbled a miner fresh from the creeks, dog-dirty, and
    loaded for bear.
He looked like a man with a foot in the grave and scarcely the
    strength of a louse,
Yet he tilted a poke of dust on the bar, and he called for
    drinks for the house.
There was none could place the stranger's face, though we
    searched ourselves for a clue;
But we drank his health, and the last to drink was
    Dangerous Dan mcgrew.

There's men that somehow just grip your eyes, and hold
    them hard like a spell;
And such was he, and he looked to me like a man who had
    lived in hell;
With a face most hair, and the dreary stare of a dog whose
    day is done,
As he watered the green stuff in his glass, and the drops fell
    one by one.

---

[1] Form: Ballad—Vocabulary: Malamute: sled dog; jag-time: drinking time;
louse: singular of lice; muck: sticky mud; poke: bag of gold.

Then I got to figgering who he was, and wondering what he'd
  do,
And I turned my head—and there watching him was the lady
  that's known as Lou.

His eyes went rubbering round the room, and he seemed in a
  kind of daze,
Till at last that old piano fell in the way of his wandering
  gaze.
The rag-time kid was having a drink; there was no one else
  on the stool,
So the stranger stumbles across the room, and flops down
  there like a fool.
In a buckskin shirt that was glazed with dirt he sat, and I
  saw him sway,
Then he clutched the keys with his talon hands—my God!
  but that man could play.

Were you ever out in the Great Alone, when the moon was
  awful clear,
And the icy mountains hemmed you in with a silence you
  most could hear;
With only the howl of a timber wolf, and you camped there in
  the cold,
A helf-dead thing in a stark, dead world, clean mad for the
  muck called gold;
While high overhead, green, yellow, and red, the North Lights
  swept in bars?—
Then you've a hunch what the music meant...hunger and
  night and the stars.

And hunger not of the belly kind, that's banished with bacon
  and beans,
But the gnawing hunger of lonely men for a home and all
  that it means;
For a fireside far from the cares that are, four walls and a
  roof above;
But oh! So cramful of cozy joy, and crowded with a woman's
  love—
A woman dearer than all the world, and true as Heaven is
  true—

(God! How ghastly she looks through her rouge,—the lady
    that's known as Lou.)

Then on a sudden the music changed, so soft that you scarce
    could hear;
But you felt that your life had been looted clean of all that it
    once held dear;
That someone had stolen the woman you loved; that her love
    was a devil's lie;
That your guts were gone, and the best for you was to crawl
    away and die.
'Twas the crowning cry of a heart's despair, and it thrilled
    you through and through—
"I guess i'll make it a spread misery," said Dangerous Dan
    mcgrew.

The music almost dies away...then it burst like a pent-up
    flood;
And it seemed to say, "Repay, repay," and my eyes were blind
    with blood.
The thought came back of an ancient wrong, and it stung like
    a frozen lash,
And the lust awoke to kill, to kill...then the music stopped
    with a crash,
And the stranger turned, and his eyes they burned in a most
    peculiar way.

In a buckskin shirt that was glazed with dirt he sat, and I
    saw him sway;
Then his lips went in in a kind of grin, and he spoke, and his
    voice was calm,
And "Boys," says he, "you don't know me, and none of you
    care a damn;
But I want to state, and my words are straight, and i'll bet my
    poke they're true,
That one of you is a hound of hell...and that one is Dan
    mcgrew."

Then I ducked my head and the lights went out, and two
    guns blazed in the dark;

331

And a woman screamed, and the lights went up, and two
    men lay stiff and stark.
Pitched on his head, and pumped full of lead, was Dangerous
    Dan mcgrew,
While the man from the creeks lay clutched to the breast of
    the lady that's known as Lou.

These are the simple facts of the case, and I guess I ought to
    know.
They say that the stranger was crazed with "hooch," and I'm
    not denying it's so.
I'm not so wise as the lawyer guys, but strictly between us
    two—
The woman that kissed him and—pinched his poke—was the
    lady known as Lou.

The Smoking Frog[1]

Three men I saw beside a bar,
Regarding o'er their bottle,
A frog who smoked a rank cigar
They'd jammed within its throttle.

A Pasha frog it must have been
So big it was and bloated;
And from its lips the nicotine
In graceful festoon floated.

And while the trio jeered and joked,
As if it quite enjoyed it,
Impassively it smoked and smoked,
(it could not well avoid it).

A ring of fire its lips were nigh
Yet it seemed all unwitting;
It could not spit, like you and I,
Who've learned the art of spitting.

---

[1] Form: Ballad—Vocabulary: rank: smelly; throttle: throat; festoon: garland
of flowers; nigh: near; sublime: majesty; guying: mocking; expectorating:
spitting; fag: cigarette.

It did not wink, it did not shrink,
As there serene it squatted'
Its eyes were clear, it did not fear
The fate the Gods allotted.

It squatted there with calm sublime,
Amid their cruel guying;
Grave as a god, and all the time
It knew that it was dying.

And somehow then it seemed to me
These men expectorating,
Were infinitely less than he,
The dumb thing they were baiting.

It seemed to say, despite their jokes:
"this is my hour of glory.
It isn't every frog that smokes:
My name will live in story."

Before its nose the smoke arose;
The flame grew nigher, nigher;
And then I saw its bright eyes close
Beside that ring of fire.

They turned it on its warty back,
From off its bloated belly;
Its legs jerked out, then dangled slack;
It quivered like a jelly.

And then the fellows went away,
Contented with their joking;
But even as in death it lay,
The frog continued smoking.

Life's like a lighted fag, thought I;
We smoke it stale; then after
Death turns our belly to the sky:
The Gods must have their laughter.

The Soldier of Fortune[1]

"Deny your God!" they ringed me with their spears;
Blood-crazed were they, and reeking from the strife;
Hell-hot their hate, and venom-fanged their sneers,
And one man spat on me and nursed a knife.
And there was I, sore wounded and alone,
I, the last living of my slaughtered band.
Oh sinister the sky, and cold as stone!
In one red laugh of horror reeled the land.
And dazed and desperate I faced their spears,
And like a flame out-leaped that naked knife,
And like a serpent stung their bitter jeers:
"Deny your God, and we will give you life."

Deny my God! Oh life was very sweet!
And it is hard in youth and hope to die;
And there my comrades dear lay at my feet,
And in that blear of blood soon must I lie.
And yet . . . I almost laughed—it seemed so odd,
For long and long had I not vainly tried
To reason out and body forth my God,
And prayed for light, and doubted—and *denied:*
Denied the Being I could not conceive,
Denied a life-to-be beyond the grave. . . .
And now they ask me, who do not believe,
Just to deny, to voice my doubt, to save
This life of mine that sings so in the sun,
The bloom of youth yet red upon my cheek,
My only life!—O fools! 'Tis easy done,
I will deny . . . And yet I do not speak.

"Deny your God!" their spears are all agleam,
And I can see their eyes with blood-lust shine;
Their snarling voices shrill into a scream,
And, mad to slay, they quiver for the sign.
Deny my God! Yes, I could do it well;
Yet if I did, what of my race, my name?

---

[1] Form: Iambic pentameter, ABAB end rhymes—Vocabulary: blear: blur;
puissant: powerful; craven: cowardly; insensate: lacking sensation.

How they would spit on me, these dogs of hell!
Spurn me, and put on me the brand of shame.
A white man's honor! What of that, I say?
Shall these black curs cry "Coward" in my face?
They who would perish for their gods of clay—
Shall I defile my country and my race?
My country! What's my country to me now?
Soldier of Fortune, free and far I roam;
All men are brothers in my heart, I vow;
The wide and wondrous world is all my home.
My country! Reverent of her splendid Dead,
Her heroes proud, her martyrs pierced with pain:
For me her puissant blood was vainly shed;
For me her drums of battle beat in vain,
And free I fare, half-heedless of her fate:
No faith, no flag I owe—then why not seek
This last loop-hole of life? Why hesitate?
I will deny . . . And yet I do not speak.

"Deny your God!" their spears are poised on high,
And tense and terrible they wait the word;
And dark and darker glooms the dreary sky,
And in that hush of horror no thing stirred.
Then, through the ringing terror and sheer hate
Leaped there a vision to me—Oh, how far!
A face, Her face . . . Through all my stormy fate
A joy, a strength, a glory and a star.
Beneath the pines, where lonely camp-fires gleam,
In seas forlorn, amid the deserts drear,
How I had gladdened to that face of dream!
And never, never had it seemed so dear.
O silken hair that veils the sunny brow!
O eyes of grey, so tender and so true!
O lips of smiling sweetness! Must I now
For ever and for ever go from you?
Ah, yes, I must . . . For if I do this thing,
How can I look into your face again?
Knowing you think me more than half a king,
I with my craven heart, my honor slain.

No! No! My mind's made up. I gaze above,

335

Into that sky insensate as a stone;
Not for my creed, my country, but my Love
Will I stand up and meet my death alone.
Then though it be to utter dark I sink,
The God that dwells in me is not denied;
"Best" triumphs over "Beast",—and so I think
Humanity itself is glorified. . . .

"And now, my butchers, I embrace my fate.
Come! Let my heart's blood slake the thirsty sod.
Curst be the life you offer! Glut your hate!
Strike! Strike, you dogs! I'll *not* deny my God."

I saw the spears that seemed a-leap to slay,
All quiver earthward at the headman's nod;
And in a daze of dream I heard him say:
"Go, set him free who serves so well his God!"

The Wee Shop[1]

She risked her all, they told me, bravely sinking
The pinched economies of thirty years;
And there the little shop was, meek and shrinking,
The sum of all her dreams and hopes and fears.
Ere it was opened I would see them in it,
The gray-haired dame, the daughter with her crutch;
So fond, so happy, hoarding every minute,
Like artists, for the final tender touch.

The opening day! I'm sure that to their seeming
Was never shop so wonderful as theirs;
With pyramids of jam-jars rubbed to gleaming;
Such vivid cans of peaches, prunes and pears;
And chocolate, and biscuits in glass cases,
And bon-bon bottles, many-hued and bright;
Yet nothing half so radiant as their faces,
Their eyes of hope, excitement and delight.

---

[1] Form: Iambic pentameter, ABAB end rhymes—Vocabulary: pathos:
sadness; blighting: deteriorating—Note: This poem could describe the failed
dreams of many would-be small business owners.

I entered: how they waited all a-flutter!
How awkwardly they weighed my acid-drops!
And then with all the thanks a tongue could utter
They bowed me from the kindliest of shops.
I'm sure that night their customers they numbered;
Discussed them all in happy, breathless speech;
And though quite worn and weary, ere they slumbered,
Sent heavenward a little prayer for each.

And so I watched with interest redoubled
That little shop, spent in it all I had;
And when I saw it empty I was troubled,
And when I saw them busy I was glad.
And when I dared to ask how things were going,
They told me, with a fine and gallant smile:
"Not badly . . . Slow at first . . . There's never knowing . . .
'Twill surely pick up in a little while."

I'd often see them through the winter weather,
Behind the shutters by a light's faint speck,
Poring o'er books, their faces close together,
The lame girl's arm around her mother's neck.
They dressed their windows not one time but twenty,
Each change more pinched, more desperately neat;
Alas! I wondered if behind that plenty
The two who owned it had enough to eat.

Ah, who would dare to sing of tea and coffee?
The sadness of a stock unsold and dead;
The petty tragedy of melting toffee,
The sordid pathos of stale gingerbread.
Ignoble themes! And yet—those haggard faces!
Within that little shop. . . . Oh, here I say
One does not need to look in lofty places
For tragic themes, they're round us every day.

And so I saw their agony, their fighting,
Their eyes of fear, their heartbreak, their despair;
And there the little shop is, black and blighting,
And all the world goes by and does not care.
They say she sought her old employer's pity,
Content to take the pittance he would give.
The lame girl? Yes, she's working in the city;
She coughs a lot—she hasn't long to live.

Gertrude Stein (1874 – 1946)

from Idem the Same, A Valentine to Sherwood Anderson, A Very Valentine[1]

Very fine is my valentine.
Very fine and very mine.
Very mine is my valentine very mine and very fine.
Very fine is my valentine and mine,
Very fine very mine and mine is my valentine.

Carl Sandburg (1878 – 1967)

Last Answers[2]

I wrote a poem on the mist
and a woman asked me what I meant by it.
I had thought till then only of the beauty of the mist, how
    pearl and gray of it mix and reel,

---

[1] Form: Free verse—Notes: Gertrude focused most of her attention on the sound of words, creating a musical effect. Meaning of the words was secondary.
[2] Form: Free verse.

And change the drab shanties with lighted lamps at evening
    into points of mystery quivering with color.

    I answered:
The whole world was mist once long ago and some day
    it will all go back to mist,
Our skulls and lungs are more water than bone and tissue
And all poets love dust and mist because all the last answers
Go running back to dust and mist.

The Junk Man[1]

I am glad God saw Death
And gave Death a job taking care of all who are tired of living:

When all the wheels in a clock are worn and slow and the
    connections loose
And the clock goes on ticking and telling the wrong time from
    hour to hour
And people around the house joke about what a bum clock it
    is,
How glad the clock is when the big Junk Man drives his
    wagon
Up to the house and puts his arms around the clock and
    says:
            "You don't belong here,
            You gotta come
            Along with me,"
How glad the clock is then, when it feels the arms of the
    Junk Man close around it and carry it away.

To Know Silence Perfectly[2]

There is a music for lonely hearts nearly always.
If the music dies down there is a silence
Almost the same as the movement of music.
To know silence perfectly is to know music.

_____

[1] Form: Free verse.
[2] Form: Free verse.

Vachel Lindsay (1879 – 1931)

The Horrid Voice of Science[1]

"There's machinery in the butterfly;
    There's a mainspring to the bee;
There's hydraulics to a daisy,
    And contraptions to a tree.

"If we could see the birdie
    That makes the chirping sound
With x-ray, scientific eyes,
    We could see the wheels go round."

And I hope all men
who think like this
will soon lie
underground.

Wallace Stevens (1879 – 1955)

The Snow Man[2]

One must have a mind of winter
To regard the frost and the boughs
Of the pine-trees crusted with snow;

And have been cold a long time
To behold the junipers shagged with ice,
The spruces rough in the distant glitter

Of the January sun; and not to think
Of any misery in the sound of the wind,
In the sound of a few leaves,

---

[1] Form: Mixture of iambic tetrameter and iambic trimeter, xAxA end
rhymes—Notes: New work with genetics makes this even more meaningful.
[2] Form: Free verse—Notes: This poem is written from the perspective of a
snow man in a lonely forest glen.

Which is the sound of the land
Full of the same wind
That is blowing in the same bare place

For the listener, who listens in the snow,
And, nothing himself, beholds
Nothing that is not there and the nothing that is.

Thirteen Ways of Looking at a Blackbird[1]

I
Among twenty snowy mountains,
The only moving thing
Was the eye of the blackbird.

II
I was of three minds,
Like a tree
In which there are three blackbirds.

III
The blackbird whirled in the autumn winds.
It was a small part of the pantomime.

IV
A man and a woman
Are one.
A man and a woman and a blackbird
Are one.

V
I do not know which to prefer-
The beauty of inflections
Or the beauty of innuendoes,
The blackbird whistling
Or just after.

---

[1] Form: Free verse—Vocabulary: pantomime: telling a story without words;
Haddam: a city; bawds: prostitutes; euphony: pleasing sound.

VI
Icicles filled the long window
With barbaric glass.
The shadow of the blackbird
Crossed it, to and fro.
The mood
Traced in the shadow
An indecipherable cause.

VII
O thin men of Haddam,
Why do you imagine golden birds?
Do you not see how the blackbird
Walks around the feet
Of the women about you?

VIII
I know noble accents
And lucid, inescapable rhythms;
But I know, too,
That the blackbird is involved
In what I know.

IX
When the blackbird flew out of sight,
It marked the edge
Of one of many circles.

X
At the sight of blackbirds
Flying in a green light,
Even the bawds of euphony
Would cry out sharply.

XI
He rode over Connecticut
In a glass coach.
Once, a fear pierced him,
In that he mistook
The shadow of his equipage
For blackbirds.

XII
The river is moving.
The blackbird must be flying.

XIII
It was evening all afternoon.
It was snowing
And it was going to snow.
The blackbird sat
In the cedar-limbs.

Marjorie Allen Seiffert (1881 – 1968)

Cubist Portrait[1]

She is purposeless as a cyclone; she must move
either by chance or in a predestined groove,
following a whim not her own, unable to shape
her course. From chance or God even she cannot escape!

Think of a cyclone sitting far-off with its head in its hands,
motionless, drearily longing for distant lands
where every lonely hurricane may at last discover
its own transcendent, implacable, indestructible lover!

What is a cyclone? Only thin air moving fast
from here to yonder, to become silent emptiness at last.

William Carlos Williams (1883 – 1963)

Danse Russe[2]

If I when my wife is sleeping
and the baby and Kathleen
are sleeping
and the sun is a flame-white disc
in silken mists

---

[1] Form: Free verse—Vocabulary: transcendent: supreme.
[2] Form: Free verse—Vocabulary: flanks; the side between the last rib and
the hip.

above shining trees,-
if I in my north room
dance naked, grotesquely
before my mirror
waving my shirt round my head
and singing softly to myself:
"I am lonely, lonely.
I was born to be lonely,
I am best so!"
If I admire my arms, my face
my shoulders, flanks, buttocks
against the yellow drawn shades,-

who shall say I am not
the happy genius of my household?

The Act[1]

There were the roses, in the rain.
Don't cut them, I pleaded.
They won't last, she said.
But they're so beautiful

---

[1] Form: Free verse.

Where they are.
Agh, we were all beautiful once, she said.
And cut them and gave them to me
In my hand.

The Last Words of My English Grandmother[1]

There were some dirty plates
and a glass of milk
beside her on a small table
near the rank, disheveled bed—

Wrinkled and nearly blind
she lay and snored
rousing with anger in her tones
to cry for food,

Gimme something to eat—
they're starving me—
I'm all right I won't go
to the hospital. No, no, no

Give me something to eat

---

[1] Form: Free verse.

Let me take you
to the hospital, I said
and after you are well

you can do as you please.
She smiled, Yes
you do what you please first
then I can do what I please—

Oh, oh, oh! she cried
as the ambulance men lifted
her to the stretcher—
Is this what you call

making me comfortable?
By now her mind was clear—
Oh you think you're smart
you young people,

she said, but I'll tell you
you don't know anything.
Then we started.
On the way

we passed a long row
of elms. She looked at them
awhile out of
the ambulance window and said,

What are all those
fuzzy-looking things out there?
Trees? Well, I'm tired
of them and rolled her head away.

The Red Wheelbarrow[1]

so much depends
upon

---

[1] Form: Free verse.

a red wheel
barrow

glazed with rain
water

beside the white
chickens.

The Three Graces[1]

We have the picture of you in mind,
when you were young, posturing
(for a photographer) in scarves
(if you could have done it) but now,
for none of you is immortal, ninety-
three, the three, ninety and three,
Mary, Ellen and Emily, what
beauty is it clings still about you?
Undying? Magical? For there is still
no answer, why we live or why
you will not live longer than I
or that there should be an answer why
any should live and whatever other
should die. Yet you live. You live
and all that can be said is that
you live, time cannot alter it—
and as I write this Mary has died.

This is Just to Say[2]

I have eaten
the plums
that were in
the icebox

and which
you were probably

---

[1] Form: Free verse.
[2] Form: Free verse—Notes: The apology which is not really an apology.

saving
for breakfast

Forgive me
they were delicious
so sweet
and so cold

To Mark Anthony in Heaven[1]

This quiet morning light
reflected, how many times
from grass and trees and clouds
enters my north room
touching the walls with
grass and clouds and trees.
Anthony,
trees and grass and clouds.
Why did you follow
that beloved body
with your ships at Actium?
I hope it was because
you knew her inch by inch
from slanting feet upward
to the roots of her hair
and down again and that
you saw her
above the battle's fury—
clouds and trees and grass—

For then you are
listening in heaven.

---

[1] Form: Free verse—Vocabulary: Actium: site of a sea battle where
Cleopatra's ships approached to reinforce, then turned and fled, and Mark
Anthony followed her in his ship, abandoning his fleet and losing the
battle.—Notes: Notice how the poem alternates between the narrator's
observations of the reality around him, both outside his windows and
reflected onto his walls (the trees, the clouds, the grass), versus the
intruding thoughts about Mark Antony.

Tract[1]

I will teach you my townspeople
how to perform a funeral
for you have it over a troop
of artists—
unless one should scour the world—
you have the ground sense necessary.

See! the hearse leads.
I begin with a design for a hearse.
For Christ's sake not black—
nor white either—and not polished!
Let it be weathered—like a farm wagon—
with gilt wheels (this could be
applied fresh at small expense)
or no wheels at all:
a rough dray to drag over the ground.

Knock the glass out!
My God—glass, my townspeople!
For what purpose? Is it for the dead
to look out or for us to see
how well he is housed or to see
the flowers or the lack of them—
or what?
To keep the rain and snow from him?
He will have a heavier rain soon:
pebbles and dirt and what not.
Let there be no glass—
and no upholstery, phew!
and no little brass rollers
and small easy wheels on the bottom—
my townspeople what are you thinking of?
A rough plain hearse then
with gilt wheels and no top at all.
On this the coffin lies
by its own weight.

---

[1] Form: Free verse—Vocabulary: dray: work cart with low or no wheels;
understrapper: underling.

No wreaths please—
especially no hot house flowers.
Some common memento is better,
something he prized and is known by:
his old clothes—a few books perhaps—
God knows what! You realize
how we are about these things
my townspeople—
something will be found—anything
even flowers if he had come to that.
So much for the hearse.

For heaven's sake though see to the driver!
Take off the silk hat! In fact
that's no place at all for him—
up there unceremoniously
dragging our friend out to his own dignity!
Bring him down—bring him down!
Low and inconspicuous! I'd not have him ride
on the wagon at all—damn him—
the undertaker's understrapper!
Let him hold the reins
and walk at the side
and inconspicuously too!

Then briefly as to yourselves:
Walk behind—as they do in France,
seventh class, or if you ride
Hell take curtains! Go with some show
of inconvenience; sit openly—
to the weather as to grief.
Or do you think you can shut grief in?
What—from us? We who have perhaps
nothing to lose? Share with us
share with us—it will be money
in your pockets.

Go now
I think you are ready.

Sara Teasdale (1884 – 1933)

There will come soft rains[1]

There will come soft rains and the smell of the ground,
And swallows circling with their shimmering sound;

And frogs in the pools singing at night,
And wild plum trees in tremulous white;

Robins will wear their feathery fire,
Whistling their whims on a low fence-wire;

And not one will know of the war, not one
Will care at last when it is done.

Not one would mind, neither bird nor tree,
If mankind perished utterly;

And Spring herself, when she woke at dawn
Would scarcely know that we were gone.

D.H. Lawrence (1885 – 1930)

From The Ship of Death[2]

I
Now it is autumn and the falling fruit
and the long journey towards oblivion.

The apples falling like great drops of dew
to bruise themselves an exit from themselves.

And it is time to go, to bid farewell
to one's own self, and find an exit
from the fallen self.

---

[1] Form: Iambic tetrameter, AABBCC. . . End rhymes—Vocabulary:
tremulous: trembling.
[2] Form: Iambic pentameter, dropping off to tetrameter then trimeter much
as the life is tapering off.

351

New Year's Eve[1]

There are only two things now,
The great black night scooped out
And this fire-glow.

This fire-glow, the core,
And we the two ripe pips
That are held in store.

Listen, the darkness rings
As it circulates round our fire.
Take off your things.

Your shoulders, your bruised throat!
Your breasts, your nakedness!
This fiery coat!

As the darkness flickers and dips,
As the firelight falls and leaps
From your feet to your lips!

---

[1] Form: Free verse—Vocabulary: pips: dots.

Snake[1]

A snake came to my water-trough
On a hot, hot day, and I in pajamas for the heat,
To drink there.

In the deep, strange-scented shade of the great dark
    carob-tree
I came down the steps with my pitcher
And must wait, must stand and wait, for there he was at the
    trough before me.

He reached down from a fissure in the earth-wall in the
    gloom
And trailed his yellow-brown slackness soft-bellied down,
    over the edge of the stone trough
And rested his throat upon the stone bottom,
And where the water had dripped from the tap, in a small
    clearness,
He sipped with his straight mouth,
Softly drank through his straight gums, into his slack long
    body,
Silently.

Someone was before me at my water-trough,
And I, like a second comer, waiting.

He lifted his head from his drinking, as cattle do,
And looked at me vaguely, as drinking cattle do,
And flickered his two-forked tongue from his lips, and mused
    a moment,
And stooped and drank a little more,
Being earth-brown, earth-golden from the burning bowels of
    the earth
On the day of Sicilian July, with Etna smoking.

---

[1] Form: Free verse—Vocabulary: carob: an evergreen tree with pods that
contain a chocolate type pulp; Etna: a volcanic mountain; paltry:
contemptible; albatross: an allusion to the albatross in "The Rime of the
Ancient Mariner"; expiate: make amends for.

The voice of my education said to me
He must be killed,
For in Sicily the black, black snakes are innocent, the gold
    are venomous.

And voices in me said, If you were a man
You would take a stick and break him now, and finish him
    off.

But must I confess how I liked him,
How glad I was he had come like a guest in quiet, to drink at
    my water-trough
And depart peaceful, pacified, and thankless,
Into the burning bowels of this earth?

Was it cowardice, that I dared not kill him?
Was it perversity, that I longed to talk to him?
Was it humility, to feel so honored?
I felt so honored.

And yet those voices:
If you were not afraid, you would kill him!

And truly I was afraid, I was most afraid,
But even so, honored still more
That he should seek my hospitality
From out the dark door of the secret earth.

He drank enough,
And lifted his head, dreamily, as one who has drunken,
And flickered his tongue
Like a forked night on the air, so black,
Seeming to lick his lips,
And looked around like a god, unseeing, into the air,
And slowly turned his head,
And slowly, very slowly, as if thrice adream,
Proceeded to draw his slow length curving round
And climb again the broken bank of my wall-face.

And as he put his head into that dreadful hole,
And as he slowly drew up, snake-easing his shoulders, and
    entered farther,
A sort of horror,
A sort of protest against his withdrawing into that horrid
    black hole,
Deliberately going into the blackness, and slowly drawing
    himself after,
Overcame me now his back was turned.

I looked round, I put down my pitcher,
I picked up a clumsy log
And threw it at the water-trough with a clatter.

I think it did not hit him,
But suddenly that part of him that was left behind convulsed
    in undignified haste.
Writhed like lightning, and was gone
Into the black hole, the earth-lipped fissure in the wall-front,
At which, in the intense still noon, I stared with fascination.

And immediately I regretted it.
I thought how paltry, how vulgar, what a mean act!
I despised myself and the voices of my accursed human
    education.

And I thought of the albatross
And I wished he would come back, my snake.

For he seemed to me again like a king,
Like a king in exile, uncrowned in the underworld,
Now due to be crowned again.

And so, I missed my chance with one of the lords
Of life.
And I have something to expiate:
A pettiness.

Ezra Pound (1885 – 1972)

A Pact[1]

I make a pact with you, Walt Whitman—
I have detested you long enough.
I come to you as a grown child
Who has had a pig-headed father;
I am old enough now to make friends.
It was you that broke the new wood
Now is a time for carving.
We have one sap and one root—
Let there be commerce between us.

Francesca[2]

You came in out of the night
And there were flowers in your hands,
Now you will come out of a confusion of people,
Out of a turmoil of speech about you.

I who have seen you amid the primal things
Was angry when they spoke your name
In ordinary places.
I would that the cool waves might flow over my mind,
And that the world should dry as a dead leaf,
Or as a dandelion seed-pod and be swept away,
So that I might find you again,
Alone.

In a Station of the Metro[3]

The apparition of these faces in the crowd;
Petals on a wet, black bough.

---

[1] Form: Free verse—Notes: Ezra Pound looked down on Walt Whitman's poetry for most of his life, but eventually recognized that his own poetry was an outgrowth of a trend away from formal verse started by Walt Whitman.
[2] Form: Free verse—Notes: The narrator resents sharing Francesca with the world, or even having them talk about her. He wishes that the world, and it's problems, would just vanish and leave him and his love.
[3] Form: Free verse—Vocabulary: apparition: act of appearing.

Lustra (from the Introduction)[1]

And the days are not full enough
And the nights are not full enough
And life slips by like a field mouse
                    Not shaking the grass.

Salutation[2]

O generation of the thoroughly smug
        and thoroughly uncomfortable,
I have seen fishermen picnicking in the sun,
I have seen them with untidy families,
I have seen their smiles full of teeth
        and heard ungainly laughter.
And I am happier than you are,
And they were happier than I am;
And the fish swim in the lake
        and do not even own clothing.

Tame Cat[3]

"It rests me to be among beautiful women
Why should one always lie about such matters?
I repeat:
It rests me to converse with beautiful women
Even though we talk nothing but nonsense,

The purring of the invisible antennae
Is both stimulating and delightful."

---

[1] Form: Free verse.
[2] Form: Free verse.
[3] Form: Free verse.

357

The Eyes[1]

Rest Master, for we be a-weary, weary
And would feel the fingers of the wind
Upon these lids that lie over us
Sodden and lead-heavy.

     Rest brother, for lo! The dawn is without!
The yellow flame paleth
And the wax runs low.

Free us, for without be goodly colors,
Green of the wood-moss and flower colors,
And coolness beneath the trees.

     Free us, for we perish
In this ever-flowing monotony
Of ugly print marks, black
Upon white parchment.

     Free us, for there is one
Whose smile more availeth

---

[1] Form: Free verse—Vocabulary: availeth: is better—Notes: The eyes of
weary of reading and would rather look on the lovely but unspecified
woman.

Than all the age-old knowledge of thy books:
And we would look thereon.

The Garden[1]

Like a skein of loose silk blown against a wall
She walks by the railing of a path
In Kensington Gardens,
And she is dying piece-meal
        of a sort of emotional anemia.

And round about there is a rabble
Of the filthy, sturdy, unkillable infants of the very poor.
They shall inherit the earth.

In her is the end of breeding.
Her boredom is exquisite and excessive.
She would like some one to speak to her,
And is almost afraid that I
        will commit that indiscretion.

The Plunge[2]

I would bathe myself in strangeness:
These comforts heaped upon me, smother me!
I burn, I scald so for the new,
New friends, new faces,
Places!
Oh to be out of this,
This that is all I wanted
        —save the new.

And you,
Love, you the much, the more desired!

---

[1] Form: Free verse—Vocabulary: skein: thread wound in a coil; anemia: low
red blood cells resulting in tiredness—Notes: The narrator is very class
conscious, and looks down on what he sees as the lower class while
mentally toying with a bored woman from the upper class.
[2] Form: Free verse—Notes: The narrator sought after a comfortable life,
but now those trappings of life are unwanted and the narrator longs for
something new, and more specifically, longs to experience something new
and foreign with his love.

Do I not loathe all walls, streets, stones,
All mire, mist, all fog,
All ways of traffic?
You, I would have flow over me like water,
Oh, but far out of this!
Grass, and low fields, and hills,
And sun,
Oh, sun enough!
Out, and alone, among some
Alien people!

The Tree[1]

I stood still and was a tree amid the wood,
Knowing the truth of things unseen before;
Of Daphne and the laurel bough
And that god-feasting couple old
That grew elm-oak amid the wold.
'Twas not until the gods had been
Kindly entreated, and been brought within
Unto the hearth of their heart's home
That they might do this wonder thing;
Nathless I have been a tree amid the wood
And many a new thing understood
That was rank folly to my head before.

Louis Untermeyer (1885 – 1972)

Long Feud[2]

Where, without bloodshed, can there be
A more relentless enmity
Than the long feud fought silently

Between man and the growing grass?
Man's the aggressor, for he has
Weapons to humble and harass

---

[1] Form: Mostly iambic tetrameter —Vocabulary: Daphne: nymph who changed into laurel tree to escape Apollo; wold: unforested plain.
[2] Form: Iambic tetrameter, AAA end rhymes—Vocabulary: enmity: deep-seated hatred.

The impudent spears that charge upon
His sacred privacy of lawn,
He mows them down, and they are gone

Only to lie in wait, although
He builds above and digs below
Where never a root would dare to go.

His are the triumphs till the day
There's no more grass to cut away,
And, tired of labor, tired of play,

Having exhausted every whim,
He stretches out each conquering limb.
And then the small grass covers him.

Rupert Brooke (1887 – 1915)

The Soldier[1]

If I should die, think only this of me:
    That there's some corner of a foreign field
The is for ever England. There shall be
    In that rich earth a richer dust concealed;
A dust whom England bore, shaped, made aware,
    Gave, once, her flowers to love, her ways to roam,
A body of England's, breathing English air,
    Washed by the rivers, blest by suns of home.

And think, this heart, all evil shed away,
    A pulse in the eternal mind, no less
        Gives somewhere back the thoughts by England given;
Her sights and sounds; dreams happy as her day;
    And laughter, learnt of friends; and gentleness,
        In hearts at peace, under an English heaven.

---

[1] Form: Sonnet.

Robinson Jeffers (1887 – 1962)

Fawn's Foster-Mother[1]

The old woman sits on a bench before the door and quarrels
With her meager pale demoralized daughter.
Once when I passed I found her alone, laughing in the sun
And saying that when she was first married
She lived in the old farmhouse up Garapatas Canyon.
(It is empty now, the roof has fallen
But the log walls hang on the stone foundation; the redwoods
Have all been cut down, the oaks are standing;
The place is now more solitary than ever before.)
"When I was nursing my second baby
My husband found a day-old fawn hid in a fern-brake
And brought it; I put its mouth to the breast
Rather than let it starve, I had milk enough for three babies.
Hey how it sucked, the little nuzzler,
Digging its little hoofs like quills into my stomach.
I had more joy from that than from the others."
Her face is deformed with age, furrowed like a bad road
With market-wagons, mean cares and decay.
She is thrown up to the surface of things, a cell of dry skin
Soon to be shed from the earth's old eye-brows,
I see that once in her spring she lived in the streaming
    arteries,
The stir of the world, the music of the mountain.

Joyce Kilmer (1887 – 1918)

Trees[2]

I think that I shall never see
A poem as lovely as a tree.

A tree whose hungry mouth is prest
Against the earth's sweet flowing breast;

---

[1] Form: Prose poem.
[2] Form: Iambic tetrameter, AABB end rhymes.

A tree that looks to God all day,
And lifts her leafy arms to pray;

A tree that may in summer wear
A nest of robins in her hair;

Upon whose bosom snow has lain;
Who intimately lives with rain.

Poems are made by fools like me,
But only God can make a tree.

Marianne Moore (1887 – 1972)

I May, I Might, I Must[1]

If you will tell me why the fen
appears impassable, I then
will tell you why I think that I
can get across it if I try.

Injudicious Gardening[2]

If yellow betokens infidelity,
    I am an infidel.
        I could not bear a yellow rose ill will
        Because books said that yellow boded ill,
White promised well.

However, your particular possession,
    The sense of privacy,
        Indeed might deprecate
        Offended ears, and need not tolerate
Effrontery.

---

[1] Form: Iambic tetrameter, AABB end rhymes—Vocabulary: fen: marsh.
[2] Form: Free verse—Vocabulary: deprecate: belittle; effrontery:
presumptuousness.

Poetry[1]

I, too, dislike it: there are things more important beyond all
this fiddle.
Reading it, however, with a perfect contempt for it, one
discovers in it, after all, a place for the genuine.

To a Steam Roller[2]

The illustration
is nothing to you without the application.
You lack half wit. You crush all the particles down
into close conformity, and then walk back and forth on
them.

Sparkling chips of rock
are crushed down to the level of the parent block.
Were not 'impersonal judgment in aesthetic
matters, a metaphysical impossibility,' you

might fairly achieve
it. As for butterflies, I can hardly conceive
of one's attending upon you, but to question
the congruence of the complement is vain, if it exists.

T.S. Eliot (1888 – 1965)

Hysteria[3]

As she laughed I was aware of becoming involved in her
laughter and being part of it, until her teeth were only
accidental stars with a talent for squad-drill. I was drawn in
by short gasps, inhaled at each momentary recovery, lost

---

[1] Form: Free verse.

[2] Form: Free verse—Vocabulary: congruence: appropriateness—Notes:
Twisted, disjointed phrases make this a hard poem, but the observations
about a steamroller (or metaphorically, any group, parents, company, etc.
that forces conformity) is contrasted with the image of a butterfly
(individuality, freedom).

[3] Form: Free verse—Notes: The waiter wants to get the hysterical woman
outside, but the narrator is only concerned with enjoying the moment in
general and her breasts in particular.

finally in the dark caverns of her throat, bruised by the ripple of unseen muscles. An elderly waiter with trembling hands was hurriedly spreading a pink and white checked cloth over the rusty green iron table, saying: "If the lady and gentleman wish to take their tea in the garden, if the lady and gentleman wish to take their tea in the garden..." I decided that if the shaking of her breasts could be stopped, some of the fragments of the afternoon might be collected, and I concentrated my attention with careful subtlety to this end.

Rhapsody on a Windy Night[1]

Twelve o'clock.
Along the reaches of the street
Held in a lunar synthesis,
Whispering lunar incantations
Dissolve the floors of memory
And all its clear relations,
Its divisions and precisions,
Every street lamp that I pass
Beats like a fatalistic drum,
And through the spaces of the dark
Midnight shakes the memory
As a madman shakes a dead geranium.

Half-past one,
The street lamp sputtered,
The street lamp muttered,
The street lamp said, "Regard that woman
Who hesitates towards you in the light of the door
Which opens on her like a grin.
You see the border of her dress
Is torn and stained with sand,
And you see the corner of her eye
Twists like a crooked pin."

The memory throws up high and dry
A crowd of twisted things;

---

[1] Form: Mostly iambic, irregular line lengths—Vocabulary: quay: wharf.

365

A twisted branch upon the beach
Eaten smooth, and polished
As if the world gave up
The secret of its skeleton,
Stiff and white.
A broken spring in a factory yard,
Rust that clings to the form that the strength has left
Hard and curled and ready to snap.

Half-past two,
The street lamp said,
"Remark the cat which flattens itself in the gutter,
Slips out its tongue
And devours a morsel of rancid butter."
So the hand of a child, automatic,
Slipped out and pocketed a toy that was running along the
    quay.
I could see nothing behind that child's eye.
I have seen eyes in the street
Trying to peer through lighted shutters,
And a crab one afternoon in a pool,
An old crab with barnacles on his back,
Gripped the end of a stick which I held him.

Half-past three,
The lamp sputtered,
The lamp muttered in the dark.
The lamp hummed:
"Regard the moon,
La lune ne garde aucune rancune,
She winks a feeble eye,
She smiles into corners.
She smoothes the hair of the grass.
The moon has lost her memory.
A washed-out smallpox cracks her face,
Her hand twists a paper rose,
That smells of dust and old Cologne,
She is alone
With all the old nocturnal smells
That cross and cross across her brain."
The reminiscence comes

Of sunless dry geraniums
And dust in crevices,
Smells of chestnuts in the streets,
And female smells in shuttered rooms,
And cigarettes in corridors
And cocktail smells in bars."

The lamp said,
"Four o'clock,
Here is the number on the door.
Memory!
You have the key,
The little lamp spreads a ring on the stair,
Mount.
The bed is open; the tooth-brush hangs on the wall,
Put your shoes at the door, sleep, prepare for life."

The last twist of the knife.

The Love Song of J. Alfred Prufrock[1]

S'io credesse che mia risposta fosse
A persona che mai tornasse al mondo,
Questa fiamma staria senza piu scosse.
Ma perciocche giammai di questo fondo
Non torno vivo alcun s'i'odo il vero,
Senza tema d'infamia ti rispondo.

Let us go then, you and I,
When the evening is spread out against the sky

---

[1] "Form: Free verse—Vocabulary: insidious: subtly harmful; malingers:
feigns illness; Lazarus: man raised from the dead by Jesus (Bible); Prince
Hamlet: from ""Hamlet"" (Shakespeare); obtuse: unintelligent; S'io credesse
che mia risposta fosse
A persona che mai tornasse al mondo,
Questa fiamma staria senza piu scosse.
Ma perciocche giammai di questo fondo
Non torno vivo alcun, s'i'odo il vero,
Senza tema d'infamia ti rispondo.
If I did think my answer would be spoken To one who could ever return
into the world, This flame would sleep unmoved.
But since never, if true be told me, any from this depth Has found his
upward way, I answer thee, Nor fear lest infamy record my words.
- from Dante's Inferno, XXVII, 61-6]

Like a patient etherized upon a table;
Let us go, through certain half-deserted streets,
The muttering retreats
Of restless nights in one-night cheap hotels
And sawdust restaurants with oyster-shells:
Streets that follow like a tedious argument
Of insidious intent
To lead you to an overwhelming question. ...
Oh, do not ask, "What is it?"
Let us go and make our visit.
In the room the women come and go
Talking of Michelangelo.

The yellow fog that rubs its back upon the window-panes,
The yellow smoke that rubs its muzzle on the window-panes,
Licked its tongue into the corners of the evening,
Lingered upon the pools that stand in drains,
Let fall upon its back the soot that falls from chimneys.
Slipped by the terrace, made a sudden leap,
And seeing that it was a soft October night,
Curled once about the house, and fell asleep.

And indeed there will be time
For the yellow smoke that slides along the street,
Rubbing its back upon the window-panes;
There will be time, there will be time
To prepare a face to meet the faces that you meet;
There will be time to murder and create,
And time for all the works and days of hands
That lift and drop a question on your plate;
Time for you and time for me,
And time yet for a hundred indecisions,
And for a hundred visions and revisions,
Before the taking of a toast and tea.
In the room the women come and go
Talking of Michelangelo.

And indeed there will be time
To wonder, "Do I dare?" and, "Do I dare?"
Time to turn back and descend the stair,
With a bald spot in the middle of my hair—

(They will say: "How his hair is growing thin!")
My morning coat, my collar mounting firmly to the chin,
My necktie rich and modest, but asserted by a simple pin—
(They will say: "But how his arms and legs are thin!")
Do I dare
Disturb the universe?
In a minute there is time
For decisions and revisions which a minute will reverse.

For I have known them all already, known them all:
Have known the evenings, mornings, afternoons,
I have measured out my life with coffee spoons;
I know the voices dying with a dying fall
Beneath the music from a farther room.
      So how should I presume?

And I have known the eyes already, known them all—
The eyes that fix you in a formulated phrase,
And when I am formulated, sprawling on a pin,
When I am pinned and wriggling on the wall,
Then how should I begin
To spit out all the butt-ends of my days and ways?
      And how should I presume?

And I have known the arms already, known them all—
Arms that are braceleted and white and bare
(But in the lamplight, downed with light brown hair!)
Is it perfume from a dress
That makes me so digress?
Arms that lie along a table, or wrap about a shawl.
      And should I then presume?
      And how should I begin?

Shall I say, I have gone at dusk through narrow streets
And watched the smoke that rises from the pipes
Of lonely men in shirt-sleeves, leaning out of windows?...
I should have been a pair of ragged claws
Scuttling across the floors of silent seas.

And the afternoon, the evening, sleeps so peacefully!
Smoothed by long fingers,

Asleep ... tired ... or it malingers,
Stretched on the floor, here beside you and me.
Should I, after tea and cakes and ices,
Have the strength to force the moment to its crisis?
But though I have wept and faster, wept and prayed,
Though I have seen my head (grown slightly bald) brought in
    upon a platter,
I am no prophet—and here's no great matter;
I have seen the moment of my greatness flicker,
And I have seen the eternal Footman hold my coat, and
    snicker,
And in short, I was afraid.

And would it have been worth it, after all,
After the cups, the marmalade, the tea,
Among the porcelain, among some talk of you and me,
Would it have been worth while,
To have bitten off the matter with a smile,
To have squeezed the universe into a ball
To roll it toward some overwhelming question,
To say: "I am Lazarus, come from the dead,
Come back to tell you all, I shall tell you all"—
If one, settling a pillow by her head,
    Should say: "That is not what I meant at all;
    That is not it, at all."

And would it have been worth it, after all.
Would it have been worth while,
After the sunsets and the dooryards and the sprinkled
    streets,
After the novels, after the teacups, after the skirts that trail
    along the floor—
And this, and so much more?—
It is impossible to say just what I mean!
But as if a magic lantern threw the nerves
    in patterns on a screen:
Would it have been worth while,
If one, settling a pillow or throwing off a shawl,
And turning toward the window, should say:
    "That is not it at all,
    that is not what I meant, at all."

No! I am not Prince Hamlet, nor was meant to be;
Am an attendant lord, one that will do
To swell a progress, start a scene or two,
Advise the prince; no doubt, an easy tool,
Deferential, glad to be of use,
Politic, cautious, and meticulous;
Full of high sentence, but a bit obtuse;
At times, indeed, almost ridiculous—
Almost, at times, the Fool.

I grow old ... I grow old ...
I shall wear the bottoms of my trousers rolled.

Shall I part my hair behind? Do I dare to eat a peach?
I shall wear white flannel trousers, and walk upon the beach.
I have heard the mermaids singing, each to each.

I do not think that they will sing to me.
I have seen them riding seaward on the waves
Combing the white hair of the waves blown back
When the wind blows the water white and black.
We have lingered in the chambers of the sea
By sea-girls wreathed with seaweed red and brown
Till human voices wake us, and we drown.

Anna Akhmatova (1889 – 1966)

Requiem – Instead of a Preface[1]
Translated by Lenore Mayherw

In the terrible years of Yezhovism I spent seventeen months
standing in line in front of the Leningrad prisons. One day
someone thought he recognized me. Then, a woman with
bluish lips who was behind me and to whom my name meant
nothing came out of the torpor to which we were all
accustomed and said, softly (for we spoke only in whispers),
    "—And that, could you describe that?"

---

[1] Form: Prose poem—Vocabulary: Yezhovism: reference to Nikolai Ivanovich
Yezhov, head of the Soviet secret police 1936-1938 during the "great
purge"; torpor: lethargy.

And I said, "Yes, I can."
And then a sort of smile slid across what had been her
    face.

April 1, 1957
Leningrad

Archibald MacLeish (1892 – 1982)

Ars Poetica[1]

A poem should be palpable and mute
As a globed fruit,

Dumb
As old medallions to the thumb,

Silent as the sleeve-worn stone
Of casement ledges where the moss has grown—

A poem should be wordless
As the flight of birds.

. . .

A poem should be motionless in time
As the moon climbs,

Leaving, as the moon releases
Twig by twig the night-entangled trees,

Leaving, as the moon behind the winter leaves,
Memory by memory the mind—

A poem should be motionless in time
As the moon climbs.

. . .

---

[1] Form: Iambic, irregular line lengths—Vocabulary: palpable: tangible;
medallions: Greek coin.

A poem should be equal to:
Not true.

For all the history of grief
An empty doorway and a maple leaf.

For love
The leaning grasses and two lights above the sea—

A poem should not mean
But be.

Not Marble nor the Gilded Monuments[1]

The praisers of women in their proud and beautiful poems,
Naming the grave mouth and the hair and the eyes,
Boasted those they loved should be forever remembered:
These were lies.

The words sound but the face in the Istrian sun is forgotten.
The poet speaks but to her dead ears no more.
The sleek throat is gone - and the breast that was troubled to
    listen:
Shadow from door.

Therefore I will not praise your knees nor your fine walking
Telling you men shall remember your name as long
As lips move or breath is spent or the iron of English
Rings from a tongue.

I shall say you were young, and your arms straight, and your
    mouth scarlet:
I shall say you will die and none will remember you:
Your arms change, and none remember the swish of your
    garments,
Nor the click of your shoe.

Not with my hand's strength, not with the difficult labor
Springing the obstinate words to the bones of your breast

---

[1] Form: Free verse—Vocabulary: Istrian: a peninsula in the Adriatic sea.

And the stubborn line to your young stride and the breath to
    your breathing
And the beat to your haste
Shall I prevail on the hearts of unborn men to remember.

(What is a dead girl but a shadowy ghost
Or a dead man's voice but a distant and vain affirmation
Like dream words most)

Therefore I will not speak of the undying glory of women.
I will say you were young and straight and your skin fair
And you stood in the door and the sun was a shadow of
    leaves on your shoulders
And a leaf on your hair—
    I will not speak of the famous beauty of dead women:
    I will say the shape of a leaf lay once on your hair.
    Till the world ends and the eyes are out and the mouths
       broken.
    Look! It is there!

Edna St. Vincent Millay (1892 – 1950)

First Fig[1]

My candle burns at both ends;
    It will not last the night;
But ah, my foes, and oh, my friends—
    It gives a lovely light!

Wilfred Owen (1893 – 1918)

Dulce et Decorum Est[2]

Bent double, like old beggars under sacks,
Knock-kneed, coughing like hags, we cursed through sludge,

---

[1] Form: Iambic, 3-3-4-3 pattern, ABAB end rhymes.
[2] "Form: Mostly iambic pentameter, some trochaic lines, ABAB end rhymes—Vocabulary: Knock-kneed: knees close together, ankles apart; lime: caustic chemical; cud: something held in the mouth and chewed, as tobacco; Dulce et decorum est Pro patria mori: It is glorious to die for your country.

Till on the haunting flares we turned our backs,
And towards our distant rest began to trudge.
Men marched asleep. Many had lost their boots,
But limped on, blood-shod. All went lame, all blind;
Drunk with fatigue; deaf even to the hoots
Of gas-shells dropping softly behind.

Gas! Gas! Quick, boys!- An ecstasy of fumbling,
Fitting the clumsy helmets just in time,
But some one still was yelling out and stumbling
And flound'ring like a man in fire or lime .
Dim through the misty panes and thick green light,
As under a green sea, I saw him drowning.

In all my dreams before my helpless sight
He plunges at me, guttering, choking, drowning.

If in some smothering dreams, you too could pace
Behind the wagon that we flung him in,
And watch the white eyes wilting in his face,
His hanging face, like a devil's sick of sin,
If you could hear, at every jolt, the blood
Come gargling from the froth-corrupted lungs,
Bitten as the cud
Of vile, incurable sores on innocent tongues,—
My friend, you would not tell with such high zest
To children ardent for some desperate glory,
The old Lie: Dulce et decorum est
Pro patria mori.

Lucian Blaga (1895 – 1961)

I will not crush the world's corolla of wonders[1]

I will not crush the world's corolla of wonders
and I will not kill
with reason
the mysteries I meet along my way
in flowers, eyes, lips, and graves.

---

[1] Form: Free verse—Vocabulary: corolla: the bloom of a flower.

375

The light of others
drowns the deep magic hidden
in the profound darkness.
I increase the world's enigma
with my light
much as the moon with its white beams
does not diminish but increases
the shimmering mystery of night—
I enrich the darkening horizon
with chills of the great secret.
All that is hard to know
becomes a greater riddle
under my very eyes
because I love alike
flowers, lips, eyes, and graves.

Miyazawa Kenji (1896 – 1933)

Daydreaming on the Trail[1]
  (Translation by Gary Snyder)

A lonely stretch, in the bind of poor fishing and drouth,
following the ocean
crossing pass after pass,
fields of wild reeds,
I've come this far alone,

dozing in the pale sun
on the sand of a dried-up riverbed
back and shoulder chilled
something bothered me—
I think at that last quartzite pass
I left the oak gate in the fence
of the cowpasture open
probably because I was hurrying—
          a white gate—
did I close it or not?

light cool sky,

---

[1] Form: Free verse.

mistletoe on chestnut floats in vision
manylayered clouds upriver
cool lattice of sunlight
some unknown big bird   calling
faintly, crork   crork

Louise Bogan (1897 – 1970)

from Beginning and End—Knowledge[1]

Now that I know
How passion warms little
Of flesh in the mould,
And treasure is brittle,—

I'll lie here and learn
How, over their ground
Trees make a long shadow
And a light sound.

Ernest Hemingway (1899 – 1960)

from Wanderings — Chapter Heading[2]

For we have thought the longer thoughts
and gone the shorter way.
And we have danced to devils' tunes,
shivering home to pray;
to serve one master in the night,
another in the day.

---

[1] Form: Dimeter lines consisting of an iamb and an anapest xAxA end
rhymes—Vocabulary: mould: earth of a grave.
[2] Form: Ballad.

Wen I-to (1899 – 1946)

Dead Water[1]
Translation by Ma Wentong

A pond despaired of any hope,
no breeze can stir up any ripples.
Better be the dump of disused brass and iron wares
and the cesspool of leftover dishes.
Maybe the brass will green into sapphire
and iron can will the rust into peach flowers;
let grease weave into colorful silky patterns,
and the mould steam out rainbows.
Let this dead water ferment into a pond of green wine,
floating with foams like pearls,
with smaller pearls simmering into larger ones
that pop out by the onslaught of wine thieving bugs.
A pond of such despair
has its own claims to freshness.
If frogs cannot put up with the silence
it is the dead water that invokes their songs.
This is a pond despaired of hope;
this is not where beauty dwells.
Better let the evil plough in all this
see what would come out of it.

Anonymous

The Anvil—God's Word[2]

Last eve I passed beside a blacksmith's door
  And heard the anvil ring the vesper chime;
Then, looking in, I saw upon the floor
  Old hammers, worn with beating years of time.

"How many anvils have you had," said I,
  "To wear and batter all these hammers so?"

---

[1] Form: Free verse—Notes: Here the pond may be a literal pond, or a symbol for anything in life that is ugly beyond redemption.
[2] Form: Iambic pentameter, ABAB end rhymes—Vocabulary: vesper: evening prayer.

"Just one," said he, and then with twinkling eye,
"The anvil wears the hammers out, you know."

And so, thought I, the anvil of God's Word,
    For ages skeptics blows have beat upon;
Yet, though the noise of falling blows was heard,
The anvil is unharmed—the hammers gone.

Langston Hughes (1902 – 1967)

Dream Deferred: Harlem[1]

What happens to a dream deferred?

        Does it dry up
        like a raisin in the sun?
        Or fester like a sore—
        And then run?
        Does it stink like rotten meat?
        Or crust and sugar over—
like a syrupy sweet?

Maybe it just sags
like a heavy load.

Or does it explode?

Evil[2]

Looks like what drives me crazy
Don't have no effect on you—
But I'm gonna keep on at it
Till it drives you crazy, too.

Maybe[3]

I asked you, baby,
If you understood—

---

[1] Form: Free verse.
[2] Form: Iambic trimeter, xAxA end rhymes.
[3] Form: Free verse.

You told me that you didn't,
But you thought you would.

Suicide's Note[1]

The calm,
Cool face of the river
Asked me for a kiss.

Stevie Smith (1902 – 1983)

Not Waving but Drowning[2]

Nobody heard him, the dead man,
But still he lay moaning:
I was much further out than you thought
And not waving but drowning.

Poor chap, he always loved larking
And now he's dead
It must have been too cold for him his heart gave way,
They said.

Oh, no no no, it was too cold always
(Still the dead one lay moaning)
I was much too far out all my life
And not waving but drowning.

Sunt Leones[3]

The lions who ate the Christians on the sands of the arena
By indulging native appetites played as has now been seen a
Not entirely negligible part
In consolidating at the very start
The position of the Early Christian Church.

---

[1] Form: Free verse.
[2] Form: Free verse—Vocabulary: larking: carefree adventure—Notes: A
metaphor, with drowning standing in for being overwhelmed in life, sinking
even as those around us think we're waving.
[3] Form: Free verse, AABB end rhymes—Vocabulary: Lions exist (Latin);
Liturgically: to do with the Church.

Initiatory rights are always bloody
In the lions, it appears
From contemporary art, made a study
Of dyeing Coliseum sands a ruddy
Liturgically sacrificial hue
And if the Christians felt a little blue—
Well, people being eaten often do.
Theirs was the death, and there's was a crown undying,
A state of things which must be satisfying.
My point which up to this has been obscured
Is that it was the lions who procured
By chewing up blood gristle flesh and bone
The martyrdoms on which the church has grown.
I only write this poem because I thought it rather looked
As if the part the lions played was being overlooked.
By lions' jaws great benefits and blessings were begotten
And so our debt to Lionhood must never be forgotten.

W.H. Auden (1907 – 1973)

Dichtung and Wahrheit[1]

XXXIII

Alas, it is as impossible that my answer to the question *Who are You?* and your answer to the question "Who am I?" should be the same as that either of them should be exactly and completely true. But if they are not the same, and neither is quite true, then my assertion *I love You* cannot be quite true either.

From Selected Shorts[2]

Whatever their personal faith,
all poets, as such,
are polytheists.

---

[1] Form: Prose poem—Vocabulary: Dichtung and Wahrheit: Sealing and truth.
[2] Form: Free verse—Vocabulary: polytheists: believers in many gods.

Marginalia (Extracts)[1]

When we do evil,
we and our victims
are equally bewildered.

***

A dead man
who never caused others to die
seldom rates a statue.

***

Animal femurs
ascribed to saints who never
existed, are still
***

more holy than portraits
of conquerors who,
unfortunately, did.

***

His thoughts pottered
from verses to sex to God
without punctuation.

***

How cheerful they looked,
the unoccupied bar-stools
in mid-afternoon,
freed for some hours from the weight
of drab defeated bottoms.

***

---

[1] Form: Free verse—Vocabulary: Marginalia: notes in the margin of a book;
femurs: leg bone; pottered: to be busy with unimportant things.

Even Hate should be precise:
very few White Folks
have fucked their mothers.

Zawgee (1907 – 1973)

The Way of the Water-Hyacinth[1]
Translated from the Burmese by Lyn Aye

Bobbing on the breeze blown waves
Bowing to the tide
Hyacinth rises and falls

Falling but not felled
By flotsam, twigs, leaves
She ducks, bobs and weaves.

Ducks, ducks by the score
Jolting, quacking and more
She spins through—

Spinning, swamped, slimed, sunk
She rises, resolute
Still crowned by petals.

Elizabeth Bishop (1911 – 1979)

Filling Station[2]

Oh, but it is dirty!
—this little filling station,
oil-soaked, oil-permeated
to a disturbing, over-all
black translucency.
Be careful with that match!

---

[1] Form: Free verse, irregular end rhymes—Vocabulary: Hyacinth: floating, flowering plant—Notes: A metaphor for inner strength or hidden support helping to overcome problems.
[2] Form: Free verse—Vocabulary: taboret: low stool; hirsute: hairy; marguerites: daisy like flower.

Father wears a dirty,
oil-soaked monkey suit
that cuts him under the arms,
and several quick and saucy
and greasy sons assist him
(it's a family filling station),
all quite thoroughly dirty.

Do they live in the station?
It has a cement porch
behind the pumps, and on it
a set of crushed and grease-
impregnated wickerwork;
on the wicker sofa
a dirty dog, quite comfy.

Some comic books provide
the only note of color—
of certain color. They lie
upon a big dim doily
draping a taboret
(part of the set), beside
a big hirsute begonia.

Why the extraneous plant?
Why the taboret?
Why, oh why, the doily?
(Embroidered in daisy stitch
with marguerites, I think,
and heavy with gray crochet.)

Somebody embroidered the doily.
Somebody waters the plant,
or oils it, maybe. Somebody
arranges the rows of cans
so that they softly say:
ESSO—SO—SO—SO
to high-strung automobiles.
Somebody loves us all.

In the Waiting Room[1]

In Worcester, Massachusetts,
I went with Aunt Consuelo
to keep her dentist's appointment
and sat and waited for her
in the dentist's waiting room.
It was winter. It got dark
early. The waiting room
was full of grown-up people,
arctics and overcoats,
lamps and magazines.
My aunt was inside
what seemed like a long time
and while I waited I read
the National Geographic
(I could read) and carefully
studied the photographs:
the inside of a volcano,
black, and full of ashes;
then it was spilling over
in rivulets of fire.
Osa and Martin Johnson
dressed in riding breeches,
laced boots, and pith helmets.
A dead man slung on a pole
—"Long Pig," the caption said.
Babies with pointed heads
wound round and round with string;
black, naked women with necks
wound round and round with wire
like the necks of light bulbs.
Their breasts were horrifying.
I read it right straight through.
I was too shy to stop.
And then I looked at the cover:
the yellow margins, the date.

---

[1] Form: Free verse—Vocabulary: arctics: rubber boots—Notes: This poem
describes the epiphany of self-awareness, and the associated relationships
with family, gender, and the human race.

Suddenly, from inside,
came an oh! of pain
—Aunt Consuelo's voice—
not very loud or long.
I wasn't at all surprised;
even then I knew she was
a foolish, timid woman.
I might have been embarrassed,
but wasn't. What took me
completely by surprise
was that it was me:
my voice, in my mouth.
Without thinking at all
I was my foolish aunt,
I—we—were falling, falling,
our eyes glued to the cover
of the National Geographic,
February, 1918.

I said to myself: three days
and you'll be seven years old.
I was saying it to stop
the sensation of falling off
the round, turning world.
into cold, blue-black space.
But I felt: you are an I,
you are an Elizabeth,
you are one of them.
Why should you be one, too?
I scarcely dared to look
to see what it was I was.
I gave a sidelong glance
—I couldn't look any higher—
at shadowy gray knees,
trousers and skirts and boots
and different pairs of hands
lying under the lamps.
I knew that nothing stranger
had ever happened, that nothing
stranger could ever happen.
Why should I be my aunt,

or me, or anyone?
What similarities—
boots, hands, the family voice
I felt in my throat, or even
the National Geographic
and those awful hanging breasts—
held us all together
or made us all just one?
How—I didn't know any
word for it—how "unlikely". . .
How had I come to be here,
like them, and overhear
a cry of pain that could have
got loud and worse but hadn't?

The waiting room was bright
and too hot. It was sliding
beneath a big black wave,
another, and another.

Then I was back in it.
The War was on. Outside,
in Worcester, Massachusetts,
were night and slush and cold,
and it was still the fifth
of February, 1918.

One Art[1]

The art of losing isn't hard to master;
so many things seem filled with the intent
to be lost that their loss is no disaster.

Lose something every day. Accept the fluster
of lost door keys, the hour badly spent.
The art of losing isn't hard to master.

---

[1] Form: Villanelle—Notes: Notice how the refrain takes on an increasingly
deep meaning as the poem progresses.

Then practice losing farther, losing faster:
places, and names, and where it was you meant
to travel. None of these will bring disaster.

I lost my mother's watch. And look! my last, or
next-to-last, of three loved houses went.
The art of losing isn't hard to master.

I lost two cities, lovely ones. And, vaster,
some realms I owned, two rivers, a continent.
I miss them, but it wasn't a disaster.

—Even losing you (the joking voice, a gesture
I love) I shan't have lied. It's evident
the art of losing's not too hard to master
though it may look like (Write it!) like disaster.

Sestina[1]

September rain falls on the house.
In the failing light, the old grandmother
sits in the kitchen with the child
beside the Little Marvel Stove,
reading the jokes from the almanac,
laughing and talking to hide her tears.

She thinks that her equinoctial tears
and the rain that beats on the roof of the house
were both foretold by the almanac,
but only known to a grandmother.
The iron kettle sings on the stove.
She cuts some bread and says to the child,

it's time for tea now; but the child
is watching the teakettle's small hard tears
dance like mad on the hot black stove,

---

[1] Form: Sestina—Vocabulary: Marvel Stove: brand of wood burning stove;
equinoctial: at the time of the equinox.

388

the way the rain must dance on the house.
Tidying up, the old grandmother
hangs up the clever almanac

on its string. Birdlike, the almanac
hovers half open above the child,
hovers above the old grandmother
and her teacup full of dark brown tears.
She shivers and says she thinks the house
feels chilly, and puts more wood in the stove.

It was to be, says the Marvel Stove.
I know what I know, says the almanac.
With crayons the child draws a rigid house
and a winding pathway. Then the child
puts in a man with buttons like tears
and shows it proudly to the grandmother.

But secretly, while the grandmother
busies herself about the stove,
the little moons fall down like tears
from between the pages of the almanac
into the flower bed the child
has carefully placed in the front of the house.

Time to plant tears, says the almanac.
The grandmother sings to the marvelous stove
and the child draws another inscrutable house.

The Armadillo[1]
      for Robert Lowell

This is the time of year
when almost every night
the frail, illegal fire balloons appear.
Climbing the mountain height,

rising toward a saint
still honored in these parts,
the paper chambers flush and fill with light
that comes and goes, like hearts.

Once up against the sky it's hard
to tell them from the stars—
planets, that is—the tinted ones:
Venus going down, or Mars,

or the pale green one. With a wind,
they flare and falter, wobble and toss;
but if it's still they steer between
the kite sticks of the Southern Cross,

receding, dwindling, solemnly
and steadily forsaking us,
or, in the downdraft from a peak,

---

[1] Form: Free verse—Notes: I read this as the fire balloons representing
Robert Lowell's poetry, shining like stars, sometimes starting a fire that
illuminates and destroys. Fire balloons are tiny hot air balloons made from
paper or thin plastic wrap using a candle as the heat source.

suddenly turning dangerous.

Last night another big one fell.
It splattered like an egg of fire
against the cliff behind the house.
The flame ran down. We saw the pair

of owls who nest there flying up
and up, their whirling black-and-white
stained bright pink underneath, until
they shrieked up out of sight.

The ancient owls' nest must have burned.
Hastily, all alone,
a glistening armadillo left the scene,
rose-flecked, head down, tail down,

and then a baby rabbit jumped out,
short-eared, to our surprise.
So soft!—a handful of intangible ash
with fixed, ignited eyes.

Too pretty, dreamlike mimicry!
O falling fire and piercing cry
and panic, and a weak mailed fist
clenched ignorant against the sky!

May Swenson (1913 – 1989)

A Couple[1]

A bee rolls in the yellow rose.
Does she invite his hairy rub?
He scrubs himself in her creamy folds.
A bullet soft imposes her spiral
and, spinning, burrows
to her dewy shadows.
The gold grooves almost match
the yellow bowl.
Does his touch please or scratch?
When he's done his honey-thieving
at her matrix, whirs free, leaving,
she closes, still tall, still
unrumpled on her stem.

David Ignatow (1914 – 1997)

The Bagel[2]

I stopped to pick up the bagel
rolling away in the wind,
annoyed with myself
for having dropped it
as if it were a portent.
Faster and faster it rolled,
with me running after it
bent low, gritting my teeth,
and I found myself doubled over
and rolling down the street
head over heels, one complete somersault
after another like a bagel
and strangely happy with myself.

---

[1] Form: Free verse.
[2] Form: Free verse—Vocabulary: portent: prophecy.

Randall Jarrell (1914 – 1965)

Bats[1]

A bat is born
Naked and blind and pale.
His mother makes a pocket of her tail
and catches him. He clings to her long fur
By his thumbs and toes and teeth.
And then the mother dances through the night
Doubling and looping, soaring, somersaulting –
Her baby hangs on underneath.
All night, in happiness, she hunts and flies.
Her high sharp cries
Like shining needlepoints of sound
Go out into the night and, echoing back,
Tell her what they have touched.
She hears how far it is, how big it is,
Which way it's going:
She lives by hearing.
The mother eats the moths and gnats she catches
In full flight; in full flight
The mother drinks the water of the pond
She skims across. Her baby hangs on tight.
Her baby drinks the milk she makes him
In moonlight or starlight, in mid-air.
Their single shadow, printed on the moon
Or fluttering across the stars,
Whirls on all night; at daybreak
The tired mother flaps home to her rafter.
The others are all there.
They hang themselves up by their toes,
They wrap themselves in their brown wings.
Bunched upside down, they sleep in air.
Their sharp ears, their sharp teeth,
Their quick sharp faces
Are dull and slow and mild.
All the bright day, as the mother sleeps,
She folds her wings about her sleeping child.

---

[1] Form: Iambic, irregular line lengths, irregular end rhymes.

Next Day[1]

Moving from Cheer to Joy, from Joy to All,
I take a box
And add it to my wild rice, my Cornish game hens.
The slacked or shorted, basketed, identical
Food-gathering flocks
Are selves I overlook. Wisdom, said William James,

Is learning what to overlook. And I am wise
If that is wisdom.
Yet somehow, as I buy All from these shelves
And the boy takes it to my station wagon,
What i've become
Troubles me even if I shut my eyes.

When I was young and miserable and pretty
And poor, I'd wish
What all girls wish: to have a husband,
A house and children. Now that I'm old, my wish
Is womanish:
That the boy putting groceries in my car

See me. It bewilders me he doesn't see me.
For so many years
I was good enough to eat: the world looked at me
And its mouth watered. How often they have undressed me,
The eyes of strangers!
And, holding their flesh within my flesh, their vile

Imaginings within my imagining,
I too have taken
The chance of life. Now the boy pats my dog
And we start home. Now I am good.
The last mistaken,
Ecstatic, accidental bliss, the blind

---

[1] Form: Free verse—Vocabulary: slacked or shorted: other shoppers
wearing slacks or shorts.

Happiness that, bursting, leaves upon the palm
Some soap and water—
It was so long ago, back in some Gay
Twenties, Nineties, I don't know . . . Today I miss
My lovely daughter
Away at school, my sons away at school,

My husband away at work—I wish for them.
The dog, the maid,
And I go through the sure unvarying days
At home in them. As I look at my life,
I am afraid
Only that it will change, as I am changing:

I am afraid, this morning, of my face.
It looks at me
From the rear-view mirror, with the eyes I hate,
The smile I hate. Its plain, lined look
Of gray discovery
Repeats to me: "You're old. "That's all, I'm old.

And yet I'm afraid, as I was at the funeral
I went to yesterday.
My friend's cold made-up face, granite among its flowers,
Her undressed, operated-on, dressed body
Were my face and body.
As I think of her and I hear her telling me

How young I seem; I am exceptional;
I think of all I have.
But really no one is exceptional,
No one has anything, I'm anybody,
I stand beside my grave
Confused with my life, that is commonplace and solitary.

The Death of the Ball Turret Gunner[1]

From my mother's sleep I fell into the State,
And I hunched in its belly till my wet fur froze.
Six miles from earth, loosed from the dream of life,
I woke to black flak and the nightmare fighters.
When I died they washed me out of the turret with a hose.

William Stafford (1914 – 1993)

Traveling Through the Dark[2]

Traveling through the dark I found a deer
dead on the edge of the Wilson River road.
It is usually best to roll them into the canyon:
that road is narrow; to swerve might make more dead.

By glow of the tail-light I stumbled back of the car
and stood by the heap, a doe, a recent killing;
she had stiffened already, almost cold.
I dragged her off; she was large in the belly.

My fingers touching her side brought me the reason—
her side was warm; her fawn lay there waiting,
alive, still, never to be born.
Beside that mountain road I hesitated.

The car aimed ahead its lowered parking lights;
under the hood purred the steady engine.
I stood in the glare of the warm exhaust turning red;
around our group I could hear the wilderness listen.

I thought hard for us all—my only swerving—
then pushed her over the edge into the river.

---

[1] Form: Free verse—Notes: The "mother's sleep" is safety at home, and here the "state" is the military.
[2] Form: Free verse—Notes: We are all sometimes faced with difficult decisions, in this case what to do about the still living, unborn fawn in the dead deer's womb.

Dylan Thomas (1914 – 1953)

Do Not Go Gentle Into That Good Night[1]

Do not go gentle into that good night,
Old age should burn and rave at close of day;
Rage, rage against the dying of the light.

Though wise men at their end know dark is right,
Because their words had forked no lightning they
Do not go gentle into that good night.

Good men, the last wave by, crying how bright
Their frail deeds might have danced in a green bay,
Rage, rage against the dying of the light.

Wild men who caught and sang the sun in flight,
And learn, too late, they grieved it on its way,
Do not go gentle into that good night.

Grave men, near death, who see with blinding sight
Blind eyes could blaze like meteors and be gay,
Rage, rage against the dying of the light.

And you, my father, there on the sad height,
Curse, bless, me now with your fierce tears, I pray.
Do not go gentle into that good night.
Rage, rage against the dying of the light.

Robert Lax (1915 – 2000)

Alley Violinist[2]

if you were an alley violinist

and they threw you money
from three windows

---

[1] Form: Villanelle.
[2] Form: Free verse.

and the first note contained
a nickel and said:
when you play, we dance and
sing, signed
a very poor family

and the second one contained
a dime and said:
I like your playing very much,
signed
a sick old lady

and the last one contained
a dollar and said:
beat it,

would you:
stand there and play?

beat it?

walk away playing your fiddle?

Gwendolyn Brooks (1917 – 2000)

A Song in the Front Yard[1]

I've stayed in the front yard all my life.
I want a peek at the back
Where it's rough and untended and hungry weed grows.
A girl gets sick of a rose.

I want to go in the back yard now
And maybe down the alley,
To where the charity children play.
I want a good time today.

They do some wonderful things.
They have some wonderful fun.

---

[1] Form: Free verse.

My mother sneers, but I say it's fine
How they don't have to be in at a quarter to nine.
My mother, she tells me that Johnny Mae
Will grow up to be a bad woman.
That George'll be taken to jail soon or late.
(On account of last winter he sold our back gate.)

But I say it's fine. Honest, I do.
And I'd like to be a bad woman, too,
And wear the brave stockings of night-black lace
And strut down the streets with paint on my face.

The Boy Died in my Alley[1]
to Running Boy

The Boy died in my alley
Without my Having Known.
Policeman said, next morning,
"Apparently died Alone."
"You heard a shot?" Policeman said.
Shots I hear and Shots I hear.
I never see the Dead.

The Shot that killed him yes I heard
as I heard the Thousand shots before;
careening tinnily down the nights
across my years and arteries.

Policeman pounded on my door.
"Who is it?" "POLICE!" Policeman yelled.
"A Boy was dying in your alley.
A Boy is dead, and in your alley.
And have you known this Boy before?"

I have known this Boy before.
I have known this boy before, who
ornaments my alley.
I never saw his face at all.

---

[1] Form: Free verse—Vocabulary: careening: rushing carelessly.

399

I never saw his future fall.
But I have known this Boy.

I have always heard him deal with death.
I have always heard the shout, the volley.
I have closed my heart-ears late and early.
And I have killed him ever.

I joined the Wild and killed him
with knowledgeable unknowing.
I saw where he was going.
I saw him Crossed. And seeing,
I did not take him down.

He cried not only "Father!"
but "Mother!
Sister!
Brother."
The cry climbed up the alley.
It went up to the wind.
It hung upon the heaven
for a long
stretch-strain of Moment.

The red floor of my alley
is a special speech to me.

Robert Lowell (1917 – 1977)

Reading Myself[1]

Like thousands, I took just pride and more than just,
struck matches that brought my blood to a boil;
I memorized the tricks to set the river on fire—
somehow never wrote something to go back to.
Can I suppose I am finished with wax flowers
and have earned my grass on the minor slopes of
    Parnassus. ...

---

[1] Form: Free verse—Vocabulary: Parnassus: mountain in Greece sacred to the muses.

No honeycomb is built without a bee
adding circle to circle, cell to cell,
the wax and honey of a mausoleum—
this round dome proves its maker is alive;
the corpse of the insect lives embalmed in honey,
prays that its perishable work live long
enough for the sweet-tooth bear to desecrate—
this open book ... my open coffin.

Keith Douglas (1920 – 1944)

Vergissmeinnicht[1]

Three weeks gone and the combatants gone
returning over the nightmare ground
we found the place again, and found
the soldier sprawling in the sun.

The frowning barrel of his gun
overshadowing. As we came on
that day, he hit my tank with one
like the entry of a demon.

Look. Here in the gunpit spoil
the dishonored picture of his girl
who has put: *Steffi. Vergissmeinnicht*
in a copybook gothic script.

We see him almost with content,
abased, and seeming to have paid
and mocked at by his own equipment
that's hard and good when he's decayed.

But she would weep to see today
how on his skin the swart flies move;
the dust upon the paper eye
and the burst stomach like a cave.

---

[1] Form: Iambic tetrameter, 2 lines rhymed per stanza—Vocabulary:
Vergissmeinnicht: forget-me-not; abased: reduced in prestige; swart: dark
skinned.

For here the lover and killer are mingled
who had one body and one heart.
And death who had the soldier singled
has done the lover mortal hurt.

Howard Nemerov (1920 – 1991)

Gyroscope[1]

This admirable gadget, when it is
Wound on a string and spun with steady force,
Maintains its balance on most any smooth
Surface, pleasantly humming as it goes.
It is whirled not on a constant course, but still
Stands in unshivering integrity
For quite some time, meaning nothing perhaps
But being something agreeable to watch,
A silver nearly silence gleaning a still-
ness out of speed, composing unity
From spin, so that its hollow spaces seem
Solids of light, until it wobbles and
Begins to whine, and then with an odd lunge
Eccentric and reckless, it skids away
And drops dead into its own skeleton.

---

[1] Form: Prose Poem—Vocabulary: gleaning: collecting bit by bit—Notes:
Perhaps a metaphor for life or for relationships?

Money[1]

AN INTRODUCTORY LECTURE

This morning we shall spend a few minutes
Upon the study of symbolism, which is basic
To the nature of money. I show you this nickel.
Icons and cryptograms are written all over
The nickel: one side shows a hunchbacked bison
Bending his head and curling his tail to accommodate
The circular nature of money. Over him arches
UNITED STATES OF AMERICA, and squinched in
Between that and his rump, E PLURIBUS UNUM,
A Roman reminiscence that appears to mean
An indeterminately large number of things
All of which are the same. Under the bison
A straight line giving him a ground to stand on
Reads FIVE CENTS. And on the other side of our nickel
There is the profile of a man with long hair
And a couple of feathers in the hair; we know
Somehow that he is an American Indian, and
He wears the number nineteen-thirty-six.
Right in front of his eyes the word LIBERTY, bent
To conform with the curve of the rim, appears
To be falling out of the sky Y first; the Indian
Keeps his eyes downcast and does not notice this;
To notice it, indeed, would be shortsighted of him.
So much for the iconography of one of our nickels,
Which is now becoming a rarity and something of
A collectors' item: for as a matter of fact
There is almost nothing you can buy with a nickel,
The representative American Indian was destroyed
A hundred years or so ago, and his descendants'
Relations with liberty are maintained with reservations,
Or primitive concentration camps; while the bison,
Except for a few examples kept in cages,
Is now extinct. Something like that, I think,
Is what Keats must have meant in his celebrated

[1] Form: Free verse—Vocabulary: Icons: image; cryptograms: writing in
code; obverse: facing side; Jupiter Ammon: Greek (Zeus), Roman (Jupiter),
and Egyptian (Amun) god with a ram's head.

Ode on a Grecian Urn.
   Notice, in conclusion,
A number of circumstances sometimes overlooked
Even by experts:(a) Indian and bison,
Confined to obverse and reverse of the coin,
Can never see each other;(b) they are looking
To opposite directions, the bison past
The Indian's feathers, the Indian past
The bison's tail; (c) they are upside down
To one another; (d) the bison has a human face
Somewhat resembling that of Jupiter Ammon.
I hope that our studies today will have shown you
Something of the import of symbolism
With respect to understanding of what is symbolized.

Snowflakes[1]

Not slowly wrought, nor treasured for their form
In heaven, but by the blind self of the storm
Spun off, each driven individual
Perfected in the moment of its fall.

Hayden Carruth (b. 1921)

Little Citizen, Little Survivor[2]

A brown rat has taken up residence with me.
A little brown rat with pinkish ears and lovely

---

[1] Form: Iambic pentameter, AABB end rhymes—Notes: Perhaps
metaphorically describing the way we are perfected through adversity?
[2] Form: Prose poem—Vocabulary: coons: raccoons; castigate: criticize
severely.

almond-shaped eyes. He and his wife live
in the woodpile by my back door, and they are
so equal I cannot tell which is which when they
poke their noses out of the crevices among
the sticks of firewood and then venture farther
in search of sunflower seeds spilled from the feeder.
I can't tell you, my friend, how glad I am to see them.
I haven't seen a fox for years, or a mink, or
a fisher cat, or an eagle, or a porcupine, I haven't
seen any of my old company of the woods
and the fields, we who used to live in such
close affection and admiration. Well, I remember
when the coons would tap on my window, when
the ravens would speak to me from the edge of their
little precipice. Where are they now? Everyone knows.
Gone. Scattered in this terrible dispersal. But at least
the brown rat that most people so revile and fear
and castigate has brought his wife to live with me
again. Welcome, little citizen, little survivor.
Lend me your presence, and I will lend you mine.

Richard Wilbur (b. 1921)

A Summer Morning[1]

Her young employers having got in late
From seeing friends in town
And scraped the right front fender on the gate,
Will not, the cook expects, be coming down.

She makes a quiet breakfast for herself.
The coffee-pot is bright,
The jelly where it should be on the shelf.
She breaks an egg into the morning light,

Then, with the bread knife lifted, stands and hears
The sweet efficient sounds
Of thrush and catbird and the snip of shears
Where, in the terraced backward of the grounds,

---

[1] Form: Iambic, 5-3-5-5- pattern, ABAB end rhymes.

A gardener works before the heat of day.
He straightens for a view
Of the big house ascending stony-gray
Out of his bed's mosaic with the dew.

His young employers having got in late,
He and the cook alone
Receive the morning on their old estate,
Possessing what the owners can but own.

Philip Larkin (1922 – 1985)

An Arundel Tomb[1]

Side by side, their faces blurred,
The earl and countess lie in stone,
Their proper habits vaguely shown
As jointed armor, stiffened pleat,
And that faint hint of the absurd—
The little dogs under their feet.

Such plainness of the pre-baroque
Hardly involves the eye, until
It meets the left-hand gauntlet, still
Clasped empty in the other; and
One sees, with a sharp tender shock,
His hand withdrawn, holding her hand.

They would not think to lie so long.
Such faithfulness in effigy
Was just a detail friends would see:
A sculptor's sweet commissioned grace
Thrown off in helping to prolong
The Latin names around the base.

---

[1] Form: Iambic tetrameter, ABBCAC end rhymes—Vocabulary: Arundel:
region in West Sussex, England; effigy: likeness; supine: laying on their
back; tenantry: tenants of an estate; skeins: a length of thread; blazon:
coat of arms—Notes: Here the spouses posed for a picture, him in armor,
while holding hands. The sculptor caught this moment, and their
expression of love is what has endured.

They would not guess how early in
Their supine stationary voyage
The air would change to soundless damage,
Turn the old tenantry away;
How soon succeeding eyes begin
To look, not read. Rigidly they

Persisted, linked, through lengths and breadths
Of time. Snow fell, undated. Light
Each summer thronged the glass. A bright
Litter of birdcalls strewed the same
Bone-riddled ground. And up the paths
The endless altered people came,

Washing at their identity.
Now, helpless in the hollow of
An unarmorial age, a trough
Of smoke in slow suspended skeins
Above the scrap of history,
Only an attitude remains:

Time has transfigured them into
Untruth. The stone fidelity
They hardly meant has come to be
Their final blazon, and to prove
Our almost-instinct almost true:
What will survive of us is love.

Talking In Bed[1]

Talking in bed ought to be easiest
Lying together there goes back so far
An emblem of two people being honest.

Yet more and more time passes silently.
Outside the wind's incomplete unrest
Builds and disperses clouds about the sky.

---

[1] Form: Blank verse (unrhymed iambic pentameter), but meter varies (falls apart) in last two lines, much as the relationship's flaws are made obvious in the last two lines.

And dark towns heap up on the horizon.
None of this cares for us. Nothing shows why
At this unique distance from isolation

It becomes still more difficult to find
Words at once true and kind
Or not untrue and not unkind.

This Be the Verse[1]

They fuck you up, your mum and dad.
    They may not mean to, but they do.
They fill you with the faults they had
    And add some extra, just for you.

But they were fucked up in their turn
    By fools in old-style hats and coats,
Who half the time were soppy-stern
    And half at one another's throats.

Man hands on misery to man.
    It deepens like a coastal shelf.

---

[1] Form: Iambic tetrameter, ABAB end rhymes—Vocabulary: soppy:
sentimental.

Get out as early as you can,
    And don't have any kids yourself.

James Dickey (1923 – 1997)

The Heaven of Animals[1]

Here they are. The soft eyes open.
If they have lived in a wood
It is a wood.
If they have lived on plains
It is grass rolling
Under their feet forever.

Having no souls, they have come,
Anyway, beyond their knowing.
Their instincts wholly bloom
And they rise.
The soft eyes open.

To match them, the landscape flowers,
Outdoing, desperately
Outdoing what is required:
The richest wood,
The deepest field.

For some of these,
It could not be the place
It is, without blood.
These hunt, as they have done,
But with claws and teeth grown perfect,

More deadly than they can believe.
They stalk more silently,
And crouch on the limbs of trees,
And their descent
Upon the bright backs of their prey

---

[1] Form: Iambic, irregular line lengths—Vocabulary: sovereign: supreme—
Notes: There is an implied acceptance of the natural order of things built
into this poem.

409

May take years
In a sovereign floating of joy.
And those that are hunted
Know this as their life,
Their reward: to walk

Under such trees in full knowledge
Of what is in glory above them,
And to feel no fear,
But acceptance, compliance.
Fulfilling themselves without pain

At the cycle's center,
They tremble, they walk
Under the tree,
They fall, they are torn,
They rise, they walk again.

The Sheep Child[1]

Farm boys wild to couple
With anything   with soft-wooded trees
With mounds of earth   mounds
Of pine straw   will keep themselves off
Animals by legends of their own:
In the hay-tunnel dark
And dung of barns, they will
Say   I have heard tell

That in a museum in Atlanta
Way back in a corner somewhere
There's this thing that's only half
Sheep   like a woolly baby
Pickled in alcohol   because
Those things can't live   his eyes
Are open   but you can't stand to look
I heard from somebody who ...

But this is now almost all

---

[1] Form: Free verse—Vocabulary: chaste: virtuous; ewe: female sheep.

Gone. The boys have taken
Their own true wives in the city,
The sheep are safe in the west hill
Pasture   but we who were born there
Still are not sure. Are we,
Because we remember, remembered
In the terrible dust of museums?

Merely with his eyes, the sheep-child may

Be saying   saying

I am here, in my father's house.
I who am half of your world, came deeply
To my mother in the long grass
Of the west pasture, where she stood like moonlight
Listening for foxes. It was something like love
From another world that seized her
From behind, and she gave, not Lifting her head
Out of dew, without ever looking, her best
Self to that great need.
Turned loose, she dipped her face
Farther into the chill of the earth, and in a sound
Of sobbing   of something stumbling
Away, began, as she must do,
To carry me. I woke, dying,

In the summer sun of the hillside, with my eyes
Far more than human. I saw for a blazing moment
The great grassy world from both sides,
Man and beast in the round of their need,
And the hill wind stirred in my wool,
My hoof and my hand clasped each other,
I ate my one meal
Of milk, and died
Staring. From dark grass I came straight

To my father's house, whose dust
Whirls up in the halls for no reason
When no one comes   piling deep in a hellish mild corner,
And, through my immortal waters,

I meet the sun's grains eye
To eye, and they fail at my closet of glass.
Dead, I am most surely living
In the minds of farm boys: I am he who drives
Them like wolves from the hound bitch and calf
And from the chaste ewe in the wind.
They go into woods   into bean fields   they go
Deep into their known right hands. Dreaming of me,
They groan   they wait   they suffer
Themselves, they marry, they raise their kind.

Alan Dugan (1923 – 2003)

How We Heard the Name[1]

The river brought down
dead horses, dead men
and military debris,
indicative of war
or official acts upstream,
but it went by, it all
goes by, that is the thing
about the river. Then
a soldier on a log
went by. He seemed drunk
and we asked him Why
had he and this junk
come down to us so
from the past upstream.
"Friends," he said, "the great
Battle of Granicus
has just been won
by all of the Greeks except
the Lacedaemonians and
myself: this is a joke
between me and a man
named Alexander, whom

---

[1] Form: Free verse—Vocabulary: Granicus: Battle in 334 BC where
Alexander defeated the Persians.

412

all of you ba-bas
will hear of as a god."

Love Song: I and Thou[1]

Nothing is plumb, level or square:
    the studs are bowed, the joists
are shaky by nature, no piece fits
    any other piece without a gap
or pinch, and bent nails
    dance all over the surfacing
like maggots. By Christ
    I am no carpenter. I built
the roof for myself, the walls
    for myself, the floors
for myself, and got
    hung up in it myself. I
danced with a purple thumb
    at this house-warming, drunk
with my prime whiskey: rage.
    Oh I spat rage's nails
into the frame-up of my work:
    It held. It settled plumb.
level, solid, square and true
    for that one great moment. Then
it screamed and went on through,
    skewing as wrong the other way.
God damned it. This is hell,
    but I planned it I sawed it
I nailed it and I
    will live in it until it kills me.
I can nail my left palm
    to the left-hand cross-piece but
I can't do everything myself.
    I need a hand to nail the right,
a help, a love, a you, a wife.

---

[1] Form: Free verse—Vocabulary: plumb; properly vertical; true: properly
aligned; skewing: tilting—Notes: The house may be read as a metaphor for
the marriage, or perhaps for some other problem area in life which
becomes a cross.

Denise Levertov (1923 – 1997)

Consulting the Oracle[1]

I asked a blind man the way east,
because I'd not seen him,
not looked before asking.
He smiled, and walked on,
sure of his felt way,
silent.

From a Plane[2]

Green water of lagoons,
brown water of a great river
sunning its muscles along intelligent
rectangular swathes of
other brown, other green,
alluvial silvers.
       Always air
looked down through, gives
a reclamation of order, re-
visioning solace: the great body
not torn apart, though raked and raked
by our claws—

Lisel Mueller (b. 1924)

Imaginary Paintings[3]

1.HOW I WOULD PAINT THE FUTURE

A strip of horizon and a figure,
seen from the back, forever approaching.

---

[1] Form: Free verse.
[2] Form: Free verse—Vocabulary: alluvial: flood plain or delta; solace: comfort.
[3] Form: Free verse.

2. HOW I WOULD PAINT HAPPINESS

Something sudden, a windfall,
a meteor shower. No—
a flowering tree releasing
all its blossoms at once,
and the one standing beneath it
unexpectedly robed in bloom,
transformed into a stranger
too beautiful to touch.

3. HOW I WOULD PAINT DEATH

White on white or black on black.
No ground, no figure. An immense canvas,
which I will never finish.

4. HOW I WOULD PAINT LOVE

I would not paint love.

5. HOW I WOULD PAINT THE LEAP OF FAITH

A black cat jumping up three feet
to reach a three-inch shelf.

6. HOW I WOULD PAINT THE BIG LIE

Smooth, and deceptively small
so that it can be swallowed
like something we take for a cold.
An elongated capsule,
an elegant cylinder,
sweet and glossy,
that pleases the tongue
and goes down easy,
never mind
the poison inside.

7.HOW I WOULD PAINT NOSTALGIA

An old-fashioned painting, a genre piece.
People in bright and dark clothing.
A radiant bride in white
standing above a waterfall,
watching the water rush
away, away, away.

Reader[1]

For Mary Elsie Robertson, author of Family Life

A husband. A wife. Three children. Last year they did not
exist; today the parents are middle-aged, one of the
daughters grown. I live with them in their summer house by
the sea. I live with them, but they can't see me sharing their
walks on the beach, their dinner preparations in the kitchen.
I am in pain because I know what they don't, that one of
them has snipped the interlocking threads of their lives and
now there is no end to the slow unraveling. If I am a ghost
they look through, I am also a Greek chorus, hand clapped to
mouth in fear, knowing their best intentions will go wrong.
"Don't", I want to shout, but I am inaudible to them; beach
towels over their shoulders, wooden spoon in hand, they keep
pulling at the threads. When nothing is left they disappear.
Closing the book I feel abandoned. I have lost them, my dear
friends. I want to write them, wish them well, assure each
one of my affection. If only they would have let me say good-
bye.

Silence and Dancing[2]

"Schweigen and tanzen" are words spoken by Elektra near
the end of the opera by Richard Strauss and Hugo von
Hofmannsthal.

Silence and dancing
is what it comes down to

---

[1] Form: Prose poem.
[2] Form: Free verse—Vocabulary: fatuous: smugly and unconsciously
foolish.

in the end for them,
as they struggle from wheelchair to bed,
knowing nothing changes,
that the poor, who are themselves,
will become even poorer
and the fatuous voices on the screen
will go on gabbling about another
war they cannot do without.

What defense against this
except silence and dancing,
the memory of dancing—

O, but they danced, did they ever;
she danced like a devil, she'll tell you,
recalling a dress the color of sunrise,
hair fluffed to sea-foam,
some man's some boy's
damp hand on her back
under the music's sweet, hot assault

and wildness erupting inside her
like a suppressed language,
insisting on speaking itself
through her eloquent body,

a far cry
from the well-groomed words on her lips.

The Story[1]

You are telling a story:
How Fire Took Water to Wife

It's always like this, you say,
opposites attract

They want to enter each other,
be one,

---

[1] Form: Free verse.

so he burns her as hard as he can
and she tries to drown him

It's called love at first
and doesn't hurt

but after a while she weeps
and says he is killing her,
he shouts that he cannot breathe
underwater—

Make up your own
ending, you say to the children,
and they will, they will

Widow[1]

What the neighbors bring to her kitchen
is food for the living. She wants to eat
the food of the dead, their pure
narcotic of dry, black seeds.
Why, without him, should she desire
the endurance offered by meat and grain,
the sugars that glue the soul to the body?
She thanks them, but does not eat,
consumes strong coffee as if it were air
and she the vigilant candle
on a famous grave, until the familiar
sounds of the house become strange,
turn into messages in the new language
he has been forced to learn.
All night she works on the code,
almost happy, her body rising
like bread, while the food in its china caskets
dries out on the kitchen table.

---

[1] Form: Free verse.

Roberto Juarroz (1925 – 1995)

Any movement kills something[1]
Translated from the Spanish by Mary Crow

Any movement kills something.

It kills the place that is abandoned,
the gesture, the unrepeatable position,
some anonymous organism,
a sign, a glance,
a love that returned,
a presence or its contrary,
the life always of someone else,
one's own life without others.

And being here is moving,
being here is killing something.
Even the dead move,
even the dead kill.
Here the air smells of crime.

But the odor comes from farther away.
And even the odor moves.

Donald Justice (1925 – 2004)

American Sketches[2]

The telephone poles
Have been holding their
Arms out
A long time now
To birds
That will not

---

[1] Form: Free verse—Notes: On a literal level physical movement, or even the movement of time, resulting in death all around us, from minute mites to large organisms. The basic idea also applies to non-physical things like ideas, where intellectual movement creates new ideas and destroys old ones.
[2] Form: Free verse.

Settle there
But pass with
Strange cawings
Westward to
Where dark trees
Gather about a
Waterhole this
Is Kansas the
Mountains start here
Just behind
The closed eyes
Of a farmer's
Sons asleep
In their workclothes

In Bertram's Garden[1]

Jane looks down at her organdy skirt
As if it somehow were the thing disgraced,
For being there, on the floor, in the dirt,
And she catches it up about her waist,
Smoothes it out along one hip,
And pulls it over the crumpled slip.

On the porch, green-shuttered, cool,
Asleep is Bertram that bronze boy,
Who, having wound her around a spool,
Sends her spinning like a toy
Out to the garden, all alone,
To sit and weep on a bench of stone.

Soon the purple dark must bruise
Lily and bleeding-heart and rose,
And the little cupid lose
Eyes and ears and chin and nose,
And Jane lie down with others soon,
Naked to the naked moon.

---

[1] Form: Mostly iambic tetrameter, ABABCC end rhymes—Notes: This poem tells a story, but really, only enough of the story to leave us speculating about what actually happened to Jane (was she seduced?, raped?) and what will ultimately happen to her?

420

Carolyn Kizer (b. 1925)

Bitch[1]

Now, when he and I meet, after all these years,
I say to the bitch inside me, don't start growling.
He isn't a trespasser anymore,
just an old acquaintance tipping his hat.
My voice says, "nice to see you,"
As the bitch starts to bark hysterically.
He isn't an enemy now,
Where are your manners, I say, as I say,
"How are the children? They must be growing up."
At a kind word from him, a look like the old day,
The bitch changes her tone: she begins to whimper.
She wants to snuggle up to him, to cringe.
Down, girl! Keep your distance
Or i'll give you a taste of the choke-chain.
"Fine, I'm just fine, "I tell him.
She slobbers and grovels.
After all, I am her mistress. She is basically loyal.
It's just that she remembers how she came running
Each evening, when she heard his step;
How she lay at his feet and looked up adoringly
Though he was absorbed in his paper;
Or, bored with her devotion, ordered in to the kitchen
Until he was ready to play.
But the small careless kindnesses
When he'd had a good day, or a couple of drinks,
Come back to her now, seem more important
Than the casual cruelties, the ultimate dismissal.
"It's nice to know you are doing so well," I say.
He couldn't have taken you with him;
You were too demonstrative, too clumsy,
Not like the well-groomed pets of his new friends.
"Give my regards to your wife," I say . You gag
As I drag you off by the scruff,
Saying, "Goodbye! Goodbye! Nice to have seen you again."

---

1 Form: Free verse.

The Ashes[1]

This elderly poet, unpublished for five decades,
Said that one day in her village a young girl
Came screaming down the road,
"The Red Guards are coming! The Red Guards. . .
Are Coming!" At once the poet
Ran into her house and stuffed the manuscript
Of her poems into the stove. The only copy.
When the guards arrived they took her into the yard
For interrogation. As they spoke
The poet's mother tried to hang herself in the kitchen.
That's all I know about the Red Guard.
It is enough.

The elderly poet is bitter—and why not?
She earned her Ph.D. At an Ivy League school
And returned to China in 1948. Bad timing.
She is bitter with me
Because i've chosen to translate a younger poet,
Young enough to be her child or mine.
The truth is, her poems are forced,
But not flowering. The good work died in the stove.
She knows this. She wants me to recompose them
From the ashes. She wants the noose
Around her mother's neck untied by me.
She wants—oh she wants!—to have her whole life over:
Not to leave America in 1948;
To know me when we are both young promising poets.
Her rusty English now is flawless,
My Mandarin, so long unused, is fluent.
No dictionaries needed. A perfect confidence
Flowing between us. And the Red Guard,
Except as the red sword-lilies
That invigilate the garden,
Unimagined by us both:
I, who believe the Reds are agrarian reformers,
She, who believes she will be an honored poet,

---

[1] Form: Free verse—Vocabulary: invigilate: Monitor.

422

Her name known to everyone, safe in her fame.

Robert Creeley (b. 1926)

Heaven[1]

Wherever they've
gone they're
not here
anymore

and all
they stood
for is empty
also.

I Know a Man[2]

As I sd to my
friend, because I am
always talking,—John, I

sd, which was not his
name, the darkness sur-
rounds us, what

can we do against
it, or else, shall we &
why not, buy a goddamn big car,

drive, he sd, for
christ's sake, look
out where yr going.

I'll Win[3]

I'll win the way
I always do

---

[1] Form: Free verse.
[2] Form: Free verse.
[3] Form: Free verse.

by being gone
when they come.

When they look, they'll see
nothing of me
and where I am
They'll not know.

This, I thought, is my way
and right or wrong,
it's me. Being dead, then,
I'll have won completely.

Old Days[1]

River's old look
from summers ago
we'd come to swim

now yellow, yellow
rustling, flickering
leaves in sun

middle of October
water's up, high sky's blue,
bank's mud's moved,

edge is
closer,
nearer than then.

Place ("There's a Way out")[2]

There's a way out
of here but it

hurts at the edges

---

[1] Form: Free verse—Notes: The season metaphorically describes the narrator's old age, and the distant bank of the river represents death. Rivers are often a passageway to death in myth.
[2] Form: Free verse.

where there's no time left

to be one if
you were and friends

gone, days seemingly
over. No one.

Thanksgiving's Done[1]

All leaves gone, yellow
light with low sun,

branches edged
in sharpened outline

against far-up pale sky.
Nights with their blackness

and myriad stars, colder
now as these days go by.

Galway Kinnell (b. 1927)

St. Francis and the Sow[2]

The bud
stands for all things,
even those things that don't flower,
for everything flowers, from within, of self-blessing;
though sometimes it is necessary
to reteach a thing its loveliness,
to put a hand on its brow
of the flower
and retell it in words and in touch
it is lovely
until it flowers again from within, of self-blessing;
as St. Francis

---

[1] Form: Free verse—Notes: The poem is a metaphor for aging.
[2] Form: Free verse—Vocabulary: fodder: coarse food; slops: leftovers served
to animals.

put his hand on the creased forehead
of the sow, and told her in words and in touch
blessings of earth on the sow, and the sow
began remembering all down her thick length,
from the earthen snout all the way
through the fodder and slops to the spiritual curl of the tail,
from the hard spininess spiked out from the spine
down through the great broken heart
to the blue milken dreaminess spurting and shuddering
from the fourteen teats into the fourteen mouths sucking
    and blowing beneath them:
the long, perfect loveliness of sow.

James Wright (1927 – 1980)

A Blessing[1]

Just off the highway to Rochester, Minnesota,
Twilight bounds softly forth on the grass.
And the eyes of those two Indian ponies
Darken with kindness.
They have come gladly out of the willows
To welcome my friend and me.
We step over the barbed wire into the pasture
Where they have been grazing all day, alone.
They ripple tensely, they can hardly contain their happiness
That we have come.
They bow shyly as wet swans. They love each other.
There is no loneliness like theirs.
At home once more,
They begin munching the young tufts of spring in the
    darkness.
I would like to hold the slenderer one in my arms,
For she has walked over to me
And nuzzled my left hand.
She is black and white,
Her mane falls wild on her forehead,
And the light breeze moves me to caress her long ear
That is delicate as the skin over a girl's wrist.

---

[1] Form: Free verse.

Suddenly I realize
That if I stepped out of my body I would break
Into blossom.

Beginning[1]

The moon drops one or two feathers into the fields.
The dark wheat listens.
Be still.
Now.
There they are, the moon's young, trying
Their wings.
Between trees, a slender woman lifts up the lovely shadow
Of her face, and now she steps into the air,
Now she is gone
Wholly, into the air.
I stand alone by an elder tree, I do not dare breathe
Or move.
I listen.
The wheat leans back toward its own darkness,
And I lean toward mine.

Lying in a Hammock at William Duffy's Farm in Pine Island, Minnesota[2]

Over my head, I see the bronze butterfly
Asleep on the black trunk,
Blowing like a leaf in green shadow.
Down the ravine behind the empty house,
The cowbells follow one another
Into the distances of the afternoon.
To my right,
In a field of sunlight between two pines,
The droppings of last year's horses
Blaze up into golden stones.
I lean back, as the evening darkens and comes on.
A chicken hawk floats over, looking for home.
I have wasted my life.

---

[1] Form: Free verse—Notes: Notice the sense of a secret shared as the moon-beams are mentally turned into something living.
[2] Form: Free verse.

Irving Feldman (b. 1928)

The Dream[1]

Once, years after your death, I dreamt
you were alive and that I'd found you
living once more in the old apartment.
But I had taken a woman up there
to make love to in the empty rooms.
I was angry at you who'd borne and loved me
and because of whom I believe in heaven.
I regretted your return from the dead
and said to myself almost bitterly,
"For godsakes, what was the big rush,
couldn't she wait one more day?"

And just so, daily somewhere Messiah
is shunned like a beggar at the door because
someone has something he wants to finish
or just something better to do, something
he prefers not to put off forever
—little pleasures so deeply wished
that Heaven's coming has to seem bad luck
or worse, God's intruding selfishness!

But you always turned Messiah away
with a penny and a cake for his trouble
—because wash had to be done, because
who could let dinner boil over and burn,
because everything had to be festive for
your husband, your daughters, your son.

---

[1] Form: Free verse.

Donald Hall (b. 1928)

My mother said[1]

My mother said, "Of course,
it may be nothing, but your father
      has a spot on his lung."
That was all that was said: My father
      at fifty-one could never
speak of dreadful things without tears.
      When I started home,
I kissed his cheek, which was not our habit.
      In a letter, my mother
asked me not to kiss him again
      because it made him sad.
In two weeks, the exploratory
      revealed an inoperable
lesion.
      The doctors never
      told him; he never asked,
but read *The Home Medical Guidebook.*
      Seven months later,
just after his fifty-second birthday
      —his eyesight going,
his voice reduced to a whisper, three days
      before he died—he said,
"If anything should happen to me . . . "

---

[1] Form: Free verse.

Names of Horses[1]

All winter your brute shoulders strained against collars,
    padding
and steerhide over the ash hames, to haul
sledges of cordwood for drying through spring and summer,
for the Glenwood stove next winter, and for the simmering
    range.

In April you pulled cartloads of manure to spread on the
    fields,
dark manure of Holsteins, and knobs of your own clustered
    with oats.
All summer you mowed the grass in the meadow and
    hayfield, the mowing machine
clacketing beside you, while the sun walked high in the
    morning;

and after noon's heat, you pulled a clawed rake through the
    same acres,
gathering stacks, and dragged the wagon from stack to stack,
and the built hayrack back, uphill to the chaffy barn,
three loads of hay a day, hanging wide from the hayrack.

Sundays you trotted the two miles to church with the light
    load
of a leather quartertop buggy, and grazed in the sound of
    hymns.
Generation on generation, your neck rubbed the window sill
of the stall, smoothing the wood as the sea smooths glass.

When you were old and lame, when your shoulders hurt
    bending to graze,
one October the man, who fed you and kept you, and
    harnessed you every morning,
led you through corn stubble to sandy ground above Eagle
    Pond,

---

[1] Form: Free verse—Vocabulary: hames: part of a harness; sledges: sled on
low runners; cordwood: wood cut to 4 feet; Glenwood: Brand of stove;
Holsteins: Species of cow; quartertop: mostly open buggy.

430

and dug a hole beside you where you stood shuddering in
    your skin,

and lay the shotgun's muzzle in the boneless hollow behind
    your ear,
and fired the slug into your brain, and felled you into your
    grave,
shoveling sand to cover you, setting goldenrod upright above
    you,
where by next summer a dent in the ground made your
    monument.

For a hundred and fifty years, in the pasture of dead horses,
roots of pine trees pushed through the pale curves of your
    ribs,
yellow blossoms flourished above you in autumn, and in
    winter
frost heaved your bones in the ground—old toilers, soil
    makers:

O Roger, Mackerel, Riley, Ned, Nellie, Chester, Lady Ghost.

The Porcelain Couple[1]

When Jane felt well enough for me to leave her
for a whole day, I drove south by the river
to empty my mother Lucy's house in Connecticut.
I hurried from room to room, cellar to attic,
opening a crammed closet, then turning
to discover a chest with five full drawers.
I labeled for shipping sofas and chairs,
bedroom sets, and tables; I wrapped figurines
and fancy teacups in paper, preserving things
she cherished—and dreaded, in her last years,
might go for a nickel on the Spring Glen lawn.
Everywhere I looked I saw shelves and tabletops
covered with Lucy's glass animals and music boxes.
Everywhere in closets, decades of dresses hung
in dead air. I carried garbage bags in one hand,

---

[1] Form: Free verse—Vocabulary: catafalque: platform for a coffin.

431

and with the other swept my mother's leftover
possessions into sacks for the Hamden dump.
I stuffed bags full of blouses, handkerchiefs,
and the green-gold dress she wore to Bermuda.
At the last moment I discovered and saved
a cut-glass tumbler, stained red at the top,
Lucy 1905 scripted on the stain. In the garage
I piled the clanking bags, then drove four hours
north with my hands tight on the Honda's wheel,
drank a beer looking through Saturday's mail,
pitched into bed beside Jane fitfully asleep,
and woke exhausted from rolling unendable
nightmares of traffic and fire. In my dreams
I grieved or mourned interchangeably for Lucy,
for Lucy's things, for Jane, and for me.
When I woke, I rose as if from a drunken sleep
after looting a city and burning its temples.
All day as I ate lunch or counted out pills,
or as we lay weeping, hugging in bed together,
I counted precious things from our twenty years:
a blue vase, a candelabrum Jane carried on her lap
from the Baja, and the small porcelain box
from France I found under the tree one Christmas
where a couple in relief stretch out asleep,
like a catafalque, on the pastel double bed
of the box's top, both wearing pretty nightcaps.

Philip Levine (b. 1928)

Belle Isle, 1949[1]

We stripped in the first warm spring night
and ran down into the Detroit River
to baptize ourselves in the brine
of car parts, dead fish, stolen bicycles,
melted snow. I remember going under
hand in hand with a Polish high-school girl
I'd never seen before, and the cries

---

[1] Form: Free verse—Notes: This poem illustrates the beauty that can be
found within the midst of ugliness.

432

our breath made caught at the same time
on the cold, and rising through the layers
of darkness into the final moonless atmosphere
that was this world, the girl breaking
the surface after me and swimming out
on the starless waters towards the lights
of Jefferson Ave. and the stacks
of the old stove factory unwinking.
Turning at last to see no island at all
but a perfect calm dark as far
as there was sight, and then a light
and another riding low out ahead
to bring us home, ore boats maybe, or smokers
walking alone. Back panting
to the gray coarse beach we didn't dare
fall on, the damp piles of clothes,
and dressing side by side in silence
to go back where we came from.

Sweet Will[1]

The man who stood beside me
34 years ago this night fell
on to the concrete, oily floor
of Detroit Transmission, and we
stepped carefully over him until
he wakened and went back to this press.

It was Friday night, and the others
told me that every Friday he drank
more than he could hold and fell
and he wasn't any dumber for it
so just let him get up at his
own sweet will or he'll hit you.

"At his own sweet will," was just
what the old black man said to me,
and he smiled the smile of one
who is still surprised that dawn

---

[1] Form: Free verse—Vocabulary: Beguine: a ballroom dance.

433

graying the cracked and broken windows
could start us all to singing in the cold.

Stash rose and wiped the back of his head
with a crumpled handkerchief and looked
at his own blood as though it were
dirt and puzzled as to how
it got there and then wiped the ends
of his fingers carefully one at a time

the way the mother wipes the fingers
of a sleeping child, and climbed back
on his wooden soda-pop case to
his punch press and hollered at all
of us over the oceanic roar of work,
addressing us by our names and nations—

"Nigger, Kike, Hunky, River Rat,"
but he gave it a tune, an old tune,
like "America the Beautiful." And he danced
a little two-step and smiled showing
the four stained teeth left in the front
and took another sip of cherry brandy.

In truth it was no longer Friday,
for night had turned to day as it
often does for those who are patient,
so it was Saturday in the year of '48
in the very heart of the city of man
where your Cadillac cars get manufactured.

In truth all those people are dead,
they have gone up to heaven singing
"Time on my Hands" or "Begin the Beguine,"
and the Cadillacs have all gone back
to earth, and nothing that we made
that night is worth more than me.

And in truth I'm not worth a thing
what with my feet and my two bad eyes
and my one long nose and my breath

434

of old lies and my sad tales of men
who let the earth break them back,
each one, to dirty blood or bloody dirt.

Not worth a thing! Just like it was said
at my magic birth when the stars
collided and fire fell from great space
into great space, and people rose one
by one from cold beds to tend a world
that runs on and on at its own sweet will.

Anne Sexton (1928 – 1974)

Her Kind[1]

I have gone out, a possessed witch,
haunting the black air, braver at night;
dreaming evil, I have done my hitch
over the plain houses, light by light:
lonely thing, twelve-fingered, out of mind.
A woman like that is not a woman, quite.
I have been her kind.

I have found the warm caves in the woods,
filled them with skillets, carvings, shelves,
closets, silks, innumerable goods;
fixed the suppers for the worms and the elves:
whining, rearranging the disaligned.
A woman like that is misunderstood.
I have been her kind.

I have ridden in your cart, driver,
waved my nude arms at villages going by,
learning the last bright routes, survivor

---

[1] Form: Trochaic, irregular line lengths, ABABCC end rhymes—Vocabulary: disaligned: unaligned—Notes: "Twelve-fingered": physical deformities in general, and extra fingers in particular, were taken as a sign that someone was a witch. "my ribs crack where your wheels": a medieval form of torture, sometimes applied to people accused of witchcraft, was to break their limbs and thread them through the spokes of a wagon wheel, then hang the wheel horizontally in the air on a pole.

where your flames still bite my thigh
and my ribs crack where your wheels wind.
A woman like that is not ashamed to die.
I have been her kind.

from The Death of the Fathers: 2.How We Danced[1]

The night of my cousin's wedding
I wore blue.
I was nineteen
and we danced, Father, we orbited.
We moved like angels washing themselves.
We moved like two birds on fire.
Then we moved like the sea in a jar,
slower and slower.
The orchestra played
"Oh how we danced on the night we were wed."
And you waltzed me like a lazy Susan
and we were dear,
very dear.
Now that you are laid out,
useless as a blind dog,
now that you no longer lurk,
the song rings in my head.
Pure oxygen was the champagne we drank
and clicked our glasses, one to one.
The champagne breathed like a skin diver
and the glasses were crystal and the bride
and groom gripped each other in sleep
like nineteen-thirty marathon dancers.
Mother was a belle and danced with twenty men.
You danced with me never saying a word.
Instead the serpent spoke as you held me close.
The serpent, that mocker, woke up and pressed against me
like a great god and we bent together
like two lonely swans.

---

[1] Form: Free verse—Vocabulary: The serpent: the father's penis in this
case.

436

With Mercy for the Greedy[1]

for my friend Ruth, who urges me to make an
appointment for the Sacrament of Confession

Concerning your letter in which you ask
me to call a priest and in which you ask
me to wear The Cross that you enclose;
your own cross,
your dog-bitten cross,
no larger than a thumb,
small and wooden, no thorns, this rose—

I pray to its shadow,
that gray place
where it lies on your letter ... deep, deep.
I detest my sins and I try to believe
in The Cross. I touch its tender hips, its dark jawed face,
its solid neck, its brown sleep.

True. There is
a beautiful Jesus.
He is frozen to his bones like a chunk of beef.
How desperately he wanted to pull his arms in!
How desperately I touch his vertical and horizontal axes!
But I can't. Need is not quite belief.

All morning long
I have worn
your cross, hung with package string around my throat.
It tapped me lightly as a child's heart might,
tapping secondhand, softly waiting to be born.
Ruth, I cherish the letter you wrote.

My friend, my friend, I was born
doing reference work in sin, and born
confessing it. This is what poems are:
with mercy
for the greedy,

---

[1] Form: Free verse—Vocabulary: wrangle: argument; pottage: stew.

they are the tongue's wrangle,
the world's pottage, the rat's star.

Thom Gunn (1929 – 2004)

Still Life[1]

I shall not soon forget
The grayish-yellow skin
To which the face had set:
Lids tight: nothing of his,
No tremor from within,
Played on the surfaces.

He still found breath, and yet
It was an obscure knack.
I shall not soon forget
The angle of his head,
Arrested and reared back
On the crisp field of bed,

Back from what he could neither
Accept, as one opposed,
Nor, as a life-long breather,
Consentingly let go,
The tube his mouth enclosed
In an astonished O.

The Reassurance[2]

About ten days or so
After we saw you dead
You came back in a dream.
I'm all right now you said.

And it was you, although
You were all fleshed out again:

---

[1] Form: Iambic trimeter, irregular but frequent end rhymes—Notes: Notice the double meaning of the title, meaning both "life yet remains" and a "still life" as in a painting, which has the appearance of life but no actual life.
[2] Form: Iambic trimeter, two end rhymes per stanza in irregular positions.

You hugged us all round then,
And gave your welcoming beam.

How like you to be kind,
Seeking to reassure.
And, yes, how like my mind
To make itself secure.

Dan Pagis (1930 – 1986)

Conversation[1]
Translated from the Hebrew by Stephen Mitchell

Four talked about the pine tree. One defined it by genus,
species, and variety. One assessed its disadvantages for the
lumber industry. One quoted poems about pine trees in
many languages. One took root, stretched out branches, and
rustled.

Izet Sarajlic (b. 1930)

Luck in Sarajevo[2]
translated from Serbo-Croat by Charles Simic

In Sarajevo
in the Spring of 1992,
everything is possible:

you go stand in a bread line
and end up in an emergency room
with your leg amputated.

Afterwards, you still maintain
that you were very lucky.

---

[1] Form: Prose poem.
[2] Form: Free verse—Vocabulary: Sarajevo: capital of Bosnia and
Herzegovina.

Gary Snyder (b. 1930)

Axe Handles[1]

One afternoon the last week in April
Showing Kai how to throw a hatchet
One-half turn and it sticks in a stump.
He recalls the hatchet-head
Without a handle, in the shop
And go gets it, and wants it for his own.
A broken-off axe handle behind the door
Is long enough for a hatchet,
We cut it to length and take it
With the hatchet head
And working hatchet, to the wood block.
There I begin to shape the old handle
With the hatchet, and the phrase
First learned from Ezra Pound
Rings in my ears!
"When making an axe handle
      The pattern is not far off."
And I say this to Kai
"Look: We'll shape the handle
By checking the handle
Of the axe we cut with—"
And he sees. And I hear it again:
It's in Lu Ji's Wen Fu, fourth century
A.D. "Essay on Literature"—in the
Preface: "In making the handle
Of an axe
By cutting wood with an axe
The model is indeed near at hand.—
My teacher Shih-hsiang Chen
Translated that and taught it years ago
And I see: Pound was an axe,
Chen was an axe, I am an axe
And my son a handle, soon
To be shaping again, model

---

[1] Form: Free verse—Vocabulary: Kai: narrator's son.

And tool, craft of culture,
How we go on.

What you should know to be a poet[1]

all you can about animals as persons.
the names of trees and flowers and weeds.
names of stars, and the movements of the planets
                    and the moon.

your own six senses, with a watchful and elegant mind.

at least one kind of traditional magic:
divination, astrology, the *book of changes,* the tarot;

dreams.
the illusory demons and illusory shining gods;

kiss the ass of the devil and eat shit;
fuck his horny barbed cock,
fuck the hag,
and all the celestial angels
                    and maidens perfum'd and golden—

& then love the human: wives   husbands and friends.

children's games, comic books, bubble-gum,
the weirdness of television and advertising.

work, long dry hours of dull work swallowed and accepted
and lived with and finally loved.   exhaustion,
                    hunger, rest.

the wild freedom of the dance, *extasy*
silent solitary illumination, *enstasy*

real danger. gambles.   and the edge of death.

---

[1] Form: Free verse—Notes: This list of things needed to be a poet includes
all forms of fundamental human experience, both the positive and the
negative.

Derek Walcott (b. 1930)

Love after Love[1]

The time will come
when, with elation
you will greet yourself arriving
at your own door, in your own mirror
and each will smile at the other's welcome,

and say, sit here. Eat.
You will love again the stranger who was your self.
Give wine. Give bread. Give back your heart
to itself, to the stranger who has loved you

all your life, whom you ignored
for another, who knows you by heart.
Take down the love letters from the bookshelf,

the photographs, the desperate notes,
peel your own image from the mirror.
Sit. Feast on your life.

Miller Williams (b. 1930)

Listen[2]

I threw a snowball across the backyard.
My dog ran after it to bring it back.
It broke as it fell, scattering snow over snow.
She stood confused, seeing and smelling nothing.
She searched in widening circles until I called her.

She looked at me and said as clearly in silence
as if she had spoken,
I know it's here, I'll find it,
went back to the center and started the circles again.

---

[1] Form: Free verse—Note: The poem addresses becoming redeveloping a
relationship with yourself after breaking up as a couple.
[2] Form: Loose iambic pentameter, unrhymed.

I called her two more times before she came
slowly, stopping once to look back.

That was this morning. I'm sure that she's forgotten.
I've had some trouble putting it out of my mind.

Etheridge Knight (1931 – 1991(

The Idea of Ancestry[1]

Taped to the wall of my cell are 47 pictures: 47 black
faces: my father, mother, grandmothers (1 dead), grand-
fathers (both dead), brothers, sisters, uncles, aunts,
cousins (1st and 2nd), nieces, and nephews. They stare
across the space at me sprawling on my bunk. I know
their dark eyes, they know mine. I know their style,
they know mine. I am all of them, they are all of me;
they are farmers, I am a thief, I am me, they are thee.

I have at one time or another been in love with my mother,
1 grandmother, 2 sisters, 2 aunts (1 went to the asylum),
and 5 cousins. I am now in love with a 7-yr-old niece
(she sends me letters in large block print, and
her picture is the only one that smiles at me).

I have the same name as 1 grandfather, 3 cousins, 3
     nephews,
and 1 uncle. The uncle disappeared when he was 15, just
     took
off and caught a freight (they say). He's discussed each year
when the family has a reunion, he causes uneasiness in
the clan, he is an empty space. My father's mother, who is 93
and who keeps the Family Bible with everbody's birth dates
(and death dates) in it, always mentions him. There is no
place in her Bible for "whereabouts unknown."

---

[1] Form: Prose poem.

The Warden Said to Me the Other Day[1]

The warden said to me the other day
(innocently, I think), "Say, Etheridge,
why come the black boys don't run off
like the white boys do?"
I lowered my jaw and scratched my head
and said (innocently, I think), "Well, suh,
I ain't for sure, but I reckon it's cause
we ain't got no wheres to run to."

Tanikawa Shuntaro (b. 1931)
Translation by William I. Elliott and Kazuo Kawamura

A Rudimentary Explanation of an Ideal Poem[2]

Called by people a poet,
I usually stay completely away from what is called poetry,
and this not just when I'm eating, reading, or chattering idly,
but even when I'm thinking about poetry.

Poetry strikes something like lightning at night.
For that split second, I see, hear and smell,
through a crack in consciousness, the world that expands
    beyond.

Unlike consciousness, poetry shines brightly,
and unlike a dream, it admits of no interpretation.

Though written with words, poetry is not words themselves.
Sometimes I think it shameful to turn it into words.
At such times I just quietly let it go,
and then I feel I have lost something.

In a world lighted up by poetic lightning, where everything
    has its place,
I feel completely relaxed (perhaps for a thousandth of a
    second).

---

[1] Form: Free verse.
[2] Form: Free verse.

It's as though I have become a single silent wildflower.

But of course the moment I have written this,
I'm far removed from poetry,

though called a poet.

from With Silence My Companion[1]

I know how worthless this poem will be
Under the scrutiny of daylight
And yet I cannot now disown my words.

While others fill their baskets at market
I drink water from a cup on the table,
Utterly idle.

I see through the trees, by the distant pool,
A white statue,
Its genitals exposed.
It is I.

I am immersed
In the past
And have become a block of dumb stone
And not the Orpheus I hoped to be.

---

[1] Form: Free verse—Vocabulary: Orpheus: Thracian poet and musician
who's music had the power to move inanimate objects.

445

From My Father's Death[1]

*

Death, coming in his sleep,
swept away with its gentle, quick hands
all the details of his life.
But there was no end of subjects for our idle talk,
while we talked away the brief hours of the night,
before the flowers withered on the altar.

Death is unknowable
and, being unknowable, lacks details,
which makes it resemble poetry.
Both death and poetry tend to sum up life,
but survivors enjoy the increasingly mysterious details
more than the summing up of life.
*

The Naif[2]

My toe tips look unusually far away.
Five toes lie coldly together
like five people strangers to one another.

There's a telephone beside my bed connected to the world,
but there's no one I want to talk to.
Since I grew *self*-conscious my life has been nothing but
     business,
          business.
Neither of my parents taught me how to make small talk.

I've relied on versification as my only guide for forty years.
Strange, but I feel most comfortable saying, "A poet"
when people ask who I am.
Was I a poet when I abandoned that woman?
Am I, eating my favorite baked sweet potato, a poet?
Am I, grown bald, a poet?

---

[1] Form: Free verse.
[2] Form: Free verse—Vocabulary: versification: writing poetry.

There are countless middle-aged men of such kind who are
  not poets

I'm but a naïve child
that has just chased the butterflies of beautiful words.
This child's soul, approaching one-hundred,
remains innocent,
unaware that he has hurt people.

Poetry is
ridiculous.

Adrian Mitchell (b. 1932)

A Puppy Called Puberty[1]

It was like keeping a puppy in your underpants
A secret puppy you weren't allowed to show to anyone
Not even your best friend or your worst enemy

You wanted to pat him, stroke him, cuddle him
All the time you weren't supposed to touch him.

He only slept for five minutes at a time
Then he'd suddenly perk up his head
In the middle of school medical inspection
And always on bus rides.

So you had to climb down from the upper deck
All bent double to smuggle the puppy off the bus
Without the buxom conductress spotting
Your wicked and ticketless stowaway.

Jumping up, wet-nosed, eagerly wagging—
He only stopped being a nuisance
When you were alone together
Pretending to be doing your homework
But really gazing at each other
Through hot and lazy daydreams.

---

[1] Form: Free verse.

447

Of those beautiful schoolgirls on the bus
With kittens bouncing in their sweaters.

Heberto Padilla (1932 – 2000)

Landscapes[1]
   Translated from the Spanish by Alastair Reid and Andrew
Hurley

You can see them everywhere in Cuba.
Green or red or yellow, flaking off from the water
and the sun, true landscapes of these times
of war.
The wind tugs at the Coca-Cola signs.
The clocks courtesy of Canada Dry are stopped
at the old time.
The neon signs, broken, crackle and splutter in the rain.
Esso's is something like this
    S O S
and above there are some crude letters
reading   PATRIA O MUERTE.

Alden Nowlan (1933 – 1983)

An Exchange of Gifts[2]

As long as you read this poem
I will be writing it.
I am writing it here and now
before your eyes,
although you can't see me.
Perhaps you'll dismiss this
as a verbal trick,
the joke is you're wrong;
the real trick
is your pretending
this is something
fixed and solid,

---

[1] Form: Free verse—Vocabulary: Esso: brand of gasoline station; PATRIA O
MUERTE: Fatherland or death.
[2] Form: Free verse.

external to us both.
I tell you better:
I will keep on
writing this poem for you
even after I'm dead.

It's Good To Be Here[1]

I'm in trouble, she said
to him. That was the first
time in history that anyone
had ever spoken of me.

It was 1932 when she
was just fourteen years old
and men like him
worked all day for
one stinking dollar.

---

[1] Form: Free verse.

There's quinine, she said.
That's bullshit, he told her.

Then she cried and then
for a long time neither of them
said anything at all and then
their voices kept rising until
they were screaming at each other
and then there was another long silence and then
they began to talk very quietly and at last he said
well, I guess we'll just have to make the best of it.

While I lay curled up,
my heart beating,
in the darkness inside her.

Weakness[1]

Old mare whose eyes
are like cracked marbles,
drools blood in her mash,
shivers in her jute blanket.

My father hates weakness worse than hail;
in the morning
    without haste
he will shoot her in the ear, once,
shovel her under in the north pasture.

Tonight
    leaving the stables,
he stands his lantern on an over-turned water pail,
turns,
    cursing her for a bad bargain,
and spreads his coat
carefully over her sick shoulders.

---

[1] Form: Free verse—Vocabulary: jute: a rough fiber.

Richard Shelton (b. 1933)

The Bus to Veracruz[1]

The mail is slow here. If I died, I wouldn't find out about it for a long time. Perhaps I am dead already. At any rate, I am living in the wrong tense of a foreign language and have almost no verbs and only a few nouns to prove I exist. When I need a word, I fumble among the nouns and find one, but so many are similar in size and color. I am apt to come up with *caballo* instead of *caballero*, or *carne* instead of *casa*. When that happens, I become confused and drop the words. They roll across the tile floor in all directions. Then I get down on my hands and knees and crawl through a forest of legs, reaching under tables and chairs to retrieve them. But I am no longer embarrassed about crawling around on the floor in public places. I have come to realize that I am invisible most of the time and have been since I crossed the border.

All the floors are tile. All the tiles are mottled with the same disquieting pattern in one of three muddy colors— shades of yellow, purple, or green. They make me think of dried vomit, desiccated liver, and scum on a pond. The floor of my room is dried vomit with a border of scum on a pond, and like most of the floors it has several tiles missing, which is a great blessing to me. These lacunae are oases in the desert where I can rest my eyes. The nausea from which I suffer so much of the time is not caused by the food or water, but by the floors. I know this because when I sit in the town square, which is covered with concrete of no particular color, the nausea subsides.

The town is small, although larger than it would seem to a visitor—if there were any visitor—and remote. It has no landing field for even small planes, and the nearest railroad is almost one hundred kilometers to the east. The only bus

---

[1] Form: Prose poem—Vocabulary: desiccated: foods preserved by drying; lacunae: missing parts; coquettish: teasing with sexual or romantic overtones; apparition: ghostly figure; circuitous: roundabout; brocade: heavy fabric with rich, raised design—Notes: The village in the story is a symbol representing any situation that is tolerable but not pleasant (for example, purgatory, a job, a location) and the bus represents the potential for escape from that place or thing.

goes to Veracruz. Often I stop at the bus terminal to ask about the bus to Veracruz. The floor of the bus terminal is scum on a pond with a border of desiccated liver, but there are many tiles missing. That terminal is always deserted except for Rafael and Esteban, sometimes sitting on the bench inside, sometimes lounging just outside the door. They are young, barefoot, and incredibly handsome. I buy them *Cocas* from the machine, and we have learned to communicate in our fashion. When I am with them, I am glad to be invisible, glad that they never look directly at me. I could not bear the soft velvet and vulnerability of those magnificent eyes.

"When does the bus leave for Veracruz? " I ask them. I have practiced this many times and am sure I have the right tense. But the words rise to the ceiling, burst, and fall as confetti around us. A few pieces catch in their dark hair and reflect the light like jewels. Rafael rubs his foot on the floor. Esteban stares out the filthy window. Are they sad, I wonder, because they believe there is no bus to Veracruz or because they don't know when it leaves?

"Is there a bus to Veracruz? " Suddenly they are happy again. Their hands fly like vivacious birds. "*Si, hay! :Por supeusto, Senor! Es verdad!* " they believe, truly, in the bus to Veracruz. Again I ask them when it leaves. Silence and sadness. Rafael studies one of the tiles on the floor as if it contains the answer. Esteban turns back to the window. I buy them *Cocas* from the machine and go away.

Once a week I stop at the post office to get my mail from the ancient woman in the metal cage, and each week I receive one letter. Actually, the letters are not mine, and the ancient woman has probably known this for a long time, but we never speak of it and she continues to hand me the letters, smiling and nodding in her coquettish way, eager to please me. Her hair is braided with colored ribbons, and her large silver earrings jingle when she bobs her head, which she does with great enthusiasm when I appear. I could not estimate how old she is. Perhaps even she has forgotten. But she must have been a great beauty at one time. Now she sits all day in the metal cage in the post office, a friendly apparition whose bright red lipstick is all the more startling because she has no teeth.

The first time I entered the post office, it was merely on an impulse to please her. I was expecting no mail, since no one knew where I was. But each time I passed, I had seen her through the window, seated in her metal cage with no customers to break the monotony. She always smiled and nodded at me through the window, eager for any diversion. Finally one day I went in on the pretext of calling for my mail, although I knew there would be none. To avoid the confusion which my accent always causes, I wrote my name on a slip of paper and presented it to her. Her tiny hands darted among the pigeonholes, and to my astonishment she presented me with a letter which was addressed to me in care of general delivery. She was so delighted with her success that I simply took the letter and went away, unwilling to disillusion her.

As soon as I opened the letter, the mystery was solved. My name is fairly common. The letter was intended for someone else with the same name. It was written on blue paper, in flawless Palmer Method script, and signed by a woman. It was undated and there was no return address. But it was in English, and I read it shamelessly, savoring each phrase. I rationalized by convincing myself that the mail was so slow the man to whom the letter had been written was probably already dead and could not object to my reading his mail. But I knew before I finished the letter that I would return to the post office later on the chance there might be others. She loved him. She thought he was still alive.

Since then I have received one letter each week, to the enormous delight of my ancient friend in the post office. I take the letters home and steam them open, careful to leave no marks on the delicate paper. They are always from the same woman, and I feel by now that I know her. Sometimes I dream about her, as if she were someone I knew in the past. She is blond and slender, no longer young but far from old. I can see her long, graceful fingers holding the pen as she writes, and sometimes she reaches up to brush a strand of hair away from her face. Even that slight gesture has the eloquence of a blessing.

When I have read each letter until I can remember it word for word, I reseal it. Then, after dark, I take it back to the post office by a circuitous route, avoiding anyone who might be on the street at that hour. The post office is always open, but the metal cage is closed and the ancient one is gone for the night. I drop the letter into the dead letter box and hurry away.

At first I had no curiosity about what happened to the letters after they left my hands. Then I began to wonder if they were destroyed or sent to some central office where, in an attempt to locate the sender and return them, someone might discover that they had been opened. Still later, the idea that some nameless official in a distant city might be reading them because almost unbearable to me. It was more and more difficult to remember that they were not my letters. I could not bear to think of anyone else reading her words, sensing her hesitations and tenderness. At last I decided to find out.

It took months of work, but with practice I became clever at concealing myself in shadowy doorways and watching. I have learned that once each week a nondescript man carrying a canvas bag enters the post office through he back door, just as the ancient woman is closing her metal cage for the night. She empties the contents of the dead letter box into his canvas bag, and he leaves by the door he came in. The man then begins a devious journey which continues long into the night. Many nights I have lost him and have had to begin again the following week. He doubles back through alleys and down obscure streets. Several times he enters deserted buildings by one door and emerges from another. He crosses the cemetery and goes through the Cathedral.

But finally he arrives at his destination—the bus terminal. And there, concealed behind huge doors which can be raised to the ceiling, is the bus to Veracruz. The man places his canvas bag in the luggage compartment, slams the metal cover with a great echoing clang, and goes away.

And later, at some unspecified hour, the bus to Veracruz rolls silently out of the terminal, a luxury liner leaving port with all its windows blazing. It has three yellow lights above the windshield and three gold stars along each side. The seats are red velvet and there are gold tassels between the windows. The dashboard is draped with brocade of the richest shades of yellow, purple, and green; and on this altar is a statue of the Virgin, blond and shimmering. Her slender fingers are extended to bless all those who ride the bus to

Veracruz, but the only passenger is an ancient woman with silver earrings who sits by the window, nodding and smiling to the empty seats around her. There are two drivers who take turns during the long journey. They are young and incredibly handsome, with eyes as soft as the wings of certain luminous brown moths.

The bus moves through sleeping streets without making a sound. When it gets to the highway, it turns toward Veracruz and gathers speed. Then nothing can stop it: not the rain, nor the washed-out bridges, nor the sharp mountain curves, nor the people who stand by the road to flag it down.

I believe in the bus to Veracruz. And someday, when I am too tired to struggle any longer with the verbs and nouns, when the ugliness and tedium of this place overcome me, I will be on it. I will board the bus with my ticket in hand. The doors of the terminal will rise to the ceiling, and we will move out through the darkness, gathering speed, like a great island of light.

The Stones[1]

I love to go out on summer nights and watch the stones grow. I think they grow better here in the desert, where it is warm and dry, than almost anywhere. Or perhaps it is only that the young ones are more active here.

Young stones tend to move about more than their elders consider good for them. Most young stones have a secret desire which their parents had before them but have forgotten ages ago. And because this desire involves water, it is never mentioned. The older stones disapprove of water and say, "Water is a gadfly who never stays in one place long enough to learn anything." But the young stones try to work themselves into a position, slowly and without their elders noticing it, in which a sizable stream of water during a summer storm might catch them broadside and unknowing, so to speak, push them along over a slope or down an arroyo. In spite of the danger this involves, they want to travel and see something of the world and settle in a new place, far from

---

[1] Form: Prose poem—Vocabulary: gadfly: nuisance; arroyo: dry gulch—Notes: The central metaphor is children's desire to leave their parents and seek adventure.

455

home, where they can raise their own dynasties, away from the domination of their parents.

And although family ties are very strong among stones, many have succeeded; and they carry scars to prove to their children that they once went on a journey, helter-skelter and high water, and traveled perhaps fifteen feet, an incredible distance. As they grow older, they cease to brag about such clandestine adventures.

It is true that old stones get to be very conservative. They consider all movement either dangerous or downright sinful. They remain comfortably where they are and often get fat. Fatness, as a matter of fact, is a mark of distinction.

And on summer nights, after the young stones are asleep, the elders turn to a serious and frightening subject—the moon. which is always spoken of in whispers. "see how it glows and whips across the sky, always changing its shape," one says. And another says, "Feel how it pulls at us, urging us to follow." And a third whispers, "It is a stone gone mad."

Amiri Baraka (LeRoi Jones) (b. 1934)

"Wise I"[1]
WHYS (Nobody Knows
The Trouble I Seen)
Traditional

If you ever find
yourself, some where
lost and surrounded
by enemies
who won't let you
speak in your own language
who destroy your statues
& instruments, who ban
your omm bomm ba boom
then you are in trouble
deep trouble
they ban your
own boom ba boom

---

[1] Form: Free verse.

you in deep deep
trouble

humph!

probably take you several hundred years
to get
out!

Rutger Kopland (b. 1934)

Natzweiler[1]
Translated from the Dutch by James Brockway

1.

And there, beyond the barbed wire, the view—
very charming landscape, as peaceful
as then.

They would need for nothing, they would
be laid down in those green pastures,
be led to those peaceful waters,

there in the distance. They would.

2.

I trace the windows of the barrack huts,
watch-towers, gas-chamber.
Only the black reflection of distance
in the panes, of a peaceful landscape,

and beyond it, no one.

---

[1] Form: Free verse—Vocabulary: Natzweiler: concentration camp in
France—Notes: The contrast between the pastoral scene and the horror of
the concentration camp make the camp even more horrible, and the last
line offers a pessimistic view of what the world has learned from those
horrors.

3.

The dead are so violently absent, as though
not only I, but they too
were standing here,

and the landscape were folding their invisible
arms around my shoulders.

We need for nothing, they are saying,
we have forgotten this world,

But these are no arms,
it is landscape.

4.

The yellowed photos in the display cases,
their faces ravaged by their skulls,
their black eyes,

what do they see, what do they see?
I look at them, but for what?

Their faces have come to belong
to the world, to the world
which remains silent.

5.

So this is it, desertion, here is
the place where they took their leave,
far away in the mountains.

The camp has just been re-painted, in that gentle
grey-green, that gentle color
of war,

it is as new, as though nothing
has happened, as though
it has yet to be.

Mark Strand (b. 1934)

Eating Poetry[1]

Ink runs from the corners of my mouth.
There is no happiness like mine.
I have been eating poetry.

The librarian does not believe what she sees.
Her eyes are sad
and she walks with her hands in her dress.

The poems are gone.
The light is dim.
The dogs are on the basement stairs and coming up.

Their eyeballs roll,
their blond legs burn like brush.
The poor librarian begins to stamp her feet and weep.

She does not understand.
When I get on my knees and lick her hand,
she screams.

I am a new man.
I snarl at her and bark.
I romp with joy in the bookish dark.

Keeping Things Whole[2]

In a field
I am the absence
of field.
This is
always the case.

---

[1] Form: Free verse.

[2] Form: Free verse—Vocabulary: In art, we talk about negative space, which is the part of the canvas not covered with images. It is always important, and sometimes more important than the images. This is about negative space in the world.

Wherever I am
I am what is missing.

When I walk
I part the air
and always
the air moves in
to fill the spaces
where my body's been.

We all have reasons
for moving.
I move
to keep things whole.

Reading in Place[1]

Imagine a poem that starts with a couple
Looking into a valley, seeing their house, the lawn
Out back with its wooden chairs, its shady patches of green,
Its wooden fence, and beyond the fence the rippled silver
    sheen
Of the local pond, its far side a tangle of sumac, crimson
In the fading light. Now imagine somebody reading the poem
And thinking, "I never guessed it would be like this,"
Then slipping it into the back of a book while the oblivious
Couple, feeling nothing is lost, not even the white
Streak of a flicker's tail that catches their eye, nor the slight
Toss of leaves in the wind, shift their gaze to the wooded
    dome
Of a nearby hill where the violet spread of dusk begins,
But the reader, out for a stroll in the autumn night, with all
The imprisoned sounds of nature dying around him, forgets
Not only the poem, but where he is, and thinks instead
Of a bleak Venetian mirror that hangs in a hall
By a curving stair, and how the stars in the sky's black glass

---

[1] Form: Free verse—Vocabulary: flicker: woodpecker—Notes: Vivid imagery creates alternate realities, one inside the other similar to those Russian dolls. There is also an implied comment on the characters and stories as having a life of their own, but a life that only exists when someone is reading them.

Sink down and the sea heaves them ashore like foam.
So much is adrift in the ever-opening rooms of elsewhere,
He cannot remember whose house it was, or when he was
 there.
Now imagine he sits years later under a lamp
And pulls a book from the shelf; the poem drops
To his lap. The couple are crossing a field
On their way home, still feeling that nothing is lost,
That they will continue to live harm-free, sealed
In the twilight's amber weather. But how will the reader
 know,
Especially now that he puts the poem, without looking
Back in the book, the book where a poet stares at the sky
And says to a blank page, "Where, where in Heaven am I?"

Paul Zimmer (b. 1934)

Zimmer's Head Thudding Against the Blackboard[1]

At the blackboard I had missed
Five number problems in a row,
And was about to foul a sixth,
When the old exasperated nun
Began to pound my head against
My six mistakes. When I cried,
She threw me back into my seat,
Where I hid my head and swore
That very day I'd be a poet,
And curse her yellow teeth with this.

David R. Slavitt (b. 1935)

Titanic[2]

Who does not love the *Titanic*?
If they sold passage tomorrow for that same crossing,
who would not buy?

---

[1] Form: Iambic tetrameter.
[2] Form: Free verse.

To go down. . .We all go down, mostly
alone. But with crowds of people, friends, servants,
well fed, with music, with lights! Ah!

And the world, shocked, mourns, as it ought to do
and almost never does. There will be the books and movies
to remind our grandchildren who we were
and how we died, and give'm a good cry.

Not so bad, after all. The cold
water is anesthetic and very quick.
The cries on all sides must be a comfort.

We all go: a few, first-class.

C.K. Williams (b. 1936)

My Fly[1]

for Erving Goffman, 1922-1982

One of those great, garishly emerald flies that always look
    freshly generated from fresh excrement
and who maneuver through our airspace with a deft
    intentionality that makes them seem to think,
materializes just above my desk, then vanishes, his dense,
    abrasive buzz sucked in after him.

I wait, imagine him, hidden somewhere, waiting, too, then
    think, who knows why, of you—
don't laugh—that he's a messenger from you, or that you
    yourself (you'd howl at this),
ten years afterwards have let yourself be incarnated as this
    pestering anti-angel.

Now he, or you, abruptly reappears, with a weightless pounce
    alighting near my hand.

---

[1] Form: Prose poem—Vocabulary: parse: Break down and understand;
felicity: great happiness; ardent: warmth of feeling.

I lean down close, and though he has to sense my looming
    presence, he patiently attends,
as though my study of him had become an element of his
    own observations—maybe it is you!

Joy! To be together, even for a time! Yes, tilt your fuselage,
    turn it towards the light,
aim the thousand lenses of your eyes back up at me; how I've
    missed the layers of your attention,
how often been bereft without your gift for sniffing out
    pretentiousness and moral sham.

Why would you come back, though? Was that other radiance
    not intricate enough to parse?
Did you find yourself in some monotonous century hovering
    down the tidy queue of creatures
waiting to experience again the eternally unlikely bliss of
    being matter and extension?

You lift, you land—you're rushed, I know; the interval in all
    our terminals is much too short.
Now you hurl against the window, skid and jitter on the
    pane: I open it and step aside
and follow for one final moment of felicity your brilliant
    ardent atom swerving through.

The Dance[1]

A middle-aged woman, quite plain, to be polite about it, and
    somewhat stout, to be courteous still,
but when she and the rather good-looking, much younger
    man she's with get up to dance,
her forearm descends with such delicate lightness, such
    restrained but confident ardor athwart his shoulder,
drawing him to her with such a firm, compelling warmth, and
    moving him with effortless grace
into the union she's instantly established with the not at all
    rhythmically solid music in this second-rate café,

---

[1] Form: Prose poem—Vocabulary: ardor: fiery intensity; athwart: from side
to side—Notes: Compare the view of inner beauty in this poem with that
expressed in "Nightclub" by Billy Collins.

463

that something in the rest of us, some doubt about ourselves,
   some sad conjecture, seems to be allayed,
nothing that we'd ever thought of as a real lack, nothing not
   to be admired or be repentant for,
but something to which we've never adequately given
   credence,
which might have consoling implications about how we
   misbelieve ourselves, and so the world,
that world beyond us which so often disappoints, but which
   sometimes shows us, lovely, what we are.

Gail Mazur (b. 1937)

In Houston[1]

I'd dislocated my life, so I went to the zoo.
It was December but it wasn't December. Pansies
just planted were blooming in well-groomed beds.
Lovers embraced under the sky's Sunday blue.
Children rode around and around on pastel trains.
I read the labels stuck on every cage the way
people at museums do, art being less interesting
than information. Each fenced-in plot had a map,
laminated with a stain to tell where in the world
the animals had been taken from. Rhinos waited
for rain in the rhino-colored dirt, too grief-struck
to move their wrinkles, their horns too weak
to ever be hacked off by poachers for aphrodisiacs.
Five white ducks agitated the chalky waters
of a duck pond with invisible orange feet
while a little girl in pink ruffles
tossed pork rinds at their disconsolate backs.

---

[1] Form: Prose poem—Vocabulary: disconsolate: beyond consolation;
anthropomorphize: give human traits to animals or objects; aviary: large
bird enclosure; ersatz: imitation—Notes: The poem begins by observing the
way December in Houston did not really feel like December to someone
used to the snow. Then, the way various animals reminded the narrator of
her separation, her isolation, and finally her feeling like the sloth, ill-
equipped to go on with her writing, but forced to by ambition, observed
metaphorically as the small, nagging monkey.

This wasn't my life! I'd meant to look
with the wise tough eye of exile, I wanted
not to anthropomorphize, not to equate, for instance,
the lemur's displacement with my displacement.
The arched aviary flashed with extravagance,
plumage so exuberant, so implausible, it seemed
cartoonish, and the birdsongs unintelligible,
babble, all their various languages unraveling—
no bird can get its song sung right, separated from
models of its own species.

For weeks I hadn't written a sentence,
for two days I hadn't spoken to an animate thing.
I couldn't relate to a giraffe—
I couldn't look one in the face.
I'd have said, if anyone had asked,
I'd been mugged by the Gulf climate.
In a great barren space, I watched a pair
of elephants swaying together, a rhythm
too familiar to be mistaken, too exclusive.
My eyes sweated to see the bull, his masterful trunk
swinging, enter their barn of concrete blocks,
to watch his obedient wife follow. I missed
the bitter tinny Boston smell of first snow,
the huddling in a cold bus tunnel.

At the House of Nocturnal Mammals,
I stepped into a furtive world of bats,
averted my eyes at the gloomy dioramas,
passed glassed-in booths of lurking rodents—
had I known I'd find what I came for at last?
How did we get here, dear sloth, my soul, my sister?
Clinging to a tree-limb with your three-toed feet,
your eyes closed tight, you calm my idleness,
my immigrant isolation. But a tiny tamarin monkey
who shares your ersatz rainforest runs at you,
teasing, until you move one slow, dripping,
hairy arm, then the other, the other, the other,
pulling your tear-soaked body, its too-few
vertebrae, its inferior allotment of muscles
along the dead branch, going almost nowhere

slowly as is humanly possible, nudged
by the bright orange primate taunting, nipping,
itching at you all the time, like ambition.

Diane Wakoski (b. 1937)

George Washington and the Loss of His Teeth[1]

the ultimate
in the un-Romantic:
false teeth

> This room became a room where your heaviness
> and my heaviness came together,
> an overlay of flower petals once new and fresh
> pasted together queerly, as for some lady's hat,
> and finally false and stiff, love fearing
> to lose itself, locks and keys become inevitable.

The truth is that George cut down his father's cherry tree,
his ax making chips of wood so sweet with sap they could be
sucked, and he stripped, the bark like old bandages
from the tree for kindling.
In this tree he defied his dead father,
the man who could not give him an education and left him to
suffer the ranting of Adams and others,
those fat sap-cheeked men who said George did not know
    enough
to be president. He chopped that tree—
it was no small one—down and the dry leaves rustled
like the feet of cows on grass.
It was then that George lost his teeth. He
fell asleep next to his pile of kindling wood and dreamed
the old father came chasing him with a large penis swung
over his shoulder. But George filled his mouth with cherries
and swallowed the bleeding flesh
and spit out the stones in a terrible torrent at his father.
With the pits of the

---

[1] Form: Free verse—Vocabulary: ossified: change into bone—Notes: This
story of child abuse told through parable can apply to a variety of physical
and verbal abuses as well.

466

cherries
came all of George's teeth,
pointed weapons to hurl from the mouth at his father,
the owner of that false cherry tree.

We all come to such battles with our own flesh,
spitting out more than we have swallowed,
thus losing part of ourselves.
You came to me thus
with weapons
         and this room is strewn with dead flowers
         that grew out of my breasts and dropped off
    black and weak.
    This room is graveled with stones I dropped
    from my womb, ossified in my own body
    from your rocky white quartz sperm.
    This room is built from the lumber of my thigh,
    and it is heavy with hate.

George had a set of false teeth
made from the cherry wood. But it was his father's tree
His lips closed painfully over the stiff set.
There is no question,
either,
where you
got the teeth in your mouth.

Robert Phillips (b. 1938)

Instrument of Choice[1]

She was a girl
no one ever chose
for teams or clubs,
dances or dates,

so she chose the instrument
no one else wanted:
the tuba. Big as herself,

---

[1] Form: Free verse.

heavy as her heart,

its golden tubes
and coils encircled her
like a lover's embrace.
its body pressed to hers.

Into its mouthpiece she blew
life, its deep-throated
oompahs, oompahs sounding,
almost, like mating cries.

Charles Simic (b. 1938)

Country Fair[1]

If you didn't see the six-legged dog,
It doesn't matter.
We did, and he mostly lay in the corner.
As for the extra legs,

One got used to them quickly

---

[1] Form: Free verse—Notes: A strength of this poem is the ambiguity as to
what the narrator thinks was the real show, the dog or the audience.

And thought of other things.
Like, what a cold, dark night
To be out at the fair.

Then the keeper threw a stick
And the dog went after it
On four legs, the other two flapping behind,
Which made one girl shriek with laughter.

She was drunk and so was the man
Who kept kissing her neck.
The dog got the stick and looked back at us.
And that was the whole show.

Fork[1]

This strange thing must have crept
Right out of hell.
It resembles a bird's foot
Worn around the cannibal's neck.

As you hold it in your hand,
As you stab with it into a piece of meat,
It is possible to imagine the rest of the bird:
Its head which like your fist
Is large, bald, beakless and blind.

Northern Exposure[2]

When old women say, it smells of snow,
In a whisper barely audible
Which still rouses the sick man upstairs
So he opens his eyes wide and lets them fill

With the grayness of the remaining daylight.
When old women say, how quiet it is,
And truly no one came to visit,
While the one they still haven't shaved

---

[1] Form: Free verse.
[2] Form: Free verse.

Lifts the wristwatch to his ear and listens.
In it, something small, subterranean
And awful in intent, chews rapidly.
When old women say, time to turn on the lights,

And not a single one gets up to do so,
For now there are loops
And loose knots around their feet
As if someone is scribbling over them
With a piece of charcoal found in the cold stove.

Prodigy[1]

I grew up bent over
a chessboard.

I loved the word *endgame.*

All my cousins looked worried.

It was a small house
near a Roman graveyard.
Planes and tanks
shook its windowpanes.

A retired professor of astronomy
taught me how to play.

That must have been in 1944.

In the set we were using,
the paint had almost chipped off
the black pieces.

The white King was missing
and had to be substituted for.

I'm told but do not believe

---

[1] Form: Free verse.

that that summer I witnessed
men hung from telephone poles.

I remember my mother
blindfolding me a lot.

She had a way of tucking my head
suddenly under her overcoat.

In chess, too, the professor told me,
the masters play bindfolded,
the great ones on several boards
at the same time.

The Old World[1]

I believe in the soul; so far
It hasn't made much difference.
I remember an afternoon in Sicily.
The ruins of some temple.
Columns fallen in the grass like naked lovers.

The olives and goat cheese tasted delicious
And so did the wine
With which I toasted the coming night,
The darting swallows,
The Saracen wind and moon.

It got darker. There was something
Long before there were words:
The evening meal of shepherds. . .
A fleeting whiteness among the trees. . .
Eternity eavesdropping on time.

The goddess going to bathe in the sea.
She must not be followed.
These rocks, these cypress trees,
May be her old lovers.
Oh to be one of them, the wine whispered to me.

---

[1] Form: Free verse—Vocabulary: Saracen: Arab.

Margaret Atwood (b. 1939)

Manet's Olympia[1]

She reclines, more or less.
Try that posture, it's hardly languor.
Her right arm sharp angles.
With her left she conceals her ambush.
Shoes but not stockings,
how sinister. The flower
behind her ear is naturally
not real, of a piece
with the sofa's drapery.
The windows (if any) are shut.
This is indoor sin.
Above the head of the (clothed) maid
is an invisible voice balloon: *Slut.*

But. Consider the body,
unfragile, defiant, the pale nipples
staring you right in the bull's-eye.
Consider also the black ribbon
around the neck. What's under it?
A fine red threadline, where the head
was taken off and glued back on.
The body's on offer,
but the neck's as far as it goes.
This is no morsel.
Put clothes on her and you'd have a schoolteacher,
the kind with the brittle whiphand.

There's someone else in this room.
You, Monsieur Voyeur.
As for that object of yours
she's seen those before, and better.

I, the head, am the only subject
of this picture.

---

[1] Form: Free verse.

You, Sir, are furniture.
Get stuffed.

Miss July Grows Older[1]

How much longer can I get away
with being so fucking cute?
Not much longer.
The shoes with bows, the cunning underwear
with slogans on the crotch—Knock Here
and so forth—
will have to go, along with the cat suit.
After a while you forget
what you really look like.
You think your mouth is the size it was.
You pretend not to care.

When I was young I went with my hair
hiding one eye, thinking myself daring;
off to the movies in my jaunty pencil
skirt and elastic cinch-belt,
chewed gum, left lipstick
imprints the shape of grateful, rubbery
sighs on the cigarettes of men
I hardly knew and didn't want to.
Men were a skill, you have to have
good hands, breathe into
their nostrils, as for horses. It was something I did well,
like playing the flute, although I don't.

In the forest of grey stems there are standing pools,
tan-colored, choked with the brown leaves.
Through them you can see an arm, a shoulder,
when the light is right, with the sky clouded.
The train goes past silos, through meadows,
the winter wheat on the fields like scary fur.

I still get letters, although not many.

---

[1] Form: Free verse—Vocabulary: pencil skirt: skirt that is narrow at the
bottom; bum: rear end; arpeggios: chords played as individual notes.

A man writes me, requesting true-life stories
about bad sex. He's doing an anthology.
He got my name off an old calendar,
the photo that's mostly bum and daisies,
back when my skin had the golden slick
of fresh-spread margarine.
Not rape, he says, but disappointment,
more like a defeat of expectations.
Dear Sir, I reply, I never had any.
Bad sex, that is.
It was never the sex, it was the other things,
the absence of flowers, the death threats,
the eating habits at breakfast.
I notice I'm using the past tense.

Through the vaporous cloud
of chemicals that enveloped you
like a glowing eggshell, an incense,
doesn't disappear: it just gets larger
and takes in more. You grow out
of sex like a shrunk dress
into your common senses, those you share
with whatever's listening. The way the sun
moves through the hours becomes important,
the smeared raindrops
on the window, buds
on the roadside weeds, the sheen
of spilled oil on a raw ditch
filling with muddy water.

Don't get me wrong: with the lights out
I'd still take on anyone,
if I had the energy to spare.
But after a while these flesh arpeggios get boring,
like Bach over and over;
too much of one kind of glory.

When I was all body I was lazy.
I had an easy life, and was not grateful.
Now there are more of me.
Don't confuse me with any hen-leg elbows;

what you get is no longer
what you see.

Variations on the Word *Sleep*[1]

I would like to watch you sleeping,
which may not happen.
I would like to watch you,
sleeping. I would like to sleep
with you, to enter
your sleep as its smooth dark wave
slides over my head

and walk with you through that lucent
wavering forest of bluegreen leaves
with its watery sun & three moons
towards the cave where you must descend,
towards your worst fear

I would like to give you the silver
branch, the small white flower, the one
word that will protect you
from the grief at the center
of your dream, from the grief
at the center. I would like to follow
you up the long stairway
again & become
the boat that would row you back
carefully, a flame
in two cupped hands
to where your body lies
beside me, and you enter
it as easily as breathing in

I would like to be the air
that inhabits you for a moment
only. I would like to be that unnoticed
& that necessary.

---

[1] Form: Free verse.

You Fit Into Me[1]

you fit into me
like a hook into an eye

a fish hook
an open eye

Seamus Heaney (b. 1939)

A Dream of Jealousy[2]

Walking with you and another lady
In wooded parkland, the whispering grass
Ran its fingers through our guessing silence
And the trees opened into a shady
Unexpected clearing where we sat down.
I think the candor of the light dismayed us.
We talked about desire and being jealous,
Our conversation a loose single gown
Or a white picnic tablecloth spread out
Like a book or manners in the wilderness.
"Show me", I said to our companion, "what
I have much coveted, your breast's mauve star."
And she consented. O neither these verses
Nor my prudence, love, can heal your wounded stare.

Clearances[3]

5
The cool that came off sheets just off the line
Made me think the damp must still be in them
But when I took my corners of the linen
And pulled against her, first straight down the hem
And then diagonally, then flapped and shook
The fabric like a sail in a cross-wind,
They'd make a dried-out undulating thwack.
So we'd stretch and fold and end up hand to hand

---

[1] Form: Free verse.
[2] Form: Free verse—Vocabulary: mauve: reddish purple.
[3] Form: Sonnet.

For a split second as if nothing had happened
For nothing had that had not always happened
Beforehand, day by day, just touch and go,
Coming close again by holding back
In moves where I was x and she was o
Inscribed in sheets she'd sewn from ripped-out flour sacks.

Punishment[1]

I can feel the tug
of the halter at the nape
of her neck, the wind
on her naked front.

It blows her nipples
to amber beads,
it shakes the frail rigging
of her ribs.

I can see her drowned
body in the bog,
the weighing stone,
the floating rods and boughs.

Under which at first
she was a barked sapling
that is dug up
oak-bone, brain-firkin:

her shaved head
like a stubble of black corn,
her blindfold a soiled bandage,
her noose a ring

---

[1] Form: Free verse—Vocabulary: nape: back of the neck; rods: stems of
wood; boughs: tree limbs; firkin: a small wooden barrel; cauled: wrapped
like an amniotic sac; connive: plot—Notes: This is one of several poems by
Seamus describing "bog people", bodies from early man preserved in bogs
and now exhumed. This one describes a woman who was found murdered
in apparent ritual punishment.

to store
the memories of love.
Little adulteress,
before they punished you

you were flaxen-haired,
undernourished, and your
tar-black face was beautiful.
My poor scapegoat,

I almost love you
but would have cast, I know,
the stones of silence.
I am the artful voyeur

of your brain's exposed
and darkening combs,
your muscles' webbing
and all your numbered bones:

I who have stood dumb
when your betraying sisters,
cauled in tar,
wept by the railings,

who would connive
in civilized outrage
yet understand the exact
and tribal, intimate revenge.

Requiem for the Croppies[1]

The pockets of our greatcoats full of barley—
No kitchens on the run, no striking camp—
We moved quick and sudden in our own country.
The priest lay behind ditches with the tramp.
A people hardly marching— On the hike—

---

[1] Form: Sonnet—Vocabulary: Croppies: Irish nationalists who revolted
against England in 1798. The name refers to the fact that they wore their
hair shortly cropped; pike: spear; conclave: secret meeting; Terraced
thousands: people on the terraces of the hillside; shroud: burial cloth.

We found new tactics happening each day:
We'd cut through reins and rider with the pike
And stampede cattle into infantry,
Then retreat through hedges where cavalry must be thrown.
Until, on Vinegar Hill, The final conclave.
Terraced thousands died, shaking scythes at cannon.
The hillside blushed, soaked in our broken wave.
They buried us without shroud or coffin
And in August the barley grew up out of our grave.

The Haw Lantern (Dedication)[1]

The riverbed, dried-up, half-full of leaves.
Us, listening to a river in the trees.

Ted Kooser (b. 1939)

At the Office Early[2]

Rain has beaded the panes
of my office windows,
and in each little lens
the bank at the corner
hangs upside down.
What wonderful music
this rain must have made
in the night, a thousand banks
turned over, the change
crashing out of the drawers
and bouncing upstairs
to the roof, the soft
percussion of the ferns
dropping out of their pots,
the ballpoint pens
popping out of their sockets
in a fluffy snow
of deposit slips.
Now all day long,

---

[1] Form: Iambic pentameter, AA end rhyme.
[2] Form: Free verse.

as the sun dries the glass,
I'll hear the soft piano
of banks righting themselves,
the underpaid tellers
counting their nickels and dimes.

Selecting a Reader[1]

First, I would have her be beautiful,
and walking carefully up on my poetry
at the loneliest moment of an afternoon,
her hair still damp at the neck
from washing it. She should be wearing
a raincoat, an old one, dirty
from not having money enough for the cleaners.
She will take out her glasses, and there
in the bookstore, she will thumb
over my poems, then put the book back
up on its shelf. She will say to herself,
"For that kind of money, I can get
my raincoat cleaned." And she will.

David Budbill (b. 1940)

Dilemma[2]

I want to be
       famous
so I can be
       humble
about being
       famous.
What good is my
       humility
when I am
       stuck
in this
       obscurity?

---

[1] Form: Free verse.
[2] Form: Free verse.

The Three Goals[1]

The first goal is to see the thing itself
in and for itself, to see it simply and clearly
for what it is.
          No symbolism please.

The second goal is to see each individual thing
as unified, as one, with all the other
ten thousand things.
          In this regard, a little wine helps a lot.

The third goal is to grasp the first and the second goals,
to see the universal and the particular,
simultaneously.
          Regarding this one, call me when you get it.

---

[1] Form: Free verse.

Thomas M. Disch (b. 1940)

The Cardinal Detoxes: A Play in One Act[1]

We are a sinful church. We are naked. Our anger, our pain, our anguish, our shame, are clear to the whole world.
—The Most Reverend Alphonsus L. Penney,
D. D. , Archbishop of St. John's,
Newfoundland, in his statement of
resignation July 18, 1990

---

[1] Form: Iambic pentameter—Vocabulary: prie-dieu: prayer kneeling bench; Mater Dolorosa: Mother of Sorrow; bereft: left desolate or alone; gall: bitter poison; Dregs: sediment from the bottom; lees: sediment at the bottom of fermenting wine; transubstantiate: change bread and wine into body and blood of Christ; heresies: belief at odds with the Church; heresiarch: proponent of a heresy; Vicar: higher ranking priest; Shroud of Turin: burial shroud with image of Christ, thought by some to be his burial cloth; basilicas: Christian church with a nave in the center; Ararat: mountain in Turkey, thought by some to be the resting place of Noah's ark; montane: related to mountains, or in this sense, like bedrock; Carnality: sexual desire; actuarial: death statistics; cotes: animal pen; wops and micks and spics and krauts: Italians, Irish, Puerto Ricans, Germans; WASP: White Anglo-Saxon Protestant; Father Coughlin: depression era priest who was an extremely popular radio personality. His message included anti-Semitic statements; Glemp: current Archbishop of Warsaw; Giacomo: Jack; gainsay: deny; Ptolemys: astronomer who believed everything revolved around the earth; chador: Garment that covers from head to toe; Autos-da-fe: public announcements of the inquisition; foetuscide: killing a fetus; casuist: a person whose reasoning is subtle, sounds true, but is false; tares: plant that looks like wheat but, when the ear appears, turns out be poisonous; Passaic: City in New Jersey; Malone: Bishop of Boston accused of covering up sexual misconduct of priests; Muggerone: fictitious name and person; bete noire: detested person; fulminates: loudly attack accusers or deny charges; Ton-ton Macoute: Haitian militia; pusillanimity: cowardly; alb, Dalmatic, chasuble, and pallium: robe, outer garment, vestment, and bishop vestment worn by a priest during Mass; sops: something to placate; crozier: Bishop's crook; legate: emissary of the Pope; imprimatur: mark of official approval; aria: solo vocal song; dollop: splash; cowl: hood; Lourdes: Town in France where Virgin Mary supposedly appeared, known for miraculous cures; exvotos: church offering; bromides: platitudes; polity: nation or state; Ratzinger: now Pope Benedict; sanguine: optimistic; conundrum: paradox or riddle; proscribed: prohibited; cellarer: person in a monastery who provides the food and drink; Homeostatic: in equilibrium; Pax vobiscum: peace be with you; consistories: assembly of Cardinals; Italian bank that collapsed in 1982. The Chairman was supposedly involved with the Masonic lodge; See: authority of a Bishop.

*The scene is a monastically bare cell in a Catholic detox center
run by the Brothers of the Most Holy Blood. There is a bed, a
small night table beside it, a desk and chair, and a prie-dieu.
On the wall above the bed, a crucifix, flanked by pictures of
the Sacred Heart and Mater Dolorosa.*

*The Cardinal and a Brother of the Most Holy Blood are
discovered as the lights come up. The Cardinal in a state of
nerves; the Brother stands by the door, attentive but
inexpressive, except at rare moments when the Cardinal has
said something particularly offensive to conventional piety or
pious convention. After any action he has been called to
perform, the Brother returns to his post of duty before the door.*

THE CARDINAL:

> God. For the most part I do without
> Him. Don't we all. He leaves us no choice,
> Having left us, bereft us, at some point
> In pre-history—say, at the moment Christ
> Particularly complained of. Was that before
> Or after the gall was proffered him? Say what?
> Oh, yes, I know, it is your vow to say
> Nothing at all. The merest sponge for all
> My vinegar. And speaking of vinegar . . . ?

*The Brother nods, leaves the room a moment and returns with
a bottle of white wine, and a wineglass on a tray. He places
this on the night table, fills the glass half-full, and gives it to
the Cardinal, who takes a sip and makes a sour face.*

THE CARDINAL:

> Where do you find this wine? The tears of Christ,
> Indeed! He would have died before he drank
> This piss. But piss is sacred, too, if it
> Is His, and I consume it reverently.
> Having—had you supposed? —whispered the words,
> The abracadabra, of consecration.
> What priest, what Catholic, does not imagine

483

Every drop as somehow holy? Dregs
Of the wedding feast, lees of the Last Supper: this
Is my blood—

[*sips*]
—or soon enough will be.
It is kind of the Abbot to accommodate
My evening need to transubstantiate.
He doubtless sees it as the loosener of
My tongue. Is the recorder on? I know
I'm being bugged, but that's all one to me.
So long as you employ corkscrews and not
Thumbscrews, I will unfold my heresies
With all due pomp, a true heresiarch.
But the Abbot ought to know I'm not
The sort of heretic the Church is prone
To burn. In matters that concern the Faith
I am as orthodox as any pope.
The Trinity, the Virgin Birth, the fall
Of Adam and the fault of Eve,
The fleshy Resurrection of the Dead,
Whatever's set down in the Creed, or been
Decreed by any Vicar of the Church—
In all this I have faith. What I believe's
Another thing. Belief's involuntary;
Faith's an act of will, more powerful
As it demands credence in what we can't
Believe. Were I the Pope, I'd elevate
The Shroud of Turin to an article
Of Faith; I would declare the round world flat
And build basilicas on Ararat.
So much for Faith; in morals, as well, I am
Ultra-montane. Priestly celibacy?
I agree. No contraception but
By abstinence. No sodomy. You look
Askance? Surely we must seal the back door,
If we lock up the front. Carnality will out,
No doubt, even among our holy few,
But all in cloistered silence, stealthily.
AIDS, alas, has made it hard to keep
Our sepulchers properly spotless. Even

484

Among you Brothers of the Holy Blood,
I hear, there have been actuarial
Anomalies. One abbot dead, another
Ailing, or so it's said. Well, there have been
Plagues before, and there'll be plagues again.
Please don't suppose I'm being holier
Than though and thine. Would I be serving time
In detox if I hadn't erred as well?

*He sits down on the bed and looks to the Brother for a glance
of permission, then pours another glass of wine.*

THE CARDINAL:

I *do* repent me of the woman's death:
Mother of four and pregnant with a fifth;
A Catholic to boot. Had I had doubts
Of God's ambition as a dramatist,
They'd be resolved with this: CARDINAL FLYNN,
INTOXICATED, REAR-ENDS PREGNANT MOM—
They're always "Moms" in newspapers—a Mom,
What's more, who was my own parishioner.
It is deplorable, and I deplore it.
Do I, as well, blame God? Who iced the road
And sent her Chevy somersaulting? No.
I doubt that God's as meddlesome as that.
Newton's laws of motion did the job

Without his intervention. God, if He's
Not dead, is deaf, indifferent, or asleep.
For me, for most of us, God is a sham—
An ancient Poetry: I Am That I Am,
As who is not? I'm what I am, too—a priest,
A whited sepulcher, a drunken beast—
According to the *Times-Dispatch* and *Sun*—
A criminal, though yet, with any luck,
The diocese will pay whatever price
The prosecution asks to drop the charge.
It wouldn't do, would it, to have My Grace
Be sent away, however many drinks
I may have had. Archbishops are not put
In jail. I wonder what they *will* have done
With me. You wouldn't know? Or wouldn't say.
Yours is the vow *I* ought to take—Silence!
But silence never was my forte. My forte
Is speech, and I will use it if I must.
I trust the tape recorder is still on?
Then this is what I mean to do, the same
As any minor Mafioso caught
And facing time: i'll sing. I'll tell those things
We Cardinals and Archbishops say
Among ourselves, the secret wisdom of
The Church, its policies and stratagems,
Beginning with the obvious. Just guess.

He pours more wine, savoring the Brother's baleful looks.

Abortion, naturally. It is the cause
To knit our ever fewer faithful few
By giving them an enemy to fight,
Those murderous liberal bitches who refuse
To be a Mom. It is the wolf who herds
The sheep; the shepherd but assists, and sheep
Know this. Wolfless, they'll stray beyond the reach
Of hook and crook. Just look at the mess we're in.
No one attends Mass but the senile poor.
Detroit has simply given up the ghost
And closed its churches as the surest way
To stanch the flow of cash. Even where there

486

Is money, Faith's extinct—and Brotherhood,
The kind that's formed by cotes and ghetto walls.
Consider Poland, Northern Ireland,
Or *my* Archdiocese before this age
Of wishy-washy tolerance, when we
Were wops and micks and spics and krauts and built
The churches that stand empty now. The WASP
Majority was our oppressor then,
But now? Who hates us? Whom have we to fear?
Jews served the purpose for a while, and still
One meets the odd parishioner who feels
A pang of loss for Father Coughlin. Glemp,
In Poland, still baits Jews—the five or six
Surviving there. But after Auschwitz, how
Shall Holy Mother Church pursue that course?
The Jews, in any case, are not our problem:
Our problem's women. Ah-ha! Your eyes agree.
It's something every cleric understands.
It's what we mean by harping on the theme
Of family values and the sanctity
Of life, i.e. , a way of bringing up
Men to be men, women to be slaves,
And priests to be their overseers. Think
Of Italy. For centuries the Church
Beneficently engineered the codes
Of gender so each Giacomo would have
His Jill, his family fiefdom, and his fill
Of sex, or if not quite his fill, his bare
Sufficiency, while she, the Mom, kept dumb
Or mumbled rosaries. Beyond the pale
Of family, the convent and the brothel
Took up the overflow of those who balked
At their Madonnament. The benefit
To all men of sufficient strength of mind
Should be self-evident; the rest could join
The Church, and practice harsh austerities
Expressive of a holy impotence
Or else become the system's managers.
Of course, it's not just Italy of which
I speak: it's you and me. It's Fatherhood
In all the Mother Church's Fatherlands.

And it's *women* who've rebelled, thrown off
The yoke of meek subservience becoming
Handmaids of the Lord Their Spouse, who would
address
The Angel of Annunciation: "No,
I've better things to do just now than bear
A child. When I am ready, *i'll* tell you. "
Women demand equality, and no one
Has been able to gainsay them. They have
The vote, the pill, the freedom of the street.
Now they'd be priests! They do not understand
When they have won their last demand, there'll be
No Church but just Detroit writ large. For why
Should men go on pretending they believe
In all our Bulls, if somehow they don't stand
To benefit? They will walk out the door.
Not all of them and all at once, of course.
Some unisex parents for a while will rear
Mini-families of one or two,
As now the wealthier Protestants do.
What's to be done? Redraw the line again?
Admit the ladies and admit the Church
Was wrong? Declare the Fathers of the Church
This age's Ptolemys, ruled out-of-date
By schoolmarm Galileos? Rather turn
Our churches into mosques! Islam, at least
Holds firm in keeping women in their place.
Within her chador, every Moslem Mom's
A nun, while *our* nuns change their habits for
A warrior garb of pants and pantyhose.
What we must do, what we have long discussed,
Is to relight the Inquisition's torch
For the instruction and delight of those
Who still can be relied on to attend
Autos-da-fe. Burn down the clinics of
Planned Parenthood. Make foetuscide a crime
Punishable, like homicide, by death,
And if the civil power's craven courts
Should balk, if legislation's voted down
Or overthrown, then we must urge our flocks
To act upon their own. One simple, just

488

Expedient would be to institute
Homes where reluctant mothers might be brought
To term; initially, for Catholic girls
Whose parents can coerce such penitence,
As once defiant daughters might be placed
In convents; then, that precedent secure,
Encourage a clandestine brotherhood
To save those fetuses whose mothers may
Reject more mild persuasion. Civil crimes
Are justified—read any casuist—
When one is acting in a Higher Cause.
Not that such deeds would make states
Change their laws:
We would be martyred, made pariahs, sent
To jail—but what a triumph for the rights
Of fetuses, and what a way to weed
The Church's fields of tares. You think I jest:
So did the bishops gathered in St. Louis,
Though after formalities, Malone
Of Boston and Passaic's Muggerone
Took me aside and asked to know if such
A league of fetal-rights revengers had
Been formed, assuring me that when it was,
They could supply recruits. Then Muggerrone
Bewailed the evils of the media,
Who had exposed his till-then secret charity
In bailing out three youths who'd raped and stabbed
A cyclist in the park. The Bishop swears
He acted only in the interest
Of inter-racial harmony, a cause
That also prompted him to champion
St. Athanasius' Orphanage
For Children Born with AIDS, a charity
That has been universally acclaimed
Except by Bishop Muggerone's *bete noire,*
The *Jersey Star,* which claims the charges paid
To the contracting firm of Muggerone
And Sons for laying the foundation of
The orphanage would have sufficed to build
A concrete pyramid upon the site.
It seems the Bishop's outlays for cement

Exceed the county's. He was furious.
"The media! " he roared—and you could see
His chins all in a tremble—"The media
Is killing us. It's Jews is what it is.
Jews hate Italians and control the news.
If you're Italian then you're in the mob.
There is no mob, the mob's a media myth! "
And all the while he fulminates and rants,
His limousine is waiting in the lot,
His chauffeur sinister as some Ton-ton
Macoute. What is so wonderful about
The Bishop is the man's unswerving and
Unnerving righteousness, his perfect Faith
That his shit and the shit of all his kin
Must smell like roses. God, what strength of mind!
Can you suppose that like aggressiveness
Would not more suit the present circumstance
Than to require this pusillanimity
Of me, those mewling statements to the press,
My sanctuary in a drying tank:
As well embroider double A's on alb,
Dalmatic, chasuble, and pallium.
Does Rome believe such sops will satisfy
The public's appetite for blood? I face
A statutory minimum of ten!
And what is being done? I must put by
My crozier, to preach from my own pulpit,
Surrender the archdiocese accounts,
As though I were another Muggerone,
Fold my hands and wait for sentencing!
I may not even speak in privacy
With my attorneys, but the legate's spy
Is crouching in the corner taking notes.
You keep me virtually a prisoner:
No telephone, no visitors, no mail
That doesn't bear the Abbot's imprimatur.
And then you counsel me to fast and pray!
Well, i'll be damned if i'll be put away
As docilely as that. I'll bleat before
I bleed. You think *my* case is scandalous?
Wait till the papers get on yours, my boys!

490

I trust this is a live broadcast, and that
The Abbot's at his intercom—with whom
Else? Let me guess: Monsignor Mallachy;
My Deputy-Archbishop Sneed; and Rome's
Own damage control team, nameless to me.
If I'm not addressing empty air,
And if you'd like to hear the aria
Through to the end, I would appreciate
A dollop of some better lubricant.
I wait Your Grace's pleasure, and my own.

He finishes the last of the wine in the bottle on the tray, then goes to the prie-dieu, kneels, and folds his hands in prayer. The Brother regards him balefully; the Cardinal lowers his eyes. The Brother cocks his head, and presses his hand to his cowl, as though better to listen to earphones. With a look of disgruntlement, he nods and takes the tray with bottle and glass from the room.

Almost as soon as the Brother is out the door, the Cardinal gets the hiccoughs. He goes through various contortions trying to stop hiccoughing, sucking in his gut, holding his breath. He still has the hiccoughs when the Brother returns with a new bottle. The hiccoughs continue for a while even after his first careful sip of wine—each one being indicated by an asterisk within parentheses in the text he speaks: (*).

THE CARDINAL:

Hiccoughs always make me (*) think of Gene
Pacelli, Pius Twelfth, who died of them
And now is offered as a candidate
For sainthood. A saint who can't stop (*) hiccoughing!
As well a holy arsonist, a saint
With clap, a blessed ex(*)ecutioner.
The present Abbot's predecessor felt
A special reverence for his (*) witheredness,
I understand, and entertained the hope
Of a mir(*)aculous remission. Yes?
It must be either Pius has no pull
With God, or sodomites can't win (*) his ear.

Imagine if his prayer'd been answered and
Instead of (*) what it is, a jail for drunks
In Roman collars, the Abbey here became
The (*) Lourdes of AIDS-infected clergymen.
I see them now, coming to hang ex(*)votos
At Pius's shrine. The statue's right hand holds
A model of a concentration camp;
The left, a water glass symbolic of
His (*) sufferings.

*In the course of these blasphemies against Pius XII, the
Brother has approached the Cardinal to refill his quickly
emptying glass. His indignation finally is too much for him,
and he slaps the Cardinal across the face, knocking off his
glasses. Immediately, remorseful, he is on his knees to retrieve
the glasses and return them to the Cardinal, who after his
initial shock seems pleased to have made a dent in the
Brother's composure.*

THE CARDINAL:

I think I touched a nerve.
And you did, too: I've stopped the hiccoughing.
I wonder if you might have saved the Pope,
If you'd been there in 1958?
Now don't explode again: keep beating me,
I may seize up, or modify my tune
To something maddeningly bland, as: jazz,
And its potential for the liturgy,
Or else a homily on nuclear arms
And how the bishops must speak up for peace.
Oh, I have bromides in reserve that could
Sedate entire senates and have done so.
It's one of a bishop's most important jobs
To demonstrate to those who wield real power
The Church's ineffectuality
In matters of much consequence. We scold
Bad boys if they make noise, but otherwise
We turn our eyes away. What if the Church
Were to attack the mafia, instead
Of sub-contracting with it, snuggling up

492

On St. Columbus Day, and saying Mass
At mobsters' funerals? You know as well
As I, the mafia would attack right back
As ruthlessly as any sovereign state.
Look at the drug lords of Columbia,
Where crime and law at last officially
Are one, the shotgun wedding of all time.
Do you think those drug lords don't intend
To decorate their polity with priests?
Their haciendas have not only taps
Of solid gold, but chapels, too, wherein
The Virgin Mother is particularly
Venerated, and with perfect piety.
For in all things relating to the heart
Criminals, poets, madmen, and lovers
Are more in touch with what they feel than we
Whose lives are ruled by prudence. I have been
Assured by Muggerone that Domenic,
His Brother, is as staunchly orthodox
As Ratzinger in Rome—the same "Fat Nick"
Who holds the strings to half the rackets on
The Jersey docks. A scandal? Not at all.
Or not according to His Eminence,
Who takes a high, Dantean view of sin.
As, in the *Inferno*, lustful lovers
Are tumble-dried forever in gusts of flame,
Which *are* the lusts that sucked them down to hell,
So Muggerone insists that every crime
Is its own punishment, and prisons are
Superfluous, especially for the rich,
Whose very riches are more punitive,
In a Dantean sense, than time served in
The cloister of a penitentiary.
A lovely theory, is it not, because
Perfectly self-contained: whatever is
Is right, even if it's wrong. Much more than I,
The Bishop's of a sanguine temperament,
Disposed to find in any seeming ill
The silvery linings of Our Savior's will.
In AIDS he sees a triple blessing: First,
As a plague selective of those most accurst;

And then in that it affords a lingering death,
Time for a true repentance to take root,
And for a good confession at the end;
And lastly, he rejoices in its horror,
Betokening the horror of lust itself
Which violates the temple of the flesh
And now is seen to do so visibly
For the enlightenment of all who might
Be tempted to the sin of sodomy.
The bishop is no less inventive in
Finding a moral advantage in the plague,
So rampant in his own community,
Of drugs. Not only alcohol.

The Cardinal holds out his cup and as the Brother fills it,
continues speaking.

THE CARDINAL:

We all,
Who celebrate the mass, find comfort in
The wine that is our savior's blood. But crack,
As well. In terms of moral theology,
Drugs are a bit of a conundrum—cheers! —
Since nowhere in the older tablets of
The law are drugs, as such, proscribed. Indeed,
Good catholics imbibed with not a twinge
Of guilt in prohibition days, and what
Is alcohol if not a drug? This bottle's
Better, by the by. My compliments
To the cellarer. So, where were we?
Oh, yes: is heroin or ecstasy
Or crack *essentially* more wrong than, say,
A bottle of chardonnay? Not logically:
It is the use to which it's put. And that,
Among the younger felons of our age
Is to release a murderous rage, and rage
Is anger heightened exponentially,
And anger is, like lust, a deadly sin,
Whose deadliness the plague of aids reveals.
This can't be the official view of aids,

494

Of course; it wouldn't play well in the press.
Sufficient that we interdict the use
Of prophylactics; sin and nature can
Be counted on to do the rest. The church
In this is like those foresters who let
A fire sweep unchecked through timberlands,
Then, when the ashes cool, move in to sow
The seedlings they have kept in readiness.
The church's view is long as his who formed
The rivers, canyons, reefs, and limestone cliffs,
Taught bees, by trial and error, to mold their nests
In tidy hexagons, and teaches man,
As patiently, to follow natural law.
I've read somewhere there are historians
Who call the new age dawning on us now
Post-history, a pregnant phrase, and one
Suggestive of that thousand years of peace
St. John foresaw in his apocalypse.
If this is so, the church must reassert
Its claim, based on its own long stability,
To be the stabilizer of the new
Homeostatic state, the *pax vobiscum*
At the end of time. Oh my, this wine
Is mellower than the first. I hope i may
Interpret it as tender of a more
Merciful, accommodating view
Toward the disposition of my case.
The laurels of authorship as little tempt
Me as the palm of martyrdom, but if
I am thrown to the wolves and made to serve
That statutory minimum, i will
Write such a book the vatican will wish
I'd never sat at her consistories,
Had not been privy to the audits of
The banco ambrosiano, nor been sent
On secret missions to the president.
Oh, i have tales to tell, and they exist
Not only in my mortal memory
But in a still unpolished form in vaults
To which my legal counsel has the key—
In the event of my untimely death

They will be published in their present form,
And i assure you, there'll be such a storm
As has not rocked the church's holy boat
Since presses multiplied what luther wrote
Like basketfuls of poisoned loaves and fish.
Such cannot be the hierarchy's wish.
These are my terms: i must retain my see,
My freedom and my cardinality.
As to the means, ask bishop muggerone
What judges currently are selling for.
Now, if you please, i'd like to use a phone.

*The Cardinal comes to stand directly in front of the Brother,
who moves away from the door. The Cardinal tries the door
and finds it locked. He stands for a while, resting his forehead
against the locked door, defeated—and unaware that the
Brother, after receiving another message through his
earphones, employs this moment of inattention to introduce
poison into the opened bottle of wine.*

THE CARDINAL:

I see. It is a kind of miracle
When those who have been blind are made to see.
Attorneys can be bought for half the cost
Of the judiciary. Muggerone
Would have known that. My aide-memoire
Can't help me now, if it is where I think.
(*faces round, smiling*)
Well, then, let me drown myself in drink.

*The Brother pours a full glass of the poisoned, wine, which the
Cardinal accepts after a moment hesitation. As at his first
taste of the earlier bottle, he makes a sour face.*

THE CARDINAL:

Between the first glass and this next, the wine
Would seem to have turned sour. Would you agree?
Ah, I forget—you're sworn to abstinence.

My tongue should have been as wise as yours. And
mute.

*He tosses back all the wine in the glass and holds it out to be
refilled. The last of the wine is poured in the glass.*

THE CARDINAL:

A toast: to my successful autopsy
And to the holy and redeeming blood
Of Christ. May it provide the evidence
To hang the lot of you! In youth I prayed
I might become a martyr for the Faith.
God has too long a memory, too cruel
A wit—which makes Him, come to think of it,
A God that I deserve, and vice versa.

*He flinches with the first effect of the poison. The Brother helps
him to sit on the edge of the bed. He begins, again, to
hiccough, and makes a desperate effort to stop.*

THE CARDINAL:

Water, damn you! Get me a glass of (*)

*The Brother takes the wineglass, goes to the door, unlocks it,
leaves the room, and returns with the glass full of water. The
Cardinal, who is doubled with cramps, and hiccoughing,
closes his eyes, holds his breath, growing red in the face and
takes twenty sips of water. To no avail. The hiccoughing
persists. The Cardinal smashes the glass on the floor. He pulls
himself to his feet by clawing at the Brother's habit.*

THE CARDINAL:

Cure me! You did before, you (*) must again:
I will not die like that damned (*) wop!

*The Brother strikes him across the face, knocking off his
glasses, but the blow has no effect against the hiccoughs.*

497

THE CARDINAL:

Again!

The Brother uses all his force. The Cardinal falls back across the bed. His face is bloody. His hiccoughs are gone. He is dead. The Brother kneels at the foot of the bed and makes the sign of the cross.

Curtain

Robert Pinsky (b. 1940)

Shirt[1]

The back, the yoke, the yardage. Lapped seams,
The nearly invisible stitches along the collar
Turned in a sweatshop by Koreans or Malaysians

Gossiping over tea and noodles on their break
Or talking money or politics while one fitted
This armpiece with its overseam to the band

Of cuff I button at my wrist. The presser, the cutter,
The wringer, the mangle. The needle, the union,
The treadle, the bobbin. The code. The infamous blaze

At the Triangle Factory in nineteen-eleven.
One hundred and forty-six died in the flames
On the ninth floor, no hydrants, no fire escapes—

---

[1] Form: Free verse—Vocabulary: yoke: around the neck and shoulders; yardage: number of yards of cloth; Lapped: overlapped; overseam: Two parallel seams with the thread alternating between them; mangle: machine that presses fabric with heated rollers; treadle: foot pedal for foot powered sewing machines; bobbin: spool of thread; Bedlamite: lunatic; placket: a piece of cloth sewn under an opening; bar-tacked: type of stitch; Houndstooth, Tattersall, Madras: patterns; tartans: plaid fabric; Ossian: legendary Gaelic hero of 3rd century A.D.; carders: machine to line up fibers in wool; calico: coarse, bright patterned cloth; culled: Check for quality and remove defective parts.

The witness in a building across the street
Who watched how a young man helped a girl to step
Up to the windowsill, then held her out

Away from the masonry wall and let her drop.
And then another. As if he were helping them up
To enter a streetcar, and not eternity.

A third before he dropped her put her arms
Around his neck and kissed him. Then he held
Her into space, and dropped her. Almost at once

He stepped up to the sill himself, his jacket flared
And fluttered up from his shirt as he came down,
Air filling up the legs of his gray trousers—

Like Hart Crane's Bedlamite, "shrill shirt ballooning. "
Wonderful how the pattern matches perfectly
Across the placket and over the twin bar-tacked

Corners of both pockets, like a strict rhyme
Or a major chord. Prints, plaids, checks,
Houndstooth, Tattersall, Madras. The clan tartans

Invented by mill-owners inspired by the hoax of Ossian,
To control their savage Scottish workers, tamed
By a fabricated heraldry: macgregor,

Bailey, macmartin. The kilt, devised for workers
To wear among the dusty clattering looms.
Weavers, carders, spinners. The loader,

The docker, the navy. The planter, the picker, the sorter
Sweating at her machine in a litter of cotton
As slaves in calico headrags sweated in fields:

George Herbert, your descendant is a Black
Lady in South Carolina, her name is Irma
And she inspected my shirt. Its color and fit

And feel and its clean smell have satisfied

499

Both her and me. We have culled its cost and quality
Down to the buttons of simulated bone,

The buttonholes, the sizing, the facing, the characters
Printed in black on neckband and tail. The shape,
The label, the labor, the color, the shade. The shirt.

Billy Collins (b. 1941)

Budapest[1]

My pen moves along the page
like the snout of a strange animal
shaped like a human arm
and dressed in the sleeve of a loose green sweater.

I watch it sniffing the paper ceaselessly,
intent as any forager that has nothing
on its mind but the grubs and insects
that will allow it to live another day.

It wants only to be here tomorrow,
dressed perhaps in the sleeve of a plaid shirt,
nose pressed against the page,
writing a few more dutiful lines

while I gaze out the window and imagine Budapest
or some other city where I have never been.

Forgetfulness[2]

The name of the author is the first to go
followed obediently by the title, the plot,
the heartbreaking conclusion, the entire novel
which suddenly becomes one you have never read, never
    even heard of,

It is as if, one by one, the memories you used to harbor

---

[1] Form: Free verse.
[2] Form: Free verse—Notes: Lethe is the river of forgetfulness in Greek mythology.

decided to retire to the southern hemisphere of the brain,
to a little fishing village where there are no phones.

Long ago you kissed the names of the nine Muses goodbye
and watched the quadratic equation pack its bag,
and even now as you memorize the order of the planets,

something else is slipping away, a state flower perhaps,
the address of an uncle, the capital of Paraguay.

Whatever it is you are struggling to remember,
it is not poised on the tip of your tongue,
not even lurking in some obscure corner of your spleen.

It has floated away down a dark mythological river
whose name begins with an L as far as you can recall,
well on your own way to oblivion where you will join those
who have even forgotten how to swim and how to ride a
    bicycle.

No wonder you rise in the middle of the night
to look up the date of a famous battle in a book on war.
No wonder the moon in the window seems to have drifted
out of a love poem that you used to know by heart.

Introduction to Poetry[1]

I ask them to take a poem
and hold it up to the light
like a color slide

or press an ear against its hive.

I say drop a mouse into a poem
and watch him probe his way out,

or walk inside the poem's room
and feel the walls for a light switch.

---

[1] Form: Free verse.

I want them to water-ski
across the surface of a poem
waving at the author's name on the shore.

But all they want to do
is tie the poem to a chair with rope
and torture a confession out of it.

They begin beating it with a hose
to find out what it really means.

Nightclub[1]

You are so beautiful and I am a fool
to be in love with you
is a theme that keeps coming up
in songs and poems.
There seems to be no room for variation.
I have never heard anyone sing
I am so beautiful
and you are a fool to be in love with me,
even though this notion has surely
crossed the minds of women and men alike.
You are so beautiful, too bad you are a fool
is another one you don't hear.
Or, you are a fool to consider me beautiful.
That one you will never hear, guaranteed.

For no particular reason this afternoon
I am listening to Johnny Hartman
whose dark voice can curl around
the concepts of love, beauty, and foolishness
like no one else's can.
It feels like smoke curling up from a cigarette
someone left burning on a baby grand piano
around three o'clock in the morning;
smoke that billows up into the bright lights
while out there in the darkness

---

[1] Form: Free verse—Vocabulary: Johnny Hartman: contemporary jazz
singer; bebop: form of jazz originating around 1940.

some of the beautiful fools have gathered
around little tables to listen,
some with their eyes closed,
others leaning forward into the music
as if it were holding them up,
or twirling the loose ice in a glass,
slipping by degrees into a rhythmic dream.
Yes, there is all this foolish beauty,
borne beyond midnight,
that has no desire to go home,
especially now when everyone in the room
is watching the large man with the tenor sax
that hangs from his neck like a golden fish.
He moves forward to the edge of the stage
and hands the instrument down to me
and nods that I should play.
So I put the mouthpiece to my lips
and blow into it with all my living breath.
We are all so foolish,
my long bebop solo begins by saying,
so damn foolish
we have become beautiful without even knowing it.

Not Touching[1]

The valentine of desire is pasted over my heart
and still we are not touching, like things

in a poorly done still life
where the knife appears to be floating over the plate
which is itself hovering above the table somehow,

the entire arrangement of apple, pear, and wineglass
having forgotten the law of gravity,
refusing to be still,

as if the painter had caught them all
in a rare moment of slow flight

---

[1] Form: Free verse.

just before they drifted out of the room
through a window of perfectly realistic sunlight.

Passengers[1]

At the gate, I sit in a row of blue seats
with the possible company of my death,
this sprawling miscellany of people—
carry-on bags and paperbacks—

that could be gathered in a flash
into a band of pilgrims on the last open road.
Not that I think
if our plane crumpled into a mountain

we would all ascend together,
holding hands like a ring of sky divers,
into a sudden gasp of brightness,
or that there would be some common spot

for us to reunite to jubilize the moment,
some spaceless, pillarless Greece
where we could, at the count of three,
toss our ashes into the sunny air.

It's just that the way that man has his briefcase
so carefully arranged,
the way that girl is cooling her tea,
and the flow of the comb that woman

passes through her daughter's hair. . .
and when you consider the altitude,
the secret parts of the engines,
and all the hard water and the deep canyons below. . .

well, I just think it would be good if one of us
maybe stood up and said a few words,
or, so as not to involve the police,
at least quietly wrote something down.

---

[1] Form: Free verse—Vocabulary: jubilize: blast trumpets.

Purity[1]

My favorite time to write is in the late afternoon,
weekdays, particularly Wednesdays.
This is how I go about it:
I take a fresh pot of tea into my study and close the door.
Then I remove my clothes and leave them in a pile
as if I had melted to death
and my legacy consisted of only
a white shirt, a pair of pants, and a pot of cold tea.

Then I remove my flesh and hang it over a chair.
I slide it off my bones like a silken garment.
I do this so that what I write will be pure,
completely rinsed of the carnal,
uncontaminated by the preoccupations of the body.

Finally I remove each of my organs and arrange them
on a small table near the window.
I do not want to hear their ancient rhythms
when I am trying to tap out my own drumbeat.

Now I sit down at the desk, ready to begin.
I am entirely pure: nothing but a skeleton at a typewriter.

I should mention that sometimes I leave my penis on.
I find it difficult to ignore the temptation.
Then I am a skeleton with a penis at a typewriter.

In this condition I write extraordinary love poems,
most of them exploiting the connection between sex
    and death.

I am concentration itself: I exist in a universe
where there is nothing but sex, death, and typewriting.

After a spell of this I remove my penis too.

---

[1] Form: Free verse—Vocabulary: carnal: earthly; flounces: a strip of
decoration.

Then I am all skull and bones typing into the afternoon.
Just the absolute essentials, no flounces.
Now I write only about death, most classical of themes
in language light as the air between my ribs.

Afterward, I reward myself by going for a drive at sunset.
I replace my organs and slip back into my flesh
and clothes. Then I back the car out of the garage
and speed through woods on winding country roads,
passing stone walls, farmhouses, and frozen ponds,
all perfectly arranged like words in a famous sonnet.

Questions About Angels[1]

Of all the questions you might want to ask
about angels, the only one you ever hear
is how many can dance on the head of a pin.

No curiosity about how they pass the eternal time
besides circling the Throne chanting in Latin
or delivering a crust of bread to a hermit on earth
or guiding a boy and girl across a rickety wooden bridge.

Do they fly through God's body and come out singing?
Do they swing like children from the hinges
of the spirit world saying their names backwards and
    forwards?
Do they sit alone in little gardens changing colors?

What about their sleeping habits, the fabric of their robes,
their diet of unfiltered divine light?
What goes on inside their luminous heads? Is there a wall
these tall presences can look over and see hell?

If an angel fell off a cloud would he leave a hole
in a river and would the hole float along endlessly
filled with the silent letters of every angelic word?

---

[1] Form: Free verse.

If an angel delivered the mail would he arrive
in a blinding rush of wings or would he just assume
the appearance of the regular mailman and
whistle up the driveway reading the postcards?

No, the medieval theologians control the court.
The only question you ever hear is about
the little dance floor on the head of a pin
where halos are meant to converge and drift invisibly.

It is designed to make us think in millions,
billions, to make us run out of numbers and collapse
into infinity, but perhaps the answer is simply one:
one female angel dancing alone in her stocking feet,
a small jazz combo working in the background.

She sways like a branch in the wind, her beautiful
eyes closed, and the tall thin bassist leans over
to glance at his watch because she has been dancing
forever, and now it is very late, even for musicians.

Toi Derricotte (b. 1941)

Allen Ginsberg[1]

Once Allen Ginsberg stopped to pee at a bookstore in New
    Jersey,
but he looked like a bum—
not like the miracle-laden Christ with electric atom juice, not
    like the one whose brain is a river in which was plunked
    the stone of the world (the one bathing fluid to wash away
    25,000 year half-lives), he was dressed as a bum.
He had wobbled on a pee-heavy bladder
in search of a gas station,
a dime store with a quarter booth,
a Chinese restaurant,
when he came to that grocery store of dreams:
chunks of Baudelaire's skin
glittered in plastic;

---

[1] Form: Free verse.

his eyes in sets, innocent
as the unhoused eyes of a butchered cow.
In a dark corner, Rimbaud's
genitals hung like jerky,
and the milk of Whitman's breasts
drifted in a carton, dry as talcum.
He wanted to pee and lay his head
on the cool stacks;
but the clerk took one look
and thought of the buttock of clean businessmen
    squatting during lunch hour,
the thin flanks of pretty girls buying poetry for school.
Behind her, faintly,
the deodorized bathroom.
She was the one at the gate
protecting civilization.
He turned, walked to the gutter,
unzipped his pants, and peed.
Do you know who that was?
A man in the back came forth.
Soon she was known as
the woman in the store on Main
who said no to Allen Ginsberg;
and she is proud—
so proud she told this story
pointing to the spot outside, as if
still flowed that holy stream.

Stephen Dobyns (b. 1941)

Tomatoes[1]

A woman travels to Brazil for plastic
surgery and a face-lift. She is sixty
and has the usual desire to stay pretty.
Once she is healed she takes her new face
out on the streets of Rio. A young man
with a gun wants her money. Bang, she's dead.
The body is shipped back to New York,

---

[1] Form: Prose poem—Vocabulary: filial: child to parent.

but in the morgue there is a mix-up. The son
is sent for. He is told that his mother
is one of these ten different women.
Each has been shot. Such is modern life.
He studies them all but can't find her.
With her new face, she has become a stranger.
Maybe it's this one, maybe it's that one.
He looks at their breasts. Which ones nursed him?
He presses their hands to his cheek.
Which ones consoled him? He even tries
climbing into their laps to see which
feels more familiar but the coroner stops him.
Well, says the coroner, which is your mother?
They all are, says the young man, let me
take them as a package. The coroner hesitates,
then agrees. Actually it solves a lot of problems.
The young man has the ten women shipped home,
then cremates them all together. You've seen
how some people have a little urn on the mantle?
This man has a huge silver garbage can.
In the spring, he drags the garbage can
out to the garden and begins working the teeth,
the ash, the bits of bone into the soil.
Then he plants tomatoes. His mother loved tomatoes.
They grow straight from seed, so fast and big
that the young man is amazed. He takes the first
ten into the kitchen. In their roundness,
he sees his mother's breasts. In their smoothness,
he finds the consoling touch of her hands.
Mother, mother, he cries, and flings himself
on the tomatoes. Forget about the knife, the fork,
the pinch of salt. Try to imagine the filial
starvation, think of his ravenous kisses.

Eamon Grennan (b. 1941)

Detail[1]

I was watching a robin fly after a finch—the smaller bird

---

[1] Form: Lineated poem.

chirping with excitement, the bigger, its breast blazing, silent in light-winged earnest chase – when, out of nowhere flashes a sparrowhawk headlong, a light brown burn scorching the air from which it simply plucks like a ripe fruit the stopped robin, whose two or three *cheeps* of terminal surprise twinkle in the silence closing over the empty street when the birds have gone about their own business, and I began to understand how a poem can happen: you have your eye on a small elusive detail, pursuing its music, when a terrible truth strikes and your heart cries out, being carried off.

Gerald Locklin (b. 1941)

Late Registration[1]

She asks me for an admissions card
to remedial English,
and I have to tell her that
we don't have any sections open.

"How come? " she asks.

So I explain that the governor provided
the money to identify those students
in need of remedial instruction,
but he did not budget any funds
for remedial instructors.

"Well, then," she says,
"put me down for creative writing."

Jack Myers (b. 1941)

Jake Addresses the World from the Garden[2]
   Rocks without ch'I [spirit] are dead rocks.
   —mai-mai sze, The Way of Chinese Painting

---

[1] Form: Free verse.
[2] Form: Free verse—Notes: Here the parent of a special needs child responds to the child using his word, but unlike the wonder the child means by the word, the parent is just saying the word without the same meaning.

It's spring and Jake toddles to the garden
as the sun wobbles up clean and iridescent.

He points to the stones asleep and says, "M'mba,"
I guess for the sound they make, takes another step

and says, "M'mba," for the small red berries crying
in the holly. "M'mba," for the first sweet sadness

of the purplish-black berries in the drooping monkey grass,
and "M'mba," for the little witches' faces bursting into
    blossom.

That's what it's like being shorter than the primary colors,
being deafened by humming stones while the whole world
    billows

behind the curtain "M'mba," the one word. Meanwhile I go on
troweling, slavering the world with language as Jake squeals

like a held bird and begins lallating to me in tongues.
I follow him around as he tries to thread the shine of a stone

through the eye of a watchful bird.
After a year of banging
his head, crying, the awful falling down, now he's trying

to explain the vast brightening in his brain by saying
    "M'mba"
to me again and again. And though I follow with the sadness

above which a stone cannot lift itself, I wink and say
"M'mba" back to him. But I don't mean it.

Nancy Vieira Couto (b. 1942)

Living in the La Brea Tar Pits[1]

Each morning she is wheeled into the picture
window of her son-in-law's house,
jammed into her selected viewing space
by the table with the lamp and bowling trophy.
The drapes sweep apart like fronds.

She stretches her neck like a brontosaurus
and watches the neighbors, whose names she doesn't
remember. Across the street
two Volkswagens line up like M&M's,
one yellow, one orange.

                At lunchtime
her daughter broils a small steak, very tender,
saying, "Ma, you *must* have meat. "But her taste runs
these days to Kellogg's Corn Flakes and baby cereals.
She leans over her plate,
stretching her neck like a brontosaurus,
and mangles a small piece between her tough
gums. The dog waits his turn.

Each evening she is wheeled up close
to the TV in her son-in-law's house.
She watches "Superman" reruns.
In the kitchen, her son-in-law
eats meat and potatoes and talks in a loud voice.
His bowling night—she will have
her daughter to herself. But the TV
picture has gone bad, and the room is dark.
Just last week she could hardly tell if there
were four lovely Lennon sisters, or three.

---

[1] Form: Free verse—Vocabulary: La Brea Tar Pits: tar pits in Los Angeles
where many dinosaur bones have been exhumed—Notes: Notice the
repeated references to "waiting their turn". The son-in-law waits his turn,
figuratively to be old and lonely. Later in time (after the tilde (~)) his
children wait their turn. They are all trapped in a cycle, much like the
animals millions of years ago trapped in the la Brea Tar Pits.

He returns late—almost eleven—
low scorer on his team. He wants his wife
but there's a dinosaur in his living room, stretching
her neck. It's past her bedtime. He waits his turn.

~

Each morning he looks out of the picture
window of his house. Across the street
the neighbors have parked their shiny new Toyotas.
He blinks, as if at something unexpected
and obscene. He moves away,
walking upright, heavy on his bare
heels. He wears pajamas.

                In the kitchen
he pours orange juice into a paper cup
and takes his medication—two shiny capsules.
His mother-in-law is extinct, and his wife, too.

There is the dog to feed, and he will think of
people to visit. He moves slow, deliberate,
but keeps on moving. The sky is full of birds,
and the Rocky Mountains all have names.

In the evening he turns on the TV
and wedges his fifty-foot frame into his favorite
chair, curling his tail over the armrest.
He watches the third rerun of the Italian
version of *Zorro*. When the horizontal
hold goes haywire, he watches diagonal stripes.

It's not easy to be a tyrannosaurus.
He stands eighteen feet tall, he thuds through life,
what's left. And when he roars, he shows his sharp
stalactites and stalagmites. His grown children
get nervous. He resents them. They wait their turn.

Stuart Dybek (b. 1942)

Brass Knuckles[1]

Kruger sets his feet
before Ventura Furniture's plate glass window.
      We're
   outlined in streetlights,
  reflected across the jumbled living rooms,
bedrooms, dining rooms,
       smelling fresh bread
   from the flapping ventilator down the alley
   behind Cross's Bakery.

His fist keeps clenching
(Our jaws grinding on bennies)
     through the four thick rings
    of the knuckles he made me in shop
   the day after I got stomped
      outside St. Sabina's.

  "The idea is to strike like a cobra. Don't follow through.
   Focus
total power at the moment of impact. "
     His fist uncoils
        the brass
whipped back a centimeter from
     smashing out my teeth,
   the force waves
       snapping my head back.
        "See? " he says,

sucking breath like a diver, toe to toe
with the leopard-skin sofa;
      I step back
   thinking how a diamond ring cuts glass;
his fist explodes.
    The window cracks for half a block,

---

[1] Form: Free verse—Vocabulary: bennies: a stimulant; spoor: track of an animal—Notes: The two are caught by the police for breaking the window but also caught in a role, a life, from which there may be no escape.

knees drop out of our reflections.

An alarm
is bouncing out of doorways,
              we cut
          down a gangway of warm bread,
              boots echoing
          through the dim-lit viaduct on Rockwell
      where I see his hand
      flinging orange swashes off the concrete walls,

blood behind us
like footprints,
              spoor for cops;
          in a red haze of switches
          boxcars couple,
  we jump the electric rail
  knowing we're already caught.

Maroon[1]

for Anthony Dadaro, 1946-1958

A boy is bouncing a ball off a brick wall after school. The bricks have been painted maroon a long time ago. Steady as a heartbeat the ball rebounds oblong, hums, sponges back round. A maroon Chevy goes by.

---

[1] Form: Prose poem—Vocabulary: alkies: alcoholics—Notes: This poem, centered on the color of blood, is all the more powerful because the final conclusion is not explicitly stated.

Nothing else. This street's deserted: a block-long
abandoned factory, glass from the busted windows on the
sidewalk mixed with brown glass from beer bottles, whiskey
pints. Sometimes the alkies drink here. Not today.

Only the ball flying between sunlit hands and shadowed
bricks and sparrows brawling in the dusty gutters. The entire
street turning maroon in the shadow of the wall, even the
birds, even the hands.

He stands waiting under a streetlight that's trying to
flicker on. Three guys he's never seen in the neighborhood
before, coming down the street, carrying crowbars.

B. H. Fairchild (b. 1942)

The Dumka[1]

His parents would sit alone together
on the blue divan in the small living room
listening to Dvorak's piano quintet.
They would sit there in their old age,
side by side, quite still, backs rigid, hands
in their laps, and look straight ahead
at the yellow light of the phonograph
that seemed as distant as a lamplit
window seen across the plains late at night.
They would sit quietly as something dense

and radiant swirled around them, something
like the dust storms of the thirties that began
by smearing the sky green with doom
but afterwards drenched the air with an amber
glow and then vanished, leaving profiles
of children on pillows and a pale gauze
over mantles and table tops. But it was
the memory of dust that encircled them now
and made them smile faintly and raise
or bow their heads as they spoke about

---

[1] Form: Free verse—Vocabulary: quintet: five instruments.

516

the farm in twilight with piano music
spiraling out across red roads and fields
of maize, bread lines in the city, women
and men lining main street like mannequins,
and then the war, the white frame rent house,
and the homecoming, the homecoming,
the homecoming, and afterwards, green lawns
and a new piano with its mahogany gleam
like pond ice at dawn, and now alone
in the house in the vanishing neighborhood,

the slow mornings of coffee and newspapers
and evenings of music and scattered bits
of talk like leaves suddenly fallen before
one notices the new season. And they would sit
there alone and soon he would reach across
and lift her hand as if it were the last unbroken
leaf and he would hold her hand in his hand
for a long time and they would look far off
into the music of their lives as they sat alone
together in the room in the house in Kansas.

Tom Hennen (b. 1942)

Soaking Up Sun[1]

Today there is the kind of sunshine old men love, the kind of
day when my grandfather would sit on the south side of the
wooden corncrib where the sunlight warmed slowly all
through the day like a wood stove. One after another dry
leaves fell. No painful memories came. Everything was lit by a
halo of light. The cornstalks glinted bright as pieces of glass.
From the fields and cottonwood grove came the damp smell
of mushrooms, of things going back to earth. I sat with my
grandfather then. Sheep came up to us as we sat there, their
oily wool so warm to my fingers, like a strange and magic
snow. My grandfather whittled sweet smelling apple sticks
just to get at the scent. His thumb had a permanent groove
in it where the back of the knife blade rested. He let me listen

[1] Form: Prose poem.

517

to the wind, the wild geese, the soft dialect of sheep, while his own silence taught me every secret thing he knew.

The Life of a Day[1]

Like people or dogs, each day is unique and has its own personality quirks which can easily be seen if you look closely. But there are so few days as compared to people, not to mention dogs, that it would be surprising if a day were not a hundred times more interesting than most people. But usually they just pass, mostly unnoticed, unless they are wildly nice, like autumn ones full of red maple trees and hazy sunlight, or if they are grimly awful ones in a winter blizzard that kills the lost traveler and bunches of cattle. For some reason we like to see days pass, even though most of us claim we don't want to reach our last one for a long time. We examine each day before us with barely a glance and say, no, this isn't one I've been looking for, and wait in a bored sort of way for the next, when we are convinced, our lives will start for real. Meanwhile, this day is going by perfectly well-adjusted, as some days are, with the right amounts of sunlight and shade, and a light breeze scented with a perfume made from the mixture of fallen apples, corn stubble, dry oak leaves, and the faint odor of last night's meandering skunk.

David Huddle (b. 1942)

Holes Commence Falling[2]

The lead and zinc company
owned the mineral rights
to the whole town anyway,
and after drilling holes
for 3 or 4 years,
they finally found the right
place and sunk a mine shaft.
We were proud

---

[1] Form: Prose poem—Notes: Notice the attention to the sense of smell to make the day real for the reader.
[2] Form: Free verse.

of all that digging,
even though nobody from
town got hired. They
were going to dig right
under New River and hook up
with the mine at Austinville.
Then people's wells
started drying up just like
somebody'd shut off a faucet,
and holes commenced falling,
big chunks of people's yards
would drop 5 or 6 feet,
houses would shift and crack.
Now and then the company'd
pay out a little money
in damages; they got a truck
to haul water and sell it
to the people whose wells
had dried up, but most
everybody agreed the
situation wasn't
serious.

Louis Jenkins (b. 1942)

A Place for Everything[1]

It's so easy to lose track of things. A screwdriver, for
instance. "Where did I put that? I had it in my hand just a
minute ago." You wander vaguely from room to room, having
forgotten, by now, what you were looking for, staring into the
refrigerator, the bathroom mirror . . . "I really could use a
shave. . . . "

Some objects seem to disappear immediately while others
never want to leave. Here is a small black plastic gizmo with
a serious demeanor that turns up regularly, like a politician
at public functions. It seems to be an "integral part," a kind
of switch with screw holes so that it can be attached to

---

[1] Form: Prose poem.

something larger. Nobody knows what. This thing's use has been forgotten but it looks so important that no one is willing to throw it in the trash. It survives by bluff, like certain insects that escape being eaten because of their formidable appearance.

My father owned a large, three-bladed, brass propeller that he saved for years. Its worth was obvious, it was just that it lacked an immediate application since we didn't own a boat and lived hundreds of miles from any large body of water. The propeller survived all purges and cleanings, living, like royalty, a life of lonely privilege, mounted high on the garage wall.

William Matthews (1942 – 1997)

A Poetry Reading at West Point[1]

I read to the entire plebe class,
in two batches. Twice the hall filled
with bodies dressed alike, each toting
a copy of my book. What would my
shrink say, if I had one, about
such a dream, if it were a dream?

Question and answer time.
"Sir," a cadet yelled from the balcony,
and gave his name and rank, and then,
closing his parentheses, yelled
"Sir" again. "Why do your poems give
me a headache when I try

to understand them? " he asked. "Do
you want that?" I have a gift for
gentle jokes to defuse tension,
but this was not the time to use it.
"I try to write as well as I can
what it feels like to be human,"

---

[1] Form: Free verse.

I started, picking my way care—
fully, for he and I were, after
all, pained by the same dumb longings.
"I try to say what I don't know
how to say, but of course I can't
get much of it down at all."

By now I was sweating bullets.
"I don't want my poems to be hard,
unless the truth is, if there is
a truth." Silence hung in the hall
like a heavy fabric. My own
head ached. "Sir," he yelled. "Thank you. Sir."

Onions[1]

How easily happiness begins by
dicing onions. A lump of sweet butter
slithers and swirls across the floor
of the sauté pan, especially if its
errant path crosses a tiny stick
of olive oil. Then a tumble of onions.

This could mean soup or risotto
or chutney (from the Sanskrit
chatni, to lick). Slowly the onions
go limp and then nacreous
and then what cookbooks call clear,
though if they were eyes you could see

clearly the cataracts in them.
It's true it can make you weep
to peel them, to unfurl and to tease
from the taut ball first the brittle,
caramel-colored and decrepit
papery outside layer, the least

---

[1] Form: Free verse—Vocabulary: nacreous: lustrous; reticent: restrained or
reserved; loam: a type of soil.

recent the reticent onion
wrapped around its growing body,
for there's nothing to an onion
but skin, and it's true you can go on
weeping as you go on in, through
the moist middle skins, the sweetest

and thickest, and you can go on
in to the core, the bud-like,
acrid, fibrous skins densely
clustered there, stalky
and incomplete, and these are the most
pungent, like the nuggets of nightmare

and rage and murmury animal
comfort that infant humans secrete.
This is the best domestic perfume.
You sit down to eat with a rumor
of onions still on your twice-washed
hands and lift to your mouth a hint

of a story about loam and usual
endurance. It's there when you clean up
and rinse the wine glasses and make
a joke, and you leave the minutest
whiff of it on the light switch,
later, when you climb the stairs.

Sharon Olds (b. 1942)

I Go Back to May 1937[1]

I see them standing at the formal gates of their colleges,
I see my father strolling out
under the ochre sandstone arch, the
red tiles glinting like bent
plates of blood behind his head, I
see my mother with a few light books at her hip

---

[1] Form: Free verse—Vocabulary: ochre: earth-tone colored—Notes: The issues alluded to in this poem form the basis for a significant amount of Sharon's confessional style poetry.

standing at the pillar made of tiny bricks with the
wrought-iron gate still open behind her, its
sword-tips back in the May air,
they are about to graduate,
they are about to get married,
they are kids, they are dumb, all they know is they are
innocent, they would never hurt anybody.
I want to go up to them and say Stop,
don't do it—she's the wrong woman,
he's the wrong man, you are going to do things
you cannot imagine you would ever do,
you are going to do bad things to children,
you are going to suffer in ways you never heard of,
you are going to die. I want to go
up to them there in the May sunlight and say it,
her hungry pretty blank face turning to me,
her pitiful beautiful untouched body,
his arrogant handsome blind face turning to me,
his pitiful beautiful untouched body,
but I don't do it. I want to live. I
take them up like male and female
paper dolls and bang them together
at the hips like chips of flint as if to
strike sparks from them, I say
Do what you are going to do, and I will tell about it.

Once[1]

I saw my father naked, once, I
opened the blue bathroom's door
which he always locked—if it opened, it was empty—
and there, surrounded by glistening turquoise
tile, sitting on the toilet, was my father,
all of him, and all of him
was skin. In an instant, my gaze ran
in a single, swerving, unimpeded
swoop, up: toe, ankle,
knee, hip, rib, nape,

---

[1] Form: Free verse—Vocabulary: nape: back of the neck; shorn lamb: lamb
with fleece removed.

shoulder, elbow, wrist, knuckle,
my father. He looked so unprotected,
so seamless, and shy, like a girl on a toilet,
and even though I knew he was sitting
to shit, there was no shame in that
but even a human peace. He looked up,
I said Sorry, backed out, shut the door
but I'd seen him, my father a shorn lamb,
my father a cloud in the blue sky
of the blue bathroom, my eye driven
up the hairpin mountain road of the
naked male, I had turned a corner
and found his flank unguarded—gentle
bulge of the hip joint, border of the pelvic cradle.

Quake Theory[1]

When two plates of earth scrape along each other
like a mother and daughter
it is called a fault.

There are faults that slip smoothly past each other
an inch a year, just a faint rasp
like a man running his hand over his chin,
that man between us,

and there are faults that get stuck at a bend for twenty years.
The ridge bulges up like a father's sarcastic forehead
and the whole thing freezes in place, the man between us.

When this happens, there will be heavy damage
to industrial areas and leisure residence
when the deep plates
finally jerk past
the terrible pressure of their contact.

                                    The earth cracks
and innocent people slip gently in like swimmers.

---

[1] Form: Free verse.

Satan Says[1]

I am locked in a little cedar box
with a picture of shepherds pasted onto
the central panel between carvings.
The box stands on curved legs.
It has a gold, heart-shaped lock
and no key. I am trying to write my
way out of the closed box
redolent of cedar. Satan
comes to me in the locked box
and says, *I'll get you out. Say*
My father is a shit. I say
my father is a shit and Satan
laughs and says, *It's opening.*
Say your mother is a pimp.
My mother is a pimp. Something
opens and breaks when I say that.
My spine uncurls in the cedar box
like the pink back of the ballerina pin
with a ruby eye, resting besides me on
satin in the cedar box.
Say shit, say death, say fuck the father,
Satan says, down my ear.
The pain of the locked past buzzes
in the child's box on her bureau, under
the terrible round pond eye
etched around with roses, where
self-loathing gazed at sorrow.
Shit. Death. Fuck the father.
Something opens. Satan says
Don't you feel a lot better?
Light seems to break on the delicate
edelweiss pin, carved in two
colors of wood. I love him too,
you know, I say to Satan dark
in the locked box. I love them but

---

[1] Form: Free verse—Vocabulary: redolent: smelling; edelweiss: small white alpine flower—Notes: A metaphorical look at child abuse, the inner destruction of evil, and the necessity to reach resolution—if not forgiveness.

I'm trying to say what happened to us
in the lost past. *Of course*, he says
and smiles, *of course. Now say: torture.*
I see, through blackness soaked in cedar,
the edge of a large hinge open.
*Say: the father's cock, the mother's
cunt*, says Satan, *I'll get you out.*
The angle of the hinge widens
until I see the outlines of
the time before I was, when they were
locked in the bed. When I say
the magic words, Cock, Cunt,
Satan softly says, *Come out.*
But the air around the opening
is heavy and thick as hot smoke.
Come in, he says, and I feel his voice
breathing from the opening.
The exit is through Satan's mouth.
Come in my mouth, he says, *you're there
already*, and the huge hinge
begins to close. Oh no, I loved
them, too, I brace
my body tight
in the cedar house.
Satan sucks himself out the keyhole.
I'm left locked in the box, he seals
the heart-shaped lock with the wax of his tongue.
It's your coffin now, Satan says,
I hardly hear;
I am warming my cold
hands at the dancer's
ruby eye—
the fire, the suddenly discovered knowledge of love.

The Pope's Penis[1]

It hangs deep in his robes, a delicate
clapper at the center of a bell.
It moves when he moves, a ghostly fish in a

---

[1] Form: Free verse.

halo of silver seaweed, the hair
swaying in the dark and the heat—and at night
while his eyes sleep, it stands up
in praise of God.

The Promise[1]

With the second drink, at the restaurant,
holding hands on the bare table,
we are at it again, renewing our promise
to kill each other. You are drinking gin,
night-blue juniper berry
dissolving in your body, I am drinking fume,
chewing its fragrant dirt and smoke, we are
taking on earth, we are part soil already,
and wherever we are, we are also in our
bed, fitted, naked, closely
along each other, half passed out,
after love, drifting back
and forth across the border of consciousness,
our bodies buoyant, clasped. Your hand
tightens on the table. You're a little afraid
I'll chicken out. What you do not want
is to lie in a hospital bed for a year
after a stroke, without being able
to think or die, you do not want
to be tied to a chair like your prim grandmother,
cursing. The room is dim around us,
ivory globes, pink curtains
bound at the waist—and outside,
a weightless, luminous, lifted-up
summer twilight. I tell you you do not
know me if you think I will not
kill you. Think how we have floated together
eye to eye, nipple to nipple,
sex to sex, the halves of a creature
drifting up to the lip of matter
and over it—you know me from the bright, blood-

---

[1] Form: Free verse—Vocabulary: juniper berry: berry used to give gin its
distinctive flavor; fume: type of wine (fume blanc).

527

flecked delivery room, if a lion
had you in its jaws I would attack it, if the ropes
binding your soul are your own wrists, I will cut them.

The Space Heater[1]

On the then-below-zero day, it was on,
near the patients' chair, the old heater
kept by the analyst's couch, at the end,
like the infant's headstone that was added near the foot
of my father's grave. And it was hot, with the almost
laughing satire of a fire's heat,
the little coils like hairs in Hell.
And it was making a group of sick noises—
I wanted the doctor to turn it off
but I couldn't seem to ask, so I just
stared, but it did not budge. The doctor
turned his heavy, soft palm
outward, toward me, inviting me to speak, I
said, "If you're cold-are you cold? But if it's on
for me. . . " He held his palm out toward me,
I tried to ask, but I only muttered,
but he said, "Of course," as if I had asked,
and he stood up and approached the heater, and then
stood on one foot, and threw himself
toward the wall with one hand, and with the other hand
reached down, behind the couch, to pull
the plug out. I looked away,
I had not known he would have to bend
like that. And I was so moved, that he
would act undignified, to help me,
that I cried, not trying to stop, but as if
the moans made sentences which bore
some human message.
If he would cast himself toward the
outlet for me, as if bending with me in my old
shame and horror, then I would rest
on his art—and the heater purred, like a creature

---

[1] Form: Free verse—Vocabulary: familiar: attendant spirit—The beginning
of a bond with the therapist that will help the narrator deal with issues
revolving around her father.

or the familiar of a creature, or the child of a familiar,
the father of a child, the spirit of a father,
the healing of a spirit, the vision of healing,
the heat of vision, the power of heat,
the pleasure of power.

Dave Smith (b. 1942)

Pulling a Pig's Tail[1]

The feel of it was hairy and coarse
like new rope in A. W. Johnson's
hardware store but I never touched it
or any part of a pig
until that day my father took me
where the farm was, woods
a kind of green stillness, the hanging
leaves from so much rain
I guess—it felt as if I was upside
down underwater trying to swim
for my life. The farmer, Uncle Bern,
said I could have one
if I could catch it. A little one
looked easy, about my size,
not so wary because he wasn't unsure
of anything yet—I must have
thought, but quick and hungry
as small lives always are
so I chased him until the foul mud
hardened on me like a skin,
the big men crying with laughter.
My father said it was just
that funny like some kind of soul's
testing to see I wanted
badly enough to catch myself, black
eyes not seeming to watch,
fixed on the horizon past the weird
way I talked to it. Finally
it listened to something and I took

---

[1] Form: Free verse.

529

a grip, held, grunting, dug
my sneakers into the shit. Why he ran
and didn't try to bite me
I don't know. By then I almost had
everything straight but felt
at last what wasn't right, the uncoiled
helplessness of anything
dragged small and screaming while
the big ones watch and grin.
I let go. I didn't say I was thinking
about school that was over
that summer, the teacher that yanked
my hair, who said she'd see
I got myself straightened out. I hid
my hands in shame. How could I
tell my father a pig's tail burns
your hands like lost beauty?
I only knew I loved school
until that raw day when she let me loose.

Wreck in the Woods[1]

Under that embrace of wild saplings held fast,
surrounded by troops of white mushrooms, by wrens
visiting like news-burdened ministers known
only to some dim life inside, this Model
A Ford like my grandfather's entered the earth.
What were fenders, hood, doors, no one washed, polished,
grazed with a tip of finger, or boyhood dream.
I stood where silky blue above went wind-rent,
pines, oaks, dogwood tickling, pushing as if grief
called families to see what none understood. What
plot of words, what heart-shudder of men, women
here ended so hard the green world must hide it?
Headlights, large, round. Two pieces of shattered glass.

---

[1] Form: Free verse—Vocabulary: rent: torn.

Sharon Bryan (b. 1943)

Beyond Recall[1]

Nothing matters
to the dead,
that's what's so hard

for the rest of us
to take in—
their complete indifference

to our enticements,
our attempts to get in touch—
they aren't observing us

from a discreet distance,
they aren't listening
to a word we say—

you know that,
but you don't believe it,
even deep in a cave

you don't believe
in total darkness,
you keep waiting

for your eyes to adjust
and reveal your hand
in front of your face—

so how long a silence
will it take to convince us
that we're the ones

who no longer exist,
as far as X is concerned,

---

[1] Form: Free verse—Vocabulary: —Notes: The narrator has unresolved
issues with someone who has died, and finds herself waiting expectantly
for the opportunity to resolve those issues — but the time will never come.

and Y, and they've forgotten

every little thing
they knew about us,
what we told them

and what we didn't
have to, even our names
mean nothing to them

now—our throats ache
with all we might have said
the next time we saw them.

Philip Schultz ((b. 1945)

The Answering Machine[1]

My friends & I speak mostly to one another's machine.
We badger, cajole, & manipulate without compunction
& often don't even remember who it is we're calling.

These machines don't counterfeit enthusiasm by raising
their volume or use a disdainful static to imply indignation.
They don't hold grudges & aren't judgmental. They're never

too busy or bored or self-absorbed. They have no conscience
& possess a tolerance for sadness which, admittedly, we lack.
Even cowardice is permitted, if enunciated clearly. I broke off

with Betsey by telling her machine I couldn't go rafting
with her in Colorado. I meant *anywhere* & it understood
    perfectly.
They appreciate, I think, how much intimacy we can bear

on a daily basis. When one becomes overburdened it buries
all pertinent information by overlapping; whatever
    happened,

---

[1] Form: Free verse—Vocabulary: supplanted: usurp; vibrato: causing slight
frequency variations in the voice.

say, to Jane's sweet birthday song, hidden now under so
   many

solicitations about my appendix operation, or Bill's news
of his father's death which was so rudely preempted by
   Helen's
wedding invitation? Yes, the conflict which evolves through

direct contact is softened & our privacy protected, but
perhaps the price we pay is greater isolation. Under all
these supplanted voices is a constant reminder of everything

we once promised & then forgot, or betrayed. The guilt
can be overwhelming, especially late at night when I replay
my messages to hear the plaintive vowels & combative
   consonants

rub like verbal sticks into a piercing vibrato of prayerlike
insistence. What is essential, after all, cannot be understood
too quickly & unessential facts get equal time. I mean

Even in our silence there is evidence of what we feared
to say or mean—that ongoing testimony of remorse &
   affection
which, however crippling, we replay nightly & then, sadly,
   erase.

Ronald Wallace (b. 1945)

Thirteen[1]

Gent, Nugget, Swank, and *Dude:*
the names themselves were lusty, crude,
as I took my small detour from school,
my breath erect, my manner cool.

In Kranson's Drugstore, furtive, alert,
stiff in my khakis I'd sneak to the back,
unzip the new issue from its thick stack,
and stick it in my quick shirt.

Oh, I was a thief for love,
accompliced by guilt and thrill,
mystery and wonder my only motive.

Oh, that old Kranson could be there still!
I'd slip in and out, liquid, unseen,
out of my mind again, thirteen.

Tom Wayman (b. 1945)

Did I Miss Anything?[2]

> *Question frequently asked by*
> *students after missing a class*

Nothing. When we realized you weren't here
we sat with our hands folded on our desks
in silence, for the full two hours;

> Everything. I gave an exam worth
> 40 per cent of the grade for this term
> and assigned some reading due today

---

[1] Form: Sonnet with constraints of meter and rhyme order relaxed—
Vocabulary: Gent, Nugget, Swank, and Dude: Magazines featuring pictures
of nude women.
[2] Form: Free verse.

on which I'm about to hand out a quiz
worth 50 per cent;

Nothing. None of the content of this course
has value or meaning
Take as many days off as you like:
any activities we undertake as a class
I assure you will not matter either to you or me
and are without purpose;

Everything. A few minutes after we began last time
a shaft of light descended and an angel
or other heavenly being appeared
and revealed to us what each woman or man must do
to attain divine wisdom in this life and the hereafter
This is the last time the class will meet
before we disperse to bring this good news to all people
on earth;

Nothing. When you are not present
how could something significant occur?

Everything. Contained in this classroom
is a microcosm of human existence
assembled for you to query and examine and ponder
This is not the only place such an opportunity has
been
gathered

but it was one place

And you weren't here.

Adam Zabajewski (b. 1945)

Electric Elegy[1]

Translated from the Polish by Renata Gorczynski,
Benjamin Ivry, and C. K. Williams

Farewell, German radio with your green eye
and your bulky box,
together almost composing
a body and soul. (Your lamps glowed
with a pink, salmony light, like Bergson's
deep self.)
Through the thick fabric
of the speaker (my ear glued to you as
to the lattice of a confessional) Mussolini once whispered,
Hitler shouted, Stalin calmly explained,
Bierut hissed, Gomulka held endlessly forth.
But no one, radio, will accuse you of treason;
no, your only sin was obedience: absolute,
tender faithfulness to the megahertz;
whoever came was welcomed, whoever was sent
was received.
Of course I know only
the songs of Schubert brought you the jade
of true joy. To Chopin's waltzes
your electric heart throbbed delicately
and firmly and the cloth over the speaker
pulsated like the breasts of amorous girls
in old novels.
Not with the news, though,
especially not Radio Free Europe or the BBC.
Then your eye would grow nervous,
the green pupil widen and shrink

---

[1] Form: Free verse—Vocabulary: Bergson: French philosopher; Wladyslaw
Gomulka (1905–1982) Polish Communist Leader; atropine: chemical used
to dilate eyes—Notes: Notice how how sound of the words fit with the
descriptions of what is on the radio. The screams of the comet are whines
as a comet flies by, it's head melting. The radio represents the history of
oppression that has gone through it's speaker, but the narrator ends on a
pessimistic note regarding the future.

as though its atropine dose had been altered.
Mad seagulls lived inside you, and Macbeth.
At night, forlorn signals found shelter
in your rooms, sailors cried out for help,
the young comet cried, losing her head.
Your old age was announced by a cracked voice,
then rattles, coughing, and finally blindness
(your eye faded), and total silence.
Sleep peacefully, German radio,
dream Schumann and don't waken
when the next dictator-rooster crows.

Moment[1]

translated from the Polish by Renata Gorczynski

Clear moments are so short.
There is much more darkness. More
ocean than firm land. More
shadow than form.

Andrei Codrescu (b. 1946)

defense of the meek[2]

the meek have taken
jesus to mean
their turn will come
jesus was merely
stating a fact the meek
will inherit the earth
there are more of them
or he may have been mean
and a Buddhist and meant
the meek will return
to the earth over
and over until they get
it right sometimes
translation is on the side

---

[1] Form: Free verse.

[2] Form: Free verse.

of the meek but never
the commentary

Two fragments from Three Types of Loss, Part 3[1]

. . .

literal translations lose music while
poetic translations lose the original

. . .

the day is a literal translation
the night is a poetic translation

. . .

Larry Levis (1946 – 1996)

The Poem You Asked For[2]

My poem would eat nothing.
I tried giving it water
but it said no,

worrying me.
Day after day,
I held it up to the light,

turning it over,
but it only pressed its lips
more tightly together.

It grew sullen, like a toad
through with being teased.
I offered it money,

my clothes, my car with a full tank.
But the poem stared at the floor.
Finally I cupped it in

my hands, and carried it gently
out into the soft air, into the

---

[1] Form: Free verse.
[2] Form: Free verse.

evening traffic, wondering how

to end things between us.
For now it had begun breathing,
putting on more and

more hard rings of flesh.
And the poem demanded the food,
it drank up all the water,

beat me and took my money,
tore the faded clothes
off my back,

said Shit,
and walked slowly away,
slicking its hair down.

Said it was going
over to your place.

Brian Patten (b. 1946)

Party Piece[1]

He said:

'Let's stay here
Now this place has emptied
And make gentle pornography with one another,
While the party goers go out
And the dawn creeps in,
Like a stranger.

Let us not hesitate
Over what we know
Or over how cold this place has become,
But let's unclip our minds
And let tumble free

---

[1] Form: Free verse—Vocabulary: woodbines: a climbing vine.

The mad, mangled crocodile of love!

So they did,
There among the woodbines and Guinness stains,
And later he caught a bus and she a train
And all there was between them then
was rain.

Maura Stanton (b. 1946)

Living Apart[1]

I leave our house, our town, familiar fields
Below me at take off when I fly to you
Deep in these shadowed mountains. Now at dawn
I wake to the horse-clop of passing carriages
As if I'd passed through time as well as space.
Yesterday we saw an Amish farmer
Bearded and calm, stroking his horse's mane
Under a flaming maple as he watched
Hang-gliders drifting down from Hyner View.
We stopped to watch them, too. I was amazed
To see men falling toward the scarlet treetops
On out-spread wings. That's when I grabbed your hand
To tell myself we were alive and human
Not lost in hell which must resemble this—
A place where souls from many centuries
Stand side by side, united but unhappy,
To watch the angels fall from fiery mountains.

Lorna Goodison (b. 1947)

Birth Stone[2]

The older women wise and tell Anna
first time baby mother,
"hold a stone upon your head and follow
a straight line go home. "

---

[1] Form: Blank verse.
[2] Form: Free verse—Vocabulary: heraldic: announcing something to come;
Gobi: desert in Mongolia; abed: in bed.

For like how Anna was working in the
field, grassweeder
right up till the appointed hour
that the baby was to come.

Right up till the appointed hour
when her clear heraldic water
broke free and washed her down.

Dry birth for you young mother;
the distance between the field and home
come in like the Gobi desert now.
But your first baby must born abed.

Put the woman stone on your head
and walk through no man's land
go home. When you walk, the stone
and not you yet, will bear down.

Kaylin Haught (b. 1947)

God Says Yes to Me[1]

I asked God if it was okay to be melodramatic
and she said yes
I asked her if it was okay to be short
and she said it sure is
I asked her if I could wear nail polish
or not wear nail polish
and she said honey
she calls me that sometimes
she said you can do just exactly
what you want to
Thanks God I said
And is it even okay if I don't paragraph
my letters
Sweetcakes God said
who knows where she picked that up

---

[1] Form: Free verse.

what I'm telling you is
Yes Yes Yes

Yusef Komunyakaa (b. 1947)

Blackberries[1]

They left my hands like a printer's
Or thief's before a police blotter
& pulled me into early morning's
Terrestrial sweetness, so thick
The damp ground was consecrated
Where they fell among a garland of thorns.

Although I could smell old lime-covered
History, at ten I'd still hold out my hands
& berries fell into them. Eating from one
& filling a half gallon with the other,
I ate the mythology & dreamt
Of pies & cobbler, almost

Needful as forgiveness. My bird dog Spot
Eyed blue jays & thrashers. The mud frogs
In rich blackness, hid from daylight.
An hour later, beside City Limits Road
I balanced a gleaming can in each hand,
Limboed between worlds, repeating one dollar.

The big blue car made me sweat.
Wintertime crawled out of the windows.
When I leaned closer I saw the boy
& girl my age, in the wide back seat
Smirking, & it was then I remembered my fingers
Burning with thorns among berries too ripe to touch.

---

[1] Form: Free verse—Vocabulary: consecrated: set apart as sacred; garland: wreath; thrashers: type of bird; Limbo: dance involving stepping under a low stick while leaning backward—Notes: The end may be read as a metaphorical statement where it is not just literal blackberries that are too ripe to touch, but the very world of the people in that car with winter crawling out of the windows that is unreachable.

Camouflaging the Chimera[1]

We tied branches to our helmets.
We painted our faces & rifles
with mud from a riverbank,

blades of grass hung from the pockets
of our tiger suits. We wove
ourselves into the terrain,
content to be a hummingbird's target.

We hugged bamboo & leaned
against a breeze off the river,
slow-dragging with ghosts

from Saigon to Bangkok,
with women left in doorways
reaching in from America.
We aimed at dark-hearted songbirds.

In our way station of shadows
rock apes tried to blow our cover
throwing stones at the sunset. Chameleons

crawled our spines, changing from day
to night: green to gold,
gold to black. But we waited
till the moon touched metal,

till something almost broke
inside us. VC struggled
with the hillside, like black silk

wrestling iron through grass.
We weren't there. The river ran
through our bones. Small animals took refuge
against our bodies; we held our breath,

---

[1] Form: Free verse—Vocabulary: Chimera: in Greek mythology, a fire
breathing monster.

ready to spring the L-shaped
ambush, as a world revolved
under each man's eyelid.

Facing It[1]

My black face fades,
hiding inside the black granite.
I said I wouldn't,
dammit: No tears.
I'm stone. I'm flesh.
My clouded reflection eyes me
like a bird of prey, the profile of night
slanted against morning. I turn
this way—the stone lets me go.
I turn that way—I'm inside
the Vietnam Veterans Memorial
again, depending on the light
to make a difference.
I go down the 58,022 names,
half-expecting to find
my own in letters like smoke.
I touch the name Andrew Johnson;
I see the booby trap's white flash.
Names shimmer on a woman's blouse
but when she walks away
the names stay on the wall.
Brushstrokes flash, a red bird's
wings cutting across my stare.
The sky. A plane in the sky.
A white vet's image floats
closer to me, then his pale eyes
look through mine. I'm a window.
He's lost his right arm
inside the stone. In the black mirror
a woman's trying to erase names:
No, she's brushing a boy's hair.

---

[1] Form: Free verse.

Ode to the Maggot[1]

Brother of the blowfly
& godhead, you work magic
Over battlefields,
in slabs of bad pork

& flophouses. Yes, you
Go to the root of all things.
You are sound & mathematical.
Jesus, Christ, you're merciless

With the truth. Ontological & lustrous,
You cast spells on beggars & kings
Behind the stone door of caesar's tomb
Or split trench in a field of ragweed.

No decree or creed can outlaw you
As you take every living thing apart. Little
Master of earth, no one gets to heaven
Without going through you first.

Heather McHugh (b. 1948)

What He thought[2]

We were supposed to do a job in Italy
and, full of our feeling for
ourselves (our sense of being
Poets from America) we went
from Rome to Fano, met
the Mayor, mulled
a couple matters over (what's
cheap, they asked us; what's
flat drink). Among Italian literati

---

[1] Form: Free verse—Vocabulary: godhead: God; Ontological: metaphysical
study of the nature of being; creed: system of belief.
[2] Form: Free verse—Vocabulary: Fano: town in Italy; literati; literary
intelligentsia; pensione: inexpensive small hotel.

we could recognize our counterparts:
the academic, the apologist,
the arrogant, the amorous,
the brazen and the glib—and there was one

administrator (The Conservative), in suit
of regulation gray, who like a good tour guide
with measured pace and uninflected tone narrated
sights and histories the hired van hauled us past.
Of all he was most politic and least poetic,
so it seemed. Our last few days in Rome
(when all but three of the New World Bards had flown)
I found a book of poems this
unprepossessing one had written: it was there
in the *pensione* room (a room he'd recommended)
where it must have been abandoned by
the German visitor (was there a bus of *them*?)
to whom he had inscribed and dated it a month before.
I couldn't read Italian either, so I put the book
back in the wardrobe's dark. We last Americans

were due to leave tomorrow. For our parting evening then
our host chose something in a family restaurant, and there
we sat and chatted, sat and chewed,
till, sensible it was our last
big chance to be Poetic, make
our mark, one of us asked
                              "What's poetry?
Is it the fruits and vegetables and
marketplace at Campo dei Fiori or
the statue there? " Because I was

the glib one, I identified the answer
instantly, I didn't have to think—"The truth
is both, it's both! " I blurted out. But that
was easy. That was easiest to say. What followed
taught me something about difficulty,
for our underestimated host spoke out
all of a sudden, with a rising passion, and he said:

The statue represents Giordano Bruno,

546

brought to be burned in the public square
because of his offence against
authority, which was to say
the Church. His crime was his belief
the universe does not revolve around
the human being: God is no
fixed point or central government but rather is
poured in waves, through all things: all things
move. "If God is not the soul itself, he is
the soul OF THE SOUL of the world. " Such was
his heresy. The day they brought him
forth to die they feared he might
incite the crowd (the man was famous
for his eloquence). And so his captors
placed upon his face
an iron mask in which

he could not speak. That's

how they burned him. That is how
he died: without a word, in front
of everyone.
        And poetry—
            (we'd all
put down our forks by now, to listen to
the man in gray; he went on
softly)—
        poetry is what he thought,
but did not say.

Agha Shahid Ali (1949 – 2001)

The Dacca Gauzes[1]

. . . for a whole year he sought to accumulate the most
exquisite Dacca gauzes.

                -Oscar Wilde, The Picture of Dorian Gray

---

[1] Form: Free verse—Vocabulary: Dacca: the capital of Bangladesh; sari: a
dress worn by women primarily in India and Pakistan; paisleys: swirled
pattern of abstract curves; Bengal: part of Bangladesh.

Those transparent Dacca gauzes
known as woven air, running
water, evening dew:

a dead art now, dead over
a hundred years. "No one
now knows," my grandmother says,

"what it was to wear
or touch that cloth. " She wore
it once, an heirloom sari from

her mother's dowry, proved
genuine when it was pulled, all
six yards, through a ring.

Years later when it tore,
many handkerchiefs embroidered
with gold-thread paisleys

were distributed among
the nieces and. daughters-in-law.
Those too now lost.

In history we learned: the hands
of weavers were amputated,
the looms of Bengal silenced,

and the cotton shipped raw
by the British to England.
History of little use to her,

my grandmother just says
how the muslins of today
seem so coarse and that only

in autumn, should one wake up
at dawn to pray, can one
feel that same texture again.

One morning, she says, the air
was dew-starched: she pulled
it absently through her ring.

Mark Halliday (b. 1949)

Get It Again[1]

In 1978 I write something about how
happiness and sorrow are intertwined
and I feel good, insightful, and it seems
this reflects some healthy growth of spirit,
some deep maturation—then
I leaf through an eleven-year-old notebook
and spot some paragraphs I wrote in 1967
on Keats's "Ode on Melancholy" which
seem to say some of it better, or
almost better, or as well though differently—
and the waves roll out, and the waves roll in.

In 1972 I often ate rye toast with peanut butter,
the toast on a blue saucer beside my typewriter,
I took huge bites between paragraphs about love and change;
today it's a green saucer, cream cheese, French bread,
but the motions are the same and in a month or so
when the air is colder I'll be back to my autumn snack,
rye toast with peanut butter, an all-star since '72 . . .
I turned around on sidewalks to stare at some woman's asses
plenty of times in the sixties and
what do you think will be different in the eighties?
In 1970, mourning an ended love, I listened
to a sailor's song with a timeless refrain,
and felt better—that taste of transcendence
in the night air
and
and here it is in 1978, the night air, hello.

My journalist friend explains the challenge
of his new TV job: you work for a week

---

[1] Form: Prose poem—Vocabulary: transcendence: surpassing others.

to get together one 5-minute feature,
and then
it's gone—
vanished into gray-and-white memory,
a fading choreography of electric dots—
and you're starting it all over,
every week that awesome energy demand:
to start over

In 1973 I played hundreds of games of catch
with a five-year-old boy named Brian.
Brian had trouble counting so we practiced
by counting the times we tossed the ball
without missing. When Brian missed
he was on the verge of despair for a moment
but I taught him to say
"Back to zero! " to give him a sense of
always another chance. I tried to make it sound
exciting to go back to zero, and eventually
our tone was exultant when we shouted in unison
after a bad toss or fumble
back to zero.

In 1977 I wrote a poem called "Repetition Rider"
and last winter I revised it three times
and I thought it was finished.

"It's not like writing," says my journalist friend,
"where your work is permanent—
no matter how obscure,
written work is durable . . . That's why
it can grow—you can move beyond
what you've already said. "

Somewhere I read or heard something good
about what Shakespeare meant in *Lear*
when he wrote: "Ripeness is all. "
I hope it comes back to me.

I see myself riding
the San Francisco subway in 1974

scrawling something in my little red notebook
about "getting nowhere fast".
I see Brian's big brown eyes lit
with the adventure of starting over
and oblivious, for a moment,
of the extent to which he is
doomed by his disabilities.
And the waves
roll out, and the waves roll in.
This poem

could go on a long time,
but you've already understood it;
you got the point some time ago,

and you'll get it again

Population[1]

Isn't it nice that everyone has a grocery list
except the very poor you hear about occasionally
we all have a grocery list on the refrigerator door;
at any given time there are thirty million lists in America
that say BREAD. Isn't it nice
not to be alone in this. Sometimes
you visit someone's house for the first time
and you spot the list taped up on a kitchen cabinet
and you think Yes, we're all in this together.
TOILET PAPER. No getting around it.
Nice to think of us all
unwrapping the new rolls at once,
forty thousand of us at any given moment.

Orgasm, of course, being the most vivid example: imagine
an electrified map wired to every American bed:
those little lights popping
on both sides of the Great Divide,
popping to beat the band. But
we never beat the band: within an hour or a day

---

[1] Form: Free verse.

we're horny again, or hungry, or burdened with waste.
But isn't it nice to be not noticeably responsible,
acquitted eternally in the rituals of the tribe:
it's only human! It's only human and that's not much.

So, aren't you glad we have such advanced farm machinery,
futuristic fertilizers, half a billion chickens
almost ready to die. Here come the loaves of bread for us
thup, thup thup thup for all of us thup thup
except maybe the very poor
thup thup
and man all the cattle we can fatten up man,
there's no stopping our steaks. And that's why
we can make babies galore, baby:
let's get on with it. Climb aboard.
Let's be affirmative here, let's be pro-life for God's sake
how can life be wrong?
People *need* people and the happiest people are
surrounded with friendly flesh.
If you have ten kids they'll be so sweet—
ten really sweet kids! Have twelve!
What if there were 48 pro baseball teams,
you could see a damn lot more games!
And in this fashion we get away
from tragedy. Because tragedy comes when someone
gets too special. Whereas,

if forty thousand kitchen counters
on any given Sunday night
have notes on them that say
I CAN'T TAKE IT ANYMORE
I'M GONE, DON'T TRY TO FIND ME
you can feel how *your* note is
no big thing in America,
so, no *horrible* heartbreak,
it's more like a TV episode,
you've seen this whole plot lots of times
and everybody gets by—
you feel better already—
everybody gets by

and it's nice. It's a people thing.
You've got to admit it's nice.

Robert Hedin (b. 1949)

The Old Liberators[1]

Of all the people in the mornings at the mall,
It's the old liberators I like best,
Those veterans of the Bulge, Anzio, or Monte Cassino
I see lost in Automotive or back in Home Repair,
Bored among the paints and power tools.
Or the *really* old ones, the ones who are going fast,
Who keep dozing off in the little orchards
Of shade under the distant skylights.
All around, from one bright rack to another,
Their wives stride big as generals,
Their handbags bulging like ripe fruit.
They are almost all gone now,
And with them they are taking the flak
And fire storms, the names of the old bombing runs.
Each day a little more of their memory goes out,
Darkens the way a house darkens,
Its rooms quietly filling with evening,
Until nothing but the wind lifts the lace curtains,
The wind bearing through the empty rooms
The rich far off scent of gardens
Where just now, this morning,
Light is falling on the wild philodendrons.

Joyce Sutphen (b. 1949)

Living in the Body[2]

Body is something you need in order to stay
on this planet and you only get one.

---

[1] Form: Free verse—Vocabulary: Bulge, Anzio, or Monte Cassino: WWII
battle sites; flak: shrapnel from anti-aircraft guns; fire storms: massive city
fires caused by incendiary bombs; philodendrons: type of plant often grown
as a house plant.
[2] Form: Mostly Iambic pentameter.

And no matter which one you get, it will not
be satisfactory. It will not be beautiful
enough, it will not be fast enough, it will
not keep on for days at a time, but will
pull you down into a sleepy swamp and
demand apples and coffee and chocolate cake.

Body is a thing you have to carry
from one day into the next. Always the
same eyebrows over the same eyes in the same
skin when you look in the mirror, and the
same creaky knee when you get up from the
floor and the same wrist under the watchband.
The changes you can make are small and
costly—better to leave it as it is.

Body is a thing that you have to leave
eventually. You know that because you have
seen others do it, others who were once like you,
living inside their pile of bones and
flesh, smiling at you, loving you,
leaning in the doorway, talking to you
for hours and then one day they
are gone. No forwarding address.

Bruce Weigl (b. 1949)

What Saves Us[1]

We are wrapped around each other in
the back of my father's car parked
in the empty lot of the high school
of our failures, the sweat on her neck
like oil. The next morning I would leave
for the war and I thought I had something
coming for that, I thought to myself
that I would not die never having
been inside her long body. I pulled
her skirt above her waist like an umbrella

---

[1] Form: Free verse.

blown inside out by the storm. I pulled
her cotton panties up as high as
she could stand. I was on fire. Heaven
was in sight. We were drowning on our
tongues and I tried to tear my pants off
when she stopped so suddenly
we were surrounded only by my shuddering
and by the school bells grinding in the
empty halls. She reached to find something,
a silver crucifix on a silver
chain, the tiny savior's head hanging
and stakes through his hands and his feet.
She put it around my neck and held
me so long the black wings of my heart
were calmed. We are not always right
about what we think will save us. I
thought that dragging the angel down would
save me, but instead I carried the crucifix
in my pocket and rubbed it on my
face and lips nights the rockets roared in.

People die sometimes so near you
you feel them struggling to cross over,
the deep untangling, of one body from another.

Claribel Alegria (b. 1950)

Documentary[1]

Come, be my camera.
Let's photograph the ant heap
the queen ant
extruding sacks of coffee,
my country.
It's the harvest.
Focus on the sleeping family
cluttering the ditch.
Now, among trees:

---

[1] Form: Free verse—Vocabulary: canasta: a card game; Izalco: a volcano in
western El Salvador.

rapid,
dark-skinned fingers
stained with honey.
Shift to a long shot:
the file of ant men
trudging down the ravine
with sacks of coffee.
A contrast:
girls in colored skirts
laugh and chatter,
filling their baskets
with berries.
Focus down.
A close-up of the pregnant mother
dozing in the hammock.
Hard focus on the flies
spattering her face.
Cut.
The terrace of polished mosaics
protected from the sun.
Maids in white aprons
nourish the ladies
who play canasta,
celebrate invasions
and feel sorry for Cuba.
Izalco sleeps
beneath the volcano's eye.
A subterranean growl
makes the village tremble.
Trucks and oxcarts
laden with sacks
screech down the slopes.
Besides coffee
they plant angels
in my country.
A chorus of children
and women
with the small white coffin
move politely aside
as the harvest passes by.
The riverside women,

naked to the waist,
wash clothing.
The truck drivers
exchange jocular obscenities
for insults.
In Panchimalco,
waiting for the oxcart to pass by,
a peasant
with hands bound behind him
by the thumbs
and his escort of soldiers
blinks at the airplane:
a huge bee
bulging with coffee growers
and tourists.
The truck stops in the market place.
A panorama of iguanas,
chickens,
strips of meat,
wicker baskets,
piles of *nances,*
nisperos,
oranges,
zunzas,
zapotes,
cheeses,
bananas,
dogs, *pupusas, jocotes,*
acrid odors,
taffy candies,
urine puddles, tamarinds.
The virginal coffee
dances in the mill house.
They strip her,
rape her,
lay her out on the patio
to doze in the sun.
The dark storage sheds
glimmer.
The golden coffee
sparkles with malaria,

blood,
illiteracy,
tuberculosis,
misery.
A truck roars
out of the warehouse.
It bellows uphill
drowning out the lesson:
A for alcoholism,
B for battalions,
C for corruption,
D for dictatorship,
E for exploitation,
F for the feudal power
of fourteen families
and etcetera, etcetera, etcetera.
My etcetera country,
my wounded country,
my child,
my tears,
my obsession.

Charles Bernstein (b. 1950)

Of Time and the Line[1]

George Burns likes to insist that he always
takes the straight lines; the cigar in his mouth
is a way of leaving space between the
lines for a laugh. He weaves lines together
by means of a picaresque narrative;
not so Hennie Youngman, whose lines are
strictly paratactic. My father pushed a
line of ladies' dresses—not down the street

---

[1] Form: Prose poem—Vocabulary: picaresque: involving rogues; Hennie Youngman: (also Henny Youngman) (1906-1998), stand-up comic specializing in one-liners; paratactic: juxtaposing thoughts or clauses without connectors; Chairman Mao: (Mao Zedong, 1893-1976, Chairman of Communist party of China; malarkey: exaggerated or foolish talk; Adam: First human (Bible), who named all things; prosodic: metrical structure of verse.

in a pushcart but upstairs in a fact'ry
office. My mother has been more concerned
with her hemline, Chairman Mao put forward
Maoist lines, but that's been abandoned
(mostly) for the East-West line of malarkey
so popular in these parts. The prestige
of the iambic line has recently
suffered decline, since it's no longer so
clear who "I" am, much less who you are. When
making a line, better be double sure
what you're lining in & what you're lining
out & which side of the line you're on; the
world is made up so (Adam didn't so much
name as delineate). Every poem's got
a prosodic lining, some of which will
unzip for summer wear. The lines of an
imaginary are inscribed on the
social flesh by the knifepoint of history.
Nowadays, you can often spot a work
of poetry by whether it's in lines
or no; if it's in prose, there's a good chance
it's a poem. While there is no lesson in
the line more useful than that of the picket line,
the line that has caused the most adversity
is the bloodline. In Russia
everyone is worried about long lines;
back in the USA, it's strictly soup-
lines. "Take a chisel to write," but for an
actor a line's got to be cued. Or, as
they say in math, it takes two lines to make
an angle but only one lime to make
a Margarita.

Jorie Graham (b. 1950)

Salmon[1]

I watched them once, at dusk, on television, run,
in our motel room half-way through
Nebraska, quick, glittering, past beauty, past
the importance of beauty,
archaic,
not even hungry, not even endangered, driving deeper and
    deeper
into less. They leapt up falls, ladders,
and rock, tearing and leaping, a gold river,
and a blue river traveling
in opposite directions.
They would not stop, resolution of will
and helplessness, as the eye
is helpless
when the image forms itself, upside-down, backward,
driving up into
the mind, and the world
unfastens itself
from the deep ocean of the given. . . Justice, aspen
leaves, mother attempting
suicide, the white night-flying moth
the ants dismantled bit by bit and carried in
right through the crack
in my wall. . . . How helpless
the still pool is,
upstream,
awaiting the gold blade
of their hurry. Once, indoors, a child,
I watched, at noon, through slatted wooden blinds,
a man and woman, naked, eyes closed,
climb onto each other,
on the terrace floor,
and ride—two gold currents
wrapping round and round each other, fastening,

---

[1] Form: Free verse—Notes: Notice the use of color tones throughout the
poem. The poem addresses issues of sexuality, sexual differences, and
overcoming obstacles.

unfastening. I hardly knew
what I saw. Whatever shadow there was in that world
it was the one each cast
onto the other,
the thin black seam
they seemed to be trying to work away
between them. I held my breath.
as far as I could tell, the work they did
with sweat and light
was good. I'd say
they traveled far in opposite
directions. What is the light
at the end of the day, deep, reddish-gold, bathing the walls,
the corridors, light that is no longer light, no longer clarifies,
illuminates, antique, freed from the body of
the air that carries it. What is it
for the space of time
where it is useless, merely
beautiful? When they were done, they made a distance
one from the other
and slept, outstretched,
on the warm tile
of the terrace floor,
smiling, faces pressed against the stone.

Michael Pettit ((b. 1950)

Driving Lesson[1]

Beside him in the old Ford pickup
that smelled of rope and grease and cattle feed,
sat my sister and I, ten and eight, big
now our grandfather would teach us
that powerful secret, how to drive.
Horizon of high mountain peaks visible
above the blue hood, steering wheel huge
in our hands, pedals at our toe-tips,

---

[1] Form: Free verse—Vocabulary: gramma grass: type of pasture grass;
Sangre de Cristos: mountain range—Notes: The driving lesson is a
metaphor for their ranch life, with the children wanting to go out into the
world while the grandfather wants them to stay in the ruts worn over time.

we heard his sure voice urge us
Give it gas, give it gas. Over the roar
of the engine our hearts banged
like never before and banged on
furiously in the silence after
we bucked and stalled the truck.
How infinitely empty it then seemed—
windy flat rangeland of silver-green
gramma grass dotted with blooming cactus
and jagged outcrops of red rock, beginnings
of the Sangre de Cristos fifty miles off.
All Guadelupe County, New Mexico,
nothing to hit, and we could not
get the damn thing going. Nothing to hit
was no help. It was not the mechanics
of accelerator and clutch, muscle and bone,
but our sheer unruly spirits
that kept us small with the great desire
to move the world by us, earth and sky
and all the earth and sky contained.
And how hard it was when,
after our grandfather who was a god
said *Let it out slow, slow* time and again
until we did and were at long last rolling
over the earth, his happy little angels,
how hard it was to listen
not to our own thrilled inner voices
saying *Go, go,* but to his saying
the *Good, good* we loved but also
the *Keep it in the ruts* we hated to hear.
How hard to hold to it—
single red vein of a ranch road
running out straight across the mesa,
blood we were bound to follow—
when what we wanted with all our hearts
was to scatter everywhere, everywhere.

Brigit Pegeen Kelly (b. 1951)

The White Pilgrim: Old Christian Cemetery[1]

The cicadas were loud and what looked like a child's
Bracelet was coiled at the base of the Pilgrim.
It was a snake. Red and black.   The cemetery
Is haunted. Perhaps by the Pilgrim. Perhaps
By another.   We were looking for names
For the baby. My daughter liked Achsa and Luke
And John Jacob. She was dragging her rope
Through the grass. It was hot. The insect
Racket was loud and there was that snake.
It made me nervous. I almost picked it up
Because it was so pretty. Just like a bracelet.
And I thought, oh the child will be a girl,
But it was not.   This was around the time
Of the dream.   Dreams come from somewhere.
There is this argument about nowhere,
But it is not true.   I dreamed that some boys
Knocked down all the stones in the cemetery,
And then it happened. It was six months later
In early December. Dead cold. Just before
Dawn. We live a long way off so I slept
Right through it. But I read about it the next
Day in the Johnsburg paper.   There is
This argument about the dead, but that is not
Right either. The dead keep working. If
You listen you can hear them.   It was hot
When we walked in the cemetery. And my daughter,
Told me the story of the White Pilgrim.
She likes the story. Yes, it is a good one.
A man left his home in Ohio and came East,
Dreaming he could be the dreamed-of rider
in St. John's *Revelations.* He was called
The White Pilgrim because he dressed all
In white like a rodeo cowboy and rode a white
Horse. He preached that the end was coming soon.
And it was. He died a month later of the fever.

---

[1] Form: Prose poem.

The ground here is unhealthy. And the insects
Grind on and on.   Now the pilgrim is a legend.
I know your works, God said, *and that is what*
I am afraid of.   It was very hot that summer.
The birds were too quiet.   *God's eyes are like*
A flame of fire, St. John said, *and the armies*
Of heaven . . . But these I cannot imagine.
Many dreams come true. But mostly it isn't
The good ones.   That night in December
The boys were bored. They were pained to the teeth
With boredom. You can hardly blame them.
They had been out all night breaking trashcans
And mailboxes with their baseball bats. They
Hang from their pickups by the knees and
Pound the boxes as they drive by. The ground
Here is unhealthy, but that is not it.
Their satisfaction just ends too quickly.
They need something better to break. They
Need something holy. But there is not much left,
So that night they went to the cemetery.
It was cold, but they were drunk and perhaps
They did not feel it. The cemetery is close
To town, but no one heard them.   The boys are part
Of a larger destruction, but this is beyond
What they can imagine. War in heaven
And the damage is ours. The birds come to feed
On what is left. You can see them always
Around Old Christian. As if the bodies of the dead
Were lying out exposed. But of course they are
Not.   St. John the Evangelist dreamed of birds
And of the White Rider. That is the one
The Ohio preacher wanted to be. He dressed
All in white leather and rode a white horse.
His own life in the midwest was not enough,
And who can blame him?   My daughter thinks
That all cemeteries have a White Pilgrim.
She said that her teacher told her this. I said
This makes no sense but she would not listen.
There was a pack of dogs loose in my dream
Or it could have been dark angels. They were
Taking the names off the stones.   St. John said

An angel will be the one who invites the birds
To God's Last Supper, when he eats the flesh
Of all the kings and princes.   Perhaps God
Is a bird. Sometimes I think this. The thought
Is as good as another.   The boys shouldered
Over the big stones first, save for the Pilgrim.
And then worked their way down to the child-
Sized markers. These they punted like footballs.
The cemetery is close to town but no one
Heard them. They left the Pilgrim for last
Because he is a legend, although only local.
My daughter thinks that all cemeteries
Have a White Pilgrim, ghost and stone, and that
The stone is always placed dead in the center
Of the cemetery ground. In Old Christian
This is true. The Ohio Pilgrim was a rich man
And before he died he sunk his wealth into
The marble obelisk called by his name. We saw
The snake curled around it. Pretty as a bracelet.
But the child was not a girl.   The boys left
The Pilgrim till last, and then took it down,
Too.   The Preacher had a dream but it was not
Of a larger order so it led to little. Just
A stone broken like a tooth, and a ghost story
For children.   God says the damage will be
Restored. Among other things.   At least
They repaired Old Christian. The Historical
Society raised a collection and the town's
Big men came out to hoist the stones. The boys
Got probation, but they won't keep it.   I
Don't go to the cemetery anymore. But once
I drove past and my babysitter's family
Was out working. Her father and mother were
Cutting back the rose of Sharon, and my red-haired
Sitter, who is plain and good-hearted, was
Pushing a lawn mower. Her beautiful younger
Sister sat on the grass beside the Pilgrim
Pretending to clip some weeds. She never works.
She has asthma and everybody loves her.
I imagined that the stones must have fine seams
Where they had been broken. But otherwise

565

Everything looked the same. Maybe better . . .
The summer we walked in the cemetery it was hot.
We were looking for names for the baby
And my daughter told me the story of the White
Pilgrim. This was before the stones fell
And before the worked-for restoration.
I know your works, says God, and talks of
The armies of heaven. They are not very friendly.
Some dreams hold and I am afraid that this
May be one of them. The White Rider may come
With his secret name inscribed on his thigh,
King of Kings, Lord of Lords, and the child
Is large now . . . but who will be left standing?

Timothy Russell (b. 1951)

In Simili Materia[1]

When she stopped on the sidewalk,
near the yellow storm drain,
near gnats swarming above the hedge,
the little girl, perhaps three,
yelled something unintelligible
at the doll in the pink carriage.
When she slapped her baby
I remembered flocks of pigeons
erupting from beams and ledges
at the Sinter Plant,
how they would flutter and circle,
flickering in the sun, and always
return to their niches to roost.

---

[1] Form: Free verse—Vocabulary: Sinter: chemicals from a mineral spring.

Nuala Ni Dhomhnaill (b. 1952)

Ceist na Teangan (The Language Issue)[1]
Translated from the Irish by Paul Muldoon

I place my hope on the water
in this little boat
of the language, the way a body might put
an infant
in a basket of intertwined
iris leaves,
its underside proofed
with bitumen and pitch,

then set the whole thing down amidst
the sedge
and bulrushes by the edge
of a river
only to have it borne hither and thither,
not knowing where it might end up;
in the lap, perhaps,
of some Pharaoh's daughter.

Sean O'Brien (b. 1952)

Rain[2]

At ten pm it starts. We can hear from the bar
As if somebody humorless fills in the dots,
All the dots on the window, the gaps in between.
It is raining. It rained and has always been raining.
If there were conditionals they too would be rain.
The future tense is partly underwater. We must leave.
There's a road where the bus stop is too far away

---

[1] Form: Free verse—Vocabulary: proofed: waterproofed; bitumen and pitch: components of tar; sedge: grasses—Notes: It is the author's hope which is sent forward in time and out via the basket of the poem.
[2] Form: Free verse—Vocabulary: swill: to flood with water; Trevor McDonald: broadcaster; Esther Williams: fashion model—best known as an actress who swam in all of her films (thanks to Julie Gamon for this information)—Notes: Here rain is a metaphor for the feeling of separation between the couple following a fight with the narrator's in-laws.

567

In the dark between streetlights. The shelter's stove-in
And a swill of old tickets awaits us.
Transitional, that's what we're saying,
But we're metaphysical animals:
We know a watery grave when we see it
And how the bald facts of brute nature
Are always entailed by mere human opinion,
So this is a metaphor. Someone's to blame
If your coat is dissolving, if rain is all round us
And feels like the threats-cum-advice of your family
Who know I am up and have come and will go to
No good.
They cannot be tempted to alter their views
In the light of that sizzling bulb. There it goes.
Here we are: a black street without taxis or buses.
An ankle-high wave is advancing
To ruin your shoes and my temper. My darling,
I know you believe for the moment the rain is my doing.
Tonight we will lie in the dark with damp hair.
I too am looking for someone to blame. O send me
A metro inspector, a stony-faced barmaid.
The library is flooding and we have not read it,
The cellar is flooding and we shall be thirsty,
Trevor mcdonald has drowned as the studio shorts
And the weather-girl goes floating past
Like Esther Williams with her clothes on,
Mouthing the obvious: raining.

Shu Ting (b. 1952)

Assembly Line[1]
   Translated from the Chinese by Carolyn Kizer

In time's assembly line
Night presses against night.
We come off the factory night-shift
In line as we march towards home.
Over our heads in a row
The assembly line of stars

---

[1] Form: Mostly iambic tetrameter.

568

Stretches across the sky.
Beside us, little trees
Stand numb in assembly lines.

The stars must be exhausted
After thousands of years
Of journeys which never change.
The little trees are all sick,
Choked on smog and monotony,
Stripped of their color and shape.
It's not hard to feel for them;
We share the same tempo and rhythm.

Yes, I'm numb to my own existence
As if, like the trees and stars
—perhaps just out of habit
—perhaps just out of sorrow,
I'm unable to show concern
For my own manufactured fate.

Mark Irwin (b. 1953)

Woolworth's[1]

Everything stands wondrously multicolored
and at attention in the always Christmas air.
What scent lingers unrecognizably
between that of popcorn, grilled cheese sandwiches,

malted milkballs, and parakeets? Maybe you came here
in winter to buy your daughter a hamster
and were detained by the bin

of *Multicolored Thongs*, four pair
for a dollar. Maybe you came here to buy
some envelopes, the light blue par avion ones

with airplanes, but caught yourself, lost,

---

[1] Form: Free verse—Vocabulary: diorama: 3-dimensional scene with painted backdrop.

daydreaming, saying *it's too late* over the glassy
diorama of cakes and pies. Maybe you came here

to buy a lampshade, the fake crimped
kind, and suddenly you remember
your grandmother, dead

twenty years, floating through the old
house like a curtain. Maybe you're retired,
on Social Security, and came here for the *Roast*

Turkey Dinner, or the *Liver and Onions*,
or just to stare into a black circle
of coffee and to get warm. Or maybe

the big church down the street is closed
now during the day, and you're homeless and poor,
or you're rich, or it doesn't matter what you are

with a little loose change jangling in your pocket,
begging to be spent, because you wandered in
and somewhere between the bin of animal crackers

and the little zoo in the back of the store
you lost something, and because you came here
not to forget, but to remember to live.

Richard Jones (b. 1953)

Certain People[1]

My father lives by the ocean
and drinks his morning coffee
in the full sun on his deck,
talking to anyone
who walks by on the beach.
And in the afternoons he works
part-time at the golf course—
sailing the fairways like a sea captain

---

[1] Form: Free verse.

in a white golf cart.
My father must talk
to a hundred people a day,
yet we haven't spoken in weeks.
As I get older, we hardly speak at all.
It's as if he were a stranger
and we had never met.
I wonder, if I
were a tourist on the beach
or a golfer lost in the woods
and met him now for the very first time,
what we'd say to each other,
how his hand would feel in mine
as we introduced ourselves,
and if, as is the case
with certain people, I'd feel
when I looked him in the eye,
I'd known him all my life.

Leaving Town after the Funeral[1]

After the people and the flowers
have gone, and before the stone
has been removed from your mother's house
and carved into a cross, I come back
on my way out of town
to visit your grave. And nothing
is there—only the ground,
roughed up a little, waiting for rain.
I sit down beside you
in my dark glasses
and put my hand on the earth
above your dead heart.
Two workmen are mowing grass
around the graves beside us.
They pretend not to see
I am crying. Quietly,
they walk over to their truck
to give me time.

---

[1] Form: Free verse.

571

The day is hot. They hold paper cups
under the water cooler on the flatbed
and drink together.
They are used to this.
The heat. The grief.
After a few minutes the younger one
walks back to work.
He gets down on his knees
and blows cut grass off a stone.
I believe he wants me to know
he will take care of you.
But hard as it is,
I know the truth:
when you drowned, your body
sank into the river forever.
Ten minutes to eight.
Darkness came down quickly.
And now it will be night
for a long, long time.
The workman gets up and goes on
with his work. I get up
and walk back to the car.
Andrew, we know the truth:
the cold child in the casket
is not the one I loved.

The Bell[1]

In the tower the bell
is alone, like a man
in his room,
thinking and thinking.

The bell is made of iron.
It takes the weight
of a man
to make the bell move.

Far below, the bell feels

---

[1] Form: Free verse.

hands on a rope.
It considers this.
It turns its head.

Miles away,
a man in his room
hears the clear sound,
and lifts his head to listen.

Wan Chu's Wife in Bed[1]

Wan Chu, my adoring husband,
has returned from another trip
selling trinkets in the provinces.
He pulls off his lavender shirt
as I lie naked in our bed,
waiting for him. He tells me
I am the only woman he'll ever love.
He may wander from one side of China
to the other, but his heart
will always stay with me.
His face glows in the lamplight
with the sincerity of a boy
when I lower the satin sheet
to let him see my breasts.
Outside, it begins to rain
on the cherry trees
he planted with our son,
and when he enters me with a sigh,
the storm begins in earnest,
shaking our little house.
Afterwards, I stroke his back
until he falls asleep.
I'd love to stay awake all night
listening to the rain,
but I should sleep, too.
Tomorrow Wan Chu will be
a hundred miles away
and I will be awake all night

---

[1] Form: Free verse—Notes: A follow-up to "The River-Merchant's Wife."

in the arms of Wang Chen,
the tailor from Ming Pao,
the tiny village down the river.

Robert Kinsley (b. 1953)

A Walk Along the Old Tracks[1]

When I was young they had already been
abandoned for years
overgrown with sumac and sour apple,
the iron scrapped, the wood long
gone for other things.
In summer my father would send us along them
to fetch the cows from the back pasture,
a long walk to a far off place it seemed
for boys so young. Lost again for a moment
in that simple place,
I fling apples from a stick and look for snakes
in the gullies. There is
a music to the past, the sweet tones
of perfect octaves
even though we know it was never so.
My father had to sell the farm in that near perfect time
and once old Al Shott
killed a six foot rattler on the tracks.
"And when the trolley was running" he said, "you could jump
her as she went by and ride all the way to Cleveland,
and oh," he said, "what a time you could have there. "

Mark Turpin (b. 1953)

Before Groundbreak[2]

Off work and going upslope for a look
I left the plans—to see the view
their money bought—weighted with a rock,

---

[1] Form: Free verse—Vocabulary: sumac: a type of shrub—Notes: This poem
explores the idealizing of things based on time and based on distance.
[2] Form: Free verse—Vocabulary: pampas: tall decorative grass; nettles: type
of weed.

574

and trampled a path of parted weeds
past pampas, nettles,
poison oak bristling in the breeze,

a weathered two-by-four nailed high up in a cedar's fork,
a haggard pair of panties waving
stiffly from a thorn,

I walked where they would walk.
Standing there, out of breath, where
they would soon stand, vacuuming

or reaching for a towel, how bare
and graspable it will seem, and ever-present,
our time and effort spent.

Don Fargo & Sons[1]

Helpless to throw them away
or to use them unaltered,
for years he crossed out *& Sons*
on the tiny invoice pads

from a cardboard box too tall
to fit beneath the seat.
His blackened mechanic's hands
turning the slip of carbon.

At seventy, he needed help up
the site's steep slope to the hoe.
Two laborers and him up
the loose hillside, or him by himself,

hauled by a cable from the loader's winch,
grasped with grim embarrassment.
Then, arriving, he spat and pissed
onto the bucket of the hoe

---

[1] Form: Free verse—Vocabulary: hoe: backhoe.

before he climbed to the seat,
as all smiled. Tall, craggy, with
a big-voiced drawl, he learned
to operate a backhoe in Korea.

There was no gentleness, only
precision in the swing of the hoe
with Don in the seat as the arm
swung from pit to pile in flowing,

boxlike movement, dripping grease.
I recall the blandness of his look in the sun
as the bucket tore the ground we
stood on and the backhoe rocked.

I never asked if he loved his work,
or if a day's glorious vulgarity
was why he still got up at seventy.
His gift was not seeming to try.

Jobsite Wind[1]

that rips paper from the walls and changes plywood into sails
staggering a bent laborer with his load—
that curves string lines, bounces grass and trees in gusts

and makes the stick-framed studs above the ledger hum.
It searches all of us moving or standing still,

---

[1] Form: Free verse—Vocabulary: ledger: a horizontal timber in a scaffold.

holding hammer or nailgun, our faces tight with cold

and hair wild. It searches us, leaning into the day,
for nothing we have, buffets the unprotected
figure atop the wall and one stooped above a half-framed
    floor

forcing blocks between the joists. Wakened
by the wind I drove deserted, limb-wreck streets to the job
and found the roofless walls awash in wind, thrashing like a
    ship

in webs of lumber and shadows waving
above raindark floors laid purposeful with wood and nails.
Wind that threaded the trembling sticks of the house

driving plastic buckets down stairs, testing the corners
of a plywood stack, smearing a dropcloth to a wall like a
    shroud—
that rolled out of the throat of the world huge and articulate
    blasts—

And shoring spreadlegged, watching my hand hammering
in rhythm to my breath, the world hidden
beyond the nailhead's own demands

while inside a focused stillness intact and undisturbed
also incessant asked Who am I? Why this action?
What is this place I am in?

Pickwork[1]

There is skill to it, how you hold your back all day, the dole
of force behind the stroke, the size of bite, where
to hit, and knowing behind each swing a thousand others
    wait
in an eight-hour day.

---

[1] Form: Free verse—Notes: Here the pick works as a metaphor for
opportunity.

And if the head suddenly comes rattling down the handle:
knowing to drive a nail for a wedge between the wood and the
    steel.
The inexperienced pretend to see in the dirt a face they hate,
and exhaust themselves. The best

measure themselves against an arbitrary goal, this much
before lunch, before break, before a drink of water, and then
do it. Some listen to the pleasant ringing
of the pick, or music, and trance-like, follow the rhythm

of the swing. Once I spent a half-hour attentive
only to my muscles triggering into motion, sweat
creeping down my chest. Ground makes the biggest
    difference.
In sandstone you feel the impact to your knees,

in mud you yank the point from the muck each throw.
The hardest part is not to let the rhythm fail,
like stopping too often to remeasure the depth, stalling
in the shithouse, losing self-respect, or beginning to doubt:

Am I cutting too wide? Is the line still straight?
Or thinking of backhoes, more help, quibbling inches
with the boss. On my job Lorenzo works in the sun all day,
his silver radio quietly tuned to the Mexican station.

Shoveling out, he shrugs and says, "No problem, Mark,"
waist-deep in the hole.
From the spot I work, I hear the strike of his pick all day.
Driving home together he has told me about his two black
    whores,

his ex and daughter in LA, and Susan Nero, "on-stage."
    Thirteen times
he's seen her. Almost reverent, he says, "She is so beautiful,"
and makes immense cups with his hands.
And driving home he has told me of his landlord who extorts
    him

for the green card he doesn't have, of his "mo-ther"
dying of cancer in Mexico city, of his son-of-a-bitch
dad who beat him, and her, and ran away, of his brother
    Michael,
and Joaquim, in Chicago, the Central Valley. In the car

he asks me if I think the boss will hold half his pay, he needs
to save something for his sister
—I hear his pick all day
and in the afternoon I go out to ask him, how's it going?

He shrugs me off. "It's no big problem, Mark.
No problem, I can do it, but the fucking pick is dull,"
and shows me the blunted steel point. "I need something—
sharper, you know: I need a sharper pick. "

Poem[1]

What weakness of mind gripped a moment's meanness
    tighter
than his?—stalling, reeling, retarding at the thought that
cupped the vision of the rope actually smoking through his
    hands

---

[1] Form: Free verse—Notes: Notice the similar initial sense of wonder and
disbelief at physical injury in this poem and in Robert Frost's "Out—Out!"

—while elsewhere and peripheral, a huge tree-limb
   plummeted.
The rope, as he observed it, was not a thing, not an object,
but a slender field of havoc twisted to a strand which, though
   he
opened the grasp of his hands from pain of it, would not
   leave his hands
(unless he thinks of something yet to do.) But he did not—
not immediately, and later he would raise his hands, and
   marvel,
grin, almost feel joy at recognition of that groove
the rope burned and furrowed across the flesh of each;
he could plainly see its path in blood, blisters, and burnished
   skin
from finger to finger as if it were something caught that was
rarely caught. He held his hands up as evidence of
   something.

Waiting for Lumber[1]

Somehow none of us knew exactly
what time it was supposed to come.
So there we were, all of us, five men
at how much an hour given to picking
at blades of grass, tossing pebbles
at the curb, with nothing in the space
between the two red cones, and no distant
downshift of a roaring truck grinding
steadily towards us uphill. Someone thought
maybe one of us should go back to town
to call, but no one did, and no one gave
the order to. It was as if each to himself
had called a kind of strike, brought a halt,
locked out any impulse back to work.
What was work in our lives anyway?
No one recalled a moment of saying yes
to hammer and saw, or anything else.
Each looked to the others for some defining
move—the way at lunch without a word

---

[1] Form: Free verse.

all would start to rise when the foreman
closed the lid of his lunchbox—but
none came. The senior of us leaned
against a peach tree marked for demolition,
seemed almost careful not to give a sign.
And I, as I am likely to do—and who
knows, but maybe we all were—beginning
to notice the others there, and ourselves
among them, as if we could be strangers suddenly,
like those few evenings we had chosen to meet
at some bar and appeared to each other
in our street clothes—that was the sense—
of a glass over another creature's fate.
A hundred feet above our stillness
on the ground we could hear a breeze
that seemed to blow the moment past,
trifling with the leaves; we watched
a ranging hawk float past. It was the time
of morning when housewives return
alone from morning errands. Something
we had all witnessed a hundred times before,
but this time with new interest. And all of us
felt the slight loosening of the way things were,
as if working or not working were a matter
of choice, and who we were didn't
matter, if not always, at least for that hour.

Kevin Hart (b. 1954)

The Room[1]

It is my house, and yet one room is locked.
The dark has taken root on all four walls.
It is a room where knots stare out from wood,
A room that turns its back on the whole house.

At night I hear the crickets list their griefs
And let an ancient peace come into me.

---

[1] Form: Blank verse—Notes: Here the room is most likely the room of a
dead child.

Sleep intercepts my prayer, and in the dark
The house turns slowly round its one closed room.

Molly Fisk (b. 1955)

Intrigue[1]

I love living in a town so small
it still has a noon whistle.
There is one stop sign,
four-way.
We have our own post office.
People here say hello
and they watch where your car is
at night,
not wanting to miss
a good story.
This makes me want
to park,
flagrantly,
outside the homes
of unsuspecting bachelors,
and lurk in the Parkside
over breakfast,
to hear news
of my own misbehavior.
I am perched
on the edge
of being familiar.

On the Disinclination to Scream[2]

If I had been a ten year old stranger
and you had tripped me in a dark alley, say,
downtown, instead of our mutual living room
I'm sure I would have screamed.

If, in the alley, you had straddled me as fast—

---

[1] Form: Free verse—Vocabulary: Parkside: restaurant.
[2] Form: Free verse.

your knees clamping my elbows into asphalt,
not the blue Chinese dragons
of our living room rug,
I might have been quiet there, too.

When you opened my mouth
with your heavy flat thumbs,
filled it with pain and flesh—
I would have choked in the alley,
as anyone would choke.

But if you had groaned then, and stood up,
walked away from the dark street
leaving me to vomit and shake alone,
I might have been saved.

I could describe you to policemen.
Perhaps their composite would match your photo
in the Harvard Reunion guide.
Your fingerprints, lifted from the collar of my dress,
might be found in Coast Guard files.

If they never found you and there was no trial
I could have gone home to people who loved me:
horrified, enraged, they would plot revenge
and rock me to sleep in soft arms.

I would have been frightened, maybe forever,
of alleys, strange men, and the dark—
but encouraged by the world, who would hate you on my
    behalf.
I would have been as safe as a ten year old can be.

Instead, I rose quietly from the Chinese rug
and went upstairs to wash.
No sound escaped me.
I couldn't afford to throw up,
and it wasn't the first time.

The Dry Tortugas[1]

They were building a house in the Dry Tortugas,
less for the solitude there than the open eyes
of a swallowtailed hummingbird they had seen once
on a fishing trip—the early Fifties, he reeling in
an oversized yellowfin, Humphrey Bogart
facing the wind, one foot on the rail in *To Have and Have Not*,
she whistling the stuttered call of the Amazonian kingfisher,
and singing in Spanish to flocks of Bonaparte gulls.
It comes to nothing in the end, though the land
is paced off and measured and two palms felled
to expand the view, a road graded the requisite mile,
and some of their friends fly down from New York
to surprise them, circle the islands all morning,
gleeful and chic
in their 4-seater Cessna (he's something exalted at Chase),
and later the bottles of Myer's and Appleton Gold sweat
dark rings on the terrace flagstones, and someone's pink
lipstick makes delicate kissprints along the rim of her glass.
No one has told me what happened—his heart attack
in Guatemala, her premonition about the wide
and empty view—or the world swinging in
with its usual brazen distractions—but they framed
the architect's plans of the house, and this
is what I inherit, a rendering in colored pencil:
what they were dreaming before I was born.

William Roetzheim (b. 1955)

Response to Emily Dickinson's "Wild Nights—Wild Nights!"[2]

We sat around a fire and drank Merlot,
A California wine called "Two Buck Chuck"
by those of us that shop at "Trader Joe's."

---

[1] Form: Free verse—Vocabulary: Dry Tortugas: islands west of Key West in Florida; kingfisher: type of large bird; Bonaparte gulls: type of gull that nests in trees; Myer's and Appleton Gold: types of rum.
[2] Form: Sonnet—Vocabulary: Two Buck Chuck: Charles Schaw Merlot, selling for $2 per bottle.

When someone asked, "If I had to be stuck

in Jimmy's mountain cabin for a night
with anyone except my wife, who would
I choose?" I thought of you, images right
and verses tight with clarity I should

achieve but never will. But more, I want
you on the night you wrote this piece, the panted
words fresh from your pen. And lest God taunt
you for *your* wish I'd have the light be slanted

such that I appeared to be the
one
inside your mind when this
piece was begun.

Stretch Marks[1]

You lie beside me,
snoring lightly, nude and tan,
your breasts relaxed. My eyes are drawn
to spider webs of lacy white along
your side, across your breasts.
The delicate patterns branch and weave,
swoop down the curves
and glide across the planes and slopes,
embossed and subtle decorations,
flesh on flesh,
The lines entwine, and seem to spell our love,
our family, our thirty years together.

Fading into Background[2]

The murmurs were the first to go,
those eavesdropped conversations
moving here and there within a crowded room.
And soon I lost discussions

[1] Form: Free verse.
[2] Form: Free verse—Notes: A poem that describes the slow loss of hearing
with aging.

from across a crowded table
at loud and boisterous weddings,
gone to background noise
like waterfalls, and for my part
just nods and smiles,
nothing but nods and smiles.

And then my wife as translator,
"What did she say?"
"What did he say?"
Until I found
it didn't really matter what they said,
when nods and smiles will say enough.

Opera Season[1]

I couldn't attend the opera this season.
The thought of your seat empty next to mine
was too much to bear.
I put our tickets in a kitchen drawer,
then mentally buried that drawer with you.

Like Therese Raquin I am haunted
by your ghost in every corner.
Like Rigoletto, that which was most precious to me
was taken away from me.
Like Butterfly, I confidently wait for our reunion
in this intermission between life and death.

---

[1] Form: Free verse—Vocabulary: Therese Raquin: protagonist in Opera of
the same name. She and her lover kill her husband, whose ghost then
haunts them; Rigoletto: Main character in opera of the same name, he
ends up mistakenly arranging to have his daughter Gilda killed; Butterfly:
main character in Madam Butterfly. She waits for the return of her lover
but to no avail, and ends up killing herself.

Shadow Friends[1]

I worship shadows like my daughter worships sun.
I don't mean those so crisp and dark
beneath a noon-time sun,
or shadow soldier squads
before a picket fence. Those underneath
a harvest moon are more my style; the way
they hide and watch
from low bushes, then dance around
the lifted skirts of swaying trees,
like witches in a forest glen.
I've lured them home with low-watt bulbs
in gargoyle sconces under overhangs.
At night my friends uncoil
on walks and walls, then call me to their yard
to stroll and see my life in grays and blacks.
And in my den the shy ones come to watch
me read by candlelight. They come, pull back,
grow bold, then sly; so while I sip my scotch
and swirl the ice I'm not alone. I'm not
depressed.

Dean Young (b. 1955)

Only One of My Deaths[2]

Because it seems the only way to save the roses
is to pluck the Japanese beetles out of
their convoluted paradise
and kill them, I think for a moment,
instead of crushing them in the driveway,
of impaling them on the thorns.
Perhaps they'd prefer that.

---

[1] Form: Iambic, irregular line lengths—Vocabulary: sconces: lights
attached to walls.
[2] Form: Free verse.

Mark Cox (b. 1956)

Geese[1]

We were in love and his uncle had a farm
where he took me hunting
to try to be in love even more.

He wanted me to have what he had:
Black coffee,
toast buttered with bad light
in a truck stop splotched with smoke,

then moonlight on the hills and snow
like a woman stepping out of her dress.

And it was good even as we killed it.
The stalks lightening,
the sun rising like a worn, yellow slicker
over us, bent over panting
because it wasn't hit cleanly
and had run us both dizzy
before settling down.

There was a particular knife he used
to make the asshole bigger.
After that, one could just reach in
and remove anything that wasn't necessary,
and thinking about it now, I see
the old school desk behind his uncle's house
put there for that reason,
see my husband sadly hosing it down,
as if regretting how and what men are taught. . .

I'm lying. . .
though the diner I see belongs
in a small town where I went to school,
the desk had no drawers, was in fact a table,
and he was whistling as he washed it.

---

[1] Form: Free verse.

The sun didn't rise
like something to keep the rain off us;
it hung, like a cold chandelier
in which I could see each filament
in each flame-shaped bulb
beating itself senseless against the light—
brilliant and hollow,

beautiful and inhumane. . .
But I wanted so badly
to forgive his hands, forgive his lovers,
and to forget how, driving home, I was fooled
by half an acre of decoys
and some camouflage netting,

how I wanted to honk but didn't,
and how the whole scene made me realize
that mannequins mate for life too,
in department stores, wearing back-to-school clothes,

made me remember that if you press hard enough
on a bird's dead breast, it will betray its own kind,
that when he took its neck and broke it
I said his first name.

Style[1]

Today, a coed with a black eye
and bruised cheek stopped me
in the hall to ask, anxiously,
where does one put "Jr."
according to standard manuals
on style?

"In jail?" I said. "No, really," she said,
"This is important."

---

[1] Form: Free verse.

Jim Daniels (b. 1956)

Wheels[1]

My brother kept
in a frame on the wall
pictures of every motorcycle, car, truck:
in his rusted out Impala convertible
wearing his cap and gown
waving
in his yellow Barracuda
with a girl leaning into him
waving
on his Honda 350
waving
on his Honda 750 with the boys
holding a beer
waving
in his first rig
wearing a baseball hat backwards
waving
in his Mercury Montego
getting married
waving
in his black LTD
trying to sell real estate
waving
back to driving trucks
a shiny new rig
waving
on his Harley Sportster
with his wife on the back
waving
his son in a car seat
with his own steering wheel
my brother leaning over him
in an old Ford pickup

---

[1] Form: Free verse—Vocabulary: Impala: model of car; Barracuda: model of
car; rig: truck; Mercury Montego: brand of car; LTD: brand of car; shammy:
soft leather cloth—Notes: Although not explicitly stated, the brother died in
a motorcycle crash.

and they are
waving
holding a wrench a rag
a hose a shammy
waving.

My brother helmetless
rides off on his Harley
waving
my brother's feet
rarely touch the ground—
waving waving
face pressed to the wind
no camera to save him.

Gu Cheng (1956 – 1993)

Ark[1]

Translated from the Chinese by Donald Finkel

The ship you've boarded
is doomed to go under—
vanish into the breathing sea.

But you still have time to stare at the flag,
or at the dark, unfolding plain,

---

[1] Form: Free verse—Notes: This poem defies simple analysis, because the
ark is a symbol and it can represent many things. Examples include your
own body (and thus, your life); a political party in power; or even the Earth.

or at the white birds twittering
over their watery grave.

You still have time to lean on the rail,
puzzled by a sound in the passageway—
though the whole ship is empty,
though every door is ajar—

till cool flames float up
from every cabin.

Li-Young Lee (b. 1957)

Eating Together[1]

In the steamer is the trout
seasoned with slivers of ginger,
two sprigs of green onion, and sesame oil.
We shall eat it with rice for lunch,
brothers, sister, my mother who will
taste the sweetest meat of the head,
holding it between her fingers
deftly, the way my father did
weeks ago. Then he lay down
to sleep like a snow-covered road
winding through pines older than him,
without any travelers, and lonely for no one.

Persimmons[2]

In sixth grade Mrs. Walker
slapped the back of my head
and made me stand in the corner
for not knowing the difference
between *persimmon* and precision.
How to choose

---

[1] Form: Free verse.
[2] Form: Free verse—Vocabulary: wolftail: brush.

persimmons. This is precision.
Ripe ones are soft and brown-spotted.
Sniff the bottoms. The sweet one
will be fragrant. How to eat:
put the knife away, lay down the newspaper.
Peel the skin tenderly, not to tear the meat.
Chew on the skin, suck it,
and swallow. Now, eat
the meat of the fruit,
so sweet,
all of it, to the heart.

Donna undresses, her stomach is white.
In the yard, dewy and shivering
with crickets, we lie naked,
face-up, face-down,
I teach her Chinese.
Crickets: chiu chiu. Dew: I've forgotten.
Naked: I've forgotten.
Ni, wo: you and me.
I part her legs,
remember to tell her
she is beautiful as the moon.

Other words
that got me into trouble were
fight and fright, wren and yarn.
Fight was what I did when I was frightened,
fright was what I felt when I was fighting.
Wrens are small, plain birds,
yarn is what one knits with.
Wrens are soft as yarn.
My mother made birds out of yarn.
I loved to watch her tie the stuff;
a bird, a rabbit, a wee man.

Mrs. Walker brought a persimmon to class
and cut it up
so everyone could taste
a Chinese apple. Knowing

it wasn't ripe or sweet, I didn't eat
but watched the other faces.

My mother said every persimmon has a sun
inside, something golden, glowing,
warm as my face.

Once, in the cellar, I found two wrapped in newspaper,
forgotten and not yet ripe.
I took them and set them both on my bedroom windowsill,
where each morning a cardinal
sang, The sun, the sun.

Finally understanding
he was going blind,
my father sat up all one night
waiting for a song, a ghost.
I gave him the persimmons,
swelled, heavy as sadness,
and sweet as love.

This year, in the muddy lighting
of my parents' cellar, I rummage, looking
for something I lost.
My father sits on the tired, wooden stairs,
black cane between his knees,
hand over hand, gripping the handle.
He's so happy that I've come home.

I ask how his eyes are, a stupid question.
All gone, he answers.

Under some blankets, I find a box.
Inside the box I find three scrolls.
I sit beside him and untie
three paintings by my father:
Hibiscus leaf and a white flower.
Two cats preening.
Two persimmons, so full they want to drop from the cloth.

He raises both hands to touch the cloth,
asks, Which is this?

This is persimmons, Father.

Oh, the feel of the wolftail on the silk,
the strength, the tense
precision in the wrist.
I painted them hundreds of times
eyes closed. These I painted blind.
Some things never leave a person:
scent of the hair of one you love,
the texture of persimmons,
in your palm, the ripe weight.

Julia Kasdorf (b. 1962)

What I Learned from My Mother[1]

I learned from my mother how to love
the living, to have plenty of vases on hand
in case you have to rush to the hospital
with peonies cut from the lawn, black ants
still stuck to the buds. I learned to save jars
large enough to hold fruit salad for a whole
grieving household, to cube home canned pears
and peaches, to slice through maroon grape skins
and flick out the sexual seeds with a knife point.

---

[1] Form: Prose poem.

I learned to attend viewings even if I didn't know
the deceased, to press the moist hands
of the living, to look in their eyes and offer
sympathy, as though I understood loss even then.
I learned to believe
that whatever we say means nothing,
what anyone will remember is that we came.
I learned to believe I had the power to ease
awful pains materially like an angel.
Like a doctor I learned to create
from another's suffering my own usefulness,
and once you know how to do this,
you can never refuse.
To every house you enter, you must offer
healing: a chocolate cake you baked yourself,
the blessing of your voice, your chaste touch.

Ruth L. Schwartz (b. 1962)

The Swan at Edgewater Park[1]

Isn't one of your prissy richpeoples' swans
Wouldn't be at home on some pristine pond
Chooses the whole stinking shoreline, candy wrappers,
condoms
     in its tidal fringe
Prefers to curve its muscular, slightly grubby neck
     into the body of a Great Lake,
Swilling whatever it is swans swill,
Chardonnay of algae with bouquet of crud,
While Clevelanders walk by saying *Look*
     at that big duck!
Beauty isn't the point here; of course
     the swan is beautiful,
But not like Lorie at 16, when
Everything was possible—no
More like Lorie at 27
Smoking away her days off in her dirty kitchen,
Her kid with asthma watching TV,

---

[1] Form: Free verse.

The boyfriend who doesn't know yet she's gonna
Leave him, washing his car out back—and
He's a runty little guy, and drinks too much, and
It's not his kid anyway, but he loves her, he
Really does, he loves them both—
That's the kind of swan this is.

Patience Agbabi (b. 1965)

Transformatrix[1]

I'm slim as a silver stiletto, lit
by a fat, waxing moon and a séance
of candles dipped in oil of frankincense.
Salt peppers my lips as the door clicks shut.
A pen poised over a blank page, I wait
for madam's orders, her strict consonants
and the spaces between words, the silence.
She's given me a safe word, a red light
but I'm breaking the law, on a death wish,
ink throbbing my temples, each vertebra
straining for her fingers. She trusses up
words, lines, as a corset disciplines flesh.
Without her, I'm nothing but without me
she's tense, uptight, rigid as a full stop.

Kate Clanchy (b. 1965)

War Poetry[2]

The class has dropped its books. The janitor's
disturbed some wasps, broomed the nest

---

[1] Form: Sonnet with relaxed form—Vocabulary: Transformatrix: a made-up word implying transformation and relationships; stiletto: slender dagger; safe word: word used in bondage games to stop the game; trusses up: ties up—Notes: The sonnet form is considered by most poets to be the most restrictive, and here that sense of the form is compared to a bondage scene.

[2] Form: Iambic, mostly tetrameter but varying.—Vocabulary: football strips: soccer uniforms; Owen: WWI British War Poet; Boche: derogatory phrase for Germans; pike: long spear; grapeshot: small iron balls used in cannons.

straight off the roof. It lies outside, exotic
as a fallen planet, a burst city of the poor;
its newsprint halls, its ashen, tiny rooms
all open to the air. The insects' buzz
is low-key as a smart machine. They group,
regroup, in stacks and coils, advance
and cross like pulsing points on radar screens.

And though the boys have shaven heads
and football strips, and would, they swear,
enlist at once, given half a chance,
march down Owen's darkening lanes
to join the lads and stuff the Boche—
they don't rush out to pike the nest,
or lap the yard with grapeshot faces.
They watch the wasps through glass,
silently, abashed, the way we all watch war.

David Berman (b. 1967)

Snow[1]

Walking through a field with my little brother Seth

I pointed to a place where kids had made angels in the snow.
For some reason, I told him that a troop of angels
had been shot and dissolved when they hit the ground.

He asked who had shot them and I said a farmer.

Then we were on the roof of the lake.

---

[1] Form: Free verse.

The ice looked like a photograph of water.

Why he asked. Why did he shoot them.

I didn't know where I was going with this.

They were on his property, I said.
When it's snowing, the outdoors seem like a room.

Today I traded hellos with my neighbor.
Our voices hung close in the new acoustics.
A room with the walls blasted to shreds and falling.
We returned to our shoveling, working side by side in silence.

But why were they on his property, he asked.

Jackleen Holton (b. 1969)

American History[1]

> First semester of my senior year,
> Mr. Severin, American History teacher,
> would wave his giant arthritic hands—
> fingers unmoving—as he spoke of past
> Presidents and foreign wars.
>   Oftentimes he'd sketch himself
> into these lectures, remembering
> how a dark theatre fell silent
> as the newsreel delivered the wreckage,
> the death toll at Pearl Harbor.
>   His wife, a sweet-faced brunette,
> had been a hard catch until the night
> he showed up at the soda fountain
> with the girl who had a reputation.
>   Against a backdrop of black-and-white

---

[1] Form: Free verse—Notes: What the narrator learned about history was learned more from the experiences the teacher shared than from the textbook, but perhaps the most important lesson was that no-one in life can avoid pain.

war footage, their courtship endured.
They had two sons, one under Eisenhower,
the other the day Kennedy was shot.
Just after Vietnam, cancer took
her far too soon.
      He looked around the silent classroom.
He told us: "Every life that has breathed
has had its tragedy." It was 1986.
Many of the cars in the student parking lot
were new. We had two more years of Reagan.
      "Something will be taken from each of you."
I could tell nobody believed him.
He raised his painful hands in the air.
His eyes searched the room, then locked
down on mine. In almost a whisper
he said—how I remember this—
"You will not be spared."

Free[1]

Behold the next-door neighbor's
Frigidaire, faithful servant
of fifteen years, now standing
at the foot of the driveway, facing
the street, a handwritten sign carelessly
taped to its freezer compartment
and fluttering in the breeze:
"Free!"

Then think of the thousands of couches
and loveseats left in the front yards
of their former houses, sometimes bearing
similar signs, otherwise their status
is implied. Evidence their worn fabrics,
outdated patterns and styles, the fact
that they've been carted outside.
They're free.

---

[1] Form: Free verse—Notes: Notice the changing meaning of the word free,
starting with available without payment, then released, the abandoned,
and finally, the forcibly cast off.

But the dumbfounded home furnishings,
the pardoned kitchen appliances
can do nothing but stand quiet vigil
outside like abandoned children
or aging, divorced wives, the downsized,
the suddenly homeless, the disenfranchised—
now free.

"Your services are no longer needed,"
their former masters have informed them
with these one-word Dear John letters
to the coffee table or the washing machine
"You can leave anytime you'd like.
You're free."

Jane Flanders (b. 1984)

The House that Fear Built: Warsaw, 1943[1]

*The purpose of poetry is to remind us how difficult it is to
remain just one person, for our house is open, there are no
keys in the doors....*
—Czeslaw Milosz, "Ars Poetica"

I am the boy with his hands raised over his head
in Warsaw.

I am the soldier whose rifle is trained
on the boy with his hands raised over his head
in Warsaw.

I am the woman with lowered gaze
who fears the soldier whose rifle is trained
on the boy with his hands raised over his head
in Warsaw.

I am the man in the overcoat
who loves the woman with lowered gaze
who fears the soldier whose rifle is trained

---

[1] Form: Free verse—Vocabulary: crone: old woman.

on the boy with his hands raised over his head
in Warsaw.

I am the stranger who photographs
the man in the overcoat
who loves the woman with lowered gaze
who fears the soldier whose rifle is trained
on the boy with his hands raised over his head
in Warsaw.

The crowd, of which I am each part, moves on
beneath my window, for I am the crone too
who shakes her sheets
over every street in the world
muttering
What's this? What's this?

Appendix A
Notes on Meter

Metered verse consists of stanzas, lines, feet, and syllables. Stanzas are optional collections of lines into the equivalent of paragraphs. Metered verse is more likely to use regular stanzas (same number of lines in each stanza) than free verse, although this is certainly not a requirement. Lines are collections of feet. In metered verse, the number of feet per line is either consistent (e.g., always 3, 4, 5, etc.) or varies in a regular pattern (e.g., 4-3-4-3). Feet are collections of syllables. Note that I haven't mentioned words. Word boundaries are irrelevant when dealing with meter.

Feet are broken down based on the accents.

da DUM is called an iamb (emphasis on the DUM part)
DUM da is called a trochee
da da DUM is called an anapest

Here are some examples:

iambs:
    the right
    abate

trochees:
    have a
    acted

anapest:
    in the snow
    violin

When poets write metered verse, they write it as iambic, trochaic, or anapestic. Each line should have more feet of the selected pattern than other types of feet. Iambic verse is the most versatile and natural. It is used for just about any subject matter. Trochaic is kind of hammering, similar to marching music. It might be used for military or forceful types of topics. Anapestic is sing-song, and works well for children's verse and funny poems. Of course, there are always exceptions to these general rules.

Here are some examples:

iambic:
    The slow are dead, however just and right.

trochaic
    Slowly hitting with a baseball bat I . . .

anapestic
    On the night before Christmas throughout the big house.

Once you've identified the pattern of feet in the lines, and the type of meter, then you should find that each line of the verse will have that number of feet and more of that type of foot than any other foot. For example, if the poem is written in iambic pentameter (iambic, 5 feet per line) then each line will have five feet and at least 3 of those five feet will be iambs. Using something other than iambs for the other two feet is called substitution, and it's what keeps the verse from getting monotonous.

Now, let's look at some exceptions to the simplified rules above:

DUM DUM is called a spondee. In iambic and trochaic verse, think of it as a wild card. In iambic verse it counts as an iamb. In trochaic verse, it counts as a trochee.

da da is called a pyrrhic, but you never have this. However, you might have a pyrrhic and a spondee, which is called a double iamb. It counts as two iambs. So da da DUM DUM is a double iamb, or two iambs.

Here are some examples:

spondee:
    big gun
    red-hot

double iamb
    in the big top
    it's an abstract

If you have a DUM as the first thing on a line, it might be the beginning of a trochee or spondee, or it can be what's called a headless iamb. In other words, an iamb without the initial da counts just like any other iamb. The author of the poem gets to pick if they want it used as a headless iamb or not, but then needs to make sure everything else in that line works out to the correct number of feet based on that assumption. One more rule: In iambic verse you shouldn't find a headless iamb on the first line. In other words, the reader needs to get into the swing of iambic reading before the poet throws a headless iamb at them.

Here are some examples:
    headless iamb
                making currents, rivers, rapids, then

    Initial trochee
        needing, then not, though each approach

If you have a da DUM da at the end of a line, you can count the da DUM as an iamb and "throw away" the trailing da, which is called a feminine ending.

Here's an example, starting with a headless iamb and ending with a feminine ending:
        scream and grab that flung me sparkling skyward

Finally, the "rule of three" says that anytime you have three of something in a row (e.g., da da da or DUM DUM DUM) the middle one gets promoted or demoted. However, it's considered bad for the poet to require that you promote (or demote) something that strongly does not want to be promoted or demoted. For example, promoting a little word like "a" with the rule of three to a stress would be a blunder.

In this example, "grandkids" could be ambiguous in its stress, but the rule of three tells us that "grand" is stressed and "kids" is weak.

> Today the kids and grandkids tempt me slowly up

Whew, that's a lot to think about. It's probably more interesting to you if you like the metered verse and you'd like to try your hand at writing some metered verse yourself.

Index by Author

Index by Title

Index by Subject

Index to Translations

Index by First Line

Index Pointing To Audio CD

	Disk A	
For Annie	Poems of Ghosts, Evil, and Superstition Disk B	13 - Death
For Once, Then, Something	Poems of Ghosts, Evil, and Superstition Disk A	09 - Ghosts
Forgetfulness	Poets Look at Growing Up and Growing Old Disk A	17 - Looking Back
Forgiveness	Poets Look at Choices in Life	29 - Anger & Forgiveness
Fork	Poems for Children of all Ages	07 - Strange
Fountain, A Bottle, A Donkey's Ears, And Some Books, A	Poets Look at Writing, Art, and Poetry	18 - Writing
Francesca	Poems of Romance	22 - Love
Free	Poems of lust, betrayal, and lost love	41 - Moving On
From A Plane	Poems of Nature	30 - Landscape
From Beginning And End - Knowledge	Poets Look at Eternity Disk A	23 - Dust unto Dust
From Fuses I - On Art	Poets Look at Writing, Art, and Poetry	35 - Art
From Fuses I - On God	Poems of Inspiration and Faith	24 - Questioning Religion
From Fuses I - On Love	Poems of lust, betrayal, and lost love	25 - Battle of the Sexes
From Idem The Same, A Valentine To Sherwood Anderson, A Very Valentine	Poems of Romance	24 - Love
From Selected Shorts	No audio version available	NA
From The Longbeards'	Poems of Romance	25 -

677

678

693

Index Pointing From Audio CD

697

698

Poems of lust, betrayal, and lost love

Poems of Nature

Poems of Romance

702

Poems of the Human Condition

Poems of Working

Poems That Make a Statement Disk B

Poets Look at Choices in Life

Poets Look at Eternity Disk A

Poets Look at Eternity Disk B

Poets Look at Growing Up and Growing Old Disk A

18 - Waiting for Death	Still Life
19 - Waiting for Death	Souvenir
20 - Waiting for Death	Place ("There's A Way Out")
21 - Waiting for Death	Misgiving
22 - Waiting for Death	On His Seventy-Fifth Birthday
23 - Waiting for Death	From The Ship Of Death
24 - Waiting for Death	Nature
25 - Waiting for Death	Mr. Flood's Party
26 - Waiting for Death	Pity Of The Leaves, The
27 - Mortal Illness	Junk Man, The
28 - Mortal Illness	Scholar, The
29 - Mortal Illness	Last Words Of My English Grandmother, The

Poets Look at War and Peace

02 - Glory	To Lucasta, On Going To The Wars
03 - Glory	Charge Of The Light Brigade, The
04 - Glory	Soldier, The
05 - Glory	Landlord's Tale, The
06 - Glory	Soldier Of Fortune, The
07 - Soldiers	Old Liberators, The
08 - Soldiers	Camouflaging The Chimera
09 - Soldiers	What Saves Us
10 - Soldiers	Requiem For The Croppies
11 - Casualties	Death Of The Ball Turret Gunner, The
12 - Casualties	Facing It
13 - Casualties	Killed At The Ford
14 - Casualties	Dulce Et Decorum Est

712

Poets Look at Writing, Art, and Poetry

Acknowledgements

All poems in this book come from copyrighted sources and the original sources retain all rights to the poems in this book. No poems from this book may be reproduced in any manner. New material created for this book is copyright 2006 by Level 4 Press, Inc. The Editor and Publisher wish to thank the following for permission to reprint copyright material.

"The Dumka" from THE ART OF THE LATHE. Copyright © 1998 by B.H. Fairchild. Reprinted with the permission of Alice James Books.

Amiri Baraka, "Wise I" Reprinted by permission of SLL/Sterling Lord Literistic, Inc. Copyright © by Amiri Baraka

Tom Hennen, "The Life of a Day" and "Soaking Up Sun" from CRAWLING OUT THE WINDOW. Used with permission of Black Hat Press, Goodhue, MN.

Andrei Codrescu, extract from "Three Types of Loss" from ALIEN CANDOR: SELECTED POEMS 1970 - 1995 (Blacki Sparrow Press. Reprinted with the permission of the author.

Lucian Blaga, "I Will Not Crush the World's Corolla of Wonders" used by permission of the translator.

"The Room" by Kevin Hart, from FLAME TREE: SELECTED POEMS, Bloodaxe Books, 2002. Reproduced by permission of the author.

Izet Sarajlic, "Luck in Sarajevo" from SCAR ON THE STONE: CONTEMPORARY POETRY OF BOSNIA (Bloodaxe Books). Reprinted with the permission of the translator.

Gwendolyn Brooks, "A Song in the Front Yard" from SELECTED POEMS, reprinted by permission of Brooks Permissions.

Gwendolyn Brooks, "The Boy Died in my Alley" from TO DISEMBARK, reprinted by permission of Brooks Permissions.

Patience Agbabi, "Transformatrix" from TRANSFORMATRIXi. First published in the UK by Canongate Books Ltd, 2000. Used with permission of Canongate Books.

Andrei Codrescu, "Defense of the Meek" from IT WAS TODAY, Coffeehouse Press. Used with permission of the author.

Mark Cox, "Geese" first appeared in "Smoulder", David R. Godine, Publisher, reprinted here by permission of the author.

Maura Stanton: "Living Apart" appeared in TALES OF THE SUPERNATURAL (David R. Godine, 1988) Reprinted with permission of the author.

W.H. Davies, "Leisure" from COLLECTED POEMS OF W.H. DAVIES. Used with permission of Mrs H M Davies Will Trust.

Toi Derricotte, "Allen Ginsberg", used by permission of the author.

Thomas M. Disch, "The Cardinal Detoxes" copyright 1993 by Thomas M. Disch. 'The Cardinal Detoxes" first appeared in "The Hudson Review". Reprinted by permission of the author.

Stuart Dybek, "Maroon" and "Brass Knuckles" used by permission of the author.

Tanikawa Shuntaro, extract from "With Silence My Companion" from WITH SILENCE MY COMPANION, Prescot Street Press. Reprinted by permission of the translator.

Rutger Kopland, "Natzweiler" from A WORLD BEYOND MYSELF. Used with permission of Enitharmon Press.

Molly Fisk, "The Dry Turtugas", "Intrigue", "On the Disinclination to Scream" used with permission of the author.

Reprinted by permission of Faber and Faber, Inc., an affiliate of Farrar, Straus and Giroux, LLC:
"Vergissmeinnicht" from THE COMPLETE POEMS by Keith Douglas. Copyright © 1978 by the Estate of Keith Douglas.

"Clearances: V", "A Dream of Jealousy", "The Haw Lantern", "Punishment", and "Requiem for the Croppies" from OPENED GROUND: SELECTED POEMS 1966-1996 by Seamus Heaney. Copyright © 1998 by Seamus Heaney. Reprinted by permission of Farrar, Straus and Giroux, LLC.

716

717

Adam Zagajewski. Translation copyright (c) 2002 by Farrar, Straus and Giroux, LLC.

Nuala Ni Dhomhnail, "Ceist na Teangan" By kind permission of the author and The Gallery Press, Loughcrew, Oldcastle, County Meath, Ireland from PHARAOH'S DAUGHTER (1990)

Charles Simic, "Fork" and "Prodigy" from SELECTED EARLY POEMS, "Detail" from NORTHERN EXPOSURE, George Braziller, Inc.. Used with permission of the author.

Lorna Goodison, "Birth Stone" reprinted with permission of the author.

Jorie Graham, "Salmon" used with permission of the author.

"Detail" copyright 2002 by Eamon Grennan. Reprinted from STILL LIFE WITH WATERFALL with the permission of Graywolf Press, Saint Paul, Minnesota.   'Detail' by Eamon Grennan, reproduced in the UK by kind permission of the author and The Gallery Press, Loughcrw, Oldcastle, County Meath, Ireland from STILL LIFE WITH WATERFALL (2001).

"Jake Addresses the World from his Garden," from "As Long as You're Happy", Graywolf Press, Saint Paul, 1986, copyright © by Jack Myers, Permission granted by the author.

"Traveling through the Dark" copyright 1962, 1998 by the Estate of William Stafford. Reprinted from THE WAY IT IS: NEW AND SELECTED POEMS with the permission of Graywolf Press, Saint Paul, Minnesota.

"Alley Violinist" from LOVE HAD A COMPASS copyright © 1996 by Robert Lax, Used by permission of Grove/Atlantic, Inc.

"To Know Silence Perfectly" from GOOD MORNING, AMERICA, copyright 1928 and renewed 1956 by Carl Sandburg, reprinted by permission of Harcourt, Inc.

"The Answering Machine" from THE HOLY WORM OF PRAISE, copyright © 2001 by Philip Schultz, reprinted by permission of Harcourt, Inc. and the author.

"Country Fair" from HOTEL INSOMNIA, copyright © 1992 by Charles Simic, reprinted by permission of Harcourt, Inc. and the author.

720

Margaret Atwood, "You Fit Into Me," from POWER POLITICS (Toronto: House of Anansi, 1971, 1996). Reprinted with permission.

Alden Nowlan, "An Exchange of Gifts" and "It's Good to Be Here" in ALDEN NOWLAN: SELECTED POEMS (Toronto: House of Anansi Press, 1996). Reprinted with permission.

Robert Phillips, "Instrument of Choice from SPINACH DAYS, pp. 81, copyright © 2000 Robert Phillips, reprinted with permission of The Johns Hopkins University Press.

Robert Kinsley, "A Walk Along the Old Tracks" used with permission of the author.

"Dream Deferred: Harlem", "Evil", "Maybe", and "Suicide's Note" are from THE COLLECTEDC POEMS OF LANGSTON HUGHES by Langston Hughes, copyright © 1994 by The Estate of Langston Hughes. Used by permission of Alfred A. Knopf, a division of Random House, Inc.

"Belle Isle, 1949" and "Sweet Will" from NEW SELECTED POEMS by Philip Levine, copyright © 1991 by Philip Levine. Used by permission of Alfred A. Knopf, a division of Random House, Inc., and the author.

"I Go Back to May 1937" and "The Pope's Penis" from THE GOLD CELL by Sharon Olds, Copyright © 1987 by Sharon Olds. Used by permission of Alfred A. Knopf, a division of Random House, Inc. and the author.

"Once" and "The Promise" from BLOOD, TIN, STRAW by Sharon Olds, copyright © 1999 by Sharon Olds. Used by permission of Alfred A. Knopf, a division of Random House, Inc., and the author.

Gerald Locklin, "Late Registration" used with permission of the author.

David Huddle, "Holes Commence Falling" from SUMMER LAKE: NEW AND SELECTED POEMS, used with permission of Louisiana State University Press and the author.

Lisel Mueller, "Reader", "Widow", "Silence and Dancing", "Imaginary Paintings", and "The Story" from ALIVE TOGETHER: NEW AND SELECTED POEMS. Reprinted with permission of Louisiana Univeristy Press.

David Slavitt, "Titanic" from BIG NOSE. Reprinted by permission of Louisiana Univeristy Press and the author.

721

Pulling a Pig's Tail, copyright Dave Smith, first appeared in THE WICK OF MEMORY: NEW AND SELECTED POEMS 1970-2000 (Louisiana State University Press, 2000). Used with permission of the author.

Dave Smith, "Wreck in the Woods" copyright Dave Smith, first appeared in FATE'S KITE: POEMS 1991 - 1995 (Louisiana State University Press, 1996). Used here by permission of the author.

Howard Nemerov, "Snowflakes" and "Gyroscope" from THE COLLECTED POEMS OF HOWARD NEMEROV, used with permission of Margaret Nemerov.

"Heaven" by Robert Creeley, from ECHOES, copyright © 1989, 1991, 1992, 1993, 1994 by Robert Creeley. Reprinted by permission of New Directions Publishing Corp.

"I'll Win,", "Old Days," and "Thanksgiving's Done," by Robert Creeley, from MEMORY GARDENS, copyright © 1986 by Robert Creeley. Reprinted by permission of New Directions Publishing Corp.

"Place (there's a way out)" by Robert Creeley, from WINDOWS, copyright © 1990 by Robert Creeley. Reprinted by permission of New Directions Publishing Corp.

"Daydreaming on the Trail", translation by Gary Snyder, from THE BACK COUNTRY, copyright © 1968 by Gary Snyder. Reprinted by permission of New Directions Publishing Corporation.

"Consulting the Oracle" and "From a Plane" are by Denise Levertov, from THE FREEING OF THE DUST, copyright © 1975 by Denise Levertov. Reprinted by permission of New Directions Publishing Corp.

"Not Waving but Drowning" and "Sunt Leones" by Stevie Smith, from COLLECTED POEMS OF STEVIE SMITH, copyright © 1972 by Stevie Smith, Reprinted by permission of New Directions Publishing Corp.

"What You Should Know to Be A Poet" by Gary Snyder, from REGARDING WAVE, copyright © 1970 by Gary Snyder. Reprinted by permission of New Directioins Publishing Corp and the author.

"Do Not Go Gentle Into That Good Night" by Dylan thomas, from THE POEMS OF DYLAN THOMAS, copyright © 1952 by Dylan Thomas. Reprinted by permission of New Directons Publishing Corp.

722

"Shorts", copyright © 1974 by The Estate of W.H. Auden, from COLLECTED POEMS by W.H. Auden. Used by permission of Random House, Inc.

William Roetzheim, "Opera Season", "Shadow Friends", "Fading into Background", "Response to Emily Dickinson's 'Wild Nights-Wild Nights!'", and "Stretch Marks" used with permission of the author.

Beyond Recall is from FLYING BLIND by Sharon Bryan, published by Sarabande Books, Inc. (c) 1996 by Sharon Bryan. Used by permission of Sarabande Books and the author.

"Before Groundbreak", "Don Fargo and Sons", "Jobsite Wind", "Pickwork", "Poem", and "Waiting for Lumber" are from HAMMER by Mark Turpin, published by Sarabande Books, Inc. © 2003 by Mark Turpin. Reprinted by permission of Sarabande Books and the author.

Irving Feldman, "The Dream" Schocken, used with permission of the author.

"How We Heard the Name" and "Love Song: I and Thou" copyright © 1961 by Alan Dugan. From POEMS SEVEN: NEW AND COLLECTED POEMS (Seven Stories Press, 2001). Reprinted by permission of Judith Shahn and Seven Stories Press.

"Axe Handles" from AXE HANDLES, copyright 1993 by Gary Snyder. Published by Shoemaker and Hoard. Used with permission of the author.

"The Sheaves", "Haunted House", and "Karma" are reprinted with the permission of Scribner, an imprint of Simon and Schuster Adult Publishing Group, from COLLECTED POEMS by Edwin Arlington Robinson. Copyright © 1925 by Edwin Arlington Robinson; copyright renewed (c) 1953 by Ruth Nivison and Barbara R. Holt.

"Fawn's Foster Mother" by Robinson Jeffers from THE COLLECTED POETRY OF ROBINSON JEFFERS, Volume 1, 1920 - 1928, edited by Tim Hunt. Copyright © 1938 and renewed 1966 by Donnan and Garth Jeffers, copyright © Jeffers Literary Properties. All rights reserved. Used with the permission of Stanford University Press, www.sup.org.

Mark Strand, "Eating Poetry" "Keeping Things Whole" and "Reading in Place" used with permission of the author.

Kaylin Haught, "God Says Yes to Me" from THE PALM OF YOUR HAND, used with permission of the author and Tilbury House Publishers.

Miller Williams, "Listen" from SOME JAZZ A WHILE: COLLECTED POEMS. Copyright 1999 by Miller Williams. Used with Permission of the poet and the University of Illinois Press.

Reprinted with Permission of the University of Arkansas Press. Copyright 1988 by Billy Collins.

Robert Creeley, "I Know a Man" from COLLECTED POEMS OF ROBERT CREELEY, 1945-1975. Copyright © 1983 by The Regents of the University of California. Used by permission of the Regents of the University of California.

"Conversation" is reprinted from THE SELECTED POETRYOF DAN PAGIS, translated and edited by Stephen Mitchell, copyright © 1996 by The Regents of the University of California. Permission granted by the Regents of the University of California and the Universityof California Press.

Gail Mazur, "In Houston" from THE COMMON, University of Chicago Press. Used with permission of the author.

Howard Nemerov, "Money" from THE COLLECTED POEMS OF HOWARD NEMEROV, University of Chicago Press. Used by permission of Margaret Nemerov.

Tanikawa Shuntaro, extract from "My Father's Death", "A Rudimentary Explanation of an Ideal Poem", "The Naif" from THE NAIF, University of Hawaii Press. Used with permission of the author and the translator.

Michael Pettit, "Driving Lesson" from CARDINAL POINTS, University of Iowa Press. Used with permission of the author.

Mark Halliday, "Get It Again" in LITTLE STAR (William Morrow, 1987), and "Population" in TASKER STREET (U. of Massachusetts Press, 1992). Used with permission of the author.

Archilochos, "Will, Lost in a Sea of Trouble" from POEMS FROM THE GREEK ANTHOLOGY (copyright © 1962), used with permission of the University of Michigan Press.

"The Poem You Asked For" is from THE SELECTED LEVIS: SELECTED AND WITH AN AFTERWORD BY DAVID ST. JOHN., by Larry Levis, © 2000. Reprinted by permission of the University of Pittsburgh Press.

"Quake Theory" and "Satan Says" are from SATAN SAYS, by Sharon Olds, © 1980 by Sharon Olds. Reprinted by permission of the University of Pittsburgh Press.

"The Bus to Veracruz" and "The Stones" are from SELECTED POEMS, 1969-1981, by Richard Shelton, © 1982. Reprinted by permission of the University of Pittsburgh Press.

"Thirteen" is from PEOPLE AND DOG IN THE SUN by Ronald Wallace, © 1987. Reprinted by permission of the University of Pittsburgh Press and the author.

"Only One of My Deaths" is from FIRST COURSE IN TURBULENCE by Dean Young, © 1999. Reprinted by permission of the University of Pittsburgh Press.

"Zimmer's Head Thudding Against the Blackboard" is from FAMILY REUNION: SELECTED AND NEW POEMS by Paul Zimmer, © 1983. Reprinted by permission of the University of Pittsburgh Press.

Jim Daniels, "Wheels" from PLACES/EVERYONE, © Madison: The University of Wisconsin Press. Used with permission of the University of Wisconsin Press.

Diane Wakoski, "George Washington and the Loss of His Teeth" used with permission of the author.

Tom Wayman, "Did I Miss Anything?" used with permission of the author.

"Blackberries," by Yusef Komunyakaa, from PLEASURE DOME (Wesleyan University Press, 2001). © 2001 by Yusef Komunyakaa. Reprinted by permission of Wesleyan University Press.

"The Dacca Gauzes" by Agha Shahid Ali, from THE HALF-INCH HIMALAYAS (Wesleyan University Press, 1987). © 1987 by Agha Shaid Ali. Reprinted by permission of Wesleyan University Press.

"The Heaven of Animals" by James Dickey, from POEMS 1957 - 1967 (Wesleyan University Press, 1967) © 1967 by James Dickey. Reprinted with permission of Wesleyan University Press.

728

Acknowledgements

Every effort has been made to trace copyright holders of the poems published in this book. The editor and publisher apologize if any material has been inadvertently included without appropriate permission or without the appropriate acknowledgement, and would be pleased to correct any oversights in future editions.